The Three-Category Ontology

An Alternative to 20th Century Analytic Philosophy

Doctoral Thesis

Damien John Spillane

Submitted in fulfilment of the requirements for the Doctorate in Philosophy

School of Philosophy and Theology

University of Notre Dame, Sydney Campus

August, 2019

Declaration

To the best of this candidate's knowledge, this thesis contains no material previously published by another person, except where due acknowledgement has been made.

This thesis is the candidate's own work and contains no material which has been accepted for the award of any other degree or diploma in any institution.

Damien John Spillane

2/8/2019

Abstract

The leading theorists of 20th century philosophy formalised their ontology on the basis of first-order logic with identity. The formal nature of such a logical conception of the world was supposed to characterise a notion of being that is maximally general and give the minimal identity conditions for a thing to be said to exist.

But as I argue in this thesis, such a logic centred approach masks the metaphysical assumptions that provide the underlying explanations of existence and our knowledge of things in the world. That foundational structure was not new but was rooted in the pre-Socratic era, Parmenides in particular. Such an assumption was assumed by these philosophers and not argued for but the later leading lights that followed in this tradition followed the formal conditions of their ontology to their logical conclusions. Those conclusions showed that what was thought to be the theory's main advantage – maximal generality – was its undoing since it was not able to explain the multifarious things in the world and the structure of perception.

Therefore a new way of doing ontology is called for. Here I offer just three non-univocal formal conditions for existence that are abstracted from – and not imposed on – the world. Three categories that exhaustively explain the structure of objects and their interactions with each other in such a way that it solves many philosophical conundrums and explains what we perceive in the world.

Acknowledgements

This is a work 3 ½ years in the making, although my initial striving for a PhD thesis began in 2010 at Macquarie University with no success. It was a thesis conceived in obscurity and must have initially baffled my supervisor. For this reason I'd like to thank Angus Brook for his open mindedness, grace and bravery in taking on this project. Hopefully the core of the thesis is much clearer and plausible now then it was when I initially proposed it. Juxtaposing it against the leading lights of 20th century philosophy must have compounded the mystery. I'd also like to thank Peter Forrest for his efforts in reviewing my work and offering helpful feedback.

I'd also like to thank Geoffrey Marnell of Abelard Consulting for his editorial work and for being so accessible for follow up questions.

Lastly I'd also like to thank my family for their support and long suffering: my wife Louise and four children: Miranda, Clelia, Harrison and Maxwell.

Table of Contents

Introduction   1

Chapter One – Gottlob Frege and the Order of Being

- **Introduction**   8

- **Parmenidean Background**   11

- **Rationalist Background**   12

- **Frege's System**

  - Function and Argument   16

  - The Whole Above the Parts   31

  - Truth-Value   41

- **Frege's Dualism**   45

- **The Transition from *Begriffsschrift* to *On Sense and Reference***   50

- **Conclusion**   64

Chapter Two – Frege and Russell on Being and Truth

- **Introduction** — 67

- **Wittgenstein Against Frege** — 69

- Truth and the World — 75

- Wittgenstein's Objections — 77

- Wittgenstein on Truth Conditions — 88

- **Russell on Being** — 91

- The Unity of the Proposition — 93

- Russell on Direct Realism — 102

- Russell on Truth via Acquaintance and Description — 105

- Logical Constructions — 113

- Russell's Image Proposition — 118

- **Conclusion** — 120

- ## Chapter Three – On Carnap and Quine and the Reconstruction of Knowledge

- **Introduction** — 122

- **Historical Background: The Cartesian Assumption**   **126**

- **The Analytic–Synthetic Distinction: Leibniz and Kant**   **130**

- **Carnap on Logical Structure**

  - Constructing a Cartesian World   132

  - The Logical Structure of the World   133

  - The Logical Structure of the World: A Rational Reconstruction   136

  - Frege–Russell Influence   139

- **Quine and Naturalism**   **154**

  - Factuality and Truth   159

  - The Analytic-Synthetic Distinction and Indeterminacy   176

- **Conclusion**   **183**

- <u>**Chapter Four – David Lewis and the Ontology of Part–Whole**</u>

- **Introduction**   **186**

- **Lewis the Humean**   **188**

- **Parthood and Mereology**   **191**

- **Composition as Identity and the Land Sale Argument**   195

- **Plural Logic and Ontological Innocence**   198

- **Lewisian Dualism**   200

- **Lewis and Identity**   202

- **Lewis on Vagueness**   208

- **Critique of Lewis on Identity**   210

- **Critique of Composition as Identity**   217

- **Critique of Lewis on Mereological Monism**   221

- **The van Inwagen Objection**   226

- **Bringing It All Together**   232

- **Conclusion**   237

- **<u>Chapter Five – Sketch of a Three-Category Ontology</u>**

- **Introduction**   239

- **Determination and Realisation**   242

- **Communication**   248

- Causation	**250**
- Truth	**254**
- Sense Data Structure	**258**
– Realism and Subsequent Debates	
- Tarski, Putnam and Field on Truth	**259**
- Structuralism	**266**
- Putnam's Case Against Realism	**271**
- Lewis' Response	**277**
– Analytic – Synthetic and A Priori – A Posteriori	**280**
– Substance and Properties	**282**
– Supervenience and Grounding	**286**
– Hierarchy of Non-Univocal Being	**293**
– Determinacy of Reference	**297**
– Conclusion	**301**

Chapter Six – Three-Category Ontology Applied to the Natural Sciences

- **Introduction**   305

- **Reduction and Non-Reductionism**   306

- **The Quantum Mechanical Challenge**   316

- **Critique of Fusion Emergentism and the Three-Category Solution**   322

- **Emergentism and the Three-Category Ontology**   326

- **Conclusion**   330

Conclusion   333

Bibliography
344

Introduction

The chief preoccupation of twentieth century analytic philosophy was formal logic and its symbols, existence expressed through quantifiers, and referring expressions such as *Fa* (where "*a*" picks out a particular and "*F*" picks out a property). The different kinds of syntax used to pick out individuals and properties within the context of a formal logical construct may give the impression, to the uninitiated, that such logic functions in concert with the particulars picked out, but that is not the case. Dispensing with the old Aristotelian logic, this new logical method is entirely "other worldly" (vis-à-vis the terrestrial domain that we inhabit). For this reason questions about the exact nature of such logical structures beckon, but they are almost never asked.

But the laws of logic and the relation of identity cannot be given any positive ontological characterisation at all but only described negatively as being orthogonal to the physical and empirical world. Everything that is subject to the referring expressions and variables is flattened into the monolithic and univocal nature of such an ontology. Such a reductionist picture I oppose in this thesis for the simple reason that it does not accord with the varied nature of the objects in the world and the empirical means by which we come to know things.

It isn't just the reductionism I am opposing but the very existence of such a logical super-structure. Such a structure does not arise from the world of experience and is not justified except ultimately on a priori grounds. Just as Francis Bacon complained that Aristotle had "utterly enslaved his natural philosophy to his logic"[1] my contention in this thesis is that the likes of Gottlob Frege, Bertrand Russell, Rudolph Carnap, and W. V. O. Quine made their ontology a slave of their logic. Giving such a structure axiological, primitive, or a priori status does not save it from the accusation that in its alienation from our common-sense

---

[1] Francis Bacon, *The New Organon,* ed. Lisa Jardine and Michael Silverthorne. (Cambridge: Cambridge University Press, 2000), 46.

knowledge, it is ultimately revealed as a fictitious entity and completely unworthy of being the basis from which we construct our knowledge of the world.

I also trace a consistent theme throughout the work of the aforementioned philosophers: that their conception of being is really just a reworking, in logical form, of the metaphysic first expounded by the ancient Greek philosopher Parmenides. Parmenides had a conception of being that was simple, univocal and primitive, and accessed independently of the senses. But such an other-worldly source of being ultimately grounds our empirical knowledge, with the individual instances of the latter deriving all ontological and epistemic being from the former.

Chapter one focuses on the first key figure, Frege, and his first-order predicate logic with identity. Frege assumed that identity was primitive, and the truth functions of his logic act in concert with identity only. Frege took the identity relation to be an a priori Humean "relation of ideas", which means that it does not pick out anything in the empirical or physical world. But from structures like this, where objects emerge by being flanked on either side of the identity symbol and the sentence that has reference to the True, he grounded and derived knowledge of particulars. This was Frege's context principle, which solidified his ontological prioritisation of the whole above its parts and in this way the sentence in its referring to the True was the ultimate source of being and its structure. The True functioned like an indivisible primitive atom from which all being springs, as parts crystallise out of the whole. In this way, Frege puts a pre-Socratic concept, accessed through the rational faculties, at the very heart of his ontology.

I also examine the transition from Frege's *Begriffsschrift* to *"On Sense and Reference"*. The opening passages of the latter spell out the shift from embodying the informativeness of identity in the signs flanking the identity sign to the sense of the reference. I argue Frege was more concerned with how it is, given the threat of scepticism imposed by his Cartesian view of the mental, that we come to know the sense – and communicate it with others – as an objective entity rather than the reference. I argue that Frege presents an external – relative to our internal mental states – account of knowledge in *On Sense and Reference* as a solution to the threat of solipsism. The three categories will emerge later as a far more natural – but still integral to our psychological states – explanation of knowledge.

The second chapter is on Frege's conception of the True and on Russell, who developed a similar conception of logic as a basis for constructing knowledge from individual units of being. Both are prime examples of Parmenidian being. The difference is that Frege's approach is rationalist whereas Russell's is more empiricist. Russell puts special emphasis on knowledge by acquaintance, where justification involves the Cartesian notions of access by introspection and indubitability. But again the unifying work ultimately derives from the one non-empirically derived conception of being. Frege starts out with structure and individual objects are derived as parts out of a whole, whereas for Russell objects are constructed from logical units of sense data. Where Frege started with structure, Russell built up his proposition with atomic building blocks he called "terms".

I find problems with both systems of being. Russell's propositions have no way of accounting for the unity of propositions, and Frege's structural derivation fails because individual propositions can only have truth derivatively. There must be, as Wittgenstein argued, an intrinsic and formal connection between propositions and truth conditions. Russell's empiricist construction of knowledge fails because it results in mere "logical fictions", which are poor substitutes for the complex structures we observe in sense experience.

The third chapter is, in a way, a coalescing of the previous two chapters. The early work of Rudolph Carnap, especially in the *The Logical Structure of the World and Pseudoproblems in Philosophy*, sought to rationally reconstruct our knowledge through Fregean logic without invoking traditional metaphysics (and having to contend with all its problems). The reconstruction sought to build, and justify in a behind-the-scenes kind of way, the knowledge we know through introspection. Quine's criticisms, however, point to this project as a failure to reconstruct our knowledge, since the formal logical apparatus did not have the specific informational basis to build the structures of our experience. Quine's indeterminacy of translation makes a similar argument by highlighting the failure of the formal mathematical-logical function operator to make any interesting distinctions that pick out the individual or the kinds of things we experience. Hence the impossibility of any uniquely correct means of translating a language. These two arguments of Quine unintentionally make the case that Frege–Russell logic lacks the resources for individuating and ultimately justifying our knowledge of particulars in the world of sense experience.

The Frege–Russell–Quine method finds more specific focus in the subject of mereology and this is the focus of chapter four. The work of David Lewis is discussed, particularly his work on the part–whole relation. Owing to the unrestricted range of the quantifier, his notion of part–whole is completely undiscriminating: parts and wholes emerge independently of any particular thing or its nature. Such an unintuitive outcome is only tolerated due to the perceived strength of Frege–Russell formal logic. Wholes are not allowed to emerge, on Lewis's conception, from their parts. Wholes and their parts are different modes of presentation of the one, underlying identity relation. In this way Lewis avoids what looks like wholes having any distinct identity *qua* as an emergent and independently individuated entity. But this, unfortunately, trades on the artificial dichotomy between the rationally derived identity relation and the formal conditions underlying the quantifier and the empirically derived mode of presentation that is Fregean in origin.

The fifth chapter presents an alternative to the Frege–Russell ontology. Specifically, it is argued that reality is exhaustively constituted by three ontological categories. The first is the *determiner*, which is the non-spatiotemporal form of the object that structures and selects its constituents such that each constituent is characterised by its role in the whole. The second is the *realiser*, which is the constituents that realise the abstract structure of the whole in space-time. The third is the *communicator*, which is the way each determiner–realiser interacts with objects other than itself. Communication functions through what we normally conceive as causation, which necessarily requires something beyond the determiner–realiser to enact the cause but the structure of the causation derives from the determiner–realiser itself (or at least one property of it).

The three categories are abstracted purely from sense experience and are a substitute for the law of identity originally found in Frege. On this model, when one observes a green tree in the back-yard, it is the sense properties that communicate – and justify – the existence of a green tree due to the fact that the sense properties are structured in concert with the way the particles of the tree are arranged (this has the added advantage of explaining the famous problem of the unity of the proposition which Russell's method does not).

Analysis, due to this newly introduced methodology, is tethered to sense experience, since an analysis of the tree comes by scientific means that reveal a structure of cellulose molecules, etc. But such a part–whole analysis reveals constituents with identities that are in part characterised by their role in the whole structure. The categories are, therefore, revealed through sense experience. They are not univocal. Every object is revealed – and knowledge of its existence justified – as *sui generis* to some extent. The determiner–realiser provides a basis for the structure of sense properties and thus the three-category method succeeds by marrying epistemic and metaphysical conditions together precisely where Quine inadvertently revealed that the Frege–Russell method of reconstruction was a failure.

The categories in this thesis are abstracted from particulars and are information rich, and thus are not vulnerable to anti-realism in the way that the Frege–Russell methods are. Hence the pitfalls that were brought out by M. H. Newman – that the theoretical structures revealed in experience depend only on the right enumeration of entities and hence are susceptible to permutation and thus a vast multitude of models can be derived by such means – in Russell's realism are avoided. The three-category ontology is derived from each particular of sense experience, connecting us to mind-external reality and prohibiting permutations. Hartry Field's naturalistic criticisms of Alfred Tarski are also discussed, not to endorse his reductionism, but to point out that Hilary Putnam's Kantian response is unsatisfactory and to point the way to the categories as providing a better naturalistic explanation of truth.

The last chapter considers the debate between reductionism and emergentism. The chief protagonist is Jaegwon Kim, whose form of reductionism is atomistic. He also formulates a *functionalist reductionism* using the Humean split between the law of identity and the empirical world. Kim is challenged by quantum theory, where the whole seems to be more fundamental than the parts. The determining–realising categories, where the constituents take on the formal nature of the whole, are much better equipped to account for such quantum phenomena as entangled states and action at a distance and avoid the pitfalls of other accounts, such as "fusionism". Kim's exclusion argument against non-reductive physicalism is also answered by the three-category ontology.

This thesis argues for a new ontology, one that provides a theoretical justification of our common sense and scientific practice and avoids the sweeping reconstructions of knowledge that come from the mainstream proponents of analytic philosophy over the last century. The three-category ontology also has the advantage of justifying the world of sense experience without needing to flatten everything down into an a priori–derived formal logical apparatus of dubious metaphysical status. It also solves a number of problems that have remained somewhat intractable up until this day.

Chapter One - Gottlob Frege and the Order of Being

Introduction

Gottlob Frege was one of the founding fathers of modern analytic philosophy. His influence is rivalled only by Bertrand Russell and Ludwig Wittgenstein. But whilst it has become commonplace to argue that much of Frege's work was innovative, the case I put forward here casts doubt on a significant portion of that contention. Frege employed new logical methods and surmounted limitations that beset the old Aristotelian logic. I do not dispute those innovations. It is his worldview as a whole, the most basic metaphysical assumptions he employed, that were not new. These assumptions hang in the background, are not argued for nor discussed explicitly, and yet they are the unmoved movers of his system.

My central argument in this chapter is that Frege's system is at core almost identical to the metaphysical system of Parmenides. Fundamental being for Parmenides either "is" or "is not". There are no alternative forms of Being. It is singular, univocal, simple and without differentiation of any kind. It also grounds the world of appearances. As such being stands in contrast to, but is also the fundamental basis of, the real world accessible to the five senses. The properties of being therefore are derived through logical deduction from its oneness not through any particular instance of knowledge. Knowledge is only possible because the world of appearances is metaphysically dependent on the world of being, which permeates the entirety of existence and is even manifest in the very act of thinking and the objects of every thought.

Frege's Parmenidian system is evident in his method of reconstructing our knowledge through logical analysis and explication, and his critique of psychologism (which was integral to his epistemology putting the rational derivation of knowledge as the basis that grounds and makes objective our sensory experience of particulars in the world). The contrasting of thoughts from their subjective mental correlates was an echo of the contrast Parmenides drew between the world of reason and the world of experience. I make the following arguments in support of such a comparison. First, I establish Frege's rationalist bona fides, which is necessary since modern scholarship is more likely to focus on his work on language and logic. I point out that Frege has been placed in the rationalist camp by Frege scholars such as Hans Sluga, and many points of emphasis in his work do parallel that of his rationalist predecessors, such as René Descartes and Gottfried Wilhelm Leibniz.

Second, Frege draws a crucial distinction between epistemic reasons and the grounds of truth. The epistemic reasons are our means of coming to know a logical law or a mathematical equation but this should not be confused with the grounds of their truth. The role of variables plays an important part here in highlighting the fact that different particulars can be substituted in and out of the various places opened up by the structures of the laws of truth. The interchangeability evident in parsing the argument and function from a sentence served the purpose of highlighting the centrality of structure – and the whole above the parts – and its opening up of sentential roles for variables to fill. In this way fundamentality belonged to the logical axioms which are supremely general among the sciences and grounds the manifestation of truth.

Third, analysis for Frege is productive in that the many particular manifestations drop out of the whole. This is where the *context principle* plays a crucial role. But the reason that analysis *is* productive is because the whole can be split up into the parts in many ways. This is because the whole is over and above the parts (the parts playing the role of accidents).

The fourth reason is closely connected with the third. Words derive their meaning within sentences and sentences, as expressions of thought, are ultimately explained by reference to the True. The old linguistic referential symbols no longer showcase the correspondence theory of truth nor refer directly in any way to particulars. They are ultimately fixed in their essential logical identity by their place in the logical structure. They emerge as parts out of the whole sentence that has as its reference in the True from which it derives its veracity and structure. The True is a simple, univocal notion that stands ontologically at the heart of

Frege's system. The identity of sentences and their parts is ultimately derived from the True. But the True exists above and beyond any parthood manifestation of it and thus the parts of it are not differentiations within it. The parts are instead *grounded in* the True in the way that Seated Socrates as an accident is grounded in Socrates. I use this metaphor throughout the thesis as a convenient analogy of the dependence of all particular being on logical being. Hence Fregean being is ultimately simple and unanalysable like Parmenidean being.

The next section highlights the dualism between form and content. Frege follows the dualism at the heart of Parmenides' system with the logical deductive system expressing the one univocal conception of being and the particulars of the world of appearances merely occupying the places opened up by the parts of the sentences of logic. But such a formal system potentially fails as a reconstruction of the rich world of sense experience. John Macfarlane attempts to defend Frege here by comparing Frege's logical mechanisms to the law of identity. But I respond that this only highlights that the structure itself is univocal and as such fails to make the adequate differentiations in the world of objects.

The last section further explores Frege's Cartesian view of the mind: the idea that thoughts are self-standing entities that are not essentially connected to the outside world. Bringing this out helps resolve a puzzle amongst Frege scholars on his use, in the *Begriffsschrift*, of linguistic expressions and whether he was able to make use of an early version of a *mode of presentation* in that work. The blindspot in these debates, however, is in not appreciating that within the *Begriffsschrift* there is no way of advancing to an objective knowledge of, and means of communicating, the mode of presentation in the first place. In other words, merely having a mode of presentation does not help since there is no account of how such an objective abstract concept is grasped in the first place. In *Sense and Reference* Frege provides a way out in essentially by-passing sense experience by placing the knower in a truth-determined relation by the laws of the True enacted through assertion.

This is an external relation – at least relative to our internal mental states – where the knower becomes a manifestation of the laws of truth. And again this is a further echo of

Parmenides, since the knower in the very act of thinking becomes a manifestation of being, which is acting in accordance with the laws of truth.

Getting clear on Frege's ultimate assumptions allows us to subject his work to a proper critique. The most fundamental problem is that the structure within his system is univocal and as such lacks the informational content to explain the world. A hint at such a critique is provided here but it will ultimately come to a climax through an examination of the work of Rudolph Carnap and W. V. O. Quine who take Frege's work to its logical conclusion. Their works will be examined in chapter three, but this chapter lays the ground work.

The last two chapters of this thesis lay out an alternative to the Fregean–Parmenidian system that does not by-pass the empirical world but instead abstracts alternative metaphysical principles. This is a metaphysical system that takes common sense and science at its face instead of an ultra-reductionistic account that seeks to flatten everything out in to the one form of being.

Parmenidean Background

Hans Sluga was one of the most prominent in emphasising the rationalist bona fides of Frege. Sluga puts Frege in the Western philosophical tradition going back to "Pythagoras, Parmenides, and Plato."[2] The Eleatic philosophers did not see ultimate being as numerous, changing and divided, which is how we see the ordinary things within our visual field. Instead, for them, being is one, eternal, homogenous, not generated or changing, not divisible, only equal to itself (not becoming), and spherical.[3] Such characteristics of being for Parmenides, specifically its oneness, simplicity and unity, are primitive since it cannot be broken up into more basic elements. Being is univocal in the sense that the "is" or "is

---

[2] Hans Sluga, *Gottlob Frege: The Arguments of the Philosophers* (London and New York: Routledge, 1980), 58.
[3] Parmenides as cited by A. H. Coxon *The Fragments of Parmenides: A Critical Text with Introduction and Translation, the Ancient Testimonia and a Commentary*, revised and expanded edition with new translations by Richard McKirahan. (Las Vegas, Zurich and Athens: Parmenides Publishing, 2009), 64-66.

not" exhausts all the possibilities of inquiry.[4] Being is not a genus that can be broken up into different species.

Parmenides, however, had to explain the host of different entities that appear, as well as change and movement within our sense experience. His idea was that being permeates all things that we perceive by being the underlying substrate that constitutes the world. Thus we perceive the world *as if* it is being broken up into different entities but that is only how it *appears to us*. Another way to put this is to say that being is the substance of the world and everything else is accidental relative to it. Accidents have their ground in a substance and in this case being is the explanation for how it is that we perceive or even think anything in the first place.

So being is the ontological ground and explanation for our epistemic grasp of anything in the world. If being did not exist then there would be no way that our sense experience could perceive appearances in the first place. In fact for him "thinking and being are the same".[5] What this means is that the very act of thought is an expression of being so that it is not possible to think what is not.

Parmenides arrives at these conclusions as a series of logical deductions from what *is*, from true being. This is the original reconstruction of knowledge on rationalist grounds. Below I will argue that Frege attempted a reconstruction very much like this only adding much more linguistic and logical details.

Rationalist Background

---

[4] Ibid, 56.
[5] Ibid, 58.

The traditional picture of Frege's contribution to analytic philosophy has been most famously advanced by the foremost Fregean scholar in recent times, Michael Dummett. That picture paints Frege as inaugurating a new era in philosophy where the old Cartesianism, which centred on epistemology, was supplanted by a theory of meaning as first philosophy. In particular, Dummett's *Frege: Philosophy of Language*, credits Frege with initiating a "linguistic turn" in philosophy that replaces the old Cartesian preoccupation with the relation between mind and world, with the relation between words and what they express.[6]

Whilst it is unquestionable that Frege focuses heavily on language and logic, I believe Dummett's approach glosses over some of the most important presuppositions and aspects of Frege's thought. It is true that the rationalist philosophers, like Descartes, did not emphasise language to the same extent as Frege, however, there is a high degree of agreement on the scope and power of reason. It is the heavy reliance on reason, which Frege subsequently takes as an ontological tool of excavation, that borrows heavily from the likes of Descartes and other rationalists (such as Leibniz).

Sluga, in his "Frege as a Rationalist", was the first to place Frege in the rationalist tradition.[7] Earlier he had criticised Dummett for not presenting a "picture of the historical Frege".[8] According to Sluga, Frege's work resembles that of Descartes and Leibniz in their use of logic in support of rationalism.[9] He equates rationalism with an emphasis on logic and a priorism, which was also the focus for Frege.

---

[6] Michael Dummett, *Frege: Philosophy of Language* (London: Duckworth, 1981). Others such as Peter Geach with G. E. M. Anscombe, "Frege," in *Three Philosophers* (Oxford: Blackwell, 1961); Anthony Kenny, *Frege: An Introduction to the Founder of Analytic Philosophy* (London: Penguin, 1995) have followed Dummett in emphasizing the linguistic component of Frege.

[7] Hans Sluga "Frege as a Rationalist," in *Studies on Frege,* vol 1., ed. Matthias Schirn, 27-47. (Stuttgart: Frommann-Holzboog, 1976) See also Sluga, *Gottlob Frege*. Others advancing a rationalist interpretation of Frege are Susan Haack, *Deviant Logic, Fuzzy Logic: Beyond the Formalism*, (Chicago: University of Chicago Press, 1996); Tyler Burge in "Frege on Sense and Linguistic Meaning," in *The Analytic Tradition: Meaning, Thought and Knowledge*, ed, David Bell and Neil Cooper (Oxford: Blackwell, 1990), 30-60 and "Frege on Knowing the Third Realm," in *Early Analytic Philosophy: Frege, Russell, Wittgenstein: Essays in Honor of Leonard Linsky* (La Salle: Open Court, 1997), 1-18.

[8] Hans Sluga, "Frege and the Rise of Analytic Philosophy," in *Inquiry* 18, no. 4 (1975): 475, https://doi.org/10.1080/00201747508601779

[9] Sluga, "Frege as a Rationalist," in Schirn, *Studies on Frege*, 27-47.

It is my position in this chapter that Sluga is right to place Frege among the rationalists. Although it is also undoubtedly true that, as Tyler Burge has argued, Frege went well beyond the rationalist "insight" in his fruitful use of inferences where it is "inextricably associated with systematic, theoretical reflection on a variety of inferences within substantive, scientific theory. So understanding is discursive rather than quasi-perceptual."[10] But although I agree with this take on Frege, it is this aspect of his thought – the preference for a totalising, discursive system over perception – and its implications for being *qua* being that I will criticise in a later section.

There are multiple facets to Frege's thought that are strongly rationalist. First, he held that knowledge of logic and mathematical objects comes primarily through reason and the understanding.[11] Second, he placed heavy emphasis on the principles of logic and mathematics, and he took these principles, as well as the presuppositions of scientific knowledge, as self-evident and primitive.[12] Third, he believed in a natural hierarchy of truths founded on mathematics and logic, and that the proof for such truths, grounded in self-evident principles, were the most fundamental proofs, with all others being derived by a chain of inference.[13] Fourth, he believed that all of scientific knowledge could be axiomotised,[14] Fifth, he believed in innate ideas.[15] And sixth, and to be argued in conjunction with my later criticisms, he held to epistemological dualism.

There is no dispute that Frege was heavily influenced by one rationalist philosopher in particular: Leibniz. Leibniz sought after a *lingua characteristic* designed to depict thoughts that would put the reasoning in metaphysics on a par with reasoning in geometry and analysis. The structure and components of this language as envisioned by Frege were to

---

[10] Tyler Burge, *Truth, Thought, Reason: Essays on Frege* (Oxford: Oxford University Press, 2005), 64.
[11] Frege concludes "that the laws of arithmetic are analytic judgments and consequently a priori." In Gottlob Frege, *The Foundations of Arithmetic* 2nd rev ed., trans. John Langshaw Austin (New York: Harper & Brothers, 1953), 99.
[12] Ibid, 102-103.
[13] See ibid, 16-17, where Frege points out that even induction – and the inductive sciences – are based deductively on logical laws.
[14] Gottlob Frege, "Logic in Mathematics," in *Posthumous Writings,* ed. Hans Hermes, Friedrich Kambartel, Friedrich Kaulbach, trans. Peter Long and Roger White (Chicago: University of Chicago Press, 1979).
[15] Frege, *Foundations*, 17.

bypass our inaccurate everyday language and mirror accurately our ideas and thoughts of ultimate reality. Such an isomorphism with reality would supposedly facilitate accurate reasoning.[16]

Frege quotes extensively from Leibniz in *The Foundations of Arithmetic* (*Foundations*) and clearly conceived of his work as an extension of Leibniz's own conceptions of logic and mathematics.[17] Frege thought Leibniz's goal was overly ambitious but he did follow him in regarding his logical system to be "the laws upon which all knowledge rests."[18] Frege's concept-script was supposed to be a system of symbols designed to express only what is essential for the correctness of inferences or proof. Logic, functioning in this way, was supposed to be central and interconnect all the other sciences, including geometry and arithmetic.

But most importantly for my purposes in this chapter is the fact that Frege follows Leibniz's dichotomy in dividing truth into truths of reason and truths of fact. In particular, truths of reason for Leibniz are grounded in the principle of contradiction and are hence necessary truths. Truths of fact, however, are contingent and based on the principle of sufficient reason. In the *Begriffsschrift* (*Bs*), Frege divides "all truths that require justification into two kinds, those for which the proof can be carried out purely by means of logic and those for which it must be supported by facts of experience."[19]

But even more basic than the principle of non-contradiction are Leibnizian identities, which are the basis on which the principle of non-contradiction depends. The classic Leibnizian identity is "a is a" and this is the foundation for other necessary truths. So for the principle of non-contradiction, where we have "a is either a or non-a", to hold, it must be the case

---

[16] Frege credits Leibniz with a "universal characteristic, of a *calculus philosophicus or ratiocinator*" in *Begriffsschrift, a Formula Language, Modeled on that of Arithmetic, for Pure Thought* in *Frege to Godel: A Source Book in Mathematical Logic, 1879-1931*, ed. van Heijenoort, trans. S. Bauer-Mengelberg (Cambridge: Harvard University Press, 1967), 6.
[17] Gottlob Frege, *The Foundations of Arithmetic*, 2nd rev ed, trans. John Langshaw Austin (New York: Harper & Brothers, 1953), 48, 50, 52, 67, and 76. See also Gottlob Frege, *Begriffsschrift*, 6-7; Gottlob Frege, "Boole's Logical Calculus and the Concept-Script," in Hermes et al, *Posthumous Writings*, 9-46.
[18] Frege, *Begriffsschrift*, 5.
[19] Ibid.

that "*a* is identical to *a*". Necessary truths of reason like the principle of non-contradiction ultimately reduce to identity propositions which are the paradigmatic embodiments of necessary truths.

It was these Leibnizian innate ideas that Frege took to be necessary in order for perception of the world outside of the mind to be possible. In his later work, "The Thought",[20] he took the objective world of thought to be, not the inner subjective world of ideas, nor the spatio-temporal world of perceivable objects, but an objective, immaterial "third realm". Frege writes regarding sense impressions that:

"These alone do not reveal the external world to us … Having visual impressions is certainly necessary for seeing things but not sufficient. What must still be added is non-sensible. And yet this is just what opens up the outer world for us; for without this non-sensible something everyone would remain shut up in his inner world."[21]

Thus although sense experience is necessary, there is an extra ingredient needed that our subjective states cannot supply, since our subjective states are stand-alone substantial entities that are not essentially connected to anything else. Frege echoes the rationalists in taking the path to objective knowledge through reason "independent of our sensations, intuition and imagination, and of all construction of mental pictures out of memories of earlier sensations…"[22] This was a distinct echo of previous rationalists and learning, for Frege, was a process of becoming aware of what is already innate.[23]

Frege's System

---

[20] Gottlob Frege "The Thought: A Logical Inquiry," *Mind* 65, no. 259 (1956): 289-311, http://www.jstor.org/stable/2251513.
[21] Ibid, 308-309.
[22] Frege, *Foundations*, 36.
[23] Ibid, 17.

i) **Function and Argument**

The work of Frege was to outline a body of axioms and rules of inference from which arithmetical propositions could be derived. It was in this field that Frege made many of his most original contributions. He did not want to discover new arithmetical truths, but to justify them on the basis of more basic laws. In this regard he took arithmetic to be reducible to logic, such that:

1) All truths of arithmetic are logical truths
2) Each fundamental arithmetical concept is translatable into general logical definitions

Importantly, for a proposition to be analytic it had to be based purely on logical laws and definitions and independent of the way in which it is psychologically held or as an object of any psychological attitude:

"When a proposition is called ... analytic in my sense, this is not a judgement about the conditions, psychological, physiological, and physical, that have made it possible to form the content of the proposition in our consciousness; nor is it a judgement about the way in which some other man has come, perhaps erroneously, to believe it true; rather it is a judgement about the ultimate ground upon which rests the justification for holding it to be true ... The problem becomes, in fact, that of finding the proof of the proposition, and of following it up right back to the primitive truths. If, in carrying out this process, we come only on general logical laws and on definitions, then the truth is an analytic one, bearing in mind that we must take account also of all propositions upon which the admissibility of any of the definitions depends."[24]

Thus Frege needs a set of logical laws that are primitive in order to ground arithmetic. So if we take the sentence "the four gospels is equal in number to the four trees in my backyard"

---

[24] Ibid, 3-4.

then we have a case where we may encounter such information empirically but ultimately such a truth is *grounded in the identity* between "the four gospels" and "the four trees in my backyard". Thus we have an arithmetical truth that is ultimately only justified because it can be traced back to an analytic truth.

In the *Foundations*, Frege sought to make the laws of arithmetic a by-product of analytic judgements and hence, a priori.[25] It is the justification for holding it to be true that distinguishes between an analytic and a synthetic proposition. An analytic proposition is purely the result of general logical laws and definitions whereas a proposition that requires appeal to any special science is a synthetic one. The former are self-standing proofs not requiring grounding whereas the latter are the opposite. Geometry, for example, is a priori – since the proofs proceed in a logical manner without appeal to empirical facts – but unlike arithmetic it is synthetic since its proofs do not involve basic logical laws.

Immanuel Kant, on the other hand, claimed that all arithmetical propositions are synthetic a priori.[26] In particular, we come to know the general truths of geometry and arithmetic by having intuitions of particular objects that are constructed on the basis of concepts. Specifically, we construct instances of a concept and then see that some of the properties of the constructed instance are exemplary of the general type. For example, we can demonstrate Kant's justification of synthetic knowledge of the number "3" through three-stroke notation "///" that illustrates the general and universal truth that every number has a successor.

A crucial distinction that Frege makes is that between the *epistemic reasons* for holding something to be true – which is the reason an individual will have for believing it – and the *reasons for truth*, which is a grounding or dependence relation between truths.[27] The first

---

[25] Ibid, 87.
[26] Immanuel Kant, *The Critique of Pure Reason*, trans. Paul Guyer and Allen W. Wood (Cambridge: Cambridge University Press, 1998)
[27] Frege, *Foundations*, 23-24. Note similarly for Kant the grounding of objective reference was the leading questions of the *Critique*; "What is the ground of the relation of that in us which we call 'representation' to the object?"; "To Marcus Herz, February 21, 1772," in *Philosophical Correspondence, 1759-1799*, ed. and trans. Arnulf Zweig (Chicago: The University of Chicago Press, 1970), 71.

concerns the *how* of coming to know something which may occur at a particular time and place and involve different reasons for different people. The second, which is preferred by Frege, concerns the natural ordering of truth grounds, that is, an ordering of truth according to its inner nature. For example, I can make the judgement that the weather is warm outside by reading a thermometer.[28] But there is another asymmetric truth-ordering relation that proceeds in the other direction: the thermometer has the particular reading that it does because the air outside it is warm. The latter is the grounds of the truth.

Here is another example to illustrate this distinction. A child might observe numerous examples of 2 + 2 = 4 and practice counting those numbers until they have mastered that example of basic addition. Given the child has engaged in a basic inductive method, does that mean the truths of arithmetic are justified based on induction from experience? No, according to Frege. Just because one comes to know something in a particular way doesn't mean there is not a more definitive proof that is independent of its empirical expression.

This leads us to a sharper focus on the chief goal of Frege's philosophy of mathematics: *that the truths of arithmetical propositions are supremely general truths.* The generality of arithmetical truths is concerned with its domain of application, most notably a complete abstraction from everything that distinguishes the different sciences. The sciences apply only to the physically or psychologically possible. Even the laws of geometry only "govern all that is intuitable", which applies to:

"The wildest visions of delirium, the boldest inventions of legend and poetry, where animals speak and stars stand still, where men are turned to stone and trees turn into men, where the drowning haul themselves up out of swamps by their own topknots – all these remain, so long as they remain intuitable, still subject to the axioms of geometry."[29]

---

[28] I borrow this example from Mark Textor. *Frege on Sense and Reference* (London and New York: Routledge, 2011), 24-25.
[29] Frege, *Foundations*, 20.

But the laws of arithmetic apply to an even larger domain than geometry: they apply to the actual, intuitable *and* the thinkable.[30] Anything thinkable is also countable. Arithmetic is a precondition of all conceptual thought. Frege's goal in this regard was to put the sciences and arithmetic on the firmest logical foundations possible by accounting for what we already know about arithmetical knowledge.

Now in what exactly does Frege's notion of truth-grounding consist? There isn't much to go on in Frege's own work, so I draw on Textor's interpretation.[31]

First, the basic or primitive truths are not grounded in further truths and are not dependent on individual instances. We can understand what the law of self-identity means by particular examples, such as the "earth = earth" or "1 = 1", but these are merely heuristics to help us understand what the general law is. The interpretations of identity statements help us to understand the law but they do not contribute to the grounds for its proof.

Second, the truth that serves in the grounding position, P, has to be more general than the truth, Q, which it grounds. As we have already seen, the law of self-identity is not grounded in individual instances such as "1 = 1" or "earth = earth". Rather it's the latter that is grounded in the generic law of self-identity. Third, and not unrelated to this, we can also say that it is the more complex truths, such as arithmetic, that are to be deduced from the less complex truths, such as the logical laws. For a set of truths to be defined in terms of another set of truths means that the former is more complex than the latter.

This is a grounding relationship. An analogy will help; seated Socrates is dependent on Socrates since the latter is a substance not dependent on anything else and cannot, *qua* substance, be broken up into more fundamental parts. We could also have other accidental states of Socrates such as running Socrates and standing Socrates but they too are just

---

[30] Ibid, 21.
[31] Textor, *Frege on Sense and Reference*, 36-37.

particular individual instances grounded in the general form of Socrates. Thus the complex gives way to the simple form of being in the order of fundamentality.

Frege's goal, however, was not to present pure formalism. He explicitly rebuffed formalism as having no sense, but involving just the arbitrary manipulation of symbols. He argued that "an arithmetic with no thought as its content will also be without possibility of application."[32] The very generality of arithmetic was in its broad applicability, not in its sheer emptiness. He states: "The same quantitative ratio (the same number) may arise with lengths, time intervals, masses, moments of inertia, etc."[33] So despite arithmetic's broad generality, it is still the case that it has substantial applications.

The development of modern logic had its foundations in Frege's *Bs* and this is where he expounds the general logical laws. Frege's primary concern is to express the laws of arithmetic in the most general manifestation so that they are not dependent on any particular manifestation. Recall his goal was to avoid the Kantian dependency on intuition. Consider the following example from Textor:

The distributive law of multiplication: $(a + b)c = ac + bc$[34]

Notice that this law is expressed without the use of particular numerals, such as "1" or "6". A reliance on specific numerals would not give the law its generality since an infinite number of examples would have to be given. Letters, on the other hand, are indeterminate in that any number can stand in place for any letter. The only requirement is that if the letter is, say, "*a*", then the same number must stand in any of its places. Textor refers to the replacement of each letter with a number as "sharpenings", since it's a move from the indeterminate to the determinate. He explains:

---

[32] Gottlob Frege, "Frege Against the Formalists," in *Translations from the Philosophical Writings of Gottlob Frege*, ed. and trans Peter Geach and Max Black (Oxford: Basil Blackwell, 1960), 187.
[33] Ibid.
[34] Textor, *Frege on Sense and Reference*, 37.

"The sentence '$(a + b)c = ac + bc$' is a law since all 'sharpenings' that make each letter determinately stand for a number yield true sentences about particular numbers. Hence, '$(a + b)c = ac + bc$' is a law of number."[35]

It is paramount for Frege's views that these laws be expressed using letters that convey generality, that is, an independence from any particular sharpening. That is, the inferences follow independent of the particulars, where each particular is generated by replacing a letter with a number. So the following is valid:

$$(a + b)c = ac + bc$$

Therefore: $(1 + 2) \times 3 = 1 \times 3 + 2 \times 3$

This gives a sense of the general structural nature of Fregean logic, and this applies equally to sentences in a way that is distinct from Aristotelian logic. Frege's antipathy to psychologism led him to reject the Aristotelian methodology. This methodology was based on abstractions from mental representation that took judgements and inferences to be concerned with how the extensions of these concepts include and overlap each other. Mental representations, on the other hand, were subjective for Frege, and true knowledge could not come through the vagaries of sense experience.

For the likes of Aristotle and some of Frege's contemporaries (such as George Boole), the errors were "essentially doctrines of inference, in which the formation of concepts is presupposed as something that has already been completed."[36] Instead Frege proposed that concepts should only be decomposable from judgeable contents, and judgements proceeded independently of sense experience. It is this generality approach where the particulars

---

[35] Ibid, 43.
[36] Frege, "Boole's Logical Calculus," in Hermes et al, *Posthumous Writings*, 15.

embodied in a sentence are posterior to a structured entity called a "thought", and here we have the birth of the famous *context principle*:

"What is distinctive about my conception of logic comes out first in that I give top priority to the content of the word 'true' and then that I immediately introduce thoughts as that concerning which the question of truth arises. I therefore do not begin with concepts that I put together into thoughts or judgements. Rather, I obtain thought-components by analysing thoughts."[37]

The role of variables in sentences is to highlight the generality of content. The variable ranges over many individual things. It is thoughts that are primary and the recognition of a name signifying an object, which are not thoughts in themselves, is inferred from the general thought. So we have a separate entity embedded in a separate domain structure that is derived by inference from the general thought. So, for example, grasping "Socrates is mortal" is to grasp this content as an instance of the more formal fundamental general expression "x is mortal".

So the variables marking out segments of sentences convey the idea that structural parts of sentences are primary and the fillers for those roles are secondary. In the *Bs*, Frege proposes notation that involves the function and argument, replacing the standard terms "subject" and "predicate". The latter pair of terms marks out logical distinctions where there shouldn't be any. For example, "Socrates loves Xanthippe" and "Xanthippe is loved by Socrates" were said to be logically distinguishable because of the differences in surface grammar. Frege's definition of function and arguments is:

"Suppose that a simple or complex symbol occurs in one or more places in an expression. If we imagine this symbol as replaceable by another (the same each time) at one or more of its

---

[37] Gottlob Frege, "[Notes for Ludwig Darmstaedter]," in Hermes et al, *Posthumous Writings*, 253.

occurrences, then the part of the expression that shows itself invariant under such replacement is called the function; and the replaceable part, the argument of the function."[38]

This generality conception comes out in two key principles of Frege's that are relevant to our discussion. The first, his guiding principle, is "never lose sight of the distinction between concept and object".[39] The second is the context principle: "Never ask for the meaning of a word in isolation, but only in the context of a sentence".[40]

Frege introduces the concept–object distinction in "On Concept and Object", which he bases on the distinction between proper names and predicates which cannot be substituted for each other in a sentence.[41] This comes out of the distinctions he draws between the uses of "is" in identity statements. If we take an identity statement like:

I) The Morning Star is Venus

The use of "is" in it should not be confused with a use of "is" in:

II) The Morning Star is a planet

The first example involves two proper names on either side of the identity sign whereas the second has a predicate asymmetrically subordinate to the subject term. In the first instance it is possible to switch terms and say that "Venus is the Morning Star" where it is not possible to say "Planet is a Morning Star". This distinction strongly reflects Leibniz's distinction between object identity seen in "a is a" type statements (as in with I) and the properties referred to under Leibniz's Law (as in II). As was argued in the last chapter, identity is at the object level, at least as it is denoted through identity statements. This is

---

[38] Frege, *Begriffsschrift*, §9.
[39] Frege, *Foundations*, xxii.
[40] Ibid.
[41] Frege, "On Concept and Object," in Geach et al, *Translations*, 42-55.

why a distinction for logical reasons can be drawn between the use of "is" in bona fide identity statements that involve proper names and the use of "is" as the copula.

It is easy now to appreciate the dichotomy between the concept and object on the basis of the linguistic distinctions in identity statements. For straight identity the object is directly involved through the use of the proper names, whereas the uses of "is" involving the copula takes the predicate as referring to the concept. The subject term stands for an object that falls under the concept where the predicate refers to the concept.

Fregean commentators take the concept–object distinction to be a straightforward result of the distinction between proper names and predicates.[42] But this is to put the cart before the horse. Fregean identity is Leibnizian and involves objects independent of any sensory routes or any quiddities that can be attributed to the object. This is evidenced when functions and arguments are isolated in sentences and such a process showcases the fundamentality of the individual over its properties or relations. First, one can take the sentence "Socrates loves Xanthippe" to isolate the proper name. We can do that by taking either "Socrates" or "Xanthippe" as the argument or taking both as arguments. If we were to remove the argument "Socrates", we would be left with the function "…loves Xanthippe". If we were to remove the argument "Xanthippe", we would be left with the function "Socrates loves …". And both "Socrates" and "Xanthippe" could be removed and the two–place relational function "… loves …" would remain.

In this example the "loving" relation clearly doesn't enter into the essence of what it means to be either "Socrates" or "Xanthippe". It may not be as clear with such an example as "Venus is a planet" because Venus must essentially be a planet if anything! But whether it is a "planet" or a "human" or any other concept under which objects may fall, neither enter into the strict logical essence of a Leibnizian identity statement which applies independently of *any* conceptual attribution. Returning to our analogy, Socrates can take on accidental states such as seated Socrates or be in accidental relations like loving Xanthippe.

---

[42] C.f. Thomas Ricketts in "Concepts, Objects, and the Context Principle," in *The Cambridge Companion to Frege*, ed. Thomas Ricketts and Michael Potter, 149-219. (Cambridge: Cambridge University Press, 2010)

As one would expect, however, function and argument take on different roles in subject–predicate or relational sentences. "Socrates" denotes an object and that object is what it is independent of any mode of presentation that allows us a sensory route or some way of knowing the object. So "…loves Xanthippe" can be removed from "Socrates" precisely because of the assumptions Frege holds about identity conditions for individuals, which in this case do not involve being in the relation of loving Xanthippe.

Such a characterisation grounds the distinction between concepts and objects, but what we also have is an intrinsic difference between both. Underlying the concept and object distinction are the properties of completeness and incompleteness, to which Frege attaches the terms "saturatedness" and "unsaturatedness". Concepts, as Frege sees them, are functions that take arguments to truth-values (more on this later), in this way they are incomplete or unsaturated. For example, we can take a sentence like "Socrates loves Xanthippe" and remove either "Socrates" or "Xanthippe", which would leave us with concepts like "x loves Xanthippe" or "Socrates loves x". So the use of variables expresses the incompleteness of such expressions where the part removed, signified by a name, is complete or saturated.

The asymmetric nature of concepts and objects fits with the Leibnizian identity conditions. An object is signified by a proper name and is a complete self-standing object with logical identity conditions. Concepts are not referred to by proper names nor do they enter into the essential objectual identity conditions of objects. They are, by their very nature, in need of an object for completion.

The concept can be compared to a piece of jigsaw puzzle that "needs" another thing in order to complete it. It is in its very nature to require completion. Another analogy: seated Socrates depends on Socrates for its existence as an accident of Socrates. It is not a part of Socrates since the latter is a primitive object being a subject representing a substance. But seated Socrates requires for its existence to be completed by Socrates. Thus there is no need for a third thing, a relation R, to unify concept and object. As Frege describes it:

"A concept is unsaturated in that it requires something to fall under it; hence it cannot exist on its own. That an individual falls under it is a judgeable content, and here the concept appears as a predicate and is always predicative. In this case, where the subject is an individual, the relation of subject to predicate is not a third thing added to the two, but it belongs to the content of the predicate, which is what makes the predicate [unsaturated]. Now I do not believe that concept formation can precede judgement because this would presuppose the independent existence of concepts, but I think of a concept as having arisen by decomposition from a judgeable content."[43]

This Leibnizian identity condition provides a basis for the most general conception of an object as a discrete, self-sufficient object. But this is the playing out of the Parmenidian metaphysic. Concepts, which can be relations or predicates, are only accidents vis-à-vis the real realm of being which underlies the self-sufficient, substantial entity, and even the proper name that picks out an individual is really only accidental relative to the structure signified by the variable and its place within the sentence.[44] Ricketts points out that even in the post-1891 period, Leibnizian identity conditions played a strong role as signifying identical objects which coincide in such a way to yield the same truth-value. Ricketts writes:

"Here is the justification for the linguistic substitutions that encode the Leibniz inference: in a true sentence, replacement of a proper name by a proper name signifying the same object yields a truth. A grasp of the inference from generalization to instance in connection with

---

[43] Frege, "Frege to Marty 29.8.1882," in *The Philosophical and Mathematical Correspondence*, ed. Gottfried Gabriel, Hans Hermes, Friedrich Kambartel, Christian Thiel, Albert Veraart, trans. Hans Kaal. (Oxford: Basil Blackwell, 1980), 101.

[44] Ricketts has argued elsewhere against the traditional interpretation of Frege as a Platonist by claiming that logical categories – judgement, assertion, inference, truth – are prior to ontological categories, including numbers. "Objectivity and Objecthood: Frege's Metaphysics of Judgment," in *Frege Synthesized: Essays on the Philosophical and Foundational Work of Gottlob Frege*, ed. Leila Haaparanta and Jaakko Hintikka, 65-95. (Dordrecht: D. Reidal Publishing Company, 1986). I take this as support for my thesis that Frege is predominantly Parmenidian above all else since his logical categories are a manifestation of the univocal notion of Parmenidian being which explains even numbers.

proper names thus includes a grasp of objects as discrete, and so a grasp of identity and the Leibniz inference."[45]

Leibnizian identity statements are therefore central for Frege and *it is this* that grounds the function of sentence structure and not the other way around. They represent the manifestation of Fregean–Parmenidian being in the world. The positions of function and argument in sentences play a role in isolating the particulars that emerge, since to know the generality of the content – as signified by the use of letters – is to know what may be substituted for those letters to form particular instances. The particular crystalises out of the whole set out by the structure of the sentence.

So it is a purely analytic move by Frege to get the particular out of the general. The linguistic functions of expressions in Frege's sentences and their univocal nature make clear that they fulfil a particular role independently of any particular expression that may occupy that role. Take Frege's example:

1) ⊢ Hydrogen is lighter than carbon dioxide[46]

Now within Frege's special logical language in the *Bs*, which he calls the concept-script, he makes use of a symbol formed from a vertical line followed by a horizontal line: ⊢.[47] The horizontal line is the "content line" and the vertical line is the "judgement line". The horizontal line alone, such as with −P, interlocks the signs that follow it, whereas the combination of both expresses the full assertion of P as true. ⊢ is the common predicate of all judgements since to assert a judgement can be paraphrased as "is a fact". So 1) is another way of stating:

1") It is a fact that hydrogen is lighter than carbon dioxide

---

[45] Ricketts, "Concepts, Objects, and the Context Principle," in Ricketts et al, *The Cambridge Companion*, 157.
[46] *Begriffsschrift*, §9.
[47] Ibid, 10-11.

Using just the content line gives us

2) – Hydrogen is lighter than carbon dioxide

This would be to state:

    2.1)   The circumstances that hydrogen is lighter than carbon dioxide

Now we can also highlight the function and argument parts of a sentence. We can highlight the argument part of the expression as follows:

1) **Hydrogen** is lighter than carbon dioxide

And as an argument, we can replace it with numerous other examples, such as:

2) **Oxygen** is lighter than carbon dioxide
3) **Nitrogen** is lighter than carbon dioxide

So the argument represents something like a slot in which different particulars can enter to complete the sentence. Alternatively we could treat carbon dioxide as the argument and retain hydrogen as the function.

4) Hydrogen is lighter than **carbon dioxide**
5) Hydrogen is lighter than **ammonia**

There are no in principle reasons why one aspect of the sentence should be taken as argument or function. Indeed even "is lighter than" can occupy the argument position and be varied with other relational expressions, such as "is heavier than", etc. The grammar may be freely interchangeable but the content remains the same. Thus we can say that "Socrates" is the subject in "Socrates loves Xanthippe", or we can say "Xanthippe" is the subject in "Xanthippe is loved by Socrates". But in either case, regardless of grammatical differences, Frege observes that we have the same content.[48]

What Frege is chiefly interested in is highlighting the positions of function and argument in the overall structure of the sentence. If we focus on the subject, say "hydrogen", we put it in contrast to a range of subjects that can be inserted into that particular place, such as ammonia or carbon dioxide. Thus we have a particular syntactical space:

() is lighter than carbon dioxide

The brackets signify an indeterminacy in the sense that it determines nothing particular but that position in the sentence can be filled by alternatives that make distinct sentences. Regardless of what we fill the spaces with, we still have the sentence categories of function and argument carrying out the same roles. The formal logical range of such categories is singular in the same way that a circle can be realised in multiple physical mediums but retains the same formal properties. The contrastive focus brings this out as well as the dispensability of the fillers for each role in the sentence structure.

The important distinction between function and argument does not touch on anything essential to the content but the distinction is only "…because we view the expression in a particular way".[49] Although function and argument are external to content, they are nonetheless indispensable to how the content is viewed since they are the linguistic tools that express the conceptual content. So they play a purely revelatory role: they reveal the underlying logical essence.

---

[48] Ibid, 12.
[49] Ibid, 22.

Function and argument tie together into a whole in a sentence in accordance with Frege's context principle. However, the actual mechanism responsible for tying them together into a whole comes from the content stroke. In the same way that we can analyse a circular pattern embodied in multiple different physical media, we can also imagine the same content stroke in front of multiple different function–argument expressions. The form is hence something distinct from its physical embodiment and hence plays a structuring role of putting the indeterminate physical medium into determinate form.

Frege's functional analyses of sentences allows him to draw out the generality at the heart of his logical analysis. It was in defining concepts as functions and objects as arguments that allowed him to highlight the structure of judgements as abstracted completely from any content. So we can formalise "Socrates loves Xanthippe" as the relation "x loves y". We can then go a step further and replace "loves" with "R" as with "xRy".

With this first foray into Frege's system we get a sketch of the role being plays in his system: it is the source of logical stability that grounds the particular that only potentially fills in for the variable. This is the grounds that underwrites knowledge in general. Similarly, the concept is held distinct from the object. This is because the former is dependent on the latter and cannot be a part of it, since that would be to break up being into parts. It is in knowing the *generality* derived from the content stroke first which is signified by the variable or empty brackets that we come to derive the particular that gets substituted in to the syntactical space in the sentence. Univocal being, known by reason, grounds the separate domain of particular known through sense.

ii)   **The Whole Above the Parts**

Dummett draws a distinction between two sorts of analysis.[50] One sort specifies the sort of entities that need to be grasped in order to grasp the whole thought. There is a unique part–whole analysis of the thought and thus to grasp the whole propositional content requires

---

[50] Dummett, *Frege*, ch. 15.

grasping its constituents. The second sort of analysis invokes a more creative mechanism, where there is no unique decomposition into constituents. This analysis is based on inferential relations where we see the various patterns embodied but none of the patterns is uniquely privileged in composing the whole.

Decomposition is like a jigsaw puzzle where the smaller pieces can be put together in different ways to make up the same content. There may be different ways to decompose a sentence without varying the content. But it is the function–argument pattern in a sentence that matters more than any particular proper name. Here's Frege's example:

"'The circumstance that carbon dioxide is heavier than hydrogen' and 'the circumstance that carbon dioxide is heavier than oxygen' are the same function with different arguments if we regard 'hydrogen' and 'oxygen' as arguments; on the other hand, they are different functions of the same argument if we regard 'carbon dioxide' as the argument."[51]

There are various inferential relations within the one whole and thus various ways to decompose it. The same pattern can determine various different expressions. So the specific proper names are just fillers for the pattern that plays the determinative role that the process of decomposition reveals. Joseph Levine explains:

"Thus in order to infer <Something is greater than 2> from <3 > 2>, we must be able to recognize the content <3 < 2> as exemplifying the pattern expressed by 'x > 2', a pattern also exemplified by the contents <1 < 2>, <2 < 2> and <4 > 2>. Likewise, in order to infer <Something is such that 3 is greater than it> from <3 > 2>, we must be able to recognize the content <3 > 2> as exemplifying the pattern expressed by '3 > x', a pattern also exemplified by the contents <3 > 1>, <3 > 3> and <3 > 4>."[52]

---

[51] Frege, *Begriffsschrift*, 22.
[52] Joseph Levine, "Analysis and Decomposition in Frege and Russell," *The Philosophical Quarterly* 52, no. 207 (2002): 195-216, http://www.jstor.org/stable/3542843.

The goal for Frege was to achieve a generality of analysis where the parts are derived from the thought but the parts are not identical with any aspect of the thought. The proper name is derived from its position in the context of the sentence so that something like "Socrates" in "Socrates loves Xanthippe" is an instance of a general quantifier such as "x" that could range over a number of other objects that could occupy the proper name position, for example, "Plato loves Xanthippe". To repeat, it is the general inferential structure that takes priority and it is in attaching that inferential structure to truth that generates concepts. Thus what are called parts should really be called accidents in the sense that seated Socrates or running Socrates are derived from Socrates but are not parts in any robust sense. The parts of the whole and the possibilities of decomposition are as multiple as the accidents derivable from a substance.

As he stated in summarising his life's work:

"What is distinctive of my conception of logic is that I began by giving pride of place to the content of the word 'true', and then immediately go on to introduce a thought as that to which the question 'Is it true?' is in principle applicable. So I do not begin with concepts and put them together to form a thought or judgement; I come by the parts of a thought by analysing the thought."[53]

Frege's logic is highly structural and sentences are holistic, where the positions in the sentence delegate proper name and concept expressions. It is also highly Leibnizian where identity is a function of anything being identical with itself and so *a* being identical with *b* means that they completely coincide, such that what holds of *a* must, of necessity, hold of *b*. There are two salient features of Frege's use of the Leibnizian inference. One is that although identity conditions for each thing in the world are supposed to be unique to that thing, the definition of self-identity *as a relation* is univocal, since it is the same relation

---

[53] Frege, "[Notes for Ludwig Darmstaedter]," in Hermes et al, *Posthumous Writings*, 253.

that is a precondition for the existence of anything whatsoever.[54] It does not admit of any definition: to know that a thing is identical with itself tells us nothing about the kind of thing that it is. The second salient feature is that for anything to exist in such an identity relation it must be discrete. So for any object to be admitted to the proper name position in a sentence, it must have determinate boundaries, that is, discreteness is built into the position in the structure of the sentence.

As will be explored in the next chapter, Frege took truth to be univocal, indefinable and rationally derived. Through the use of identity, reason gives us the law of identity which forms the backbone of sentences and allows us to parse out the various particulars that can be permuted whilst retaining the overall structure. Thus knowledge does not proceed through particular to sentence, but the other way around. The judgement and content strokes logically precede, and are foundational to, the sentence and its content.

We may attempt to narrow down the conditions of truth to some particular instance. However, applying truth to any instance would be illegitimate, since truth, like Leibnizian identity, is *external* to any particular in the world, and applying it would invite the further question as to whether that particular application is itself true. Thus a vicious regress threatens. Frege writes:

"And any other attempt to define truth also breaks down. For in a definition certain characteristics would have to be specified. And in application to any particular case the question would always arise whether it were *true* that the characteristics were present. So we should be going round in a circle."[55]

Fregean analyticity, however, is not like Kant's in not being able to advance knowledge. His broader conception of logic meant it had a genuine content. The logical definitions and laws are productive in that the analytic propositions grow out of the definitions and are "as

---

[54] Throughout the *Begriffsschrift* identity is taken as one of the basic identity symbols so that logic suffices for general application.
[55] Frege, "The Thought," 291.

plants are contained in their seeds, not as beams are contained in a house".[56] Frege complains about Kant's definition of analyticity:

"[Kant] seems to think of concepts as defined by giving a simple list of characteristics in no particular order; but, of all ways of forming concepts, that is one of the least fruitful. If we look through the definitions given in the course of this book, we shall scarcely find one that is of this description. The same is true of the really fruitful definitions in mathematics, such as that of the continuity of a function. What we find in these is not a simple list of characteristics; every element in the definition is intimately, I might almost say organically, connected with the others.

What we shall be able to infer from [the definition] cannot be inspected in advance; here we are not simply taking out of the box what we have just put into it. The conclusions we draw from it extend our knowledge, and ought therefore, on Kant's view, to be regarded as synthetic; and yet they can be proved by purely logical means and are thus analytic. The truth is that they are contained in the definitions, but as plants are contained in their seeds, not as beams are contained in a house."[57]

For Frege particular sentences are mere embodiments and expressions of much broader patterns of logical deduction that give rise to them. The inferential patterns that attach to the True are thus highly determinative of the particular instances that give rise to objects delineated by proper names and concept expressions. As we have seen, the function and argument expressions are just that: expressions external to the real essential nature of the logical relations that underlie and give rise to them.

Frege later articulates a view of content that is more structured than what we get in the *Bs*, articulating concepts in terms such as "incomplete" and "unsaturated": where to count as a

---

[56] Frege, *Foundations*, 101.
[57] Ibid, 100-101.

concept something must "fall under it".[58] Such a conceptual approach was very much integral to the generality of logic and the concomitant derivation of concepts from judgements. Earlier he used similar language where the variable is "holding a place open for" the argument.[59] Contrasting his view of concept formation with that of Boole, he writes:

"For in Aristotle, as in Boole, the logically primitive activity is the formation of concepts by abstraction, and judgement and inference enter in through an immediate or indirect comparison of concepts via their extensions. . . . As opposed to this, I start out from judgements and their contents, and not from concepts. . . . I only allow the formation of concepts to proceed from judgements. If, that is, you imagine the 2 in the content of possible judgement

$$2^4 = 16$$

to be replaced by something else, by (–2) or by 3 say, which may be indicated by putting an *x* in place of the 2:

$$x^4 = 16,$$

the content of possible judgement is thus split into a constant and a variable part. The former, regarded in its own right but holding a place open for the latter, gives the concept '4th root of 16'."[60]

Again, instead of abstracting concepts en route to true judgements, Frege is proposing that concepts can be derived from true judgements. The use of a variable along with a proper

---

[58] Frege, "Frege to Marty 29.8.1882," in Gabriel et al, *The Philosophical and Mathematical Correspondence*, 101.
[59] Frege, "Boole's logical Calculus," in Hermes et al, *Posthumous Writings*, 16.
[60] Ibid, 15-16.

name on the right-hand side are to fit together like hand-in-glove according to the logical demands of the whole sentence organised to give rise to the identity condition. The variable functioning to hold the place open for the argument is Frege's way of eliminating what is superfluous to the underlying identity function and what is subsequently permitted to be abstracted out of the sentence as an already articulated whole. The substitutability or interchangeability of functions in the variable position signals their indeterminacy vis-à-vis the whole sentence structure whilst finding completion and ultimately elimination in the context of the sentence.

The concept, which is a functional expression, finds completion in the self-subsistent object. This is elaborated by Frege's distinction between the *sense* (Sinn) and *reference* (Bedeutung) of an object. The *sense* of an object is a way in which it presents itself. Using numbers as an example, the two sentences "4^2" and "$(2 \times 2)^2$" are different senses of the one object. The sense of a predicate is a concept that maps an object to a truth-value. The concept, in effect, finds completion in the combination of the object and the truth-value. This is the elegance of the Fregean program: he has the determinate identity sign, truth functional symbols and truth-value on the one hand, and the epistemically individuative criteria – which are the ways they are presented or expressed – on the other hand. So the expression of the object–truth-value function can be called "functions-in-intensions".[61] The mode of presentation for each example can be given as follows:

"…to one who understands the expression '4^2', this expression presents an object as the number that results if the successor of 3 is multiplied by itself. The expression '$(2 \times 2)^2$' presents that same object in a different way, namely, as the number that results if the successor of one is multiplied by the successor of one and then this intermediary results is multiplied by itself."[62]

An obvious consequence of the numbering relation is that each number occupies a successor relationship and this would appear to be an essential characteristic of numbers if

---

[61] Richard Heck and Robert May, "The Composition of Thoughts," *Nous* 45, no. 1 (2011): 126-166, https://doi.org/10.1111/j.1468-0068.2010.00769.x
[62] Ibid, 159.

ever there was. But this is not the case, as it turns out, for the implications of Frege's functions. These successor functions are mere modes of presentations for the Leibnizian object that Frege plugs in as the occupier for the reference of each numeral. So if we take the function "e^2" which maps the same object in the case of both "4" or "(2 × 2)" we return the value "16" in both cases as the value of that function. We have a function from objects to objects in both cases. But if we take two identity statements such as:

1) "$4^2 = 16$"
2) "$(2 \times 2)^2 = 16$"

In both cases we have an identity statement where the same object is referred to on both sides of the identity sign. This *is* an instance of identity, the classic case being self-identity "a = a", but where 1) and 2) are distinct modes of presentation of the one logical object. Going back to functions and the mapping of objects to objects – the function maps the object denoted by "4" to "16" in the first example and "(2 × 2)" in the second – we have a case of Fregean objectual identity which is a "relation between objects . . . in which each thing stands to itself but to no other thing."[63] We have here numbers as logical objects and the distinctly mathematical functions are modes of presentation – senses – of the logical object.

The univocal notions of identity and truth provide no distinctions, nor is there any differentiation within them, so a place must be carved out by Frege that is distinct from these categories. Intensions are meant to play both an individuative and an expressive role. Frege applied this as much in arithmetic as with any other cases of identity. Take a simpler example: "2 + 3 = 5" is a statement where the relation of sense can be distinguished from reference. What is significant about this statement, above and beyond a bland statement of self-identity, is that the thought of the sum operation of 2 + 3, the sense, carries the mathematically significant information. We have the same reference but the left-hand side is designated via its sense, which carries cognitive significance, and thus means something

---

[63] Gottlob Frege, "On Sense and Reference," in Geach et al, *Translations*, 56.

above and beyond just "5 = 5". Frege brings the tools of sense and reference to mathematical statements. He wrote:

"one cannot fail to recognize that the thought expressed by '5 = 2 + 3' is different than that expressed by the '5 = 5', although the difference only consists in the fact that in the second sentence '5', which designates the same number as '2 + 3', takes the place of '2 + 3'. So the two signs are not equivalent from the point of view of the thought expressed, although they designate the very same number. Hence I say that the signs '5' and '2 + 3' do indeed designate the same thing, but do not express the same *sense*. In the same way 'Copernicus' and 'the author of heliocentric view of the planetary system' designate the same man, but have different senses; for the sentence 'Copernicus is Copernicus' and 'Copernicus is the author of the heliocentric view of the planetary system' do not express the same thought."[64]

What we have is a vast web of logical interrelations that derive their status and essential nature in connection to their truth-value. Burge spells out these two aspects – the Leibnizian inference and the truth conditions – of Frege's thought: "One understands the structural nature of thoughts and components of thoughts ... by reflecting discursively on a large number of deductive inferences among sentences."[65] And: "The key to understanding such structure lies in understanding the contribution of such components to determining truth conditions and to preserving truth in deductive inference."[66] But as we have seen these logical deductions are not multiple manifestations in the sense of being distinct *kinds* of things but are rather all manifestations of the single univocal identity and truth conditions.

The priority Frege gives to these categories reveals a particular part–whole conception. Going back to Dummett's distinction between analysis and decomposition, he holds Frege to a univocal notion of parthood and hence restricts the parthood relation to any analysis of sentences. He points to the indeterminacy of values of function–argument expressions:

---

[64] Gottlob Frege, "Logic in Mathematics," in Hermes et al, *Posthumous Writings*, 225.
[65] Burge, *Truth, Thought, Reason*, 14.
[66] Ibid.

"Given only the value of a function for some argument, it is not possible to recover the function or the argument. For this reason, it is inappropriate to regard either the argument or the function as a *constituent* or *part* of the value, since we naturally suppose that anything is uniquely analyzable into its ultimate constituents."[67]

Hence it is impossible to work backwards from truth-value to any determinate selection of function or argument. In the same way that Socrates does not determine seated Socrates since the latter is not a part of, but is rather grounded in, the former, and Socrates could just as easily manifest a different accident such as running Socrates. Others such as James Levine disagree, pointing out that Frege held to a broader conception of parthood than would have been found in a more atomistic type of mereology where only one unique set of parts is possible for any whole.[68] Frege speaks of the same thought as being "split up in different ways…" and "put together out of parts in different ways."[69] And there are passages where he contrasts the uniqueness of the elements of a class with the parthood relation itself which can be involved in different decompositions:

"… if we are given a whole, it is not yet determined what we are to envisage as its parts. As parts of a regiment I can regard the battalions, the companies or the individual soldiers, and as parts of a sand pile, the grains of sand or the silicon and oxygen atoms. On the other hand, if we are given a class, it is determined what objects are members of it…. The only members of the class of companies of a given regiment are the companies, but not the individual soldiers."[70]

So a given whole does not, in fact, determine a particular part–whole outcome. This is as it should be, since, as we have seen for Frege, different wholes are decomposed through an interchange of the parts via the substitution into variable positions in the sentence. This is a result of the ontological distinction between the structural features of the sentence that are

---

[67] Michael Dummett, "An Unsuccessful Dig," *The Philosophical Quarterly* 34, no. 136 (1984): 377-401, http://doi.org/10.2307/2218768.
[68] James Levine, "Analysis and Decomposition,"
[69] Gottlob Frege, "A brief Survey of My logical Doctrines," in Hermes et al, *Posthumous Writings*, 201-202.
[70] Gottlob Frege, "Frege to Russell 28.7.1902," in Gabriel et al, *The Philosophical and Mathematical Correspondence,* 140.

intimately connected to truth-values, on the one hand, and the occupiers of those slots in the sentence, on the other. The whole for Frege is inevitably univocal whilst the parts are dispensable to the whole's identity. The locus for inferential relations which characterises its essence lies in the structure of the whole. The whole, then, is pregnant with different possibilities of different parthood manifestations.

Again, this is a concept of being that is separate from its *parthood manifestations*. Whole and parts are in two separate domains. The parts being accidents merely present the structural positions of the whole. This is even the case in mathematics where, say, the successor relation or identities like $4^2 = (8 + 8)$, just give different modes of presentation of the one manifestation of being. The whole grounds the parts precisely because the former is more fundamental than the latter.

iii) **Truth-Value**

Sentences are then able to derive their identity conditions from referencing truth-values. The meaning of a sentence is its truth-value which is expressed by its sense. The truth-value plays a determinative role out of which the sentence is constructed and can be then decomposed in multiple directions through substitutions. As Frege puts it "sense attaching to a truth-value corresponds its own manner of analysis."[71] Thus parts are posterior to determination by truth-value and this is why he also defines parts in a "special", non-literal sense.[72]

In other words, what it means to be a part is contextual – and hence derivative – inhabiting a certain context derived from a truth-value. The filler for that particular sentential "slot" could have occupied a different part of a different whole as dictated by the context principle. This lends weight to Levine's position, as clearly this is not a part–whole relation that just involves a set of concatenated items.

---

[71] Frege, "On Sense and Reference," in Geach et al, *Translations*, 65.
[72] Ibid.

But playing such a determinative role means the truth-value must in some way be constitutive of what it means for each sentence to be a whole. But it is more than just constitutive of each whole. The truth-value determines positions within the whole rendering fillers of each role essentially epiphenomenal to the whole and its function as a judgement. The motivating intuition behind this is that extrinsic properties tell us nothing about the nature of the relata. For example, any duplicate of me would have the same height and mass that I do but may well differ in not being a brother or father as I am. Edward Kanterian explains:

"If I am told that there is a certain true thought about Thomas Aquinas, without being told what thought that is ('Aquinas had mystical insights'), I know that the Meaning of the sentence expressing that thought is the True and, also, apparently, that a 'part' of that truth-value is Aquinas himself, but I still can't determine the remaining bit of the thought, the predicate or concept ('had mystical insights')."[73]

The metaphysical picture painted by Frege is that we have these objects, the True and the False, and they occupy a central position in the order of knowledge. We do not name these objects and identify their properties as we would ordinarily do when we want to know what the sentence is about. But the order of knowledge proceeds in the opposite direction. First we find out whether a sentence is true *and then* we determine the object that the sentence stands for. Thus we have an ontological order of being that proceeds from the True category to all the other objects that are the derivatives of true sentences. This is why Kurt Gödel believed that Frege's supreme category of the True to be "reminding one somewhat of the Eleatic doctrine of the 'One'."[74] Likewise Richard Mendelsohn said, "The resemblance is certainly striking. For the True – or the Great Fact or Reality – appears to be an undifferentiated totality much like Parmenides' being."[75]

---

[73] Edward Kanterian, *Frege: A Guide for the Perplexed* (London and New York: Continuum, 2012), 185.
[74] Kurt Godel, "Russell's Mathematical Logic," in *Philosophy of Mathematics, Selected Readings* 2nd ed., ed. Hillary Putnam and Paul Benacerraf (Cambridge: Cambridge University Press, 1983), 214.
[75] Richard Mendelsohn, *The Philosophy of Gottlob Frege* (Cambridge: Cambridge University Press, 2005), 137.

Frege's idea of the content of logic arises from its potential to generate content out of positions delimited by sentence structures. It's a fruitfulness of determination that involves charting the waters between the empirical derivation of arithmetic from observations in the world and the formalist methods that involve the manipulation of empty symbols. Instead Frege offers a program that involves the context principle, a particular conception of logic, and the distinction between the concept and object that express the determinative role set out by the logical laws and the univocal notion of truth. Thus in contradistinction to empty symbols or empirically derived objects we have here what seems to resemble transcendental categories that express themselves as the essential and determinative conditions of sentence structures.

The opposition between the determining conditions and their particular embodiments in sentences also clarifies the apparent tension between the context principle and the compositionality principle. The latter principle states that the senses of the ingredients of a sentence are more basic than the sentence as a whole. Thus in contradistinction to the context principle the individual words are more basic since they can occupy different sentences and carry their meaning with them. Dummett was the first to bring attention to this dilemma where he writes:

"It [my solution] was meant to epitomize the way I hoped to reconcile that principle [Context], taken as one relating to sense, with the thesis that the sense of a sentence is built up out of the senses of the words. This is a difficulty which faces most readers of Frege. . .The thesis that a thought is compounded out of parts comes into apparent conflict, not only with the context principle, but also with the priority thesis…"[76]

Recall that the context principle involves opening up positions within the sentence that give the proper name and the identity conditions of the individual. Remember, too, that in a sentence like "Socrates loves Xanthippe" it is the particulars that are derived from the structural features of the sentence that are signalled through the use of variables, such as with "x loves Xanthippe". But it is not that "Socrates" could not find meaning in other

---

[76] Michael Dummett, *The Interpretation of Frege's Philosophy* (London: Duckworth, 1981), 547.

sentences, such as in "Socrates taught Plato", but that within the context of a sentence "Socrates" derives a meaning peculiar to, and derived out of, that sentence whole.

The context principle is the expression of the determining conditions of the truth-value and the logical laws and it is these features that set the structure that is embodied and realised in the particular sentence. But we cannot come to know such contextual features except through the particulars that fill the roles set for them in the sentence. So what we have here are parts-in-context and thus no conflict between the context and compositionality principles. Dummett writes:

"Frege's account, if it is to be reduced to a slogan, could be expressed in this way: that in the order of *explanation* the sense of a sentence is primary, but in the order of *recognition* the sense of a word is primary. Frege was unwaveringly insistent that the sense of a sentence – or of any complex expression – is made up out of the senses of its constituent words. This means we understand the sentence – grasp its sense – by knowing the senses of the constituents. . It is this which I intended to express by saying that, for Frege, the sense of the word is primary, and that of the sentence secondary, in the order of recognition: any theory of meaning which is unable to incorporate this point will be impotent to account for the obvious and essential fact that we can understand new sentences. But, when we come to give any general explanation of what it is for sentences and words to have a sense, that is, of what it is for us to grasp their sense, then the order of priority is reversed."[77]

Thus Dummett's distinction between the "explanation" and the "recognition" reflects complementary factors that together influence the identity conditions of a sentence and its parts. The sentence is explanatory in that it sets out the positions that play a determinative role in what the particular names or concepts will mean. But to grasp the sense of the whole it is necessary that we grasp the senses of the parts the identities of which have been fixed antecedently by the whole. Thus the identity conditions fixed by the sentence are not absolute, since that would preclude us from recognising the same words in different sentences. The whole is thus dependent on the particular words to be realised and hence

---

[77] Dummett, *Frege*, 4.

recognised where the individual words have their identity conditions fixed in part by the structure.[78]

Thus the central position the True occupies in Frege's system is the most explicit expression of how his sentences express Parmenidian being in its primitiveness and all-pervasive generality. The True gives structure to sentences which in turn grounds the particulars that can be substituted for the variables. Frege rejects the correspondence principle precisely because he gives pride of place to the True in *the reconstruction of knowledge* rather than taking knowledge as it is.

Frege's Twin System

As argued in the opening section of the chapter, Frege's position and influences are fundamentally Parmenidian in nature. Reason and logic, for Frege, are univocal and normative, and as such are ontologically distinct from, but fundamental relative to, the physical objects of perception (or their mental correlates, such as sense data, imaginings, or memories). The ontological dualism that Frege sets up commits him to oppose any form of linguistic meaning that is isolated inside the subjective cognition of any perceiver. The derivations of meaning which proceed through thought must be distinguished from their unlimited and varyingly associated subjective ideas and their material counterparts in the external world. Recall that substitution is demanded where the variable, marking out the proper name, and predicates and relations being unsaturated entities, find completion in the whole of the sentence.

The context principle and the function–argument segmentation of a sentence have traditionally led the majority of Frege scholars to place his sentence structure at the heart of his ontology. But this is to ignore the strict rationalist strictures that Frege follows in

---

[78] This distinction between the context principle which determines the identity of individual constituents and the composition principle where the whole requires each word to be reusable in different contexts and is necessary for the recognition of the sense of a word finds parallels with the *determiner* and *realiser* categories I will expound in later chapters.

drawing the distinction between reason and the laws of logic on the one hand, and the material and sensual world, on the other. There are no necessary internal connections between the subjective world of ideas and the objective world of thoughts and thus no way for our mental impressions to figure in knowledge justification. Thus Frege situates meanings in the context of sentence structure as a way of deriving them internally from thought and thus grounding – the way accidents are grounded in substance – their existence. Our epistemic states have to be reconstructed and not taken at face value.

Frege's dualism is found in the area of truth where he divides between two kinds of justification: "…those for which truth can be carried out purely by means of logic and those for which it must be supported by facts of experience."[79] The former kind are concerned with the nature and grounds of truth, the laws of inference (or deductive logic), and reflect the rational method of analysis we find in Descartes. Non-foundational knowledge is derived by deduction from foundational instances of knowledge. The latter are themselves known by intuition, when we "grasp"[80] abstract or logical objects. This act of "grasping" was never properly explained by Frege but the grasp of sense is a necessary precondition for referring.[81]

The intellect's drawing of inferences is immediate, transparent and absolute. There is no segmenting the inferential process into distinct kinds. Nor does it depend in any way on the variables of sense data. This was the point of the variables Frege inserted into his logical laws where different subjects and concepts can be substituted, since the laws of logical inference are independent of anything taking the place of those variables. The knowledge that is drawn from the senses has gaps but there can be no gaps in logic. The laws of logic are univocal. This Cartesian foundationalism at the heart of Frege's epistemology can be seen in this passage from an unpublished essay:

"Now the grounds which justify the recognition of a truth often reside in other truths which have already been recognized. But if there are any truths recognized by us at all, this cannot

---

[79] Frege, *Begriffsschrift*, 5.
[80] Frege, "The Thought," 309.
[81] The mystery of how the knower hooks on to the sense will be explored in the next section.

be the only form that justification takes. There must be judgments whose justification rests on something else, if they stand in need of justification at all.

And this is where epistemology comes in. Logic is concerned only with those grounds of judgment which are truths. To make a judgment because we are cognizant of other truths as providing justification for it is known as *inferring*. There are laws governing this kind of justification, and to set up these laws of valid inference is the goal of logic."[82]

Now it could be asked at this point how it is that such a logic seen as a monolithic block could make the vital distinctions that grounds the variable knowledge gained through sense experience. In other words, how is a rigidly general view of logic supposed to give us an understanding of the various objects and natures that make up our everyday folk ontology? But Frege's aim *was* for substantial information to be derivable from identity contexts. Different names flanking the identity sign, for example "a = b", are two different modes of presentation by which the same content or object is revealed. The symbols for identity of content are not just incidental grammatical features, as is the difference between "At Platea the Greeks defeated the Persians" and "At Platea the Persians were defeated by the Greeks".

It is in moving from purely formal modes of identity judgements, like "x is x", to the exact same identity relation, expressed materially, as in "x is y", that we see how the generality in Frege's logic can yield substantive identities where the different names are identities but cloaked in different modes of presentation. The chaotic flux of varying appearances and perceptions can be reduced to identities signalled by two different names. It is the entering into such identity relations by objects signalled by different names that yields the substantive production of new synthetic truths. There is nothing internal to the occupants of either side of the identity sign that grounds the identity but it is the generic identity condition itself that plays such a role. For example, if we have an identity statement like "Hesperus = Phosphorus" then the identity is fixed because they are extensionally the same – that is, they are occupying either side of the identity sign – and not because of any unique

---

[82] Gottlob Frege, "Logic," in Hermes et al, *Posthumous Writings*, 3.

descriptive features of either "Hesperus" or "Phosphorus" (which are merely picked out epistemically).

But logics like Frege's are permutation invariant. In other words, the chain of deduction follows through independently of the difference between any particulars that take the place of any variable. But attribuiting such permutation invariance to Frege's system is incorrect according to John Macfarlane, and as such, the accusation that the generality of Fregean categories are insufficiently discriminatory misfires:

"But even apart from his commitment to logicism, Frege could not demarcate the logical notions by their permutation invariance. For he holds that *every sentence* is the name of a particular object: a truth-value. As a result, not even the *truth functions* in his logic are insensitive to differences between particular objects: negation and the conditional must be able to distinguish the True from all other objects. Finally, every one of Frege's logical laws employs a concept, the 'horizontal' (–), whose extension is {the True}. The horizontal is plainly no more permutation-invariant than the concept *identical with Socrates*, whose extension is {Socrates}."[83]

But this is to miss the heart of Frege's rationalism, namely the dualism he draws between rational principles and the way they are instantiated (as expressed by particular names and their modes of presentation). The univocal notions of the True, or the horizontal stroke, or any of the logical apparantus Frege makes use of, bear no structural congruity to the particular objects that express them. The very fact of permutation invariance means the logical structure of the laws of deduction are *indifferent* to the structure of the objects that enter into those relations.

Take the last example Macfarlane gives. Certainly the concept "identical with Socrates" is permutation invariant as a whole since, for example, Plato cannot occupy the other side of

---

[83] John Macfarlane, "Frege, Kant, and the Logic in Logicism," *The Philosophical Review* 111, no. 1 (2002): 34, http://doi.org/10.1215/00318108-111-1-25

the identity sign to Socrates. But Plato *can* enter into the the relation of being self-identical. And since being identical with oneself is a relation that any object enters into just by virtue of *being*, then, *a fortiori*, that relation certainly *is* permutation variant in the broadest possible sense.

Identity for Frege refers to "the essence of things"[84] which is what is expressed by the symbols of logic, but such essences bear no structural affinities either with the linguistic symbols or the modes of presentation through which they are expressed. This follows quite naturally from the univocallity of the logical laws which means that there can be no differentiation within them that would allow for a structural isomorphism – and hence any intelligible internal relation – with the objects that substitute into those laws. Such an isomorphism with any particular, that would demarcate it *qua* that particular, would necessarily exclude any isomorphism with any other particular, but this would be impossible for a univocal notion of truth. What is more, the formal notion of identity is the same definitionally as the material mode and so, in terms of structure, the condition of identity is indifferent to any particular that enters into the identity relation.

Frege tries to walk the tight rope between purely formal logic and its content. He states "as far as logic itself is concerned, each object is as good as any other, and each concept of the first level as good as any other and can be replaced by it."[85] But he denies that logic is "unrestrictedly formal" and the reason he gives has a whiff of question-begging about it: "if it were, then it would be without content".[86] To support his point he compares logic to the basic concepts of geometry: "Just as the concept *point* belongs to geometry, so logic, too, has its own concepts and relations; and it is only in virtue of this that it can have a content. Toward what is thus proper to it, its relation is not at all formal . . . To logic, for example, there belong the following: negation, identity, subsumption, sub-ordination of concepts. And here logic brooks no replacement".[87]

---

[84] Gottlob Frege, "Conceptual Notation," in *Conceptual Notation and Related Articles*, ed. and trans. Terrell Ward Bynum (Oxford: Clarendon Press, 1972), 126.
[85] Gottlob Frege, *On the Foundations of Geometry and Formal Theories of Arithmetic*, trans. Eike-Henner Kluge (New Haven: Yale University Press, 1971), 109.
[86] Ibid.
[87] Ibid.

So just like the sciences and geometry, logic has its own concepts and relations that are indespensable to it in so far as it is just these concepts under which fall the concepts and relations of the special sciences. But still, it is through intuitive and deductive means that conclusions are drawn. The variables in any particular subject area can be supplied by the sciences, but such deductions as structured logical propositions employing truth functions and identity are essentially indifferent to the subject matter supplied by the sciences.

What we have here is a system of logical deduction that is Parmenidian to the extent that the deduction occurs independently of the empirical world and yet it is all pervasive in the sense that derivation can be made of particulars that are substituted in for variables (which is most notable in the case of identities). In other words, like Parmenides, Frege seeks to make knowledge only possible due to logical deduction. But the question of whether such a logical system can explain the many and varied nature of the world is a challenging one. The permutation invariance of the structure of logic makes it indifferent to the entities that populate the world, and this calls into question whether or not it has the explanatory power to do the reconstruction of the world of appearances that Frege wants it to do. We will see in later chapters that this dilemma reaches a climax in the work of Carnap and Quine, a dilemma that leads the latter to reject intensions altogether.

The Transition from *Begriffsschrift* to On Sense and Reference

In the *Bs*, Frege was clearly dissatisfied with the lack of rigor and precision in ordinary language, making it unable to contribute to the goals of a) deriving arithmetic truths in a gap-free manner from purely logical laws and b) reducing all concepts and definitions to the concepts and definitions of logic. The *Bs* was a semantic theory where sentences were designed to stand for their content. The overall goal of his concept-script language was to purge all psychological aspects and influences. He wrote:

"Now all aspects of language which result only from the interaction of speaker and listener – for example, when the speaker considers the listener's expectations and tries to put them on the right track even before speaking a sentence – have nothing corresponding to them in my formula language, because here the only thing considered in a judgement is that which influences its possible consequences. Everything necessary for a correct inference is fully expressed; but what is not necessary usually is not indicated; nothing is left to guesswork."[88]

The sentence stands for the content, and the parts of the sentence stand for the corresponding parts of the content. The *Bs* theory of function–argument, as discussed, was distinct from the content which it represents. Conceptual content was designed to be the content that contributes to the truth-value. Thus the replacement of a part of a sentence with another part with the same content would yield a sentence with the same content. Frege had in mind the rationalist goal of relying on "logical deductions alone" and to "transcend all particulars" so that there would be no contaminating influence from intuition.[89] The goal of his "conceptual notation" was "to test in the most reliable manner the validity of a chain of reasoning and expose each presupposition which tends to creep in unnoticed, so that its source can be investigated."[90] It was here in the *Bs* that he pointed to the "conceptual content" as that signified by the sentence capturing what is solely necessary for inference. Frege outlines the conditions for sameness of content despite a reversal of the roles of subject and predicate:

"Note that the contents of two judgments can differ in two ways: either the conclusions that can be drawn from one when combined with certain others also always follow from the second when combined with the same judgments, or else this is not the case. The two propositions 'At Plataea the Greeks defeated the Persians' and 'At Plataea the Persians were defeated by the Greeks' differ in the first way. Even if a slight difference in sense can be discerned, the agreement predominates. Now I call that part of the content that is the

---

[88] Frege, "Conceptual Notation," in Bynum, *Conceptual Notation and Related Articles*, 113.
[89] Ibid, 104.
[90] Ibid.

same in both the *conceptual content*. Since *only this* has significance for the *Bs*, no distinction is needed between propositions that have the same conceptual content."[91]

Conceptual content is integrally tied up with inferential potential and it is the inferential role that concerns Frege the most in the *Bs*. For example, if A and B have the same content, then they will play the same role in any ordering of inference in which they are involved. But there is a problem here. The *Bs* theory of content has it that the circumstances that are referred to *just are* the content referred to. Consider Frege's identity relation "$\equiv$" and examples such as:

1) "The evening star $\equiv$ The evening star"

2) "The evening star $\equiv$ The morning star"

In each reference, both to "the evening star" and "the morning star", we have the planet Venus involved and the content of the identity relation. So on this basis, the content of 1) and 2) must be the same. But this is manifestly not the case. We can infer from "the evening star is a planet" and "the evening star is the morning star" to the conclusion "the morning star is a planet". But we cannot follow the same inferential order from "the evening star is a planet" and "the evening star is the evening star" to the conclusion that "the morning star is a planet". Frege proposes a move out of this in the *Bs*:

"Identity of content differs from conditionality and negation by relating to names, not to contents. Although symbols are usually only representatives of their contents – so that each combination [of symbols usually] expresses only a relation between their contents – they at once appear in *propria persona* as soon as they are combined by the symbol for identity of content, for this signifies that the names have the same content. Thus, with the introduction of a symbol for identity of content, a bifurcation is necessarily introduced into the meaning

---

[91] Frege, *Begriffsschrift*, 12.

of every symbol, the same symbols standing at times for their contents, at times for themselves."[92]

So in the special cases of identity sentences, Frege is saying that there is no involvement of objects – as would typically be the case for any judgement involving negation or conditionality – with the relation of content identity. Instead, the symbols on either side of "≡" indicate themselves and this is supposed to ground the difference in inferential potential. So if we take the sentence "the morning star ≡ the evening star", "morning star" does not refer to the planet Venus but rather to itself, the word "morning star". So the sentence is actually saying that the term "morning star" is referring to different content than the term "evening star" and this explains the difference in inferential potential.

It should be noted that the whole point of the formulas of the concept-script was to mirror the formulas of mathematics: representing by something analogous to pictorial form the elements represented. So just as the parts of a painting can be broken up and analysed as standing for and corresponding to the parts of the object depicted, so too can something like "1 + 2" be broken up into "1", "2", and "+" with each representing an individual thing. So although the concept-script was a means to purge the inessentials from a representative language, the connection could not be merely incidental to the characteristics of the language. An isomorphic relation is necessarily an internal relation, a relation of forms between the representation and the represented.

But locating the source of identity in the relation between words created a tension that did not escape Frege. His goal was ultimately a rationalist one of defining a language of *pure thought* and thought in turn had to connect with the identity of content in a way that was not merely arbitrary. The whole point of introducing symbols was so that those symbols would refer *beyond themselves*. He notes:

---

[92] Frege, "Conceptual Notation," in Bynum, *Conceptual Notation and Related Articles*, 124.

"This makes it appear at first as if it were here a matter of what pertains to the *expression* alone, *not to the thought*, and as if there were no need at all for different symbols for the same content and hence for a symbol for identity of content either."[93]

Moreover, as Mendelsohn points out, if the conceptual content of a judgement exhausts the full inferential potential, and the two signs figuring in an identity statement by definition signify the same conceptual content, then it renders the symbol for identity of content superfluous.[94] Mendelsohn compares the superfluous state of the identity sign to that between the active and passive voices in sentences such as "At Platea the Greeks defeated the Persians" and "At Platea the Persians were defeated by the Greeks": they both contain the same conceptual content. So the grammatical distinctions are purely incidental to the conceptual content of the judgement.

Another weakness for the *Bs* identities is the imputing of signs with representative power. We take "Hesperus" as signifying the brightest star in the evening sky and "Phosphorus" as signifying the brightest star in the morning sky. But equally there is nothing stopping us from allocating *both* "Hesperus" and "Phosphorus" as different stylistic alternative ways of expressing the brightest star in the morning sky. Or aside from these terms we could come up with a completely different term such as "Lucifer" to refer to the same phenomena as "Phosphorus", the brightest star in the morning sky.

On the second alternative, we can have two different terms, "Lucifer" and "Hesperus", signifying the one phenomena, the brightest star observed to shine in the morning. What we have in this case is merely a stylistic difference between two terms: a difference in the physical manifestation of the terms used to signify the one mode of presentation. But in learning that "Lucifer" and "Hesperus" signify the same observed phenomenon there is no extension in astronomical knowledge, but merely an extension in meta-linguistic knowledge, namely that these two terms signify the same thing.

---

[93] Frege, *Begriffsschrift*, 21.
[94] Richard Mendelsohn, "Frege's *Begriffsschrift* Theory of Identity," *Journal of the History of Philosophy* 20, no. 3 (1982): 279-299, http://doi.org/10.1353/hph.1982.0029

The dilemma Frege saw was in accounting for how it is that names make reference in a way that signifies real knowledge that is cognitively significant and not just any arbitrary stipulations of a language community. It is at this point that Frege introduces his geometrical example where we have a "way of determining" (*Bestimmungsweise*) which is a description given by Frege of a situation that is signified by two different names representing two different ways in which the one geometric point is determined. Point A is given immediately through perception where point B has to be inferred by following various geometric instructions where eventually B is determined to be the same point as A. Frege writes:

"The need for a symbol for equality thus rests on the following fact: the same content can be fully determined in different ways; and *that*, in a particular case, *the same* content is actually given by *two ways of determining [Bestimmungsweisen] it*, is the content of a *judgement* …It is clear from this that different names for the same content are not always a trivial matter of formulation; if they go along with different ways of determining the content, they are relevant to the essential nature of the case."[95]

Mendelsohn considers Frege's use of a *Bestimmungsweisen* in the Begriffsschrift as challenging those critics, such as Leonard Linsky and William and Martha Kneale, who took his identity statements to be based purely on the arbitrary conventions of language, and that it was only in later works that Frege had a basis for proper knowledge with the sense of a term, a "mode of presentation".[96] So identity statements, far from telling us something significant about the world, would be merely a matter of philological interest rather than conveying anything of real scientific interest. But clearly, according to Mendelsohn, with his use of the *Bestimmungsweisen*, Frege has the resources to base identity on something of more substance than the trivialities of linguistic items.

---

[95] Frege, *Begriffsschrift*, 21.
[96] Richard Mendelsohn, *The Philosophy of Gottlob Frege*, 49-52.

Frege gives us a condensed summary of the *Bs* theory of identity statements and his grounds for rejecting it thirteen years later in his "On Sense and Reference" (*SaR*):

"But this relation would hold between the names or signs only in so far as they named or designated something. It would be mediated by the connexion of each of the two signs with the same designated thing. But this is arbitrary. Nobody can be forbidden to use any arbitrarily producible event or object as a sign for something. In that case the *Satz* a=b would no longer refer to the subject matter, but only to its mode of designation; we would express no proper knowledge by its means."[97]

Aside from the Linksy–Kneale criticisms, however, very little attention has been given to this passage in the literature and thus little effort put in to understanding such a key pivot point for Frege in the move from linguistics to sense in his theory of knowledge. Mendelsohn's counterargument to Linsky and Kneale is to point out that they simply ignore Frege's *Bestimmungsweisen* in the *Bs* and it is precisely Frege's emphasis on identity *expressions* that prevented him from distinguishing between the trivial identities and those that signal real differences (the *Bestimmungsweisen*) in knowledge. According to Mendelsohn's defence, Frege *has* the repertoire to defend a real theory of knowledge. It is just that his stunted identities, based on linguistic expressions, prevented him from making the crucial distinctions.

But this interpretation is completely unfaithful to Frege's own criticisms in the passage from *SaR*. Clearly he saw the identity expressions as providing the *sign* that is central in mediating the identity of the one designated object. Rendering the = superfluous was surely unacceptable to Frege. There is no mention of the *Bestimmungsweisen* there and this is telling. Mendelsohn is quite right to emphasise its centrality to the *Bs* theory of identity statements that "touch the very heart of the matter". But if it is *so* central then why wasn't it mentioned in the *SaR* mea culpa quoted earlier?

---

[97] Frege, "On Sense and Reference," in Geach et al, *Translations*, 36-37.

My suggestion is that Frege wasn't so much concerned with the identity of the object referred to by expressions but *the means* by which *we* come to know the *Bestimmungsweisen* and logical laws and in turn the means by which we communicate objective knowledge with each other. As inhabitants of sensory worlds and the fact that those sensory worlds carry no information about the laws of logic then this presents a hurdle for how we obtain objective knowledge and communicate from person to person.

It is the differences in sense that are supposed to give rise to different names which in turn contain different modes of presentation. Modes of presentation, for all practical purposes, are not essentially different to the *Bs* term *Bestimmungsweisen*. It is the different modes of presentation that give rise to the different names – physical inscriptions – with unique geometrical properties.

The first two sentences of the *SaR* tells us that it is the *arbitrariness* of the name's designation that explains the failure of statements like "a = b". Having a *Bestimmungsweisen* doesn't help even though it is integral to reference, since what he is concerned with is how exactly it is that *signs for us* hook on to the *Bestimmungsweisen* in the first place. It is the word-to-world relation – or rather word-to-*Bestimmungsweisen*[98] – that presents the dilemma since physical words are only arbitrarily associated with their modes of presentation. The *Bestimmungsweisen* is an objective object in the world that is not interpreted. It is the designating names that are in question.

Special emphasis is placed in *SaR* on the nature of a sign as opposed to just a physical inscription (such as a figure that is not invested with any *intent* to refer to any particular thing). The physical properties of a figure are not enough, there has to be a way in which a name designates such that any two signs that are identical in shape and designate in the same way are two *tokens* of the same sign *type*. Textor explains:

---

[98] Recall the example given earlier in this section where the term 'Lucifer' can be used to refer to the same sense as 'Phosphorus'. Linguistic inscriptions are indifferent between same and different senses.

"*a* is a token of the same sign as *b* if, and only if, *a* and *b* have the same shape, and *a* and b are used with the intention to designate an object determined in the same way."[99]

What Mendelsohn omits is the crucial link between *knowing subject* and the mode of designation that works hand-in-glove to present the same object in the world. Sense itself does not refer to an object, but requires the *act* of the knower and the object: the mysterious act of grasping integral to this process. Linguistic expressions, though obviously not essential to the objects referred to, are still essential as a gateway from the knower to the thing known. And it is precisely *in this role* that Frege found insurmountable difficulties.

Recall that the concept-script was supposed to be a unique language that purged the non-essential elements of ordinary language that overlayed the pure logical language that was isomorphic with the objects represented by its symbols. The complaint in the *SaR* passage of the arbitrariness in the relation of designation arises precisely because it is the conventions of language that play the determinative role and not any isomorphic relation. The mode of determination may be fundamental to reference but there is no non-arbitrary connection between it and the sign in itself. It is in the *intent* of the use of the sign and not something inherent to the sign itself that gives it its referential power.[100]

It is vital at this point to recall Frege's commitment to metaphysical dualism: the strong opposition between the world of Platonic determinacies of forms and concepts and the Heraclitian world of flux where physical objects are essentially of an indeterminant nature. In the *Foundation* he distinguishes what is "objective from what is handleable or spatial or real".[101] So it is through mental activity that we come to grasp the objective objects of the mind and not the physical language inscriptions.

---

[99] Textor, *Frege on Sense and Reference,* 120.
[100] Frege's concept of the mind was implicitly of an inner homunculus interpreting the inner symbols of sense experience which are intentionally inert in themselves. This view of the mind will receive further attention and critique in later chapters as we discuss the work of Russell and Quine.
[101] Frege, *Foundations,* 35.

Returning to the passage discussed from *SaR* it should be clear why it is not possible to attain reliable knowledge from the straight observation of physical symbols (which are indeterminant objects in space). He provides further details in his "Letter to Jourdain" where he notes that objectivity of meaning and content is necessary for communication where without it "a common science would be impossible."[102]

Frege's entire formal system was based on the most basic signs, such as in judgeable content, where the primitive and indefinable logical entities are related by basic axioms and inference rules like conditionality. But it was later, after the *Begriffsschrift*, where he describes primitive indefinables as "explications" and it is these that scientists use to communicate with one another. These explications, however, are indefinable because they are inscrutable, owing to their status as *assumed competencies* among knowers. Their ultimate ground, instead, seems to be pragmatic:

"We must admit logically primitive elements that are indefinable . . . . Once the investigators have come to an understanding about the primitive elements and their designations, agreement about what is logically composite is easily reached by means of definition. Since definitions are not possible for primitive elements, something else must enter in. I call it explication. It is this, therefore, that serves the purpose of mutual understanding among investigators. . . . [Explication] has no place in the system of a science . . . . Someone who pursued research only by himself would not need it. The purpose of explications is a pragmatic one; and once it is achieved, we must be satisfied with them. And here we must be able to count on a little goodwill and cooperative understanding, even guessing."[103]

Perhaps the most prominent example of an indefinable, which was also *sui generis* for Frege, was his concept of truth. Truth cannot be given any definition. This is not because it

---

[102] Gottlob Frege, "Frege to Jourdain undated," in Gabriel et al, *The Philosophical and Mathematical Correspondence*, 80.
[103] Gottlob Frege, "On the Foundations of Geometry: Second Series," in *Collected Papers on Mathematics, Logic, and Philosophy*, edited by Brian McGuinness. Translated by Max Black, V. H. Dudman, Peter Geach, Hans Kaal, E. –H. W. Kluge, Brian McGuinness, R. H. Stoothoff. (Oxford: Basil Blackwell, 1984), 300-301.

is an integral part of the content of any judgement but because it has to be presupposed in the very act of judging itself. It is the judgement stroke which "contains the act of assertion".[104] It is our very actions as rational beings that require us to follow in accordance with the laws of truth in our acts of assertion. Thus the philosopher is externally driven according to the norms of truth and prescriptions for illocutionary acts of truth,[105] prescribing how we, as rational creatures, ought to submit to the basic laws of thought rather than to any internal justifiable mental grasp of truth.

It is because we are all walled off from each other behind a Cartesian subjectivist mind, and because the physical world is subject to Heraclitean flux, that we have such difficulty knowing the meaning each of us fixes to judgeable content:

"Science needs technical terms that have precise and fixed meanings, and in order to come to an understanding about these meanings and exclude possible misunderstandings, we give elucidations [explications]. Of course in so doing we have again to use ordinary words, and these may display similar defects . . . So it seems that new elucidations [explications] are necessary. Theoretically one will never really achieve one's goal in this way. In practice, however, we do manage to come to an understanding about the meanings of words."[106]

It is only "in practice" that we are able to overcome our limited subjectivist states. In fact Frege thinks that an empiricist view of cognition collapses into idealism because there is nothing inherent in the ideas in individual minds or anything material that could be true or false. Thus after concluding that judgements cannot be identified with mental states,[107] and hence nothing psychophysical can explain their status as objective truths, he writes:

---

[104] Gottlob Frege, *The Basic Laws of Arithmetic*, trans. and ed. Montgomery Furth (Berkeley: University of California Press, 1964), 39.
[105] A similar take on truth as unanalysable and simply an illocutionary act of assertion is given by A. J. Ayer; "...to say that a proposition is true is just to assert it, and to say that it is false is just to assert its contradictory. And this indicates that the terms "true" and "false" connote nothing, but function in the sentence simply as marks of assertion and denial. And in that case there can be no sense in asking us to analyse the concept of 'truth'." *Language, Truth, and Logic* 2nd ed. (New York: Dover Publications, 1946), 88-89
[106] Frege, "Logic in Mathematics," in Hermes et al, *Posthumous Writings*, 207.
[107] In fact it is an utter mystery how the incongruous mental processes and abstract world of thoughts come together in the apprehension of true thoughts. He writes; "For in grasping the law something comes into view whose nature is no longer mental in the proper sense, namely the thought; and this process is perhaps the most

"Standing by a river, swirls of water are often observed. Wouldn't it be absurd to claim that such a swirl was valid or true, or even false? And even if the atoms or molecules in my brain danced around each other a thousand times more spirited and frenzied than gnats on a nice summer night, would it not be just as absurd to maintain that this dance was valid or true? And if explanations were such dances, could they be said to be true? And finally, is it any different, if the explanations were jumbles of idea?"[108]

On the basis of Frege's Cartesian view of the mind, we can see the *SaR* passage as an allusion to the subjective space that Frege conceives as an insurmountable barrier in carrying us from the inscription to the mode of determination. Thus the only way to rescue our knowledge of truth comes through the right disposition to truth,[109] through the assertion of a judgement. This is the progressive line of thought worked out in the first pages of *SaR*.[110] Truth is neither contained in, nor a part of, the content, but is manifest in the mental *attitude* that asserts that content linguistically.[111] Ricketts and Levine explain:

"The relationship between a thought and its truth-value is not describable in a sentence – it is not a matter of a thought's falling under a concept or of a relation's holding between two objects. Rather, the relationship between the thought that Socrates is mortal and the True is linguistically expressed by an indication of the asserting force with which a sentence

---

mysterious of all…It is enough for us that we can grasp thoughts and recognize them to be true; how this takes place is a question in its own right."; Gottlob Frege, "Logic," in Hermes et al, *Posthumous Writings*, 145.
[108] Ibid, 144.
[109] Frege does say that in thought "there must be something in his consciousness that is aimed at the thought."; "The Thought," 308. So internal mental processes are somehow involved, but the important point is the condition of thought in its *determination of that thought* lays essentially outside the mental processes.
[110] See also his "Frege to Husserl 30.10-1.11.1906," "Frege to Husserl 9.12.1906," and "Letter to Jourdain 28.1.1914" in Gabriel et al, *The Philosophical and Mathematical Correspondence*, 66-69, 70-71, 81-84.
[111] Gareth Evans points to such a cognitive and psychological test for the distinguishing and identification of senses in Frege "the Intuitive Criteria of Difference"; "…the thought associated with one sentence S as its sense must be different from the thought associated with another sentence S` as its sense, if it is possible for someone to understand both sentences at a given time while coherently taking different attitudes towards them, i.e. accepting (rejecting) one while rejecting (accepting), or being agnostic about, the other." *The Varieties of Reference*, (Oxford: Oxford University Press, 1982), 18-19. However, more accurately this should be a criteria that identifies the *manifestation* of sense (thought) since for Frege thoughts are clearly entities that pre-exist and, are unaffected by, their grasp; see Frege, "The Thought," 310-311.

expressing the thought is uttered by someone who has recognized-the-truth of the thought."[112]

A second look at the way the *SaR* passage has been translated also provides support for my interpretation. As Makin points out, *"unsere Bezeichnungsweise"* has been inaccurately translated as "…but only to its mode of designation", where the "it" refers to the names or the sentence as a whole. The more accurate rendering of that passage is "…but only to *our* mode of designation".[113] The failure of knowledge, according to Makin, is attributable to our subjective investment of reference in the sign more so than anything to do with the sign itself. Makin's point is well taken but this improved translation can service a slightly different point: that it is in the subjective mode of picking out signs qua physical inscriptions accessed through the sensory world that presents the dilemma and not taking them as merely a sign of our *intent* to take senses in pursuit of a reference.

In conclusion, Mendelsohn's interpretation overlooks a major facet of Frege's theory of judgement, namely the subjective state of cognition and the way our subjective states interpret the signs within identity statements. The symbols in the *Bs* are supposed to play a representative role vis-à-vis the mode of designation and the object of reference. Highlighting this third facet to Frege's judgement allows us to more naturally interpret the *SaR* criticism of the *Bs* and fits such a development within Frege's overall Cartesian-rationalist worldview.

In *SaR* Frege asks us to consider the case of "Odysseus was set ashore at Ithaca while sound asleep".[114] This mythical account has a sense but obviously no reference. But how are we to know this? Under sceptical assumptions Frege assumes there is nothing about the sense data itself that tells us whether a reference is fixed. Likewise, in veridical cases there is nothing about the sense data that imposes itself on the knower. The key to veridical

---

[112] Thomas Ricketts and James Levine, "Logic and Truth in Frege," *Aristotelian Society Supplementary Volume* 70, Issue 1, (1996): 135, https://doi.org/10.1093/aristoteliansupp/70.1.121
[113] Gideon Makin, *The Metaphysics of Meaning: Russell and Frege on Sense and Denotation* (London and New York: Routledge, 2000), 97. (My emphasis).
[114] Frege, "On Sense and Reference," in Geach et al, *Translations*, 42.

knowledge, for Frege, is not in any internal accessibility to the outside world, but in our attitude: it is in the "striving for truth that drives us always to advance from the sense to the reference."[115] And in veridical cases that reference is the True.

From what has been reviewed it should be obvious that a form of Cartesian solipsism threatens for Frege and his solution appears to be a form of pragmatic external realism. This forces Frege to locate reference ultimately in *the intent* of the truth seeker that is driven from the sense of a sentence to its reference (which in the appropriate cases it will be the True). The seeker after truth is determined to go after truth much the same way the external forces of gravity drives a falling body. Nothing about the intrinsic psychological structure of the state of cognition *qua* the nature of that structure fixes the reference.

This theme will be taken up further in the next chapter, but it is important to recognise the Parmenidian themes here as well. For Parmenides, empiricism is not a genuine epistemic route to being. As discussed, for him the very act of thought itself is a direct expression of being: the True *is* being in the world and this is manifested through our acts of assertion. It is precisely in this way that the True manifests itself in the domain of our world: by acting on us in our sincere striving for true thoughts through truth-seeking actions.

But the Fregean system leaves any role for our ordinary perceptual capacities out of the picture. Internal perceptual states *do not* impress their truth-value on the knower. An alternative to such a solipsistic frame of reference will be given in the last chapters where the newly introduced categories will provide a far more straightforward and arguably natural explanation for how we acquire knowledge of the mind-external world.

Conclusion

---

[115] Ibid.

Throughout this chapter we have situated Frege firmly within the rationalist camp. But even at a more fundamental level, we have exposed his system as thoroughly Parmenidian. Frege, like Parmenides, eschews the psychological in favour of the rational. But such an attempt at reconstructing our knowledge means that ultimately everything we know through the means of appearances must be based on what can be justified by reason. But the question left is whether such a grounding relationship between the accidents of the empirical world and the substance of being possesses the explanatory power to account for the world of appearances.

Frege's employment of variables, and the permutations that can occur within the slots opened up by his logical structure, show that the structure is univocal and thus doubtful that it can make the differentiations that we demand given our empirical engagement with objects. In by-passing the internal world of sense – and thereby inviting an unwelcome solipsism – Frege had to cast the knower as seeking truth *in action* rather than knowing it through internal psychological means. But such a division may seem artificial and the final chapters of this thesis will much more closely tie together the means of our coming to knowledge and the justification of that knowledge.

So are we not better off taking the world of appearances at face value and instead extracting our metaphysical principles from the world? Instead of bringing our metaphysical principles to the discussion and assuming what should be argued for, should we not, rather, extract those principles from science and common sense? The final chapters of this thesis will answer "yes" to both questions and elucidate alternative metaphysical categories that do not require morphing the world of appearances into something they are not.

The consequences of Frege's system re-emerges later in 20th century philosophy most conspicuously with the work of Quine and his mentor Carnap. Within the works of these two philosophers we will see that the structure–content relationship spelled out by Frege lacks the resources to justifiably reconstruct our knowledge of the sensory world. Quine took this to imply that intensions and mental representations as entities ought to be omitted from our ontology. I will instead propose new categories that marry our epistemology and metaphysics, along with a way of looking at the structure and justification of knowledge that extends naturally from subjectivity to objectivity and which is in accordance with, not dismissive of, our common sense knowledge of objects.

Chapter Two – Frege and Russell on Being and Truth

Introduction

The previous chapter made the case that Frege's metaphysical system was just a more elaborate version of that laid out by Parmenides. That was evident from the simple, univocal, supremely general, structure of the logical laws that are the primitive foundation of Frege's entire system. Frege's shunning of psychologism also paralleled Parmenides' antipathy to empirical knowledge and the material world. For both philosophers logical deduction occurs in a unitary fashion independently of the material world and its division into multiple entities with multiple natures.

In this chapter I look more closely at the metaphysical nature of Frege's central notion: the True. I also look at the logical atomism that is central to Bertrand Russell's answer to scepticism during his post-idealist phase. Both philosophers share the same fundamental metaphysical principles: that ultimate being is simple, primitive, unitary and one. For Frege it is manifest in the True, whereas for Russell it is the oneness expressed through proper names and the ultimately unifying principle behind the objects of acquaintance.

Frege's notion of the True runs into problems since he must state a condition for a sentence to be true – which finds paradigmatic expression under the identity predicate – and then once reference is made to the True, that predicate is merged with a name. The root of the problem is that the conditions of truth, being purely derivative, demands reduction: with truth requiring a name for the True and thus merging with the True completely.

Wittgenstein marshals a series of arguments purporting to integrate truth into the proposition itself in an absolute as opposed to a merely derived sense. First, truth-values cannot be referenced by means that are not true themselves. Second, the simple and univocal nature of Frege's True fails to select the unique sense of a thought. Thus there is no intrinsic connection between the truth-value of a sentence p and its negation: –p. Wittgenstein's picture theory of the proposition, on the other hand, does purport to tie truth essentially to the proposition precisely in the picturing relation. However, a major drawback of that view is that there seems to be no privileged medium which we would normally ascribe to sense data over other media, such as written prose or a musical score.

The second half of the chapter focuses on Russell. Russell's "terms" are the constituents of propositions and are self-subsistent, substantial entities. As such, there is no way to account for the unity of the proposition with only such singular atomic entities – a point which Russell readily acknowledged. This is very important because, in the final two chapters of this thesis, I propose a way of unifying the proposition by supplying precisely what is lacking in Russell's account – a formal, unifying category.

Firstly, I outline Russell's theory of direct realism which eschewed the need for a sense as something that threatens realism. I also point out that behind the epistemological certainty of acquaintance exists the metaphysical grounding by Parmenidian being. Further, the act of naming is an expression of being for Russell.

Knowledge by description presents fresh dilemmas, however, since it is an inference from the world of sense data to the orthogonal world of entities revealed by physics. A further issue is the substantial nature of sense data which, as substances they cannot refer beyond themselves or be dependent on any entities other than themselves. Russell finds a way out for the realist by logical construction which is the construction of objects in the world out of sense data. Here we have a construction of an object out of a series of immediately juxtaposing perspectives all connected under the logical relation of "similarity".

But such a construction ultimately substitutes the unities of sense experience for the "logical fictions" constructed out of sense data. Such a construction is really nothing over and above the atomic units. Thus the little packages of Parmenidian being are ultimate for Russell. But such a model lacks the resources to explain the complex and varied structures we see in sense experience. The failure to explain our experiences will become clearer as this picture is elaborated and brought to further fruition by Carnap and Quine's work detailed in the next chapter.

Lastly I discuss a step in the right direction: Russell's image theory of the proposition. Picturing here is an isomorphism between the structure of the image and the object pictured. This is a positive move for two reasons: first, it respects the structure of appearances by taking them at face value and second, because it accounts for the unity of the proposition by it being a reflection of the unity of the objects pictured. However, this leaves the unity of the object unexplained. But as I will argue in the final chapters, it is precisely here that my own categories will explain such a unity.

Ultimately my goal is to offer up an alternative form of analysis that relies on categories in competition to that offered by Parmenides. The three categories put forward will be abstracted from the unities observed in sense experience instead of imposing other-worldly logical structure on them. As such, the categories will not be univocal. There is also no prioritising the one, simple (partless), whole as we see in Parmenidian unity, but rather there will be a reciprocal dependency – supervenience – between parts and whole. Furthermore, the third category will be in competition with the substantial entities of sense data and have the capacity to refer beyond themselves to the world and hence subvert the threat of anti-realism.

Wittgenstein Against Frege

Frege was an absolutist on truth and held that truth was indefinable. To give a definition in such a way would be to give necessary and sufficient conditions for a sentence to be true and hence reduce its definition to more basic concepts and hence make *those* concepts more fundamental. He states that "it is probable that the content of the word 'true' is unique and indefinable."[116] Hence he took the True to be the most basic concept of logic, in the same way as "the beautiful" is for aesthetics, and "the good" is for ethics.

Kant divides the concept of the good between that which is good in itself and that which has merely derived goodness. And it is the good will that attains that lofty status as good in itself. But its goodness is not conditional on "what it effects or accomplishes,..." or "...because of its fitness to attain some proposed end," but because "...of its volition, that is, it is good in itself and, regarded for itself, is to be valued incomparably higher than all that could merely be brought about by it in favor of some inclination and...the sum of all inclinations."[117]

In the same way, G. E. Moore took such an uncompromising view of the good in ethics.[118] Moore argued that anyone attempting to define goodness would be treating it as a natural property and thus committing the naturalistic fallacy. In other words, it is the good for Moore, and the good will for Kant, that count as good just as they are in themselves and *not* as they are in relation to any other external criterion.

It is crucial to have this split between the true and the merely derived true in mind to appreciate Frege's entire approach to truth and judgement. The fact that truth cannot be defined in anyway gets spelled out in his description of the interplay between judgement and truth:

"From the laws of truth there follow prescriptions about asserting, thinking, judging, inferring. And we may very well speak of laws of thought in this way too. But there is at once a danger here of confusing different things. People may very well interpret the expression 'law of thought' by analogy with 'law of nature' and then have in mind general features of thinking as a mental occurrence. A law of thought in this sense would be a

---

[116] Frege, "The Thought," 291. He also said "Truth is obviously something so primitive and simple that it is not possible to reduce it to anything simpler."; "Logic," in Hermes et al, *Posthumous Writings*, 129.
[117] Immanuel Kant, *Kant: Groundwork of the Metaphysics of Morals*, ed. and trans. Mary Gregor (Cambridge: Cambridge University Press, 1997), 8.
[118] G. E. Moore, *Principia Ethica* (Cambridge: Cambridge University Press, 1903)

psychological law. And so they might come to believe that logic deals with the mental process of thinking and with the psychological laws in accordance with which this takes place. That would be misunderstanding the task of logic, for truth has not been given here its proper place. Just as 'beautiful' points the way for aesthetics and 'good' for ethics, so do words like 'true' for logic. In order to avoid any misunderstanding and prevent the blurring of the boundary between Psychology and Logic, I assign to Logic the task of discovering the laws of truth, not the laws of taking things to be true or of thinking. The meaning of the world 'true' is spelled out in the laws of truth."[119]

Note the difference between "the laws of truth" and mere "taking things to be true" or "thinking".[120] Frege is drawing a sharp distinction between the truth and the associated laws of truth – which are intrinsically true – and the mere taking something to be true and thinking which can only be true in a derived sense. Thus in his formulation of the judgement-stroke he is careful not to give it any role in actually making true but merely asserts that it is a precondition for judging: "The *judgement-stroke* is placed vertically at the left hand end of the content-stroke, it converts the content of possible judgement into a judgement".[121] Thus ⊢"$3^2=9$" is an assertion of its truth but does not make "$3^2=9$" true. It may be more correct to say that assertion is an act in accordance with truth. Elsewhere he is even clearer about the statements that are not prefixed by the judgement stroke:

"If we write down an equation or inequality, e.g. 5>4, we ordinarily wish at the same time to express a judgement; in our example, we want to assert that 5 is greater than 4. According to the view I am here presenting, '5>4' and '1+3=5' just give us expressions for truth-values, without making any assertion."[122]

---

[119] Frege, "Thoughts," in McGuiness et al, *Collected Papers,* 351-352.
[120] Elsewhere he makes a similar comparison between logic and the "true": "Logic is concerned with the predicate 'true' in a quite special way, namely in a way analogous to that in which physics has to do with the predicates 'heavy' and 'warm' or chemistry with the predicates 'acid' and 'alkaline'." Frege, "Logic," in Hermes et al, *Posthumous Writings*, 128.
[121] Ibid, 11.
[122] Gottlob Frege, "Function and Concept," in McGuiness et al, *Collected Papers,* 149.

Thus true statements are independent of the subjects judging and asserting their truth. The function of the judgement stroke is within the frame of reference of the judger or asserter and thus its chief role according to Nicholas J. J. Smith is that it "effects assertion".[123] Thus the act of assertion isn't just distinct from the subject matter of the assertable content but the formulation of such content as designating a truth-value is distinct from the act of judging, which is an act in accordance with the laws of truth. Thus the act of assertion is like a falling rock acting in accordance with gravity. The rock is not gravity nor responsible for gravity's actions. The judgement stroke brings the *act of judging* into the equation, linking the true statement and judger together. The judger gets put on to the "rails of truth", so to speak – the way a rock will fall according to the precepts of gravity – but plays no essential role in the creation of truth.

Thus the behaviour of the judger and their attitude in the act of assertion is determined in the same way that a rock falling is determined by the law of gravity. Just as the rock is acting in accordance with the law of gravity yet is ontologically distinct from the law of gravity so the actor in the act of assertion is acting in accordance with the laws of truth yet is distinct from the laws of truth. Smith states: "When the judgement stroke is present, something is *being done* (an assertion is being made)."[124]

So for Frege a judgement is an addition *of sorts* to the predicate. Without such a judgement we just have a thought that is offered for consideration. It may well be true but it carries no force beyond that. The insertion of the intentional agent doing the asserting is the additional semantic information provided by the judgement stroke. It marries the agent with the true statement.

As discussed in the previous chapter, "the True" has fundamental, primitive, and indefinable status for Frege. It is all pervasive in that every true thought is *intrinsically true* since "predicating [truth] is always included in predicating anything whatever."[125] But in

---

[123] Nicholas J. J. Smith, "Frege's Judgement Stroke and the Conception of Logic as the Study of Inference not Consequence," *Philosophy Compass* 4, issue 4, (2009): 642, https://doi.org/10.1111/j.1747-9991.2009.00219.x
[124] Ibid.
[125] Frege, "Logic," in Hermes et al, *Posthumous Writings*, 129.

order to effect such a neat principle *as* fundamental, he needs to tidy up some of the loose ends in the form of the complexity of sentences.

This he does in the *Foundations* under what Peter Sullivan calls the "merger theory".[126] The merging comes about through the reduction of sentences to names. Thus Frege's example of "$E^2 = 4$" is a sentence that functions as a name, denoting either the True or the False depending on what value is substituted in. But this, as Sullivan explains, conflicts with the motivation he gives for the two truth values in the first place where he assumes that identity is playing the role of a predicate. Frege writes, "'$\Gamma=\Delta$' shall denote the True if Γ is the same as Δ; in all other cases it shall denote the False".[127] A predicate must of its very nature combine with a name, but as Sullivan points out the predicate is lost in *Foundations* since sentences are merged into names.

But Frege's overall goal, as is most clear in *Foundations*, is a reductionistic one. Specifically, he endeavours to reduce all semantic functions to either the True or the False. Sentences that count as true cannot take on complex conditions and qualifications in order to count *as true*, since this would reduce truth to more fundamental concepts. Thus a true statement in the *Foundations,* as Sullivan writes, cannot take the following form "'…' refers to the True iff …. That form, of course, leaves open the question 'And what if not?'"[128] The absolute simplicity and fundamentality of truth means it can't be split up. Instead, concepts in a sentence that segment it into complex and varying functions need to be reduced to the True. Sullivan again:

"Objects in *Grundgesetze* fall into three classes: the True, the False, and the rest. If a functional expression is to be defined in a way that makes it (at most) two-valued – if it is to be a concept-word – then this three-way division must be pressed into two. So the horizontal is defined to yield the True for the True, and the False for the-False-and-the-rest;

---

[126] Peter Sullivan, "The Sense of a Name of a 'Truth-Value'," *The Philosophical Quarterly* 44, no. 177 (1994): 476-481, http://doi.org/10.2307/2220246.
[127] Frege, *Basic Laws*, I §7.
[128] Sullivan, "The Sense of a Name," 478.

negation yields the False for the True, and the True for the-False-and-the-rest; similarly for material implication."[129]

In the case of the identity condition mentioned earlier, it seemed a definite condition was being laid for a sentence to refer to the True. But then Frege's system merges the predicate into a name as a precondition of functioning as a reference. It turns out that he must do this in order to reduce everything ultimately to the truth-value, but then he seems to have removed the very conditions to refer to that truth-value in the first place. He has sawed off the branch that was supporting him.

So we have a clear line drawn between the subjective state of judgement and its public correlate, assertion, on the one hand, and that of truth, on the other. Additionally, returning to the comparison with Kant's concept of "the good", we can see then that "the rest" for Frege, with predication figuring among them, are ultimately separate semantic functions and play a role in truth only to the extent that they can express that truth via denoting sentences. They are true only in a derived sense and Frege is anxious to press them into the omnipresent and univocal concept of the True. Sullivan spells out the unfortunate consequences of such a theory:

"To say that there are 'no predicates' in Grundgesetze is to say that it recognizes no forms of complexity, characteristic of thoughts and their expression, which carry with them this intrinsic involvement with truth. Then, having no longer an anchor in the inner structure of thoughts, truth was 'dissociated' from them along with assertion. It is astonishing that Frege did not recognize what he had done."[130]

The only means by which Frege could respond to such an objection is to say that there is an association but it plays the role of *determination* vis-à-vis individual thoughts and as such is a separate category from each thought which is a *realising condition* (The way a rock may

---

[129] Ibid.
[130] Ibid, 481.

realise the force of gravity). This explains the mere derived status of any particular thought having a truth-value, derived because it is determined so, externally to itself. Sullivan even hints at such a distinction himself: "The distinction of predication and assertion is of a piece with the distinction of truth and its recognition…"[131] That is so if we substitute "recognition" with "realisation".

So this is the natural route out of the quandary Sullivan paints for Frege that is still in accordance with his overall theory. But because of the univocality of truth for him, the association with any individual thought must come via a different means, and as we have seen last chapter, it is the *act of assertion* under the correct attitude that plays such a role. Thus a strong hint of a behaviourist element finds its way into Frege's account of truth. But this leaves no place for any internal justification of knowledge states involving perception. Where does the informational content of our ordinary empirical encounters come into it? This seems to be the real dilemma for Frege which Sullivan's objections come close to pinpointing.

i) **Truth and the World**

Frege takes the status of the word "true" to be redundant in a sentence.[132] In other words, it adds nothing to the content of any sentence. For example:

1) Scott Morrison is the Prime Minister of Australia

2) It is true that Scott Morrison is the Prime Minister of Australia

---
[131] Ibid, 480.
[132] Frege, "The Thought,"

The content of both sentences are equivalent and hence the "it is true" in 2) functions redundantly.

The rationalist picture of truth drawn by Frege is counter to the correspondence theory of truth. In maintaining a boundary between psychology and logic, he rules out any subjective ideas as being the locus for truth bearing. Truth cannot consist of any kind of internal picturing relation, for example. Picturing is a correspondence between the picture and a particular state of affairs. And any notion of correspondence illicitly devolves the nature of truth into a two-place relation with something that is not of the same category. Here is a definition of the correspondence theory:

"x is true:= there is a y such that x corresponds to y."

We have here a definition of truth, x, involving a term, y, distinct from itself. Thus we have an analysis of truth into different terms. Presumably for a correspondence between two things to exist, there has to be some sort of likeness between the two things. But for ideas to represent, they could only be related to other ideas and not anything in the physical world. For Frege in order to judge the veridicality of a picture, it is necessary to view the relation "side-on" so to speak. But this is impossible under the solipsistic picture of the mental Frege has painted for himself. Thus the picture doesn't *present* the object it is about – it doesn't give the object to the perceiver in any way. Rather it is necessary, though impossible, to have prior, *mind-independent* knowledge of what the picture is representing. Hence Frege's second objection to the correspondence theory:

"Correspondence is a relation. This is contradicted, however, by the use of the word 'true', which is not a relation-word and contains no reference to anything else to which something must correspond. If I do not know that a picture is meant to represent Cologne Cathedral then I do not know with what to compare the picture to decide on its truth. A correspondence, moreover, can only be perfect if the corresponding things coincide and are, therefore, not distinct things at all."[133]

Thus perfection in correspondence demands complete coincidence, an identity. He gives the example of comparing a bank-note with another to test if it's genuine where it would be illegitimate to compare it to something unlike it such as a gold piece.[134] Again, Frege's reliance on a rationalist theory of identity is evident in his theory of truth. He does not permit any "ontological gap"[135] in the correspondence relation, the kind you would get between things of different kinds. The incomparable identity conditions as a marker for pure being is the only permitted condition for truth.

But then how can the identity relation play such an integral role in setting out the limiting case for truth when, as Sullivan argued, identity is a predicate that gets absorbed in its role as a name standing for the True? Again it can only be that the identity predicate plays the realising role where the True plays the determiner. In determining truth the predicate gets absorbed but as far as the realising conditions are concerned identity is indispensable. The lack of a perfect identity in the correspondence relation permits relative truth in violation of Frege's central conviction of absolute truth. Truth, for Frege, in its absolute and universal nature exists as a solitary substantial entity that cannot permit completion by anything complementary. Any conditionals are ruled out by an absolute, simple conception of being that merely *is what it is* and not anything else.

ii) **Wittgenstein's Objections**

Contrary to the rationalism of Frege, Wittgenstein situates his philosophical system in a way that is far more answerable to immediate experience. He brings his philosophy down to earth from the Fregean heights, tying logic to the world of linguistics and sense data. The notion of truth is one area where this comes across particularly strongly. As spelt out

---

[133] Frege, "The Thought," 291.
[134] Ibid.
[135] This term comes from John McDowell characterising the relation between proposition and reality in *Mind and World* (Cambridge, MA: Harvard University Press, 1994), 27.

already Frege's indefinable concept of truth is not metaphysically integral to the content of any judgement, but has to be presupposed in the act of judgement. The thought is recognised as true or false and expressed in a public manner in the act of assertion.

Note too that for the Platonic, psychologically averse Frege, meaning does not reside in psychological states or any spatiotemporal entities. Thus a sentence, as a series of raw marks or sounds, can only derive its meaning externally, the specific locus for its "truth" or "falsity" being the public act of assertion in accordance with the "laws of thought". This fact is indicated by the judgement-stroke plus the horizontal which is the designation of a truth-value, a sign that prefixes the sentence and hence stands external to its content.

Wittgenstein strongly opposed this Fregean picture and this opposition is illustrated in the central theme of the *Tractatus Logico-Philosophicus*[136] and earlier works. For him sense can only be spoken in a determinate way about the world on the assumption that there is an internal, formal connection between language and the external world. As he states: "A sentence can be true or false only by being a picture of reality."[137]

For Wittgenstein, it is in the making of true and false statements about the world where that internal, formal connection is based. Wittgenstein marshals various objections to Frege's concept of truth and sense from early in his writing. It will be recalled that Frege's ontology begins with the True as the most fundamental and simple entity in the order of being. The True is in turn determinative of basic sentences where the parts of the sentence can be abstracted out as deriving from the truth-value, the reference of the sentence. These sentences and their particular senses can only be regarded as true in a derived sense. Wittgenstein attacks this outlook in the following passages:

"An illustration to explain the concept of truth. A black spot on white paper; the form of the spot can be described by saying of each point of the plane whether it is white or black. To

---

[136] Ludwig Wittgenstein, *Tractatus Logico-Philosophicus*, trans. David F. Pears and Brian F. Mcguinness (London: Routledge, 2002)
[137] Ibid, 4.06.

the fact that a point is black corresponds a positive fact; to the fact that a point is white (not black), a negative fact. If I indicate a point of the plane (a truth-value in Frege's terminology), this corresponds to the assumption proposed for judgment, etc. etc.

But to be able to say that a point is black or white, I must first know under what conditions a point is called white or black; in order to be able to say 'p' is true (or false) I must have determined under what conditions I call 'p' true, and thereby I determine the sense of the proposition.

The point at which the simile breaks down is this: we can indicate a point on the paper, without knowing what white and black are; but to a proposition without a sense corresponds nothing at all, for it signifies no thing (truth-value) whose properties are called 'false" or 'true'; the verb of the proposition is not 'is true' or 'is false' – as Frege thought – but that which 'is true' must already contain the verb."

"Every proposition must *already* have a sense; assertion cannot give it a sense, for what it asserts is the sense itself. And the same holds of denial, etc."[138]

The analogy is this: the abstract coordinate system corresponds to assertion and the black and white spots correspond to the truth-values. It is the coordinate system itself that gets us to the points on the paper and thus the points are designated by a means that are not themselves coloured. Analogously, it is assertive behaviour that give us the truth value of sentences and lead us "blindly" to the truth referred to by sense. Thus the disanalogy consists in that a point can be singled out without making use of any concepts of black or white. But the same cannot occur when picking out a truth-value, which requires, according to Wittgenstein, that we have prior understanding of truth and falsity. Michael Potter points out the absurdity that Wittgenstein had uncovered in Frege's naming:

---

[138] Ibid, 4.063-4.064.

"It should therefore be possible, by analogy with the case of the sheet of paper, for the first stage, that of constructing a name which expresses what we wish to assert, to be done by someone who does not know what truth and falsity are. And that is ridiculous. In order to express a thought, I have to realize that thoughts aim at truth. It is incoherent to imagine someone coming to an understanding of language as a device for picking out one or other of the truth-values while still ignorant of what the point of this practice is."[139]

Wittgenstein thus sees the need to reverse the order of priority between sentences and truth-values. Instead of maintaining Frege's absolute version of truth – that confers truth on sentences that then have it in only in a derived manner – he instead proposes that in order to grasp truth we have to grasp how that truth applies to a proposition and that proposition's sense in particular. Truth has to be inherent to the sense of the sentence itself, *qua* individual representation, in order to refer to the truth-value in the first place, that is, in order to find its way to the individual and variegated true or false manifestations scattered amongst the different sentences. Thus Wittgenstein's take on truth is intimately tied to particular sentences in ways that Frege's would never have permitted.

His chief objection to Frege's judgement stroke is that it is "logically altogether meaningless"[140] and does not belong to the proposition. In particular there is no way to say that Fregean sentences are true or false in themselves and their status as derived truth means they are outside the realm of sense altogether and hence meaningless. Wittgenstein concludes from this that the truth status of propositions has no objective basis and hence the assertion sign merely establishes that the authors (Frege and Russell) hold the propositions to be true.[141]

Wittgenstein wants true sentences to be something that model reality. But he objects to Frege's assigning the judgement stroke to transform the sentence – coupled with the horizontal that already designates a truth-value – into the designation of the True. Sentences shouldn't be designating their truth conditions, for they contain truth in themselves as

---

[139] Michael Potter, *Wittgenstein's Notes on Logic* (Oxford: Oxford University Press, 2009), 89.
[140] Wittgenstein, *Tractatus* 4.442.
[141] Ibid.

things that "already contain the verb",[142] that is, the verb that specifies "the true" or "the false" within the sentence. He also registers another objection in the *Tractatus*, regarding how Frege moves from truth-conditions to sense in the context of logical connectives:

"Only Frege's explanation of the truth-concept is false: if 'the true' and 'the false' were really objects and were the arguments ¬p etc. then Frege's determination of the sense of '¬p' would be no determination at all."[143]

The argument is brief and hence has been the source of much confusion. The essence of his complaint is that truth conceived as a separate object is indeterminate vis-à-vis the sense of logical propositions. Unlike Ian Proops, however, I don't believe it "is unclear…why conceiving of truth and falsity as objects is supposed to have these dire consequences"[144] at least not if one appreciates the central role the True plays in determining sentence structures. The case of the all determinative role for the True has already been made in the previous chapter but an appreciation of this will help understand what Wittgenstein is driving at and this goes to the heart of Frege's system.

The upshot of Wittgenstein's complaint is that Frege's propositions being either true *or* false as names of distinct objects precludes them from holding bipolarity in truth-value status. As such, a proposition can either signify the True *or* signify the False, it cannot be jointly capable of being true *and* capable of being false. This means that whichever truth-value is specified by any particular sentence, the sentence is fixed by that truth-value. It is not a matter of that sentence having equal capacity to change its truth-value. There is nothing about the exact circumstances or truth conditions of a sense, say "¬p", that would make it true *as opposed to false* and the same could be said vice-versa. The fixing of truth conditions, for Frege, is entirely external to it.

---

[142] Ibid. 4.063.
[143] Ibid 4.431.
[144] Ian Proops, *Logic and Language in Wittgenstein's Tractatus* (New York: Garland Publishing, 2000), 42.

But that leaves it an open question as to what a Fregean sense of a truth-value is and what role it plays. In particular what conditions are laid down by a sense for the fulfilment of a truth-value? Consider, for example:

A signifies the True iff (…)

How does this square with Frege's indefinability criterion for truth? The answer is that there is no way of specifying any conditions of a descriptive kind. Indeed truth cannot feature in the content of any sentence at all. The judgement-stroke precludes any means of actually specifying the word "true" in a sentence, certainly if one wants to replace a sentence like "A is true" with a specific condition like correspondence, or coherence, that seeks to define that truth. The problem with such a methodology, according to Frege, is that one has to presuppose the notion of truth in order to apply such conditions.

Thus truth cannot be identified with anything psychological or anything physically embodied such as sentences. Instead, for Frege, truth is a matter of action or attitude, performed in the act of assertion. There are strict norms of use that he specifies as a condition for such an act of assertion. It is in no way a mere feeling of truth but, as Smith points out, one's condition must be one of "*justified with certainty*".[145] This is obviously not a representative state or any kind of correspondence with truth. It must be a condition of *embodiment* of truth. This is why the judgement-stroke does not play a naming role but is "a sign of its own special kind"[146] and "contains the act of assertion".[147]

Thus the only real way to express truth is in the act of assertion according to the laws of truth. But even this cannot *constitute* truth in anyway, so it is difficult to characterise the intimacy of the relationship that Frege is certain exists. But in any case there must be a strictly asymmetric, determinative relation proceeding from the True to the assertive act that issues in a relation of sorts. The necessity of the connection between the True and the

---

[145] Smith, "Frege's Judgment Stroke," 655.
[146] Frege, *Basic Laws*, 82.
[147] Ibid, 39.

assertive sentence is integral to Frege's system but it is obscure precisely because the nature of the True itself is obscure.

Returning now to *Tractatus* 4.431, Elizabeth Anscombe explains the argument in this way: Since reference cannot determine sense under Frege's system, then "¬p" must remain undetermined. But Proops thinks this fails to capture the heart of the disagreement.[148] However, it does have at least prima facie plausibility, since the reason the sense of "¬p" remains undetermined is because "the True" and "the False" are separate objects and thus not intrinsically connected to any single sense. This points back to the difficulty of squaring the all determinacy of the True with its necessarily distinct referring sentence. This means the universe is carved up into a truth-value dualism in which one category of propositions refer to the True, and another lot, the False. This is why there can never be anything about individual propositions themselves that sets out the conditions for their truth or falsity. Thus the necessary connection between sentence and truth-value must be blind to each sentence's distinct form, ultimately independent of the natures of each sentence's specific content.

It is unsurprising then that the uniquely substantial character of the True has a value range that does not specify any specific circumstance or object but rather takes names for truth-values that are indeterminate for anything else. As Peter Simons explains:

"…the course of values of that function which takes the True to the True and all other objects to the False, and this is indeterminate *both* because of the indeterminacy of 'the course of values of' *and* because of that of the reference of 'the True' and 'the False'. If we do not know which objects the True and the False are to start with, the stipulations in §10 will not help us to determine them, because the functions in terms of which they are stipulated are themselves only determined when the truth-values are determined."[149]

---

[148] For example, Proops, *Logic and Language*, 42.
[149] Peter Simons, "Frege and Wittgenstein, Truth and Negation," in *Wittgenstein: Eine Neubewertung*, ed. Rudolf Haller and Johannes Brandl (Vienna: hpt, 1990), 124.

Along these lines there is no way of moving from the intimacy between a sentence and its truth-condition to its counterpart truth-value in a way that preserves the original sense. True and False, for Frege, are not bipolar concepts with any intelligible gradient between them. There is no truth-value spectrum and thus no intelligible connection between the two and hence no path from the sense of one proposition to its negation via its truth-values.

The inherent arbitrariness of the truth conditions explain why, for Wittgenstein, sentences *must be* essentially bipolar, that is, either true or false. Sense is identified with truth-condition and thus sense ties the true and false together. Anscombe puts it: "[F]or Wittgenstein 'having a sense' was one and the same thing with being true-or-false."[150] There is an intimacy between sentence and truth here that we do not see in Frege.

Sentences are pictures of the world and sense does not require a further model to establish truth or falsity. Thus, for example, the sentence "*aRb*" is true by virtue of being a model of the world since "*a*" is to the left of "*b*". But this modelling process cannot itself be represented, as truth is already given in the modelling itself. Wittgenstein does not see the need that Frege saw for characterising the correspondence relationship horizontally. Thus sense is self-sufficient as he states in the Notebook, "logic must take care of itself".[151]

In a sentence like "It is asserted: Such-and-such is the case", the clause "it is asserted" is, accordingly, made redundant by the second half of the sentence. The *saying* that a situation is the case is laid bare by the sentence itself in the *Tractatus* and hence it is incorrect, on this methodology, to specify any criterion of truthfulness external to the sentence itself. It is inherent in the very being of the sentence to depict a possible state of affairs. The situation

---

[150] G. E. M. Anscombe, *An Introduction to Wittgenstein's Tractatus* (London: Hutchinson University Library, 1959), 58-59.

[151] Wittgenstein, *Tractatus* 5.473. In later passages Frege does seem to acknowledge that assertion is not a necessary condition for the redundancy of the truth predicate in a statement and locates it in content or "thought" itself: "If I attach ['true'] to the words 'that sea-water is salty' as a predicate, I likewise form a sentence that expresses a thought. For the same reason as before I put this also in the dependent form 'that it is true that sea-water is salty.' The thought expressed in these words coincides with the sense of the sentence 'that sea-water is salty.' So the sense of the word 'true' is such that it does not make any essential contribution to the thought." "My Basic Logical Insights," in Hermes et al, *Posthumous Writings*, 251

it depicts is contingent owing to its embodying of the two poles, truth and falsity. But the possibility that the state of affairs obtains is intrinsically given by the sentence.

Wittgenstein stresses that the sense of a sentence is necessary for it to be a sentence at all[152] and Frege's assertion sign cannot give a proposition any sense at all. All the assertion sign achieves is signalling that Frege (and Russell) holds the sentence to which it is affixed to be true.[153] Instead, the truth conditions are supposed to supervene on the sense of the sentence itself. The lesson of the illustration given earlier is that the truth of a sentence cannot be attributed to the meaningful sentence *after* it has fixed its reference. According to Wittgenstein, the expressing of a thought and the thought's aiming at truth are, contra Frege, inseparable.

So where does this leave the sense-to-reference relation for Frege, especially in light of *Foundation*'s leaving the reference to the truth-value in sentences? As is well known, sense plays a determinative role for Frege by determining or picking out a word's referent. But "indentifying" may be a better term to use than "determine" since the former recognises that it is *only* in our mental grasping of a thing that we are identifying what it is and that it has distinct individuative criteria.

Truth is a simple, unary, Platonic object. It exists in stark contrast to the Heraclitian world of flux that characterises sense impressions and matter. This is not to say that sense impressions were of no interest to Frege. The role of sense impressions is to epistemically identify objects in the world. The sense impressions and other subjective criteria constitute the intensional states that play an individuating role, but to derive truth requires sentences where, in *Foundations* most notably, functions are reduced to wholes (sentences) naming truth-values.

---

[152] Ibid, 4.064.
[153] Ibid, 4.442.

Thus the objectivity of thought and judgement for Frege depends on an ontological distinction between the subjective world of ideas and the objective world of thoughts. Ideas are things that "are had" whereas the laws of thought are independent of our mental states:

"And their effect is brought about by an act of the thinker without which they would be ineffective, at least as far as we can see. And yet the thinker does not create them but must take them as they are. They can be true without being apprehended by a thinker and are not wholly unreal even then, at least if they could be apprehended and by this means be brought into operation."[154]

Frege is careful to qualify that "acknowledging" is not a subjective process. He has to appeal to the sui generis cognitive process of grasping. In the same vein he describes judgement as "peculiar and incomparable".[155]

But given the derived nature of the truth of all things outside of truth-values, and the reductionist approach he takes to anything outside of the True, it is little wonder he had to appeal to vague notions such as grasping. But even worse, it creates a schizophrenic view of understanding where the "laws of thought" operate on a different track to our subjective understanding. Simons spells out such a consequence for cognition:

"…that it should be possible for me fully to grasp or understand a sense which, as the sense of a name of a truth-value, is a thought, while it is no part of my understanding that *what* I have grasped *is* a thought. It cannot be demanded that this should be a part of my understanding, because whether a sense is a thought is a matter, not of its internal form or nature, but of its particular semantics. It is a matter of what object in particular it determines as its referent, and it cannot be a requirement of understanding that I must know that."[156]

---

[154] Frege, "The Thought," 311.
[155] Frege, "On Sense and Reference," in Geach et al, *Translations*, 65.
[156] Simons, "The Sense of a Name," 479.

The reason we can understand the sense of a truth-value is that we are acting in accordance with the "laws of truth". But we have no idea *what* it is because, unlike sense properties, we have no ownership over that thought. It does not constitute our thought processes in any way. This is why elsewhere Frege stated that the sense that the True does have is "devoid of content".[157] Thus I conclude that Frege's understanding of human cognition leaves us totally in the dark as to how it is that the judging subject is in a position to know anything that is true.

What does not seem to be appreciated by Wittgenstein, however, is that this dilemma – where sense is inseparable from truth-value – is a result of Frege's metaphysical assumptions, assumptions never really spelt out. By conceiving sentences as akin to arithmetical equations and making senses the names of truth-values, he prioritises the latter *functionally*: Take the function $f(x^2)$ which is a function that maps the argument 3 to the value 9. In this case the lack of any independent identity of the 3 becomes obvious since it is mapped by the function, f, into the 9. The 3 is identity dependent on the one, self-subsistent entity, revealed as the 9 in this case. The function here is external to the 3 – it is the *same* function that occurs in all arithmetical equations – and thus the reduction occurs in a way that does not involve any essential feature of the 3.

Now there is no way to reverse such a function and extract the 3 from the 9. That is because, for Frege, there is no way, *qua* substantial entity, of breaking up the 9. Even if we represent it as the equation $9 = 3^3$ all we have is an identity with two different modes of presentation flanking the identity sign with two entities on either side simple in their being and hence unanalysable into parts. The reason sense is not determined for Frege is simply because the real work of turning the sentence into a name of a truth-value – assimilating the meaning of the thought to the truth-value – is done by the truth-value itself via the grounding relationship. And that truth-value is a quintessential example of Parmenidian being: a simple, opaque and ultimately meaningless entity outside of the generic stipulations given to it by Frege. This is *why*, in its determination, truth cannot draw an intelligible connection between the same sense prefixed by negation.

---

[157] Frege, "My Basic Logical Insights," in Hermes et al, *Posthumous Writings*, 252.

Wittgenstein was right to criticise Frege in these ways. In my final two chapters I detail an alternative theory of truth with alternative categories that essentially identifies truth with propositions. Importantly, it is a conception of truth that is not univocal and is an essential function of sense data rather than being some unknown entity that abides in Plato's third realm.

iii) Wittgenstein on Truth Conditions

Wittgenstein famously held to a picture theory of the proposition, the model he proposed in the *Tractatus* for how it is that a proposition represents reality. More specifically, it is an account of how truth and falsehood are possible. Without the picturing relation, a proposition cannot be true or false.[158] It is intrinsic to a proposition that it represents reality either rightly or wrongly, truly or falsely:

"A picture agrees with reality or fails to agree; it is correct or incorrect, true or false"[159]

"'True' and 'false' are not accidental properties of a proposition, such that, when it has meaning, we can say it is also true or false: on the contrary, to have meaning *means* to be true or false: the being true or false actually constitutes the relation of the proposition to reality, which we mean by saying that it has meaning."[160]

Immediately we can see this as a remedy for Frege's dependence on the judgement stroke to derive the truth of a sentence. Instead, the truth or falsity of a picturing proposition is intrinsic to it.

---

[158] Wittgenstein, *Tractatus*, 4.06.
[159] Ibid, 2.21.
[160] Ludwig Wittgenstein, *Notebooks, 1914-1916*, ed. and trans. G. E. M. Anscombe, ed. George Henrik von Wright (Oxford: Blackwell, 1979),112.

However, picturing can conjure up misunderstandings as to the exact nature of the resemblance since one is inclined to think in terms of a *material* resemblance in the way that a map or a drawing will tend to represent according to the ratio of physical dimensions. Indeed Wittgenstein gives this impression with the famous car accident experiment from which he derived the idea of the picture theory in the first place. As Georg Henrik von Wright describes it:

"Wittgenstein was reading in a magazine about a lawsuit in Paris concerning an automobile accident. At the trial a miniature model of the accident was presented before the court. The model here served as a proposition; that is, as a description of a possible state of affairs. It has this function owing to a correspondence between the parts of the model (the miniature-houses, -cars, -people) and things (houses, cars, people) in reality. It now occurred to Wittgenstein that one might reverse the analogy and say that a *proposition* serves as a model or *picture*, by virtue of a similar correspondence between *its* parts and the world. The way in which the parts of the proposition are combined – the *structure* of the proposition – depicts a possible combination of elements in reality, a possible state of affairs."[161]

Thus the exact resemblance of the model cars and the physical arrangement of the parts resembles the arrangement of the cars depicted in the accident. But such a resemblance isn't a necessary condition for picturing, as this can take far broader forms:

"At first sight a proposition—one set out on the printed page, for example—does not seem to be a picture of the reality with which it is concerned. But neither do written notes seem at first sight to be a picture of a piece of music, nor our phonetic notation (the alphabet) to be a picture of our speech. And yet these sign-languages prove to be pictures, even in the ordinary sense, of what they represent."[162]

---

[161] George Henrik von Wright "A Biographical Sketch," in Norman Malcolm *Ludwig Wittgenstein: A Memoir*, 2nd ed. (Oxford: Oxford University Press, 1984): 8, quoted in David Stern *Wittgenstein on Mind and Language* (Oxford and New York: Oxford University Press, 1995), 35.
[162] Wittgenstein, *Tractatus*, 4.011.

Hence picturing extends to means that take on forms that do not initially appear to be "picturing" as we normally understand it.

Another crucial feature of the picture theory of the proposition is that it fulfils its criterion as a representation independently of whether or not it succeeds in successfully representing how the world is. In particular, Wittgenstein states: "What a picture represents it represents independently of its truth or falsity, by means of its pictorial form."[163] Thus, for example, to think truly "that *p*" is the same as to think falsely "that *p*". In both instances one is thinking the same thing: "that *p*". In an earlier publication, Wittgenstein put the problem as follows:

"If a picture presents what-is-not-the-case ... this only happens through its presenting *that* which *is* not the case. For the picture says, as it were, '*This* is how it is *not*' and to the question '*How* is it not?' just the positive proposition is the answer."[164]

The picture theory of the proposition is an important step in the right direction. My theory of intentionality will resemble it in some important respects. However, unlike the *Tractatus* model, it will prioritise the natural signs of sense impressions over that which are merely conventional. In addition, truth or falsity will be tied in with the content of the proposition so that saying "how something is" will be equivalent to saying that it is true. In other words, the very content which is true in any particular case is fixed by the formal identity between proposition and fact and it is not possible that such a proposition could have been false.

Russell

We saw in previous chapters how influential the rationalist tradition was in the work of Frege. For Russell there is an overriding theme that stems from Leibniz, a principle guiding

---

[163] Ibid, 2.22.
[164] Wittgenstein, *Notebooks*, 25.

him in his search for ultimate principles, namely *quodlibet ens est unum*: "whatever is, is one."[165] This is what makes Russell's logical atomism atomic. Russell embarked on a quest for true unities, but these were not just unities abstracted from an amalgamation of objects placed in proximity to each other. In mereological terms, he thought "parts have no direct connection *inter* se".[166] As he states in his commentary on Leibniz:

"'Where there are only beings by aggregation,' Leibniz says, 'there are not even real beings. For every being by aggregation presupposes beings endowed with a true unity, since it only derives its reality from that of those of which it is composed, so that it will have none at all if every component is again a being by aggregation.' What is not truly one being, is not truly a being." [167]

Elsewhere Russell sets the criteria for what counts as an entity in his ontology:

"If there is such an object as a class, it must in some sense be one object."[168]

And:

"What was wrong was assuming individuals which have no being….I now extend this to all classes. The error seems to me to lie in supposing that many entities ever combine to form one new entity."[169]

---

[165] Bertrand Russell, *Principles of Mathematics* (London and New York: Routledge, 2010), 133. See also his 1910 letter to Bradley in *The Collected Papers of Bertrand Russell*, Vol. 6: *Logical and Philosophical Papers 1909-1913* (London: Routledge, 1992), 350. The case for this principle's overriding influence on Russell comes from Jan Dejnozka *The Ontology of the Analytic Tradition and its Origins: Realism and Identity in Frege, Russell, Wittgenstein and Quine* (New York: Rowman and Littlefield, 1996)
[166] Russell, *Principles*, 141.
[167] Bertrand Russell, *A Critical Exposition of the Philosophy of Leibniz* (Nottingham: Spokesman, 2008), 103.
[168] Bertrand Russell, "Letter to Philip Jourdain," 1 Jan 1906, quoted in *The Ontology of the Analytic Tradition*, 185.
[169] Ibid.

But these unities are also substantial entities and, in this section, I expound and refute these key elements of his metaphysics. The pivot upon which much of his metaphysics and epistemology turns is his conception of substance. His view of substance is one of self-subsistence and independence. In this way he follows Aristotle in taking substance to be essentially non-predicative and non-relational.

But the notion of substance is also Parmenidian according to Russell.[170] Substance, as a metaphysical category, which is normally thought to originate with Aristotle, has an absolute and atomic nature reminiscent of Parmenidian being. As Russell writes:

"What subsequent philosophy, down to quite modern times, accepted from Parmenides, was not the impossibility of all change, which was too violent a paradox, but the indestructibility of substance."[171]

It is important to keep this influence in mind as one reads Russell and to discern that such substances are integral to his whole worldview. For example, sense data are substances in their nature and thus cannot depend on objects beyond themselves. As we will see later, such a metaphysical posit leads to dilemmas for direct realism and the unity of the proposition.

i) **The Unity of the Proposition**

There are several commonly thought functions of propositions, such as bearers of truth-values, objects of belief and the meanings of sentences. But in playing such roles it is vital that propositions be able to form unities that are not merely just a function of their parts, or the individual words that make up the sentence. Thus a proposition differs from a mere list

---

[170] The case for the influence of Parmenides on Russell is laid out by Dejnoka, *The Ontology of the Analytic Tradition*, 135-143.
[171] Bertrand Russell, *A History of Western Philosophy* (New York: Simon and Schuster, 1945), 52 quoted in Ibid, 138.

or random concatenation of words. We can see this in Russell's example: the difference between "A difference B" and "A differs from B".[172] There is a natural unity in the latter not in the former.

One useful way to start an exposition of Russell's account of the unity of the proposition is to compare his account with the accounts of Moore and Frege. Moore took the constituents of propositions to be concepts. Concepts were Platonic entities for Moore – eternal, immutable and abstract – and hence not dependent on our psychological means of apprehending them:

"Concepts are possible objects of thought; but that is no definition of them. It merely states that they may come into relation with a thinker; and in order that they *may* do anything, they must already *be* something. It is indifferent to their nature whether anybody thinks them or not."[173]

Intelligibility for Moore meant analysing a thing into its constituent concepts, but it was the synthesis of concepts into a proposition that gave it its truth-bearing status. In this way concepts made up the fundamental components of all that exists. Thus propositions were not about separate entities, but about the very objects that made them up. Such an intimate identity relation followed naturally from Moore's Platonism and meant the objects of intentionality went directly to the objects themselves and skipped any mediation from our psychological processes. Indeed, the immediacy with which truth presents itself entailed a rejection of the correspondence theory of truth:

"What kind of relation makes a proposition true, what false, cannot be further defined, but must be immediately recognized."[174]

---

[172] Russell, *Principles*
[173] G. E. Moore, "The Nature of Judgment," *Mind* 8, no. 30 (1899): 180, http://www.jstor.org/stable/2247657.
[174] Ibid.

Thus with Moore we have propositions built up out of concepts. But the constituents were also eternal and abstract and also atomistic. Thus in order to protect the integrity of such independent building blocks required that they only acquire external relations to each other. Both the relata and relations exist independently of each other. Thus we have Moore's general metaphysical and epistemological system: the world is made up of concepts externally related to each other and bearing truth-conditions that exist independently of any knowing agent.

Whilst Moore's account greatly influenced Russell in this early period, it was not so with Frege. Both Russell and Moore rejected Frege's intermediates, the senses between knower and reference. Like Russell, however, Frege held propositions to be made up of their constituents arranged in a certain way. An expression that is complete has no gaps in it. But what holds the parts of a sentence together for Frege? To answer this he drew a fundamental ontological distinction between complete and incomplete expressions. For a thought to be complete, Frege believed that an unsaturated sense had to be completed by a saturated sense. So if we take the parts of a complex phrase, they are held together because the unsaturated sense "glues" the parts of the thought together. In a simple sentence such as "Frege is smart", we have the complete sense expressed by "Frege" and the unsaturated sense expressed by "smart". So "Frege" completes the unsaturated sense, "smart", to give us the whole complete sense of the sentence, "Frege is smart". Or we could take a sense like "Jim loves Jane". The incomplete component in this case is "loves" which picks out two incomplete entities: in this case the expression is "x loves y". So Jim and Jane saturate these two gaps.

The logical subject is a substantial independent entity; it is decisively *not* unsaturated. There is no way of characterising it in any way that is essentially relational or predicative. Hence concepts and relations, being unsaturated functions, have a completely different nature. As a corollary to this, there is no half-way house for a predicate concept to be a substance-in-relation, for it cannot be a "something-in-itself" as well as a "something-for-others". Thus we either have a predicate or we have reference to a concept that in fact makes it into an object.

Now Frege, like Russell and Moore, ensured that propositions were not tainted with subjectivity. Unsaturated and saturated entities were neither subjective nor physical but belonged to an objectively real third realm of entities.[175] They are in no way dependent on our perceptions nor would they in any way go out of existence if there were no rational beings in the universe.

Now it might seem that Frege is at an advantage since, contrary to Moore and Russell, he starts with the whole and derives the unsaturated and saturated parts. But invoking a third realm makes it a mystery just how it is that the predicate plays such an important role of gluing the parts of the proposition together. We are told *that* they are incomplete and in need of completion and that we get a distinct, complete thought as a result, but this really tells us nothing of the mechanism by which it happens. As Donald Davidson argues, this merely labels the problem rather than solves it.[176]

Russell rejected Frege's solution since it makes any sentence with adjectives false on the basis that for the adjective to refer would necessarily involve turning it into a substantive, which it is not. Thus no sentence with adjectives could refer accurately.[177] Hence the unstable states of Frege's situation led Russell to reject the ontological distinction between objects and concepts, but doing so deprived him of what seemed like a prima facie solution to the unity problem.

Russell decided instead to follow Moore in maintaining one singular ontological entity that he called a *term*. A term just refers to anything that is the subject of a proposition. They are the ordinary objects that we talk about. Thus the things referred to are directly involved in our propositions about them. Furthermore, they are not a linguistic or psychological entity, but simply the broadest category of any entity. In fact it covers every conceivable object of

---

[175] On Frege's use of the "third realm" see Burge who documents many references he makes to numerous non-spatial, atemporal, and causally inert entities such as concepts, functions, relations, numbers, thought contents etc, that inhabit this realm; "Frege on Knowing," in *Early Analytic Philosophy*, 1-18

[176] Donald Davidson, "Truth and Meaning," *Synthese* 17, no. 1, (1967): 304, http://www.jstor.org/stable/20114563.

[177] See in Russell, *Principles*, §49 and §52 for a more complete argument against Frege's position.

thought. As he states: "A man, a moment, a number, a class, a relation, a chimaera, or anything else that can be mentioned, is sure to be a term".[178] These terms, as the meanings of individual linguistic expressions, go together to make up propositions.

Russell thus sought a solution that avoided Frege's difficulties, by making terms complete entities that *can* occupy the subject of a proposition. As is obvious from the previous quote, Russell took surface grammatical form for granted as a guide to logic. He had not, at the time of writing the *Principles*, drawn a distinction between grammatical and logical form.

But in addition to terms, Russell also drew a distinction between things and concepts. A thing, for example "Socrates", can be used exclusively as a subject, whereas a concept has amphibious use: it can occupy the subject of a proposition but also the predicate.[179] Thus the concept "wisdom" occupies the subject position where the concept denoted by "wise" would occupy the predicate.

Introducing concepts such as relations gave Russell the means to explain propositional unity for the simple reason that relations relate things. Consistent with the dual functional role of a concept, a relation relates but it can also function as a term, that is, as a self-subsistent entity. So we could have a relation actually relating as in "John loves Jane" or we could express the relation as a term in a set such as {John, Jane, loves}. Russell states the difference succinctly: "The fact seems to be that a relation is one thing when it relates, and another when it is enumerated as a term in a collection."[180] So in the latter case, "loves" functions in the same way as the other two terms and there is no relational unity.

It may appear on this account that a proposition's being true is quite trivial. For A and B to be related by the relation of difference just means that A and B are different. Recall that Russell's propositions contain the objects they are about. Thus if A and B are related by the

---

[178] Ibid, 45.
[179] Ibid, 46.
[180] Ibid, 141.

relation of difference in the proposition that A is different from B, then that proposition is a fact. Thus there is no distinction between fact and a true proposition.

Now the difficulty with this is that it doesn't allow for false propositions. If A is not different to B but instead they are the same thing then there is no relation of difference relating A and B. There could not be any fact that A is different from B and thus there could be no proposition that A is different to B. Thus *ex hypothesi* there can be no false propositions since a false proposition must be a unity in order for it to be a proposition. But if it did relate its objects in a false proposition, it would be a true proposition!

Russell's account precluded him from accepting any form of the correspondence theory since there is no gap between true proposition and fact. Thus there are no two objects for the correspondence theory to relate. Instead Russell, like Moore, took truth to be a primitive, unanalysable notion. In this way his account of truth resembled Frege's. But the important difference is that he took truth to also be a property of propositions. As he states: "some propositions are true and some are false, just as some roses are red and some are white."[181] Notably he doesn't state anything like a supervenience relation between propositions and truth which would tie the latter to the particular characteristics of the former and hence make truth analysable and possibly equivocal. Instead he is forced to attribute a brute, unexplained, unanalysable, primitive property to any true proposition.

The trouble for unity, as Russell conceded, was that there was no way even in principle to draw a distinction between the relation-as-term, on the one hand, and the relation-relating that was actually responsible for bringing the terms together, on the other. He concedes that "The verb, when used as a verb, embodies the unity of the proposition, and is thus distinguishable from the verb considered as a term, though I do not know how to give a clear account of the precise nature of the distinction."[182]

---

[181] Bertrand Russell, "Meinong's Theory of Complexes and Assumptions," in *Essays in Analysis*, ed. Douglas Lackey (London: Allen & Unwin, 1973), 75.
[182] Russell, *Principles*, 51.

Whilst some have argued that this was a serious problem for Russell,[183] that is disputable. But in either case it is important to recognise that Russell was boxed into this corner by his rejection of internal relations and his atomistic doctrine based on self-subsistent entities. Internalism takes relations to be grounded in the natures of each of the relata so that in a sense it can be said that the nature of each is written into the nature of the other. The inherent instability of internal relations was one of the arguments that lead F. H. Bradley to monism.[184] Since every object is related to every other object in the universe then every object contains within itself the same complexity as inhabits the entire universe. Indeed it is difficult to see how objects can even be distinguished at all. One consequence of this is that in analysing the objects out of the whole, we falsify that whole since, *ex hypothesi*, those objects are identified with the whole.

Russell rejected such a picture and embraced logical atomism along with its corollary, external relations. His view was that objects existing in relations are simple and that any given entity in a relation can also exist in many different relations as well. But such a pluralist outlook was threatened by a well-known objection from Bradley, called *Bradley's Regress*.[185] Given the relation acts on two entities only as an abstraction from the complexity of such an entity's parts, then as simples there is nothing intrinsically tying the entities together.

Consider "John loves Jane" as an example of a complex. Since John and Jane are related by an external relation – loves – then as simples in a relation there is nothing intrinsic to either John or Jane that relates each to the other. Compare this with, say, two blue balls existing in *the same colour as* relation which is internal and hence grounded in the nature of the two balls. But there is no comparable quality in either John or Jane relating each to each other; that is to say, there is nothing in John's nature that requires that he must love Jane. And

---

[183] See Bernard Linsky, "The Unity of the Proposition," *Journal of the History of Philosophy* 30, no. 2 (1992): 243-273, https://muse.jhu.edu/article/226223; Donald Davidson, *Truth and Predication* (Cambridge, MA: Belknap Press, 2005), 103-106.

[184] As he says, "You cannot, in any sense, know, or perceive, or experience, a term as in relation, unless you have also the other term to which it is related." F. H. Bradley, *Appearance and Reality* (Oxford: Clarendon Press, 1893), 322. And he also says, "internal relations...point towards a higher consummation beyond themselves"; F. H. Bradley, "Coherence and Contradiction," in *Essays on Truth and Reality* (Oxford: Clarendon Press, 1914), 239-240.

[185] Bradley, *Appearance and Reality*, 32-33.

there is also nothing in the loving relation which ties either of its constituents in such a way. So what ties John and Jane into this particular loving relation? Clearly it has to be another external relation brought in to relate loving to its two constituents in order to ensure a unity. But what relates *that* external relation to loving and the two constituents? Hence an infinite and vicious regress ensues since the logical gap always has to be plugged by further external relations and unity is never accounted for.

Bradley avoided the problem of unity by denying *any* independent existence to the parts of the one, unified, absolute. This meant that Bradley had no explaining to do on how many parts become one since the whole is ontologically prior to the parts. Russell had more difficulty accounting for unities because of the different way he conceived of judgement. "John", "loving", and "Jane" are all separate individual pieces of the one proposition. As Stewart Candlish writes: "For Russell, a judgment is not like a single piece of wood, whose individual pieces are notional rather than real; rather, it is like a model assembled from pieces existing in their own right, all of which are in Frege's terms 'saturated'."[186]

Bradley pointed out later the contradictory nature of relational facts: relations hold between terms and the terms must uphold their integrity as independent entities. Hence to become a whole the parts must become something other than they are since to become whole something beyond what is immediately experienced must be included. Hence "no term … can itself simply be or become a 'between'".[187] Therefore a relational fact must be and not be something more than its constituents. He writes: "A relation both is and is not what may be called the entire relational situation, and hence in this respect contradicts itself."[188]

Russell concurred with Bradley that analysis is falsification – since after analysis we lose information when the verb is transformed into a verb noun – but it still played a prominent role in linguistic analysis for him. But he was forced to skirt the issue of unity and the objection of Bradley's regress by positing unity as a primitive that is assumed in analysis:

---

[186] Steward Candlish, *The Russell/Bradley Dispute and its Significance for Twentieth Century Philosophy* (New York: Palgrave Macmillan, 2007), 52.
[187] F. H. Bradley, "Relations," in *Collected Essays*, vol. 2 (Oxford: Clarendon Press, 1935), 634.
[188] Ibid, 635.

"[A] relating relation is distinguished from a relation in itself by the indefinable element of assertion…"[189]

But aside from Russell's obvious difficulties in these areas he at least has a way of decomposing concepts, something that has fairly straightforward appeal to our intuitions and on this note he criticises Bradley:

"…it is important to realize the very narrow limits of this doctrine [that analysis falsifies]. We cannot conclude that the parts of a whole are not really its parts, nor that the parts are not presupposed in the whole in some sense in which the whole is not presupposed in the parts … In short, though analysis gives us the truth, and nothing but the truth, yet it can never give us the whole truth. This is the only sense in which the doctrine is to be accepted. In any wider sense, it becomes merely a cloak for laziness, by giving an excuse to those who dislike the labour of analysis."[190]

Russell is here conceding metaphysical ground to whole propositions above and beyond their parts but he may have surrendered any explanation of that unity to begin with. Having said that Russell was still able to aim the accusation of laziness at Bradley, since in Bradley's system there was no way to do analysis given that what was left over were mere relations-as-appearances. Russell at least had parts leftover from analysis. This was a big plus in his favour given the utility and broad appeal of analysis in general (as in rudimentary chemical analysis). But nonetheless there remained the awkwardness of the verb and noun verb distinctions and Bradley was quick to point out the inconsistency that threatened his pluralism:[191]

"Mr. Russell's main position has remained to myself incomprehensible. On the one side I am led to think that he defends a strict pluralism, for which nothing is admissible beyond simple terms and external relations. On the other side Mr. Russell seems to assert

---

[189] Russell, *Principles,* 100.
[190] Ibid, 142.
[191] Russell Hylton actually argues his inability to account for unity threatens his opposition to idealism; *Russell, Idealism, and the Emergence of Analytic Philosophy* (Oxford: Clarendon Press, 1990), 177-178.

emphatically, and to use throughout, ideas which such a pluralism surely must repudiate. He throughout stands upon unities which are complex and which cannot be analysed into terms and relations. These two positions to my mind are irreconcilable, since the second, as I understand it, contradicts the first flatly. If there are such unities, and, still more, if such unities are fundamental, then pluralism surely is in principle abandoned as false."[192]

There is tension here for Russell. Although he is a pluralist in accepting only terms into his ontology, he clearly wants to maintain a role for propositional unity. But when we form unities of facts we require something more than the constituents. *The problem is there is nothing in Russell's ontology to play the role of a unifier, to explain that unity.* Further, the terms in his ontology are independent entities that are not suited to playing a predicative or relational role. Specifically, they maintain their identity independent of context or position in a whole. The fifth chapter of this thesis will supply such unity without sacrificing a detailed analysis of the parts. This will require new principles and ontological categories.

ii) **Russell on Direct Realism**

In moving away from idealism, Russell went to the opposite extreme and embraced direct realism, and it was direct realism that led him to reject Fregean senses. Russell agreed with Frege that propositions are not subjective entities, that is, they are not constituents of mental states or language. But the two differed on just how the symbols representing propositions relate to the objects of reference. The senses for Frege were Platonic entities that inhabited a half-way house between the thinking subject and referent. Russell, on the other hand, was rejecting the neo-Kantian idealism that was around at the turn of the 20th century and was emphatic in emphasising the directness of the relation between truth and object.

---

[192] F. H. Bradley, "Supplementary Note to 'On appearance, error and contradiction'," *Mind*, reprinted as "Supplementary Note II" in *Essays in Truth and Reality*. (Oxford: Clarendon Press, 1914), 281, quoted in *The Russell/Bradley Dispute*, 57.

But Russell recognised that there was a major hurdle to any form of realism, one that had stalked every form of realism since the scientific revolution: that the objects of our perception as described by physics are really nothing like the objects we directly perceive. Physics describes objects as mostly empty space and even the few heterogeneous atoms that do reside in that space hardly resemble the homogeneity of, for example, the feel of a dense wooden table. Given such incongruence between the world of our perception and the world described by physics, how can we posit a strong enough connection between the two that will guarantee reliable knowledge? The incongruence guarantees that it is impossible in principle to ascertain any kind of correlation for the simple fact that the physical object is completely unknowable:

"The supposed contents of the physical world are *prima facie* very different from these: molecules have no colour, atoms make no noise, electrons have no taste, and corpuscles do not even smell.

If such objects are to be verified, it must be solely through their relation to sense data: they must have some kind of correlation with sense data, and must be verifiable through their correlation *alone*.

But how is the correlation itself ascertained? A correlation can only be ascertained empirically by the correlated objects being constantly *found* together. But in our case, only one term of the correlation, namely, the sensible term, is ever *found*: the other term seems essentially incapable of being found. Therefore, it would seem, the correlation with objects . . . is itself utterly and for ever unverifiable."[193]

Russell sums up the argument in a much later publication:

---

[193] Bertrand Russell, "The Relation of Sense-data to Physics," in *Mysticism and Logic and Other Essays* (London: Allen and Unwin, 1917), 145-146.

"Naïve realism leads to physics, and physics, if true, shows that naïve realism is false. Therefore, naïve realism, if true, is false; therefore it is false."[194]

Now whereas Frege held that the sense – as opposed to the object it designates – expressed by a name is a constituent of the thought (or sense) expressed by the entire sentence that contains that name, as discussed in the last section, Russell held that the object *is* a constituent of the proposition expressed by the sentence. Russell's notion of a proposition is that it actually contains the objects of reference whereas for Frege the parts of sense remain at the level of sense only.

For the mind to come to know an object, it proceeds, according to Frege, by the symbolic functions of proper names. There are twin symbolic functions: the expression of a sense and the designation of an object.[195] The sense is a way of knowing for Frege and its sharp distinction with reference reflects a paralleled split in Frege between the epistemic and metaphysical domains. Hence the distinction between knowing that "the morning star is the morning star" – known purely a priori – and knowing that "the morning star is the evening star" – which necessarily involves its mode of presentation to the knower.

Russell strongly opposed such a split between the epistemic and ontic domains and hence the content of a Russellian proposition directly involves what the proposition is about. A famous example was given by Frege in a letter he wrote to Russell in 1904.[196] Taking the sentence, "Mont Blanc is over 4,000 metre's high", we can say the function, "is over 4,000 metre's high", maps "Mont Blanc" to its reference, which is the True in this case. But crucially the sense occupies Frege's abstract third realm and hence the mountain itself, Mont Blanc, is not a direct part of the sense. Frege writes:

---

[194] Bertrand Russell, *An Inquiry into Meaning and Truth* (London and New York: Routledge, 1992), 15.
[195] See Frege, "On Sense and Reference," in Geach et al, *Translations*, 56-78.
[196] Gottlob Frege, "Frege to Russell 13.11.1904," in Gabriel et al, *The Philosophical and Mathematical Correspondence*, 160-165.

"I agree with you that 'true' is not a predicate like 'green.' For at bottom, the proposition 'It is true that 2 + 3 = 5' says no more than the proposition '2 + 3 = 5.' Truth is not a component part of a thought, just as Mont Blanc with its snowfields is not itself a component part of the thought that Mont Blanc is more than 4,000 metres high."[197]

Russell's response to this is to argue that we do not grasp any intermediary, such as a sense, but rather that Mont Blanc is directly a constituent of the proposition "Mont Blanc is over 4,000 metre's high". He writes:

"I believe that in spite of all its snowfields Mont Blanc itself is a component part of what is actually asserted in the proposition 'Mont Blanc is more than 4,000 metres high.' We do not assert the thought, for this is a private psychological matter: we assert the object of the thought, and this is, to my mind, a certain complex (an objective proposition, one might say) in which Mont Blanc is itself a component part. If we do not admit this, then we get the conclusion that we know nothing at all of Mont Blanc."[198]

Thus in order to secure a basis for knowledge, Russell insists that the objects of a proposition be direct parts of that proposition. Intermediary entities would be an epistemic barrier between knower and known since we may know the sense itself but unless the reference is actually part of that sense, which for Frege it is not, then we have no direct basis for knowledge. Later Russell reiterates such a concern in involving "ideas" in judgements where "ideas become a veil between us and outside things – we never really, in knowledge, attain to the things we are supposed to be knowing about, but only to the ideas of those things."[199]

It might seem strange that something generally conceived as abstract as a proposition could contain real physical things, the things that it is about. But Russell was heavily influenced

---

[197] Ibid, 163.
[198] Ibid 169.
[199] Bertrand Russell, *The Problems of Philosophy* (Indianapolis, Cambridge: Hackett Publishing Company, 1912), 119.

by Moore in his early post-Kantian years and he took propositions and the "terms" that make them to be something like Platonic entities. So reference to Mont Blanc would take in its enormous weight but weight is merely a Platonic concept considerably lightening the burden!

iii) **Russell on Truth via Acquaintance and Description**

In contrast to Frege's rationalism, Russell takes the direct contents of experience as the starting point for knowledge and in particular draws a distinction between two forms of knowledge: *knowledge by acquaintance* and *knowledge by description.* For Russell, acquaintance is the gold standard in knowledge and is the most fundamental in a *foundationalist epistemology*. But it also, as I will argue in this section, reflects Russell's prized hierarchy in being, with the epistemological ordering reflecting the metaphysical ordering: the most simple, independent, abstract elements being the grounds for the plural, descriptive, dependent, instances of sense experience.

The defining characteristics of acquaintance is *direct* and *infallible* knowledge.[200] In this way, acquaintance is immediate and does not involve mental representations; that is, there are no cognitive intermediaries, such as mental ideas, between the knower and object known. Russell characterises the flip side of acquaintance, from the object to the knower as a *presentational* relationship, that is, there is a direct and unmediated giving of the object in knowledge.[201]

The infallibility of acquaintance means that if S is acquainted with object O, then O must exist as a matter of necessity. It is also signified by a logically proper name which picks it out directly and not via any description. As he states "[w]hatever we are acquainted with

---

[200] On acquaintance see his "Knowledge by Acquaintance and Knowledge by Description," in *Mysticism and Logic*, 209-232; Russell, *The Problems of Philosophy*, ch. 5.
[201] Russell, "Knowledge by Acquaintance," in *Mysticism and Logic*, 209.

must be something; we may draw wrong inferences from our acquaintance, but the acquaintance itself cannot be deceptive."[202] Likewise there is no possibility for error such that when "we are acquainted with an object, there certainly is such an object, and the possibility of error is logically excluded".[203]

Now it is important to emphasise that the objects of acquaintance are not physical objects but special items such as sense data, abstract objects, and perhaps the self.[204] One can be acquainted with something and yet draw the wrong inference in *what* we are acquainted with. So a round penny may appear elliptical if looked at from a particular angle. However, this is still not deceptive because it is the elliptical sense-datum that we are acquainted with and not the penny itself. In this regard illusions and even hallucinations can be objects of acquaintance, since the something *is* the appearance.

The objects of acquaintance also exhibit the Parmenidian principles of simplicity and independence. This is what Proops calls the "Independence Thesis".[205] As Russell writes:

"Knowledge of things, when it is of the kind we call knowledge by *acquaintance*, is essentially simpler than any knowledge of truths, and logically independent of knowledge of truths, though it would be rash to assume that human beings ever, in fact, have acquaintance with things without at the same time knowing some truth about them."[206]

Now we may have a judgement, for example, that S judges "*aRb*". The acquaintance relation guarantees the existence of each constituent of the judgement individually such that any judgement must presuppose an act of acquaintance.[207] So judgement is more than acquaintance but must presuppose it. However, error *can* arise in the case of judgement if

---

[202] Russell, *Problems of Philosophy*, 119.
[203] Ibid, 16.
[204] Ibid, ch. 5.
[205] Ian Proops, "Russellian Acquaintance Revisited," *Journal of the History of Philosophy* 52, no. 4 (2014):796, https://doi.org/10.1353/hph.2014.0098
[206] Russell, *Problems of Philosophy*, 72.
[207] Ibid, 75.

the constituents are not united in a way that gives a right judgement. Russell explains the difference between the two forms of knowing as follows:

"From the fact that presentation is a two-term relation, the question of truth or error cannot arise with regard to it; in any case of presentation there is a certain relation of an act to an object, and the question whether there is such an object cannot arise. In the case of judgment, error can arise; for although the several objects of the judgment cannot be illusory, they may not be related as the judgment believes that they are. The difference, in this respect, between judgment and presentation is due to the fact that judgment is a multiple relation, not a two-term relation."[208]

Now what commentators have noted regarding acquaintance is that particular instances such as being "brown" or "red" may be presentations of something beyond themselves, which have been called "truthmakers".[209] But this is really just the underlying substantial being, the source of unity of the experience and that *unity* is, in fact, distinct from the particular quality that it unifies.

There are, in Russell's writings, cases where acquaintance appears to fail indubitable tests. Russell advances an atomistic system of knowledge. We can know the parts of the system individually, one step at a time, but not all at once. So for *aRb* we can know each part individually, but to know *a* does not entail knowing *Rb*, and to know *b* does not entail knowing *Ra*. This is what Peter Hylton calls "Platonic Atomism".[210] But there is a strong objection from experience and Russell's answer seems to imperil acquaintance. The objection is that experience does not appear to divide up into discrete units:

"It is often urged that, as a matter of immediate experience, the sensible flux is devoid of divisions, and is falsified by the dissections of the intellect. Now I have no wish to argue

---

[208] Bertrand Russell, "The Nature of Sense-data: A Reply to Dawes Hicks," *Mind* 22, no. 85, (1913): 76, https://doi.org/10.1093/mind/XXII.1.76
[209] Mark Johnston, "Better Than Mere Knowledge?: The Function of Sensory Awareness," in *Perceptual Experience*, ed. Tamar Szabo Gendler and John Hawthorne (Oxford: Oxford University Press, 2006), 281.
[210] Hylton, *Russell, Idealism and the Emergence of Analytic Philosophy*, 105-116.

that this view is contrary to immediate experience: I wish only to maintain that it is essentially incapable of being proved by immediate experience."[211]

Russell responds to this by pointing out cases of phenomenal continua where sense data fail to discriminate changes in identities, such as in the gradual accumulation of weight and the change in colour over time.[212] So a colour may be identified as A at time t_1. At t_2 the colour is changed to B, which is only slightly different from A, and the difference is not noticed. Then, at t_3 the colour is changed to C, which is only slightly different from B, and the difference between B and C is not noticed *even though C is judged to be different from A*.

The lesson is that we should reject the assumption that in order for a difference in colour to be the case, there has to be an appearance of difference of colour. Cases of phenomenal continua undermine such a supposition, which arises from an unwarranted conflation of knowledge by acquaintance of an object and the knowledge of truth *about* that object. Russell writes:

"It is unconsciously assumed, as a premise for reductio ad absurdum of the analytic view, that, if A and B are immediate data, and A differs from B, then the fact that they differ must also be an immediate datum. It is difficult to say how this assumption arose, but I think it is to be connected with the confusion between 'acquaintance' and 'knowledge about.' Acquaintance, which is what we derive from sense, does not, theoretically at least, imply even the smallest 'knowledge about,' i.e. it does not imply knowledge of any proposition concerning the object with which we are acquainted."[213]

The "data" here are sense data that Russell elsewhere defines as "fleeting, vague, without sharp boundaries, without any clear plan or arrangement".[214] He goes on to say that we

---

[211] Bertrand Russell, *Our Knowledge of the External World* (New York: The New American Library, 1960), 114.
[212] Ibid, 113.
[213] Ibid, 115. He also makes statements like this: "To know that two shades of colour are different is knowledge about them; hence acquaintance with the two shades does not in any way necessitate the knowledge that they are different." Ibid, 151.
[214] Russell, *Problems of Philosophy*, 100.

might have acquaintance with a particular white patch but it is only after observing several more instances that we learn to abstract the universal underlying this particular sense-datum.[215] So there are two key ingredients involved in acquaintance: the sense data and the universal. The qualitative aspect of a particular sense datum gives us epistemic access to the universal that grounds each instance.

The quote above may give the job of differentiating objects to "knowledge about" which may come as a surprise given Russell's definitions present the impression that the identity conditions are laid out by acquaintance. But I would argue that it is the vital distinction between the sense data and the universal, the epistemic and grounding conditions that are crucial here. The epistemic factors are caught up with fleeting sense data – as shown by the phenomenal continua cases – and thus not always reliable guides to the underlying universals and this is the case even with acquaintance. With the example of the phenomenal continua it is the "knowledge about"[216] that is best able to get us access to the underlying individuating conditions.

Now Proops calls attention to a possible conflict between the Independence Thesis and what he calls the "Perfect Knowledge Thesis"[217] of acquaintance which is drawn from passages from Russell such as: "I know the colour perfectly and completely when I see it, and no further knowledge of it itself is even theoretically possible."[218] And the sense data in the presence of a table exhibit "things immediately known to me just as they are."[219] Proops defines the principle thus:

"We (nonomniscient beings) can – and sometimes do – have perfect and complete knowledge of particulars and other proper parts of the universe."[220]

---

[215] Ibid, 101.
[216] Which is founded on acquaintance anyway; Ibid, 75
[217] Proops, "Russellian Acquaintance Revisited," 797.
[218] Russell, *Problems of Philosophy*, 42.
[219] Ibid.
[220] Proops, "Russellian Acquaintance Revisited," 797.

The first tension Proops points out is between the knowledge given by acquaintance of sense data "just as they are" and the Independence Thesis. The former would seem to require knowing all the propositional truths about the sense datum but such a requirement would seem to threaten the latter. Proops' suggestion is that Russell's statement is a polemical point against the Monistic Idealists and their adherence to internal relations between knower and known. The knowledge of sense data "just as they are" would exclude any internal relation with the knower.

Proops considers ways to interpret Russell's exact definition of perfect and complete knowledge such as it involving acquaintance with every intrinsic fact about the object known by acquaintance. Another would be an acquaintance with every part of the sense datum. Proops' own suggestion is again that Russell is defining perfect and complete allusively as a polemic against his idealist opponents like Bradley.

But mere polemics would seem to sell short one of the most prodigious metaphysical system builders of the 20th century. I would suggest the answer is far simpler than this and involves the distinction between the epistemic conditions and the simple metaphysical grounds of those conditions. Perfect and complete knowledge is not a matter of acquaintance with intrinsic facts of the object since the ground that *is* the object is independent and hence not "of" anything. Nor is it an acquaintance with every part of the sense-datum since that is a violation of simplicity and begs the question as to how those parts relate to the whole.

What about Russell's description that the knowledge of acquaintance is a knowledge of objects "just as they are"? I would suggest that far from a suggestion of knowledge of all truths about the intrinsic nature of the object I would suggest that such a possibility is metaphysically impossible for Russell even if we qualify the so-called truths as truths of the object's intrinsic nature. Acquaintance does not involve "ofness" at all since the ground of knowledge accessed through the epistemic conditions given by the qualities is independent of any other entity, fact or not. What we have communicated here by terms like "just as they are" and "in itself" instead is a communion with simple and independent being given access by the qualities of the sense data. Thus there is a very close connection between knowledge by acquaintance being independent and perfect which could both be described together as self-sufficient:

"In the same way, in order to understand a name for a particular, the only thing necessary is to be acquainted with that particular. When you are acquainted with that particular, you have a full, adequate, and complete understanding of the name, and no further information is required. No further information as to the facts that are true of that particular would enable you to have a fuller understand of the meaning of the name."[221]

But what about "knowledge by description"? This knowledge comes indirectly since it is knowledge that demands more than just a dyadic relation between knower and known and thus this knowledge is propositional and subject to truth or error. Knowledge by description allows us to go beyond the things known by acquaintance, but it is dependent on such knowledge. We saw with the penny example that different perspectives give different shapes of the same penny to observers. We can give a description of the penny and be certain that we are being appeared to in an elliptical fashion and then from another angle given another description and be certain we are being appeared to in a circular fashion – but the shape of the penny itself hasn't changed.

Russell's demand was for a certainty in knowledge such that for a thought to be registered as a thought, it has to have a reference and one has to be certain about the reference. This naming relation towards the objects of acquaintance makes a demand for certainty precisely because it is the law of identity – actually the manifesting of simple and independent being in the naming process – that is underwriting such knowledge in the first place. Thus in order to think directly about x one has to be acquainted with x, and in order to do so one has to be able to name x.

---

[221] Bertrand Russell, "The Philosophy of Logical Atomism," in *Logic and Knowledge* (London: Unwin Hyman, 1956), 202.

It follows from this that if Russell restricts logic and the law of identity to the confines of such relations and their logically atomic natures, then the threat of scepticism will emerge for any item outside such a relation. It is no coincidence that Humean scepticism vis-à-vis induction emerged under similar conditions, as he drew a dichotomy between "relations of ideas" and "matters of fact". The former were examples such as "*a* is *a*" and the latter were all contingent, non-analytic in nature. But for Russell such contingencies do not just threaten induction, but the very possibility of having a referring thought in the first place. It is a result of making simple, Parmenidian being the metaphysical grounds of his epistemological system.

In *The Problems of Philosophy* (*PP*), Russell uses knowledge by description in *inferring* the existence of a mind-independent object, such as a table, from its various appearances. So the table becomes "the physical object which causes such-and-such sense data."[222] But soon after the publication of *PP* Russell abandons the approach of inferring physical objects from sense data. In the *PP*, Russell admits that "we can never prove the existence of things other than ourselves and our experiences".[223] The reason for this is the epistemological gulf between the world of appearances – of colours, tastes, sounds, smells, and feelings – and the world of things-in-themselves (namely that described by physics and which contains none of the objects of appearances). And for Russell at this stage in his career it was the simplicity behind the objects of appearance that conferred epistemological certainty.

iv) **Logical Constructions**

So how does Russell justify knowledge outside the sphere of acquaintance? By a priori means it may be that we can draw inferences to objects as *causes* of our sense impressions. But the lessons of the previous section rule this out for Russell since there is no reliable or even intelligible connection between sensations and cause. This seems to be the common intuitive response, since we would ordinarily say that it is *because* the world is such and

---

[222] Russell, *Problems of Philosophy*, 47.
[223] Ibid, 22.

such that we have such and such an experience. But the inconsistency between the world of appearances and the world described by physics seems to rule out such inferences for Russell.

Given the logically atomic nature of sense data, it follows that appearance reveals nothing but the data of immediate sense. Sense data are "the hardest of hard data"[224] of experience and "all that we directly and primitively know of the external world".[225] Hence we are dealing with objects that are epistemologically atomic and therefore of a substantial, that is, non-dependent nature. Aristotelian substances[226] are self-contained entities that cannot by their very nature be dependent on objects beyond themselves. For these reasons sense data cannot have any sort of status that is intentional or in any way a "being-for-others".

The solution Russell proposed, however, is not an intuitive one. Instead of explaining sense data and their structure in terms of the objects they represent, he attempts to define the objects of experience as a function of sense data. This is a decidedly logical turn for Russell, replacing the use of induction to justify knowledge of the external world. Such a method he calls "logical construction" since the objects of acquaintance are formally logical atoms and his new approach is to construct objects out of such logical atoms and thus enfold objects of experience within the certainty of fundamental being. As he famously asserted:

"The supreme maxim in scientific philosophising is this: Wherever possible, logical constructions are to be substituted for inferred entities."[227]

Avoiding inferred entities beyond the immediate objects of acquaintance was Russell's goal. He wanted to avoid positing an unknown world of "things in themselves". As noted earlier, acquaintance was underwritten by the immediacy of logical knowledge and the method of logical construction was to move from beyond this using the paradigm already

---

[224] Russell, *Our Knowledge of the External World*, 78.
[225] Ibid, 141.
[226] Humean and Lockean sense impressions also resemble Aristotelian substances.
[227] Russell, "The Relation of Sense-data to Physics," in *Mysticism and Logic*, 155.

developed in partnership with Alfred North Whitehead in *Principia Mathematica*.[228] According to the work of Russell and Whitehead, a number is nothing more than a class of classes whose members bear a one-to-one correlation with each other. In this way numbers can be logically constructed from classes whose members are related under equivalencies.

Hence the solution Russell sought was to enfold the entities beyond acquaintance and the certainty of identity back into the epistemological sphere of logical certainty – into simple and atomic packets of Parmenidian being. In addition, this was also the solution that was in accordance with Ockham's Razor, namely that entities should not be multiplied beyond necessity. Thus it is better if entities supposed to be inferred from other entities can be defined as disguised versions of those latter entities and thus avoid an unnecessary multiplication of entities.

Russell does not, however, eliminate all inferred entities. He introduces what he calls "sensibilia" which are so-called because they are "objects which have the same metaphysical and physical status as sense data, without necessarily being data to any mind".[229] There is nothing in his system, according to him, that prevents such an inference since it is only inferences to entities that are completely incommensurable with sense data – such as the Kantian things-in-themselves – that are unwarranted.[230]

Now the benefit of sensibilia is that they can be purely *potential* sense data. They can be either sensed sensibilia, which are objects of acquaintance, or unsensed sensibilia. They both have the same ontological status even if only in the former role are they of epistemological use. Sensibilia puts the objects of experience on firmer ground, accommodating the fact that sense data are fleeting. Since there is an objective basis on which we can say that every object is potentially an object of acquaintance, there is no threat of objects going out of existence, or never existing at all, if they are unsensed by

---

[228] Bertrand Russell and Alfred North Whitehead, *The Principia*, 2nd ed. 3 vols. (Cambridge: Cambridge University Press, 1910-1913)
[229] Russell, "The Relation of Sense-data to Physics," in *Mysticism and Logic*, 142.
[230] Ibid, 150.

some perceiver. Sensibilia are not dependent ontologically on perceivers, they are not limited in the same way as traditional sense data.

Now how does Russell go about the constructive process? He starts within the perspective of the Cartesian observer. Imagine different people sitting around a room looking at the same table. No matter how close to each other the observers are "[n]o two of these people have exactly the same sense data".[231] Every person is at a slightly different angle or distance from the object and is operating under different psychological conditions, so every observer sees the object slightly differently. Now the definition of a perspective is the sum total of all the data presented to not only the one perceiver but to all possible perspectives even where there is no perceiver.[232]

Each perspective differs ever so slightly which threatens the continuity of the series. So Russell introduces a technical term called "similarity" which can bridge two juxtaposed lots of data since the difference between the lots may be indistinguishable and yet fail transitivity: A may be similar to B and B similar to C but A not similar to C. This is the formal principle which joins the different perspectives involved in moving at different angles and distances from the same object into a continuous series. This is essentially how Russell justifies a move from knowing sensibilia to knowing the objects in the world.

Now Russell is quite clear in denying that there is any kind of Lockean substratum or bare particular underlying the series, which is as should be expected given that he is defining the object in terms of sense data.[233] But he is not denying the identity conditions that individuate the sense data themselves. It is not an equivalence relation between perspectives as witnessed by the failure of transitivity. But surely it is the data themselves underwritten by the law of identity with equivalence functioning as the limiting case. An example of this may be a series of concentric spheres overlapping each other to such a great extent that one

---

[231] Ibid 147.
[232] Russell, *Our Knowledge of the External World,* 95.
[233] Ibid, 110.

must observe several spheres to notice that it is only a partial overlap emerging. And of course overlap is a relationship that every object can have with itself.

Thus the differences that emerge in a series are departures from equivalences and as such they are lacking in real being, at least as Russell defines it. This means that the real differences between the objects that go together to make up a series of different perspectives of an object like a table are departures from real being and not manifestations of any real substantial unity. Now some have sought to defend Russell's description of objects as "logical fictions", as in passages like the following that suggest the objects are not real in any substantial sense:

"We can now define the momentary common sense 'thing,' as opposed to its momentary appearances. By the similarity of neighbouring perspectives, many objects in the one can be correlated with objects in the other, namely with the similar objects. Given an object in one perspective, from the system of all the objects correlated with it in all the perspectives; that system may by identified with the momentary common sense 'thing'. Thus an aspect of a 'thing' is a member of the system of aspects which is the 'thing' at that moment . . . . All the aspects of a thing are real, whereas the thing is a merely logical construction."[234]

Sajahan Miah, citing Michael Bradie in agreeance, argues that the use of "merely", which is contrasted with the "real" here, does not imply that Russell thinks of these constructions as unreal or fictitious, but only that real is defined "in a special technical sense which is only applicable to sense data."[235] But this is not a mere technical matter for Russell at all, but the definition of being at play here goes to the very heart of Russell's philosophy. The sense of real that applies to sense data is the real of logical atomic entities. These are the locus of real being and anything outside of that – that is, outside the enclosed unity of being itself – is a considerable downgrading in the being stakes. However, Miah goes on to reproduce the following quote from Russell in support of his interpretation:

---

[234] Ibid, 96.
[235] Citing Michael Bradie "Russell's Scientific Realism," typescript, 1–32. Paper presented at the Russell Conference '84 in Toronto, in Sajahan Miah, *Russell's Theory of Perception 1905-1919* (London and New York: Continuum, 2006), 133.

"The world we have constructed can, with a certain amount of trouble, be used to interpret the crude facts of sense, the facts of physics, and the facts of physiology. It is therefore a world which may be actual. It fits the facts, and there is no empirical evidence against it; it also is free from logical impossibilities. But have we any good reason to suppose that it is real?"[236]

As Maher points out, Russell goes on to show that there is no good reason to deny the constructed objects. But it is interesting that in this passage Russell clearly acknowledges considerable doubt over the ontological status of the constructed objects, which prompted the question in the first place. So in what sense *are* they real? I suggest the only way we can make sense of their reality is as accidents of a concatenation of logical objects, in the same way that seated Socrates is still *something* even though its ontological status is ultimately derived from the fundamental, primitive status of Socrates.

In defining physics in the terms of sense data, Russell is generally credited with initiating the verificationist movement. And Quine as we will see in the next section takes Rudolph Carnap to be following and improving on Russell's work. But as I have tried to show here, it is the Frege–Russell logical machinery and the law of identity that is really doing all the work behind the empirical scenes. As we will see in the next section, Carnap tries to marry Frege's emphasis on structure to Russell's atomic empiricism. But ultimately the question will be whether or not such structure is able to explain the experiences we have and ground our objective shared knowledge with other perceivers. Quine will show this to be unsuccessful.

Russell's dilemma is also a result of accepting Parmenidian being as the real source of grounds behind his Cartesian view of the mind and its lack of intrinsic connection with the outside world. To Russell, only the sensible "is ever, *found*". But this is just a symptom of his atomistic worldview which, as we saw, lacked the resources to account for the unity of

---

[236] Ibid.

the proposition. Being atomic and independent, sense data have no necessary connection with anything beyond themselves, which meant that Russell, in constructing the outside world, was forced to forge connections with *other sense data*. And having to construct objects out of sense data meant that their status as aggregated unities put them in only a tenuous connection with Russell's conception of ultimate atomic being. But again what comes into focus here is the Parmenidian conception of being at the heart of Russell's use of substantial entities in his account of realism. Ironically, this conception of being posed a threat to his realism, but the next section will show a step in the direction of a correspondence theory which, I will argue, is far more in line with common sense realism.

v) **Russell's Image Proposition**

The unity of the proposition was an ongoing dilemma for Russell in his 1919 work "On Propositions: What They Are and How They Mean",[237] he sought a solution in a new conception of the proposition. The proximate cause of this new conception was his acknowledged failure of the Multiple Relation Theory of Judgement.[238] The failure was due to its linguistic forms requiring separate representations of relations, which created further problems as to how those relations could be unified with the rest of the proposition and in the correct order so as to rule out non-sense judgements.

By introducing propositions as images of their truth-makers, however, it provided the advantage that no further answers need to be given as to how the constituent parts should be related together. Russell explains this with an example:

"In this case, I have a complex image, which we may analyse, for our purposes, into (a) the image of the window, (b) the image of the fire, (c) the relation that (a) is to the left of (b).

---

[237] Bertrand Russell, "On Propositions: What They Are and How They Mean," in *Logic and Knowledge*, ed. Robert Charles Marsh, 283-320. (London: Unwin Hyman, 1956)

[238] The year before he concludes, clinging tenuously to the Multiple Relation Theory of Judgement under the weight of Wittgenstein's objections, that belief must be "a new sort of thing, a new beast for our zoo, not another member of our former species but a new species"; Russell, "The Philosophy of Logical Atomism," in *Logic and Knowledge*, 226.

The objective consists of the window and the fire with the very same relation between them. In such a case, the objective of a proposition consists of the meanings of its constituent images related (or not related, as the case may be) by the same relation as that which holds between the constituent images in the proposition."[239]

Russell seems to be just avoiding the question of unity by appealing to an identity between the unity of the truth-bearer and the unity of the truth-maker. But there is a deeper point he is making here: that the image ties together the two objects in the one relation rather than representing the relation as an object itself. The linguistic form *must* mention the relation as if it is a separate entity juxtaposed with the relata, but the image only represents the objects together organised under the formal conditions set out by the relation acting in a behind-the-scenes manner.

But does this really solve the problem? Graham Stevens, rightly to my mind, points out that this really just pushes the unity problem back a step, so that now we have a unity of the truth-maker problem.[240] As I will detail in chapter five, my own three-category ontology will draw on such an image-model of the proposition to explain the unity of the proposition. But the difference is that the three-category ontology provides the *explanatory basis* for how to get unity at the level of the object that will in turn explain the unity at the level of the proposition.

Conclusion

Throughout this chapter we have focused heavily on Frege's and Russell's fundamental conceptions of being, the bare bones of which reflect Parmenidian primitive being: the rationalist-derived concepts of oneness, simplicity and unity. This was reflected in Frege's concept of the True, and also in Russell's logically atomic sense data and the "terms" of his

---

[239] Russell, "On Propositions," in Marsh, *Logic and Knowledge*, 315-316.
[240] Graham Stevens, "Russell and the Unity of the Proposition," *Philosophy Compass* 3, issue 3. (2008): 491-506, https://doi.org/10.1111/j.1747-9991.2008.00142.x

propositions. Analysis ultimately serves to reduce individual propositions to fundamental substantial being.

Given the simplicity of Frege's True, propositions could only be true in a derived sense. That is because truth cannot be broken up into many and varied pieces. The flaw that Wittgenstein found in Frege's view was with propositions that were not intrinsically tied to truth. For Russell, the problems arose because the individual units of being were all he had in his repertoire, leaving nothing to act on those units as a unifying agent. Russell's construction of objects from sense data was overly reductionist. Taking complex and varied structures of our experience and transforming them into "logical fictions" calls into question the explanatory power of his logical method of construction since such unities cannot substitute for the more complex unities of our experience.

In the next chapter we will consider Carnap's *The Logical Structure of the World and Pseudoproblems in Philosophy* and the reconstruction of knowledge. The elaborate methods used, and the tying of Frege's logic to sense data, will be identified as a failure by Quine. Quine's famous indeterminacy of translation thesis will also target intensions as largely indeterminate vis-à-vis the univocal conception of being. Quine's banishment of intensions, however, will be taken by myself to be a *reductio ad absurdum* for the whole Frege–Russell project, as it does not contain the informational content to objectively discriminate the intensions of our experience.

The last chapters of this thesis will present alternatives to the Frege–Russell methods of analysis, based on categories that are extracted from experience rather than being metaphysical principles of being force-fitting the world of experience into its unitary structure. Analysis under these new categories will present an alternative to substantial sense data with a metaphysical function that connects them to the objects of their reference. Along with a "being in-itself" they will have a "being for-others". Tying the categories so close to each particular sense experience will preclude any univocal notion of the categories. The objects themselves, in turn, will not be simple and ultimate wholes but rather break into parts – but the parts and wholes will be mutually dependent. Such a metaphysical scheme will respect empiricist demands and comport with common sense.

Chapter Three - On Carnap and Quine and the Reconstruction of Knowledge

Introduction

Quine was perhaps the most important philosopher of the mid-twentieth century and has had an enormous impact on analytic philosophy in recent decades. Carnap has also had a significant impact, both directly and through his influence on Quine. It is Carnap's *The Logical Structure of the World and Pseudoproblems in Philosophy* (*LSW*) and Quine's naturalism that will concern us in this chapter. More specifically, it will be the efforts of both at reconstructing empirical knowledge. These philosophers continued in the tradition of Frege and Russell – employing their logical methods and attempting a total reconstruction of knowledge – and so this chapter continues the trajectory of the previous chapters.

The first section presents the epistemic situation vis-à-vis our knowledge of the outside world that derives ultimately from Descartes and passed on by modernist philosophers to Carnap and Quine. The threat of scepticism is two-fold: the knowing self is a substance which is not intrinsically connected to the internally present objects of cognition that are representations of the world *and* those representations are not structured in any way that is internally connected to the outside world.

The possibility of scepticism looms large in the attempts at reconstructing knowledge made by both Carnap and Quine. New approaches to the *LSW* have taken the work, in its effort to justify empirical and scientific knowledge, to be Kantian in nature. I argue, contrary to this, that Carnap's attempt involves trying to marry Frege's logical system as a grounding basis for particular knowledge instances with Russell's empiricism. Carnap goes further than Russell, however, by denying anything beyond the auto-psychological. I argue it is precisely Frege's logic and the marrying of that logic – through the grounding relationship – to Russell's objects of acquaintance that is the driving force behind the construction of knowledge in the *LSW*. Thus the real inspiration for the constructive work is Fregean and

Russellian and not Kantian. The elaborate attempt Carnap makes to marry Fregean rationalism to Russellian empiricism provides an instructive test for the entire Frege–Russell system of logic and knowledge reconstruction. Thus this chapter represents a culmination of the last two chapters.

Quine, however, argues forcefully that Carnap's project is a failure. The reason the construction of our empirical knowledge is unsuccessful, according to Quine, is because the formal conditions of Frege–Russell logic fail to eliminate the "is at" connective that places the sense data in the first place. I argue that the reason for this is due to the fact that the Frege–Russell formal logical machinery cannot do the constructive work required of it. Thus the reconstruction and justification of our inter-subjective knowledge states are not due to the inadequacies of empiricism, as Quine thinks, but to a lack in formal logic to have the informational content to make any such construction and thus to justify any individual state of knowing.

I go on to review the work of Quine and attempt to present the metaphysical assumptions at the heart of his entire naturalistic system of knowledge reconstruction. On one level this is obvious from his Cartesian starting point since mental phenomena are internal entities lacking any inherent dependence on anything outside itself.[241] But more fundamentally it is revealed in individual acts of knowing where true individual declarative sentences are really just accidental states of knowledge and epiphenomenal to naturalistic behavioural states. Like Frege, metaphysical grounding takes primacy over epistemic states of knowing. This is expressed through the marrying of philosophy and science where truth is immanent in the act of clarification through regimentation of theories and the striving towards simplicity that puts one in a state of resonance with the fundamental realm of being. It is in acting in accordance with the being behind the natural realm that our mental representations and a priori knowledge are by-passed – actually rendered epiphenomenal to use more modern parlance – and dispensed with in Quine's ontology.

---

[241] Note that I have referred to mental phenomena and not any substantial Cartesian self and thus not, absurdly, attributing a full-blown Cartesian dualism to Quine.

Thus Quine borrows his metaphysics from Parmenides (under the gloss of naturalism) just like Frege and Russell. It is a system of being where, in its univocality, cannot make distinctions between individual entities, be they individual facts or mental representations. It is precisely in being at a level of analysis more fundamental to individual representations where naturalism is found to be more to be pre-eminent in the order of being. Quine's behaviourism, through which such being is made manifest, is the true basis for our construction of knowledge. It is also the reason why one manual of translation cannot be preferred over another that is behaviourally consistent. Thus given that such behavioural manifestations cannot make distinctions between intensions, ultimately there is no basis for placing intensionally distinct terms on either side of the identity sign, which in turn means there is no basis for the analytic–synthetic distinction nor the reality of intensional entities at all.

Lastly, I find Quine's system to be inadequate and point the way to an improved system. First, his system is fundamentally incoherent since it is supposed to be science-based and purports to dispense with a priori metaphysics and yet he assumes a conception of being that is just a naturalistic repackaging of Parmenidian being. Second, the Cartesian dichotomy between mental states and being – which is also a reflection of Parmenides' elevation of being over the empirical world – requires a basic denial of the real being of our internally accessed mental states.

This is a heavy price to pay and may mean that Quine has been too quick to grasp simplicity – the taste for desert landscapes – at the cost of explanatory power. It also leads to a situation where our cognitive representational states are placed against a background that is in radical opposition to what they reveal. Thus Hillary Putnam, not without good reason, draws a parallel between Quine's naturalism and Kantian transcendentalism. I argue that this is really a symptom of the dichotomy between the world accessed by perception and the world of Parmenidian being pulling the strings of Quine's naturalism.

The point of this chapter is ultimately to point the way to a better metaphysical system, one that is abstracted from our empirical and scientific accounts and not imposed on them, and does not eliminate mental representations but takes them as data to be preserved and explained. This will require dispensing with univocal being, but taking structures as they are revealed in perception and proposing a psychological model of mental intentionality that is not a self-subsistent substance. The advantage of such an approach will be in presenting a credible alternative integrated with mental representation and not one based purely on naturalistic behavioural actions.

Historical Background: The Cartesian Assumption

The move Quine made towards naturalism came on the back of a tradition that was heavily influenced by Cartesian dualism. As is well known Descartes' focus was on epistemology, most notably his fixation on finding a firm foundation for knowledge. But the mere positioning of the knowing subject and its epistemic relation to the outside world requires substantial metaphysical assumptions. In this section on Quine I spell out those assumptions and how they influenced his thought.

Descartes' chief concern is knowledge that is certain or incorrigible.[242] Certainty and incorrigibility were for him tests as to whether a belief can in any way be doubted. The mind is intimately connected to the "ideas" that it gains from perception – such "ideas" are modes or attributes of the mind – and knowledge of them is direct and veridical.[243] But such incorrigible knowledge is only of the ideas themselves and *not* what they are representative of. Thus it is possible to imagine both a goat or a chimera but *only* in the sense that both can be immediately grasped – though the latter is devoid of any fact in the world – before the mind.[244]

---

[242] See the *First* and *Second Meditations* in René Descartes, *Meditations on First Philosophy*, trans. Michael Moriaty (Oxford: Oxford World's Classics, 2008)
[243] Ibid, 25.
[244] Ibid, 27.

Although ideas, for Descartes, can be known with certainty, there is nothing about them that fixes any particular state of reference beyond themselves. The believing in objects outside our veil of ideas derives purely from a "blind inclination".[245] After establishing the existence of God in the *Third Meditation*, Descartes goes on to argue that because our ideas of material things are often imposed on us against our will, and because material things do not presuppose thought, then beliefs in the existence of external objects cannot come from us.[246] But because God is not a deceiver, he has granted Descartes an inclination to believe that the idea of an external object is produced by that external object.

For Descartes, the meaning of our ideas is derived in a purely non-logical manner by some sort of judging psychological faculty. Ideas are akin to mere scratches or noises that are meaningless except as they derive their meaning externally. That meaning is supplied by God and his non-deceiving nature. In the passive perception of ideas themselves, we are in no danger of error. Only when we judge that something exists in the mind-independent world purely on the basis of our sensations and not on the guiding premise of God's good nature do we fall into error.

Some modern commentators believe they have found a split in the cognitive processes described by such early modern philosophers as Descartes and John Locke, one that entails the existence of a further inner substantial self, called a "homunculus",[247] that look up at what Daniel Dennett metaphorically calls a "Cartesian Theatre".[248] This is how it is for Descartes that we exist in a state of incorrigibility towards our own ideas. The homunculus is an existing entity distinct, in a sense, from the intrinsically unintelligible ideas that it has to interpret as representations. Dennett finds this account to be futile. Its either circular, since understanding external objects requires understanding at the homunculus level, or it

---

[245] Ibid, 29.
[246] Ibid, 27.
[247] See Anthony Kenny, "The Homunculus Fallacy," in *The Legacy of Wittgenstein* (Oxford: Basil Blackwell, 1984) 125-136. Kenny applies the homunculus fallacy to Descartes and traces the same assumptions in modern neuroscience.
[248] Daniel Dennett, *Consciousness Explained* (New York: Black Bay Books, 1991)

results in a regress, since the little homunculus' understanding will require a further littler homunculus to account for its own knowledge of ideas.[249]

Fred Wilson, drawing on the work of David and Alan Hausman on Berkeley's idealism, divides the inner representations of perception into two forms of information: semantic and syntactic.[250] The former is the referencing of ideas beyond themselves and the latter is the way in which those simpler ideas are arranged. This creates two dilemmas for the early modern philosophers like Descartes and Locke: the objects in the outside world are completely unlike ideas and the ideas themselves have no intrinsic meaning. How does the homunculus grasp a meaning that isn't accessible to it? How does it interpret outside objects in light of internal mental ideas?

The state of knowing can thus be divided into four elements: the inner homunculus, the ideas, the interpretation of the ideas, and the referent. Scepticism arises due to the lack of any intrinsic meaning in the inner arrangement of ideas. A further scepticism looms large due to the substantial self-subsistent status of the inner homunculus. Its status as an inner knowing self bears no intrinsic connection to the inner ideas occupying consciousness. In such a state there is no intelligible sense as to *how it is* that one can have knowledge of one's own ideas.

Such scepticism was brought to the fore in the early 20th century most notably by Russell and Wittgenstein in giving an account of how we can be sure of using a word to refer to an idea in the same way in the present as we did in the past. For example, how do we know that our use of the phrase "that is green" refers to the same idea now as it did when we used that phrase in the past? Any recollection of such a definition can only be by our *present* experience of memory. Russell writes:

---

[249] Daniel Dennett, "Artificial Intelligence as Philosophy and as Psychology," in *Brainstorms: Philosophical Essays on Mind and Psychology*, (Cambridge, MA: MIT Press, 1978), 122.
[250] Fred Wilson, "On the Hauseman's 'A New Approach'," in *Berkeley's Metaphysics: Structural, Acquaintance, Ontology, and Knowledge: Collected Essays in Ontology*, ed. Robert Muehlmann (University Park, PA: Pennsylvania State University Press, 1995), 73.

"Why do we believe that images are, sometimes or always, approximately or exactly, copies of sensations? What sort of evidence is there? And what sort of evidence is logically possible? The difficulty of this question arises through the fact that the sensation which an image is supposed to copy is in the past when the image exists, and can therefore be known only by means of memory, while, on the other hand, memory of past sensations seems only possible by means of present images. How, then, are we to find any way of comparing the present image and the past sensation? The problem is just as acute if we say that images *differ* from their prototypes as if we say that they *resemble* them; it is the very possibility of comparison that is hard to understand. We think we can know that they are alike or different, but we cannot bring them together in one experience and compare them… In this way the whole status of images as 'copies' is bound up with the analysis of memory."[251]

Wittgenstein makes a similar case for the unreliability of direct knowledge made clear by memory as an example:[252] Fregean recognition is an understanding grasped by the individual but there is no criterion by which we can verify something like "this is brown".[253] Using a word according to some rule or means of interpretation doesn't guarantee correct use. There is therefore no way of checking that our recognition of the meaning of a term is veridical or just a faulty memory.[254] Later in the *Philosophical Investigations* he explains the difficulty that knowing a private object poses:

"Let us imagine the following case. I want to keep a diary about the recurrence of a certain sensation. To this end I associate it with the 's' and write this sign in a calendar for every day on which I have the sensation. I will remark first of all that a definition of the sign cannot be formulated. But still I can give myself a kind of ostensive definition. How? Can I point to the sensation? Not in the ordinary sense. But I speak, or write the sign down, and at the same time I concentrate my attention on the sensation – and so, as it were, point to it inwardly. But what is this ceremony for? For that is all it seems to be! A definition surely

---

[251] Bertrand Russell, *The Analysis of Mind* (PA: Pennsylvania State University, 2001), 110.
[252] Credit for many of the references in this section to John Cook's *The Metaphysics of Wittgenstein* (Cambridge: Cambridge University Press, 1994)
[253] Ludwig Wittgenstein, *Wittgenstein's Lectures: Cambridge, 1930 – 1932* (from the notes of John King and Desmond Lee,) ed. Desmond Lee (Oxford: Basil Blackwell, 1980) 61, quoted in Cook, *The Metaphysics of Wittgenstein,* 291.
[254] Ludwig Wittgenstein, *Philosophical Grammar*, trans. Anthony Kenny, ed. Rush Rhees, (Berkeley, CA: University of California Press, 1974), 168.

serves to establish the meaning of a sign. Well, that is done precisely by the concentrating of my attention; for in this way I impress on myself the connexion between the sign and the sensation. But 'I impress it on myself' can only mean: this process brings it about that I remember the connexion *right* in the future. But in the present case I have no criterion of correctness. One would like to say: whatever is going to seem right to me is right. And that only means that here we can't talk about 'right'."[255]

Here we have an implication for knowledge from the model of consciousness assumed by both Russell and Wittgenstein where the knowledge of our inner ideas are presented before the inner homunculus. The images presented before the unencumbered homunculus are not interpreted and thus lacking intrinsic intelligibility and hence there is no direct and unmediated knowledge of the outside world. There is no epistemically reliable pathway from homunculus to outside world owing to the lack of any intrinsic relation. Carnap and Quine inherit such a situation from Descartes and each details a route to knowledge of the external world that does not proceed through the means of sense data. Carnap's work follows in the footsteps of Frege's rationalism whereas Quine's naturalistic alternative is behaviourism.

The Analytic-Synthetic Distinction: Leibniz and Kant

The first clear distinction drawn that foreshadows the analytic–synthetic distinction comes from Leibniz: the distinction between what he calls "truths of reason" and "truths of fact". He explains:

"Truths of reason are necessary, and their opposite is impossible: Truths of fact are contingent, and their opposite is possible."[256]

---

[255] Ludwig Wittgenstein, *Philosophical Investigations*, ed. G. E. M. Anscombe and Rush Rhees, trans G. E. M. Anscombe (Oxford: Blackwell, 1953), § 258.
[256] Gottfried Wilhelm Leibniz, *The Monadology*, trans. Robert Latta. Adelaide: ebooks@adelaide, 2014, accessed 1st June 2019: 33 https://ebooks.adelaide.edu.au/l/leibniz/gottfried/l525m/

Here he relies on the principle of contradiction as a test for truths of reason. But the formal argument is the basic identity statement "*a* is *a*" which if declared false entails a contradiction such as "*a* is non-*a*". Likewise truths of geometry are of such a nature that they are not derived apart from reason. But a truth of fact is contingent and hence can be negated without contradiction. Such truths are empirical, or derived a posteriori, such as "trees exist", or "that dog is brown".

Kant referred to Leibniz's truths of reason as "analytic" truths and adopted the principle of non-contradiction as a test for analyticity. He introduces a metaphor called "containment" as a test for an analytic judgement where the predicate is contained in the subject. A synthetic judgement on the other hand is defined in opposition to an analytic judgements; for example, "all bodies are extended", where the predicate is not already contained in the subject.[257]

In the next section we will see that Carnap attempts a construction of the empirical world on the basis of analytic logical forms and the law of identity. In the second half of the chapter we will go over Quine's famous rejection of such a distinction and how it is a natural consequence of the interplay of various metaphysical assumptions that grow out of his overall system.

Carnap on Logical Structure

---

[257] Kant, *The Critique of Pure Reason*, A 6-7.

i) Constructing a Cartesian World

Carnap represents an interesting segue from Kant, his scientific empirical emphasis had a profound impact on Quine. In fact Quine considered Carnap to have had the greatest influence on his philosophy.[258] Carnap situates the knower within a state very much resembling the homunculi, with knowledge depending – as with science and empiricism – on the experience, interpretation and construction of sense data. Along these lines he prioritises drawing up linguistic frameworks with semantic rules that the situated knower employs to interpret its expressions and posit truth conditions.

The early Carnap took it to be his chief goal to provide a logical method for justifying knowledge, by providing it with a firm basis. He followed a reductionist pathway, already blazed by empiricists like Russell, in reducing all statements referring to the exterior world to statements about sense data (the immediately given). In this he held firmly to the principle of verifiability, where all observation purporting to be empirical ultimately reduce to the indubitable basis of the immediately given observable concepts.

But as we will see, the Cartesian assumptions provide a very consequential hurdle for Carnap in the *LSW* precisely in formulating a *realist* structuralism that is sufficiently grounded in objectivity. This dilemma is evident in the various interpretations of the *LSW*. The original interpretation was that of Quine, who focused on the empirical side of the *LSW* and saw it chiefly as a work that justifies knowledge through empirical foundationalism. In this chapter, however, I follow Christopher Pincock in arguing that Carnap's chief thesis is structural realism. But I also argue that the Cartesian assumption means that he cannot provide an immediate justification of sense experience à la verificationism. But he must, instead, proceed via intersubjective logical structures. This is the Kantianism that Michael Friedman argues is central in the *LSW*. Along these lines, I argue that each interpretation,

---

[258] W. V. O. Quine, "On Carnap's Views on Ontology," in *The Ways of Paradox and other Essays* (New York: Random House, 1966), 126.

the Quinean and the Friedmanite, whilst making valuable contributions, both leave out something vital.

ii) **The Logical Structure of the World**

In *LSW* Carnap introduces his "constitution theory".[259] His goal is to build a hierarchical system of concepts, step by step, building from the lowest level to the higher level concepts. But even though it is constructive, it is still reductive in terms of analysis. Statements of science that involve predicates can be broken up into more primitive relations between the more basic concepts.

The key difference between Carnap's systematic reduction of language and Russell's is that his logical manipulations allow him to proceed from an auto-psychological basis. The elementary experiences that make up the auto-psychological are purely Cartesian products confined to the individual. Russell, on the other hand, attempted to reduce talk of physical objects to talk of sensibilia, which involved the sensibilia of individuals *and* unsensed sensibilia. For Carnap elementary experiences do not involve any questions of veridicality. Experiences are taken as given and hence there is no question of whether *they could be* veridical or hallucinatory. As he explains:

"At the beginning of the system, the experiences must simply be taken as they occur. We shall not claim reality or nonreality in connection with these experiences; rather, these claims will be 'bracketed'"[260]

As an aside, I find Carnap to be more consistent than Russell in eliminating sensibilia. Recall that for Russell unsensed sensibilia were objects outside the mind that had the potential to be sense data and provided the advantage of not making objects of perception

---

[259] Rudolph Carnap, *The Logical Structure of the World and Pseudoproblems in Philosophy*, trans. Rolf A. George (Chicago and La Salle, Illinois: Open Court, 1967)
[260] Ibid, § 64.

dependent on perceivers. Russell justified their existence since they were immediately proximate and commensurate with sense data. But sense data are self-subsistent entities that are immediately known by the mind's eye. On what basis could there be to make *any* inference beyond them, even to a close proximity? If they are truly self-subsistent as Russell believed, there is no way for them to possess any internal connection to objects immediately proximate or not. Thus sensibilia could literally be anything and there is no way to rule this out on the basis of sense data alone.

It might seem, just on the basis of these points, that Carnap's sole concern in the *LSW* is epistemic; that is, his aim was to justify the verificationist project of deriving all knowledge from experience. This was, in fact, Quine's interpretation in his famous essay "Two Dogmas of Empiricism".[261] Quine saw Carnap as continuing Russell's project of constructing the external world from sense data:

"To account for the external world as a logical construct of sense data – such, in Russell's terms, was the program. It was Carnap, in his *Der Logische Aufbau der Welt* of 1928, who came closest to executing it".[262]

And going even further, Quine took it as "radical reductionism" where "the rest of significant discourse" is translated into "a sense-datum language".[263]

Given the eminence in 20th century philosophy of Quine it is of little surprise that that interpretation prevailed for some years after the *LSW* was translated into English in 1967. This changed in 1987 when Michael Friedman, in his essay "Carnap's *Aufbau*

---

[261] Quine, "Two Dogmas of Empiricism," in *From a Logical Point of View: Logico-Philosophical Essays* (New York: Harper and Row, 1963), 20-46.
[262] W. V. O. Quine, "Epistemology Naturalized," in *Ontological Relativity and Other Essays* (New York: Colombia University Press, 1969), 74.
[263] Quine, "Two Dogmas," in *From a Logical Point of View,* 39.

Reconsidered",[264] offered a different interpretation, one that sought to conceive the epistemic project in the *LSW* along Kantian lines.

In one sense, a re-analysis was called for owing to Quine's lack of serious engagement with the entirety of the *LSW*. He focuses almost entirely on the experiential basis and neglects Carnap's attempt at objectivity. Another snag emerges from the heavy influence of Frege on Carnap, with his adoption of the view that meaning is located in whole sentences rather than individual terms. Hence for Carnap it is whole sentences that are to be translated into sense-datum sentences. This was a step away from the empiricist reductionism of Locke and David Hume.

Friedman takes a look at the objects of immediate experience, those at the lowest level of the reductionist picture. The puzzling thing about this level is that whilst it is the lowest level in the phenomenal framework, it is not entirely clear why Carnap devotes such attention to constructing this level in the first place. If the autopsychological objects are fundamental, why do they need to be constructed?[265]

The other problem posed by Friedman for Quine's interpretation involves the freedom the constructionist has to build from the autopsychological basis in the first place. There is nothing mandatory about building it in the way set out in the section of the *LSW* that Quine focuses on. Both of Friedman's challenges to the Quinean view suggests that there is an emphasis on objectivity in the *LSW* that is even more fundamental than the particular empirically based hierarchy. In fact, there is nothing in any construction system that imposes itself as necessary to the selection of a system. Any construction system is merely a means of revealing the underlying logical structure that is objective and the basis from which different systems can be constructed.

---

[264] Michael Friedman, "Carnap's *Aufbau* Reconsidered," in *Reconsidering Logical Positivism* (Cambridge: Cambridge University Press, 1999), 89-93.
[265] Ibid, 522-523.

Hence the distinction between the subjective and objective domains is integral to a proper understanding of the *LSW*.[266] Even the system focused on most heavily by Carnap, the autopsychological, is tainted with, as Friedman puts it, the "purely ostensive" but can be "characterized through its logical structure alone".[267] Thus to use language banished by Carnap, the individual constructional systems are accidental to the essential underlying logical nature integral to the unity of science. Friedman puts it like this:

"For any such system contributes equally well to the goal of revealing the logical structure of, and logical relations among, our concepts. What construction theory primarily seeks is a characterization of all concepts through their formal or structural properties, and, as we have seen, what this requires is the unity of science – the unity of the object domain."[268]

Thus the logical form of knowledge grants objectivity to experience. And the most basic form of logical knowledge is manifested in what Carnap calls "purely structural definite descriptions" that individuate objects in a way that is completely independent of their ostensive or intrinsic qualities.[269] Carnap argues for a pluralism throughout the *LSW*, that aside from phenomenalism, there are multiple alternative languages suitable for constructing the world. Each language offers its own description of the logical form but ultimately the logical form doesn't involve any language in its nature.

iii) **The Logical Structure of the World: A Rational Reconstruction**

Is logical form and the unity of science really so central to the *LSW*? Is his emphasis on formal descriptions of an intersubjective nature so important that the verificationist aspects are really just a superficial cloak masking what he really thinks are at the heart of constructivism? There are two ways of looking at the rational reconstruction in that work:

---

[266] In fact Alan Richardson raises this distinction as the chief interpretative difficulty of the work; Alan Richardson, *Carnap's Construction of the World: The Aufbau and the Emergence of Logical Empiricism* (Cambridge: Cambridge University Press, 1998), 2.
[267] Friedman, *Reconsidering*, 100.
[268] Ibid.
[269] Carnap, *The Logical Structure of the World*, § 12-16.

the first focused on the subjective nature of our knowledge and draws on neo-Kantianism with an emphasis on a specific logical form of experience and the second focuses on the objective basis of our knowledge which is grounded in the logic of Frege and Russell. As a result, it becomes evident that there are both objective and subjective tensions that have to be reconciled with the whole process of rational reconstruction.

There are passages in the *LSW* where Carnap seems to place the subjective and objective in direct juxtaposition. He states:

"If the basis of the constructional system is autopsychological then the danger of subjectivism seems to arise. Thus, we are confronted with the problem of how we can achieve objectivity of knowledge with such a system form."[270]

This danger is one of solipsism, where sense data being exclusively subjective provides no basis for extending knowledge into the mind independent world.

The solution to this dilemma for Carnap was structure – scientific structure, to be precise. This structure provides an objective backstop to subjective experience. He states:

"A system form with an autopsychological basis is acceptable only because it is recognized that *science is essentially concerned with structure and that, therefore, there is a way to construct the objective by starting from the individual stream of experience*. Much of the resistance to an autopsychological basis (or 'methodological solipsism') can probably be traced back to an ignorance of this fact."[271]

---

[270] Carnap, *The Logical Structure of the World*, 106.
[271] Ibid, 107. Emphasis in the original.

The structuralist method was already Russell's view. Pincock has pointed out that Carnap approved of Russell grounding objectivity in structure.[272] For Russell, the physical objects of experience were unknowable. Only the *relations* in which those entities entered into were known, due to the corresponding *relations* between the immediately known sense data. Carnap, accordingly, cites Russell with crediting structure as the basis for objective knowledge: "It was not until Russell that the importance of structure for the achievement of objectivity was pointed out".[273]

Profound similarities with Russell are hardly surprising given that both adhered to what Russell initially called "the supreme maxim in scientific philosophizing" which is "wherever possible, logical constructions are to be substituted for inferred entities." Pincock makes the case that the reconstruction that occurs in the *LSW* derives from Russell and not Kant. So for Russell, it is not primarily a reduction of objects to sense data but an independent construction much like Carnap's. My interest here does not lie in fleshing out all the details of Pincock's case for the rehabilitation of the "received view", but in his interpretation over their differences vis-à-vis the supreme maxim. Carnap states:

"In questions of detail, construction theory diverges very considerably from Russell, but it, too is based on his methodological principle: 'The supreme maxim in scientific philosophizing is this: Wherever possible, logical constructions are to be substituted for inferred entities'. We shall, however, employ this principle in an even more radical way than Russell (for example, through the choice of an autopsychological basis, in the construction of that which is not seen from that which is seen, and in the construction of the heteropsychological objects)".[274]

Pincock points to a commonality of method between Russell and Carnap in that both look for a reordering of our knowledge based on science. Pincock references Russell's *Our*

---

[272] Christopher Pincock, "Russell's Influence on Carnap's *Aufbau*," *Synthese* 131, no. 1, (2002): 1 – 37, https://doi.org/10.1023/A:1015066427566
[273] Rudolph Carnap, *Der Logische Aufbau der Welt*, (Felix Meiner, 1928) quoted in ibid, 14-15.
[274] Carnap, *The Logical Structure of the World*, 8.

Knowledge of the External World for information on what the reconstruction project meant. Russell writes:

"We start from a body of common knowledge, which constitutes our data. On examination, the data are found to be complex, rather vague, and largely interdependent logically. By analysis we reduce them to propositions which are as nearly as possible simple and precise, and we arrange them in deductive chains, in which a certain number of initial propositions form a logical guarantee for all the rest. These initial propositions are *premises* for the body of knowledge in question."[275]

This is a neat statement of Russellian analysis which prizes such scientific virtues as precision and simplicity in the form of logical deduction. Pincock also notes there is no requirement for the basic premises to be self-evident. In fact, Carnap's project is thoroughly Russellian–Fregean. We noted in the last chapter that the essential nature of objects of acquaintance was logical: it was the structure of the truth-functional machinery of first-order logic that was the driver behind the inferential relations of variables. Logical structure takes precedence over variables that merely happen to fill the role set out by that structure. This logical priority was no less the basis behind Russell's knowledge by acquaintance and his "logical fictions" were structured entities built up from its logical atoms. So it is a mistake to fixate on the subjective qualities of the autopsychological base at the expense of their grounds. It is upon such a structure of being that Carnap builds his constructional system and it is in this respect that he was influenced by Russell's structuralism.

As will be explored further in the next section, Carnap employs the logical machinery of both Russell and Frege, but the key difference is that he marries Frege's project to Russell's by starting from the basic logical axioms and working his way up to Russell's objects of acquaintance, providing a justification of the identities and structure of the latter based on the former. Thus the building up of sense data from logic is, far from contradicting

---

[275] Bertrand Russell, *Our Knowledge of the External World as a Field for Scientific Method in Philosophy* (Oxford, England: Open Court, 1915), 211, quoted in "Russell's Influence on Carnap's *Aufbau*", 20.

Russell's empiricism, a fulfilment of it, and in accordance with the real logical essences of the objects of acquaintance.

iv) Frege–Russell Influence

We saw in the first chapter that Frege drew a line between the chaotic world of sense experience and the intelligible Platonic world of logic. Frege rejected psychologism in order to preserve the latter from being tainted by the subjectivity of the former thereby compromising the very meaning of the laws of logic and their claim to objective truth. Importantly, when it comes to arithmetic, Frege wanted the laws of logic alone to be the sole justifier in conjunction with indubitable premises that abstract from all particularity. This is the important distinction between the grounds of truth and the epistemology of truth. The context in which such laws are discovered were of no relevance to how they are justified.

In a very similar way to Frege, Carnap in the *LSW* stresses the logical justification of belief in opposition to psychologism. Indeed the logic of the *LSW* is thoroughly Fregean: it operates over a maximally general domain and its use of variables is intrinsically unrestricted in range. That is to say, the operations of logic do not essentially involve any particular thing. What is more, the *LSW* reconstructions are not intended to involve psychological states in their reconstructions, which is strongly reminiscent of Frege's antipathy to psychologism.

Now this creates a significant challenge for Carnap, a challenge that Frege avoided due to his rational epistemology that by-passed sense experience entirely. The key challenge that motivates the *LSW* is how, given the solipsistic nature of subjective experience, it is possible to have intersubjective knowledge of the objective world? The Cartesian dilemma for Carnap is to find a common ground for individuals trapped inside a world that is subjective, private and incommunicable.

Carnap's solution is similar to Russell's: scientific knowledge involves descriptions not of subjective experiences but of the relations between them. But the Cartesian dilemma ensures that this isn't a straightforward mapping of our unreconstructed experiences on to the objective world. The lawless[276] and unintelligible nature of sense experience denied them and their surface relations from being the bearers of anything like a logical law. As Carnap states: "Relations themselves, in their qualitative peculiarity, are not intersubjectively communicable."[277] Hence considerable work needs to be done to elucidate the identity of relations in such a context that disabuses one from any initial psychological frame of reference.

In this vein Carnap restricts knowledge to the structures of the range of relations themselves, specifically to formal properties such as transitivity, symmetry and reflexivity.[278] Thus Carnap is seeking to eliminate the material – which is just to say the subjective or intensional – characteristics of the structure. For example, the relation "being the father of" can be represented as $<a1, a2>$ and the intension of that relation is true where $a1$ is the father of $a2$. But extensionally this relation only holds if we abstract from any intensional content and take the relation as simply a set of tuples. The structure can be instantiated in many different ways. So any particular r can take the value of, say, "the father of", or "taller than", or "larger than", etc. But however many instances there are the definition of the structure is entirely independent of each and every one of them.

The relation between structure and instance bears considerable resemblance to the Fregean relation between the logical laws and definitions and their particular instances. The structure can be seen here as the ground for any particular r that is an instance. Hence a description that picks out the structural properties of experiences – and hence the grounds of that experience – displays objective scientific knowledge. To base that description in the structural essence is to ground experience in objective, intersubjective knowledge.

---

[276] Thomas Uebel notes earlier writings such as the 1922 manuscript "Von Chaos zur Wirklichkeit," in which Carnap refers to the lawlessness of the psychological domain in "Neurath's Influence on Carnap's *Aufbau*," in *Influences on the Aufbau*, ed. Christian Dambock, 51-76. (Dordrecht: Springer, 2016)
[277] Carnap, *The Logical Structure of the World*, 30.
[278] Ibid, 21-22.

Now purely formal structural descriptions just picking out certain n-place structures do not serve to individuate objects in a domain. For this Carnap utilises what he calls a "structural definite description" which individuates an object on the basis of its relation to other objects in the domain. The objective is to identify the individual without appealing to the subjectively laden ostensive process: "On the basis of a structural description, we can frequently provide a definite description of individual objects merely through structural statements and without ostensive definitions."[279]

At the base of the system Carnap introduces the basic relation Rs - the "recollection of similarity" – which is the sole non-logical constant that occupies the only position as a primitive, undefined concept from which all others are constructed and reduced. Thus epistemologically, the base as whole units serves as primary relative to "the final constituents of experience at which one arrives through psychological or phenomenological analysis".[280] We see here Carnap's conspicuous goal of placing structure above elements that occupy subjective roles and are infected with subjective intensional properties.

Again we see similarities with Frege's work: the context principle – which was a constructive principle of sorts since it provides distinct definitions conferred on concepts by virtue of their place within the sentence – and the variables used that confer generality on judgement. The places within the basic relation structure likewise take precedence in reflecting the correct epistemic order. This is why Carnap introduces the basic relation[281] before the basic element.[282]

Following on from this, it may be easy to dismiss the Quinean verificationist interpretation of the *LSW* as seeing a strong connection between the epistemic system and empiricism.

---

[279] Ibid, 27.
[280] Ibid, 107.
[281] Ibid, 178-179.
[282] Ibid, 179.

This seems especially true where Carnap establishes the aloofness of the structural descriptions as:

"We saw earlier that it was possible to draw conclusions concerning properties of individuals from relation descriptions. In the case of structure descriptions, this no longer holds true. They form the highest level of formalization and dematerialization".[283]

The methodology employed requires working from the top in delineating the structural description alone in a way that fails to select for any particular empirical state of affairs. There is no way of knowing that a structural description picks out any individuals own experiences. Even with the basic relation, the extension of each place in the structure is just a pair list of the items laid down in the application of such a condition. It bears no essential connection to psychological reality.

But how does Carnap maintain what he calls "the conceptual purity of the operation rules and thus of the constructional definitions"[284] whilst also maintaining a strict empiricism and, with it, what may appear to be a structuralism beholden to the nature and configuration of sense data? We saw with Frege that all particulars were prone to the substitution rules laid out by the structure of the laws of logic and the places occupied by the variables. In this way he maintained prime place for logical structure and the grounds of any particular embodiment.

Carnap borrows the tools of Frege and Russell to turn the similarity relation into a reduction of the terms – which are merely substitution instances – of such a relation into an equivalence class. For example, the colour green gets analysed into the relation description of "the same colour as" which exhibits both reflexivity and symmetry. The similarity relation is not transitive, however, since we are only dealing with objects with colours in common. Thus objects that may only be, say, partially green may be constructed out of such

---

[283] Ibid, 23.
[284] Ibid, 161.

an equivalence relation. However, the equivalence relation takes precedence over any particular occupying the relata in that, definitionally, they can be reduced to the coloured object and the equivalence relation. This lies at the heart of constructionism and it is thoroughly Russellian and Fregean *not* Kantian, analysis. That is, objects are constructed and identified based on an equivalence relation and to the extent they are embedded in such a grounding system.

There is a sense in Carnap's system of going back to the drawing board in grounding our experiences in a way that usurps how we may ordinarily make surface empirical judgements. Quasi-analysis proceeds empirically such that empirical facts determine what goes into the similarity circles and their subsequent independence from one another. However, the autopsychological is infected with the self and subjectivity, though not to an irredeemable extent. Redemption comes through reconstruction. So just having an inventory of qualities does not allow us to work up, in a direct manner, from familiar empirical objects to constructed objects. Carnap writes:

"We who know the sense of the basic relation, and thus also the sense of the constructed entities, know that the quality classes are the individual visual qualities, tones, fragrances, etc.. but we do not as yet have a way of telling A whether a given quality class that he has formed is a tone, let alone which tone it represents. Eventually, we must come to the point where we can give him such information even though we do not know his inventory lists. For this is precisely the central thesis of construction theory, that each object about which a meaningful scientific statement can be made can be constructed."[285]

Thus there is an ambiguity inherent in the empirical knowledge states of an individual in that it is only by a process of intersubjective logical construction that that individual is able to identify their states with constructed objects. Therefore a suspension of intuitive knowledge is necessary before a constructional account can be worked up to the point of replacing familiar empirical objects.

---

[285] Ibid, 181-182.

It is important at this point to recall that Russellian acquaintance at its heart was actually logical; that is, it was *really* rationally derived logical conditions that individuated and identified objects of acquaintance and not their surface sense data qualities. Logical construction, for Russell, *did* involve the construction of objects out of sense data but sense data are fundamentally logical entities. And the quasi-wholes – "logical fictions" – were produced by the same logical methods of utilising equivalences that Carnap employed. These entities were logical structures and this is the conception of structure that Carnap is following. The difference lies in the rejection of sensibilia, but as I argued earlier, Russell could have begun on the same auto-psychological basis and probably should have, given his own worldview.

But further to this, Russell situates the perceiver in a spatial context vis-à-vis the object of perception in order to make the constructions. Thus the perceiver stands at the termination of a causal chain that proceeds from the object via the unsensed sensibilia to the sense data manifest to the perceiver.[286] The construction process then proceeds by comparing perception to perception under the "similarity" relation. But what basis is there for such an image of perception in the first place based on the Cartesian view of the mind assumed by Russell? It seems as if he is helping himself to ill-gotten assumptions and hence it can be argued that Carnap's autopsychological basis constructed by the pure logical system of Frege is a more consistent position.

Carnap's construction basis, by contrast, is purely rationalist and no first-person vantage point is assumed. His aim is to lay out a rational justification of intuition in a way that sets the parameters for such a justification without at the same time essentially involving intuition. Intuition plays no part for Carnap and hence does not exist except in raw, uninterpreted form. As he states: "the 'given' is never found in consciousness as mere raw material, but always in more or less complicated connections and formations."[287]

---

[286] Russell, "The Relation of Sense-data to Physics," in *Mysticism and Logic*, 145-179.
[287] Carnap, *The Logical Structure of the World*, 158.

Intuition does play a guiding role for the scientist in an initial recognition of a particular object for further scientific and rational analysis. Consider his example of the botanist who "forms the object of an individual plant as a physical object, without thereby engaging in any conscious thinking activity; most of the time, he recognizes intuitively this thing as a plant of such and such a species."[288] However it is clear that intuition plays a purely epistemic role: "intuitive recognition (e.g., of a plant) can become useful for further scientific work only because it is possible to give, in addition, the indicators (of the particular species of plant), to compare them to the perception and thus to give a rational justification of intuition."[289] He gives a succinct summary of the totalising role of the justificatory scheme:

"The fact that we take into consideration the epistemic relations does not mean that the syntheses or formations of cognition, as they occur in the actual process of cognition, are to be represented... with all their concrete characteristics. In the constructional system, we shall merely reconstruct these manifestations in a rationalizing or schematizing fashion; intuitive understanding is replaced by discursive reasoning."[290]

The role of construction theory is to be the justificatory base that is common to the different systems that are studied by the various specialist sciences. This is another significant parallel with Frege, where the processes of rational justification must abstract completely from the particular differences of each system. Thus the same basic relation underlies all systems and serves as their reductive base. This also serves as a demonstration of the unity of science which Carnap labels "the fundamental thesis of construction theory".[291]

The flashpoint of contention is over whether such a seemingly holistic system of knowledge, where experiences depend on their relations to other points in the system, can be said in anyway to be verificationist? Central to Carnap's project is a system of principles that would appear to exclude immediate sense experience as the final arbiter of knowledge.

---

[288] Ibid, 158.
[289] Ibid.
[290] Ibid, 89
[291] Ibid, 29.

One solution that presents itself is by splitting Carnap's system into the phenomenological, which plays a realising or communicative role on the one hand, and the similarity relation, a univocal reconstructive mechanism that plays a determinative role, on the other. There has to be an objective determination of our subjective states. Carnap's form of structuralism requires an objective structure untainted by subjectivism, hence his account of the structuring process does not involve any spelling out of such states. This gives the impression that Carnap cannot possibly stand in line with the empiricists let alone be the ultimate fulfilment of that tradition, as Quine argued.

But Carnap's structuralism is *highly reductionist.* In order to effect such a revolutionary worldview he has to reconstruct our phenomenal experience in such a way that renders it unrecognisable as a reconstruction of our subjective states. His form of analysis, in fact, makes it difficult to see it as anything less. He adopts a form of analysis that comes straight from Russell and Frege. Hence property descriptions – such as two objects being a shade of blue – can be reanalysed as knowledge admissible because of their grounding within the equivalence class.

Russell's similarity relation plays an integral role in how he defines numbers. Two classes that are similar are said to have the same number. This definition is non-circular since, by defining similarity as a one-to-one correspondence between objects, a knowledge of number is not presupposed. For example, one may not know how many forks and plates there are on a given dinner table, but one may know that for each plate there is a fork, in which case we know that the class of forks and the class of plates are similar even if we do not know their number. It is also abstractive since any given number is what is held in common between similar classes. Thus two is defined as the class of all couples, which will include all the married couples, two eggs, two trees in the backyard, two cars on a given road, etc. All that each has in common – and hence the similarity – is the property *two*. The definition is also exclusionary, as Russell's explanation of the "one-one" relation makes clear:

"A relation is said to be 'one-one' when, if *x* has the relation in question to *y*, no other term *x'* has the same relation to *y*, and *x* does not have the same relation to any term *y'* other than *y*."[292]

But this is an exclusionary relation that only functions in a way that abstracts from all differentia. Hence uniqueness is purely linguistic, a function of occupying the place of the variable. The relation is univocal and uniqueness results *only* in the same way that being self-identical marks one off as unique. Self-identity is univocal and purely linguistic, and any object can occupy the place in the relation by virtue of structural invariance through permutation.

But given the unambiguous definition of the structure, what differentiates objects in Carnap's structural definite description that are supposed to be purely analytic? Carnap gives an illustration of providing the identity of the stations of a railway network based entirely on the network's structure. He follows the lessons of the *Principia* by drawing the system based just on the structural account of relations. He asks whether, given a topological map of the network, names can be derived for the unnamed stations:

"…we look up the intersections of highest order, i.e., those in which the highest number of lines meet. We will find only a small number of these. Assume that we find twenty intersections in which eight lines meet. We then count, for each such point, the number of stations between it and the next intersection on each of the eight lines, and we will hardly find two of the eight to coincide in all eight numbers. Thus, we have identified all twenty points. But if there are still two, or even all twenty, which have the same numbers, then all we have to do is consider the connections between each of the eight neighboring intersections.... We proceed in this way until we find characteristics which no longer coincide, even if we have to survey our entire net. But once we have discovered the name for even one point on the map, the others are easily found, since only very few names qualify for the neighboring points."[293]

---

[292] Bertrand Russell, *Introduction to Mathematical Philosophy* (New York: Dover Publications, 1919), 15.
[293] Carnap, *The Logical Structure of the World*, 25-26.

The starting points are the twenty points where the eight lines meet and they are an example of developing unique structural criteria for concepts. These points become concepts distinguished by being the only ones with eight overlapping lines. Further eliminative criteria are introduced by counting the number of stations from each intersection to the next along each of the eight lines to see if any coincide in *all* eight numbers. If two resonate in such a way then further criteria are introduced and the web of relations is expanded until a definite description is attained.

This is an analytic procedure which should be obvious by the parallels with the Russellian definitions of numbers. Contingent features external to the definitions such as the distance between stations are excluded from the analysis. The topological map where the structural criteria have been used to isolate each of the twenty points are then compared to the ordinary map which has the same twenty points with the same characteristics and then the names of those points are fed back into the topological map. The structural maps are expanded from the points of equivalence to points of non-equivalence which differentiates each object description.

This form of structuralism is radically at odds with how we may ordinarily think of reference based on our ordinary phenomenological experiences. In perceiving the tree in my backyard, I may see it as a construction of millions of smaller phenomenological points to such an extent that it may seem to take on a life of its own. And that new emergent form may be seen as grounded in the structure that exists non-phenomenologically among the scientific objects of atoms and molecules.

This may in fact be the unreconstructed version of Russell's structuralism but this sort of model is impossible for Carnap for one main reason: he doesn't nearly have as rich an information base as needed. All the objects of science are, for Carnap, quasi-objects in the sense that they are like Russellian and Fregean numbers: classes of objects already constructed by the primitive unanalysable basic relation. Carnap sees the unity in the tree example – a series of co-located objects – the same way that Russell does: as a faux unity and therefore entirely analysable into the nodes of a structure that is univocal in nature.

But as I have already stated Carnap's goal was to achieve definite descriptions guided by pure structure in a way wholly in concert with the acquisition of empirical knowledge. But even in this we see a parallel with Frege. Consider Hume's Principle which was the basis for Frege's definition of numbers: x is the number of class $y =_{def} x$ is the class of all classes equinumerous with y. Such a definition *requires* real concrete examples such as the number of cats or the number of trees in one's backyard. But such a requirement is just a result of the equivalence relation in the same way that something's being self-identical requires just that thing to be identical to itself. As Alan Richardson writes:

"That is, the uniqueness of the described relation is logically presupposed in the definition but is only empirically ascertainable. The empirical nature of the guarantee of the uniqueness of reference of the structural definite description is meant to give content to the idea that the constructional system is a constructional system for empirical concepts, as opposed to the formal concepts of mathematics. It is this empirical uniqueness of the described relations which is in principle unavailable on the implicit definition account given by Schlick."[294]

But in Frege's number case what is "empirically ascertainable" are really just empirical cues to the logical superstructure that plays the real role in grounding the equivalence relation. The anti-psychologism demands that empirical concepts play no such integral role in the logical laws, and in the case of numbers there is nothing in the individual objects and their empirical representations that play any integral role in the definition. The role of the empirically ascertained properties is purely epiphenomenal.

The impoverished information base of Carnap's system – which is purely equivalence and non-equivalence – resembles more the states of Parmenides' being and non-being. Carnap's

---

[294] Richardson, *Carnap's Construction of the World*, 50.

state of being is purely univocal, which means no genus–species differentiations are possible, just the ever expanding web of the system conferring individuation, based purely on the categories of equivalence and non-equivalence.

Thus the topological map serves as a grounds for an empirical description of reality where the structural descriptions are designed to purge all ambiguity. And thus we have a genetic conception of empirical concepts that is underwritten by a unified structure of logical forms designed to give them their identity. In the preface to the *LSW*, Carnap emphasises laying a rational foundation for scientific concepts which must not be confused with how those concepts are initially arrived at. The structural descriptions are designed to give an account of how our scientific concepts are justified by their logical basis, but given that logical space is orthogonal to the chaotic state of our ordinary sense experience, a new account had to be given that required suspending intuitive gained knowledge.

Thus the purely logical grounds utilises the elements of sense experience to reconstruct the world. And thus the sense experiences have to cleave tightly to the logical form to act as a realising condition for the determining structure. Recall that Russell's original idea for structuralism was that we have intrinsic knowledge of sense data but not of the structure that gives it its particular form. Hence we have sense data playing something of a realising role, where the structure is a determining precondition and both act in a kind of collaborative unity.

But crucially for the *LSW*'s project is how to transition from such a holistic network of structures to the particular sensory items that might come together to make, for example, a tree concept out of various patches of brown and green. Stated again, such a conceptualisation would seem to be extremely information rich, but Carnap has merely the equivalent of being and non-being through which to make distinctions. To put it another way, he only has the distinction between p and $\neg p$ as instruments of discrimination in the passages where he moves from the auto-psychological to the intersubjective illustrated with the railway example. His construction principles have various virtues, such as simplicity and consistency that act on his holistic construction basis, but the question is whether or not the structures are rich enough to ground all empirical knowledge.

Carnap begins his epistemology from a Cartesian perspective, so individual sense data do not come self-interpreted. An experience in isolation may be a hallucination or it may be genuine, but there is no way of discriminating between the two. It is only by seeing if that experience fits in to the web of other beliefs that I will know if it is a hallucination or not. For example, I might observe the experience in better light or from a closer vantage point and see that it is inconsistent with other experiences. Only *then* do I know if the knowledge is veridical or not. More specifically, the assignment of various sensory qualities to world points proceeds holistically. As Quine explains: "the plan was that qualities should be assigned to point-instants in such a way as to achieve the laziest overall world compatible with our experience."[295]

Sections 126 and 127 of the *LSW* are Carnap's attempt to move beyond the autopsychological undivided elementary experiences and where Quine directs his most prominent challenge to the empirical project. The details need not detain us (and he is sketchy on them anyway) but the goal is to show how the various elementary experiences constructed can be assigned to various points in the four dimensional space-time world. But every single assignment requires the employment of broadly applicable desiderata such as simplicity and consistency which ultimately depend on the single similarity relation between basic experiences. Carnap calls for an eliminative reduction where the designation of experiences at the four spatio-temporal co-ordinates can be reduced to purely subjective experiences. But it is here that Quine identifies a problem with the eliminative reduction since there is no way to eliminate the connective "is at" by translating those sentences into ones that refer purely to subjective mental experiences. Quine complains that Carnap:

"Provides no indication, not even the sketchiest, of how a statement of the form 'Quality Q is at x;y;z;t' could ever be translated into Carnap's initial language of sense data and logic.

---

[295] Quine, "Two Dogmas," in *From a Logical Point of View*, 40.

The connective 'is at' remains an added undefined connective; the canons counsel us in its use but not in its elimination."[296]

It should be obvious to this point that Quine's assessment leaves out a large chunk of the epistemological machinery employed by Carnap in the *LSW*. But that machinery, although playing the role of grounding empirical experiences, was purported to explain the realising conditions of experience. This was the whole point of Carnap's use of Fregean and Russellian relations. Thus a kind of intimacy between sense data and grounding conditions was a necessity for Carnap and therefore Quine is not out of order in demanding the elimination in the translations of objects into sense data. Where Quine fails is in looking purely to sense data alone and not the single univocal relation of similarity that lacks the richness in structure to provide any means of eliminative translation. In other words, the elimination does not occur so much because the sense data themselves do not contain the conditions for the connective, but because they are not found in the similarity relation and the attendant structures built up in accordance with the guiding desiderata.

Thus Carnap's entire system draws heavily from the logical machinery of Frege and Russell whilst trying to tie that logical machinery to auto-psychological sense data. Frege almost entirely ignored sense data throughout his work, whereas Russell was thoroughly within the empiricist tradition and made explicit the need to construct the objects of acquaintance. Carnap attempts to make the construction of sense data exclusively from the auto-psychological and thus shuns Russell's project that starts with perspectives at the end of a causal chain based on sensibilia. This creates the need to construct the empirical base through the pure Fregean logical system.

The importance of the *LSW* project is that it represents a completeness of the Frege and Russell projects by marrying the two together. It engages the Fregean logical system with experience and forces consistency in Russell's system by eliminating everything except the auto-psychological. This creates a best-of-all-possible worlds amalgamation between the two major philosophical systems that inaugurated 20th century analytic philosophy and is

---
[296] Ibid.

thus a test of their adequacy as total philosophical systems. Quine's objections, however, show that project to be a complete failure for the simple reason that it fails to explain the data of our experiences.

But tracing back the worldview of Carnap through Russell and Frege we can see that at its heart this is a failure owing to the dichotomy Parmenides drew between the rational and sensory world. The former lacks the information content, since it is incongruent with the latter. There is only one form of being for Parmenides and that is justified through rationalist insight gained through non-empirical means. Therefore the determining conditions for the rich informational content of our experience is lacking and hence any true empiricism – much less verificationism! – should rule out such a conception of being. In the last chapters, alternative non-univocal categories will be introduced that fill such an explanatory vacuum.

Quine and Naturalism

Quine was an avowed and perhaps even dogmatic naturalist, and this presupposition is generally recognised to permeate a good portion of his corpus. He immerses the human knower thoroughly within the world of science and empiricism. To the extent that epistemology becomes a branch of the natural sciences and philosophy, it is denied a domain of its own. He stated his position succinctly in his 1969 Dewey Lectures:

"Philosophically, I am bound to Dewey by the naturalism that dominated his last three decades. With Dewey I hold that knowledge, mind and meaning are part of the same world that they have to do with, and that they are to be studied in the same empirical spirit that animates natural science. There is no place for a prior philosophy. When a naturalistic philosopher addresses himself to the philosophy of mind, he is apt to talk of language. Meanings are, first and foremost, meanings of language. Language is a social art which we all acquire on the evidence solely of other people's overt behavior under publicly recognizable circumstances. Meanings, therefore, those very models of mental entities, end up as grist for the behaviorist's mill. Dewey was explicit on this point: 'Meaning... is not a psychic existence; it is primarily a property of behavior.'"[297]

Quine's naturalism is very much intertwined with his behaviourism, and language is to be subject to the same rigors of scientific analysis as any other discipline of science, such as physics. To the extent that there are meanings for Quine, they are identified with the overt behaviour of individuals. Behaviourism is an inevitable consequence of naturalism, and in fact, in the field of linguistics, "one has no choice".[298] Quine's behaviourism is, crucially, his key area of departure from Russell, Carnap and the philosophers traditionally associated with empiricism, such as Locke, George Berkeley and Hume. Russell and Carnap, it will be recalled, represented the culmination of the Cartesian project where knowledge was still answerable, in one way or another, to immediate sense experience. Quine, whilst still purporting to continue the verificationist tradition, deploys behaviourism to subvert any notion of meaning that is special, private or mysterious from a scientific point of view.

In fact, it can be all too tempting to see in Quine an aversion to verificationism given his famous departure from Carnap and Russell on various doctrines. But Quine did, in fact, embark on a constructive, systematic project which he intended to be very much within the empiricist tradition. But the problem that arose for Carnap's project was that the adoption of the auto-psychological as the basis of the domain did not follow from the formal logical apparatus or the scientific considerations he employed but rather was derived *a priori*.

Quine's approach, by contrast, is to reject any appeals to first principles independent of scientific naturalism. There is no purely philosophical terrain to appeal to justify scientific knowledge. One of the most prominent of Quine scholars, Roger Gibson, has pointed to Quine's naturalism as fundamental to his whole philosophy and that it is, in fact, "a key to unlocking a correct interpretation of Quine."[299] However, it is a strongly reductionist kind

---

[297] W. V. O. Quine, "Ontological Relativity," in *Ontological Relativity and Other Essays* (New York: Columbia University Press, 1969), 26.
[298] W. V. O. Quine, *The Pursuit of Truth* (Cambridge MA: Harvard University Press, 1992), 37-38.
[299] Roger Gibson, "The Key to Interpreting Quine," *The Southern Journal of Philosophy* 30, no. 4, (1992): 17, https://doi.org/10.1111/j.2041-6962.1992.tb00644.x

of naturalism the basis of which is the machinery of first-order logic with identity. And underwriting the character of the variable is the univocal notion of identity: "what sense can be found in talking of entities which cannot meaningfully be said to be identical with themselves and distinct from one another?"[300] Here he is very much following Frege in positing a condition of identity as a mark of legitimacy for any given kind of thing.

Quine's *criteria of identity* undergirds his naturalist epistemology by supplying the conditions under which entities of a certain kind – be they sets, meanings, propositions, material objects, etc. – can be counted as the same individual or different. This is evident in the workings of naturalised epistemology in the following way. The first requirements are observation sentences. These are sentences that are directly connected to our stimulations (for example, "it is raining" or "there is a green tree"). Now the way that reference is applied by Quine is through a subset of observation sentences known as observation categoricals.[301] These typically take the form of "whenever *this*, then *that*". Scientific knowledge is of a general nature for Quine and these sentences are common in drawing scientific inferences, such as "when a hydrate is heated, it changes colour".

The linguistic basis that guarantees reference follows from the marrying together of a relative clause and a general or categorical assertion. Knowledge of objects does not come directly through the introspection of our referential experiences but from the role they play in the laws of broader theories. Pronouns in order to be objectively referential, have to take up an indispensable role in categorical propositions, as in the case, says Quine, of the "substantivized relative clause 'things which . . .' . . . preceded by 'every' or 'some'."[302] In keeping with the tradition of modern predicate logic, a relative predicate like "things which are red" cannot be applied to a subject like "all fire trucks" since that is not an appropriate semantic or syntactic subject.

---

[300] W. V. O. Quine, "On What there is," in *From a Logical Point of View*, 4.
[301] W. V. O. Quine, "Empirical Content," in *Theories and Things* (Cambridge, MA: Harvard University Press, 1981), 28.
[302] W. V. O. Quine, "The Variable and its Place in Reference," in *Philosophical Subjects: Essays Presented to P. F. Strawson*, Z, ed. van Straaten (Oxford: Clarendon Press, 1980), 165.

We start to see the identity conditions emerging as integral to the overall global role of objective quantified logic. Objects are not initiated into our knowledge base following as grammatical subjects but only when the general quantifier lays the initial formal conditions. Contrast this with a singular relative pronoun which Quine labels – borrowing a term from Peter Geach – a pronoun of "laziness". It is dispensable. Quine states:

"In the sentence 'I bumped my head and it hurts' the pronoun is one of laziness. It could be supplanted by its grammatical antecedent 'my head': 'I bumped my head and my head hurts.' By contrast, in the focal categorical 'Whenever there is a raven, it is black' the pronoun is essential."[303]

Lazy pronouns don't function as referential and hence are at the heart of substitutional quantification. Thus truth in these cases is a matter of substituting the correct linguistic expressions to form complete sentences as in a sentence like "If … drives a truck, then … has black hair". Thus the truth of such an open sentence is just a matter of substituting the appropriate term for the variable to yield the truth sentence. There is no objectual reference occurring here. In the case of the focal categorical, however, the "it" refers beyond the linguistic item "a raven" and into the environment. Another example is "for any thing found on Crown land then that thing belongs to the government". Here we have two pronouns that refer to the same object given by identity, which is picked out by "any thing" and "that thing". The substitutional construal of sentences is enough to give us understanding, but for full reference to occur – that is, for there to be obtaining truth conditions – then reference is needed through the use of identity. Identity marked out in a sentence is the condition under which pronouns are construed referentially. Converting our sentence into one with a bound variable we have something like:

"$\forall x$ (If x is found on Crown land then x belongs to the government)"

---

[303] W. V. O. Quine, *From Stimulus to Science* (Cambridge: Harvard University Press, 1998), 27-28.

Thus for any thing – absolutely anything falling under the identity condition – then for that thing if it is found on Crown land, it belongs to the government. Thus the bound variable playing the role of the pronoun is a guarantee of ontological existence. Already we see the influence of Parmenides argument which, as Russell describes it:

"When you think, you think of something; when you use a name, it must be the name of something. Therefore both thought and language require objects outside themselves."[304]

This is the reasoning that led to Quine's use of the existential quantifier in order to make ontological commitments. It is this conception of immanent truth, whereby the use of predicate logic renders the subject of the sentence a variable. For Quine the variable is chiefly involved in "linking and permuting" the positions in the sentence.[305] The monistic nature of the variable is evident in its ability to "range over objects of any sort" and even in their various uses "they are not so various after all when we probe their inner nature."[306]

Mere linguistic relations – or, presumably, associations of ideas in one's head that might be made through substitutional quantification – do not result in objective reference. Nor is this like Russellian acquaintance, which depended on the logical apparatus that was ultimately known a priori. We will spell out Quine's rejection of the a priori – a posteriori distinction later, but for now it is important to understand his placing the law of identity – Parmenidian being – as the naturalistic grounds from which the justification of knowledge is built up. In other words, it is naturalism expressed through the general quantifier and the range of the variable within a natural environment that give the conditions for ontological commitment and not anything internal to our cognitive states.

i) **Factuality and Truth**

---

[304] Bertrand Russell, *A History of Western Philosophy* (London and New York: Routledge, 2004), 56.
[305] W. V. O. Quine, *Quiddities: An Intermittently Philosophical Dictionary* (Cambridge, MA: Harvard University Press, 1987), 238.
[306] Ibid, 237.

Situating the knowing agent vis-à-vis truth represents *how* Quine situates us within the structure of ultimate being. Thus his emphasis is on epistemology, following in the tradition of Descartes. But his ontology, like that of Frege and Russell, is pure Parmenides. The key difference is being is embodied in the naturalistic world and acts externally on us through the mechanism of first-order logic with identity.[307] We are not able to apprehend being in any internally given, a priori manner, but instead we *act* in accordance with its nature, which is ultimately given in the virtues of scientific theory, namely clarity and simplicity.

In order to understand Quine on truth and knowledge, it is paramount to understand the knowing self and its relation to ideas of the outside world. Although he rejects Cartesian dualism, he still situates the self in an epistemologically unencumbered state such that knowledge claims can be deliberated in a way that allows freedom of decision. Quine conceives the knowing subject as a substantial entity. He is certainly no dualist, but dialectically he still assumes that the judgemental relation is accidental vis-à-vis the knower. That is to say, the knower isn't compelled into a state of knowledge that is in any way prescriptive or normative in the encounter with the manifest image or what we might say are the pre-theoretically recognised ordinary bodies of our experience. Thus the ontologies in works such as *Word and Object*,[308] *Ontological Relativity*,[309] and *Roots of Reference*[310] are intended to be descriptive accounts of how we come to have the ontologies we have arrived at. They are not prescriptions on how we *ought* to do ontology.

Quine is quick to disavow idealism and attempts to put in place a robust realism. However, when it comes to knowing bodies in the mind-independent world it is a matter of *positing* them as a means of organising our sense experiences. Quine, loyal to Hume, takes the individual sense experiences to bear no necessary connection with each other. Thus any given experience does not wear unity on its face; rather bodies must be posited in accordance with our theorising and hence are the product of our constructions or inventions.

---

[307] The external acting of being on the knowing agent was already there in primordial form in Frege's assertion but becomes more explicitly behaviouristic in Quine.
[308] W. V. O. Quine, *Word and Object* (Cambridge, MA: MIT Press, 1960)
[309] Quine, *Ontological Relativity*.
[310] W. V. O. Quine, *Roots of Reference* (LaSalle, Il: Open Court, 1974)

This doesn't stop Quine from talking about evidence for theories or reality in a robust sense. In fact he sees science "as pursuing and discovering truth rather than as decreeing it."[311] He elsewhere writes:

"Having noted that man has no evidence for the existence of bodies beyond the fact that their assumption helps him organize his experience, we should have done well, instead of disclaiming evidence for the existence of bodies, to conclude: such then, at bottom, is what evidence is, both for ordinary bodies and for molecules."[312]

However, this is reminiscent of the idealist Berkeley's refusal to disavow "matter". The details of just how Quine defines truth in accordance with reality is crucial. The first thing to note is that Quine embraces Frege's redundancy theory of truth where mention of the truth predicate is unnecessary in asserting the truth of a sentence. Any mention of a sentence itself is only a temporary reprieve from the real business of that sentence, which is talking about the world. As he states, the point of the truth predicate is "to point through the sentences to the reality."[313] So to say that "snow is white" is true is simply to dis-quote the sentence and say that snow is white. Regarding disquotation, Quine writes:

"It tells us what it is for any sentence to be true, and it tells us this in terms just as clear to us as the sentence in question itself. We understand what it is for the sentence 'snow is white' to be true as clearly as we understand what it is for snow to be white. Evidently one who puzzles over the adjective 'true' should puzzle rather over the sentences to which he ascribes it. 'True' is transparent."[314]

Quine's relinquishing of first philosophy was not accompanied by a rejection of what he called the "old epistemological problem" and by this he means the problem of scepticism. He writes that such old epistemologists:

---

[311] Quine, *From Stimulus to Science*, 67.
[312] W. V. O. Quine, "The Ways of Paradox" in *The Ways of Paradox and Other Essays* (Cambridge, MA: Harvard University Press, 1976), 251.
[313] W. V. O. Quine, *Philosophy of Logic* 2nd ed. (Cambridge, MA: Harvard University Press, 1970), 11.
[314] Quine, *Pursuit of Truth*, 82.

"... saw their problem as one of challenging or substantiating our knowledge of the external world. Appeal to physical sense organs in the statement of the problem would have seemed circular ...

A far cry, this, from the old epistemology. Yet it is no gratuitous change of subject matter, but an enlightened persistence rather in the old epistemological problem. It is enlightened in recognizing that the skeptical challenge springs from science itself, and that in coping with it we are free to use scientific knowledge. The old epistemologist failed to recognize the strength of his position.

The epistemologist thus emerges as a defender or protector. He no longer dreams of a first philosophy, firmer than science, on which science can be based; he is out to defend science from within, against its self doubts."[315]

As we saw in the first chapter, the challenges to a correspondence theory of truth, such as the *regress problem,* were readily apparent to Frege. It is also extremely problematic to provide a definition of "reality" or "correspondence" when there is no mind-independent immediate access to such a reality. Tarski's method is a solution to such problems since there is no need to refer to any realm beyond what is immediate to the sentence itself and to truth-functional connectives like the biconditional. Thus truth and reality are said to be *immanent*:

"Disavowing as I do a first philosophy outside science, I can attribute reality and truth only within the terms and standards of the scientific system of the world that I now accept; only immanently..."[316]

---

[315] Quine, *The Roots of Reference*, 3.
[316] W V. O. Quine, "Reply to Harold N. Lee," in *The Philosophy of W. V. O. Quine* expanded edition, ed. Lewis Edwin Hahn and Paul Arthur Schilpp (La Salle, Il: Open Court, 1998), 316.

Measuring knowledge against the certainty of sense data was the way first philosophy grounded our knowledge of the external world. Thus the doing of science is within the Cartesian theatre and there is no external vantage point much less a "supra-scientific tribunal", to anchor it. It is inherent in our state as knowers that we are only able to work from within any given theory and to work from such a vantage point that brings improvements in clarity and understanding:

"I see philosophy and science as in the same boat – a boat which, to revert to Neurath's figure … we can build only at sea while staying afloat in it. There is no external vantage point, no first philosophy."[317]

"The naturalistic philosopher begins his reasoning within the inherited world theory as a going concern. He tentatively believes all of it, but believes also that some unidentified portions of it are wrong. He tries to improve, clarify, and understand the system from within. He is the busy sailor adrift on Neurath's boat."[318]

It is the case that truth, as set out by Tarski, is immanent to sentences, which means that the truth conditions are laid down by, and thereby limited to, the sentences of that particular language. It is also the case that truth, for Quine, is immanent at the theoretical level. Truth is dispensable when it is "equated to the sentence itself" à la Tarski, but in a sentence with the variable functioning in a way analogous to the pronoun then truth "is not to be lightly dismissed."[319] Truth is accidental at the former level but intrinsic to the latter.

At first it may seem odd for Quine to hold both these positions together so that truth conditions are a matter set out by a given language *and* a given theory at any particular time. But this is more a matter of getting clear regarding how sentences fit together with theories held by any given community of knowers and how that all fits together and interacts with the external world.

---

[317] Ibid, 316.
[318] W. V. O. Quine, "Five Milestones of Empiricism," in *Theories and Things*, 72.
[319] Quine, *Quiddities*, 214.

Eve Gaudet points out that in Quine's system it is important to make a distinction between saying what it is for a sentence to be true and saying *that* the sentence is true.[320] In the first instance we are talking about what it is for a sentence to be true in a given language. Thus what it is to identify any given true sentence involves going no further than the sentence itself and its language so that truth fails to go translinguistic. In the second case, saying *that* a sentence is true at the theoretical level means saying *which* sentences are true and which sentences are false. It means "accepting a given theory is accepting a systematic assignment of truth-values to a set of related sentences."[321]

Observation sentences are the port of entrance for our knowledge of the outside world. They supply evidence for theoretical sentences, since they are so closely associated with our stimulations.[322] Importantly they operate at the level of the knower in commanding "assent or dissent outright, on the occasion of a stimulation in the appropriate range, without further investigation and independently of what he may have been engaged in at the time."[323] But they are a by-product of the speech community and are those sentences that command unanimous assent. This is how they obtain an intersubjective status. This is one level of truth and it is precisely here and not beyond the language community that we find evidence for a given theory.

There is also a semantic function for observation sentences. This seems to be what links them to sense experience and from which they derive meaning. This is the entrance point to science. It is here that Quine's behaviourism especially comes to the fore since it is precisely in the learning of the observation sentence that an evidential link is established with the theoretical level, for the latter are systems of sentences.

---

[320] Eve Gaudet, *Quine on Meaning: The Indeterminacy of Translation* (London: Continuum International Publishing Group, 2006), ch. 3.
[321] Ibid, 27-28.
[322] Quine, *Pursuit of Truth*, 2-3.
[323] Ibid, 3.

To explain at a more succinct level, we can say following Gaudet's interpretation of Quine's Tarskian approach to truth, that the sentences of theories are indeed true and determined to be so from within a given theory held at the time. However, that truth has a *derived* status in that it is the outside world of factuality that occupies a privileged determining condition of the truth status of those sentences. And what is the exact nature of this relationship? It is of a distinctly behavioural nature, the conditioning that takes place in the learning of the observation sentence which in turn supplies meaning and evidence through their many and varied relations to theoretical sentences.[324]

Quine's rejection of facts as the objects of states of affairs and what he calls the "copy"[325] theory of language fits together with his embrace of Tarski where true statements do not demand an object of correspondence.[326] Quine's solution in his characteristic move to avoid first philosophy is to embrace naturalism, which is the:

"… abandonment of the goal of a first philosophy. It sees natural science as an inquiry into reality, fallible and corrigible but not answerable to any supra-scientific tribunal, and not in need of any justification beyond observation and the hypothetico-deductive method."[327]

In addition, he defines the natural philosopher as one who "begins his reasoning within the inherited world theory as a going concern".[328] That philosopher is in a position of complete ownership of his beliefs and "emerges as a defender or protector"[329] of those beliefs. And most importantly they seek to "improve, clarify, and understand the system from within".[330] Thus we get strong hints just from these passages that Quinean naturalist knowledge is very

---

[324] Another way to look at this; Tarski sentences are indeed true but they are truth derived and determined by the conditions of the natural world; "Here the truth predicate serves, as it were, to point through the sentence to the reality; it serves as a reminder that though the sentences are mentioned, reality is still the whole point." Quine, *Philosophy of Logic,* 11. The sentence here points to reality since it is grounded in reality in the same way that seated Socrates points to Socrates because it is grounded in the being of Socrates.
[325] Quine, "Ontological Relativity," in *Ontological Relativity*, 27.
[326] The parallels with Frege are striking since he also embraced a redundancy view of truth and rejected the correspondence theory of truth with the true sentences being determined by the external conditions manifest in assertion.
[327] Quine, "Five Milestones of Empiricism," in *Theories and Things,* 72.
[328] Ibid.
[329] Quine, *Roots of Reference,* 3.
[330] Quine, "Five Milestones of Empiricism," in *Theories and Things,* 72.

much a goal-orientated activity. It isn't about having a stock of set beliefs but rather having the right disposition.

Instead of demanding the ontologist believe according to the demands of immediate sense data, or as a result of being in the right sort of mental state, Quine stresses that one should acquiesce to the highest tribunal of scientific knowledge, which is currently physics. Although it may be possible that "telepathic" laws could be established over and above the microphysical states, Quine reiterates that it would remain the responsibility of the "physicist to go back to the drawing board and have another try at full coverage, which is his business."[331]

In fact the very nature of science is that it is evolving, so it is not possible to affirm any particular ontology. As Quine says:

"We can switch our own ontology too without doing violence to any evidence, but in so doing we switch from our elementary particles to some manner of proxies and thus reinterpret our standard of what counts as a fact of the matter. Factuality, like gravitation and electric charge, is internal to our theory of nature."[332]

Thus Quine's physicalism, which he calls "bluntly monistic",[333] as an explored notion constitutes an ongoing deference to broader and broader conceptions of the world. It is difficult to nail down an ontology, not only because of this sort of progress but because it is a structural conception in which individual things are not permanent occupiers. But his conception of ontology, what constitutes an object, and what is ultimately true defers closer and closer to the ideal of physics. As Gaudet writes:

---

[331] W. V. O. Quine, "Reply to Hillary Putnam," in *The Philosophy of W. V. O. Quine*, 430-431.
[332] Quine, "Things and Their Places in Theories," in Moser, *Materialism*, 23.
[333] Quine, *From Stimulus to Science*, 15.

"...for Quine, the ontology of the *overall conceptual scheme* is physical – primacy of microphysical states – which means that the factuality of a regimented idiom also increases as the idiom comes closer to the idiom of physics. Chemistry, for instance, being closer to physics than is biology, is thus the more factual of the two."[334]

Quine describes his ultimate goal of "limning the true and ultimate structure of reality."[335] The entire aim of his regimenting ontology is to systematise and clarify[336] in a way which gets beyond common sense and the potential misleading ontology implicit in ordinary language. This means, as Gaudet points out, that physicalism is *"an enterprise"* with aims, as she quotes Quine, for "a minimum catalogue of states—elementary states, let us call them—such that there is no change without a change in respect to them."[337]

This seems to place Quine's behaviourism and his naturalistic epistemology in an interesting light since there seems to be a significant parallel with Fregean assertion. For the natural epistemologist to know in accordance with the facts is to be disposed to behave in a manner that grants factuality to our theoretical sentences and the way to do this is through a system of regimentation with the goal of achieving the greatest level of systematic clarity possible. This is a goal orientated activity according to the norms and methods of scientific truth seeking where physics serves as the normative standard for attaining knowledge. It is the process of enlightened behaviour where we attain, for Quine, the level of concordance with facts.[338]

---

[334] Gaudet, *Quine on Meaning*, 10.
[335] Quine, *Word and Object*, 221.
[336] On the other hand Quine describes the elementary physical states as "inscrutable"; "Facts of the Matter," in *Confessions of a Confirmed Extensionalist and other Essays*, ed. Dagfinn Follesdal and Douglas B. Quine (Cambridge, MA: Harvard University Press, 2008), 285-286. The apparent discrepancy can be explained if we recognise that physics deals in concepts that give the clearest exposition of what an object is in the most monistic terminology of first-order logic where *what* that monistic being is, independently of language and mental predicates, must be simple and opaque.
[337] Gaudet, *Quine on Meaning*, 13. He also describes science as an "institution or process in the world..."; "Epistemology Naturalized," in *Ontological Relativity*, 84.
[338] He states: "normativity comes in with the conjuring of hypothesis. Five virtues to seek in hypothesis are: Conservatism, generality, simplicity, refutability, modesty"; *The Pursuit of Truth*, 20.

Carnap's failure to build his reconstructionist project is another key to understanding Quine. As we saw in the last section, Carnap's logical apparatus wasn't able to eliminate the basic "is at" distinctions in building the objects of sense data. In short there is an indeterminacy that runs from theory to sense experience and this is evident in many of Quine's best known doctrines. Understanding these doctrines is essential to understanding Quine's realism, that is, his explanation for how our thoughts come to have sufficient contact with the outside world as to be counted as genuine knowledge.

Language is to be taken as a social art that needs to be studied empirically and independently of private meanings and private references. A private language, where meaning is to be a purely mental entity subject to introspection, needs to be abandoned. The subjective view of meaning Quine describes disparagingly as "the myth of a museum".[339] He goes on to explain that:

"...the naturalist's primary objection to this view is not an objection to meanings on account on their being mental entities, though that could be objection enough. The primary objection persists even if we take the labeled exhibits not as mental ideas but as platonic ideas or even as the denoted concrete objects. Semantics is vitiated by a pernicious mentalism as long as we regard a man's semantics as somehow determinate in his mind beyond what might be implicit in his dispositions to overt behavior. It is the very facts about meanings, not the entities meant, that must be construed in terms of behavior."[340]

So it isn't the subjective private nature of mental entities themselves that is the problem, per se. It is the indeterminacy that infests mental and Platonic entities and indeed *any* concrete reference. In other words, it is the particular and variegated nature of intensional meanings that are problematic as opposed to the univocality of first-order logic with identity that finds full expression in a public language.[341] This sort of reductionism was very much evident in

---

[339] Quine, "Ontological Relativity," in *Ontological Relativity*, 27.
[340] Ibid.
[341] The advantage of my account is that it marries Quine's behaviourism to the extensionality behind the Frege-Russell system of logic Quine presupposes. In arguing that the simplicity of such a system is the guiding virtue for naturalistic behaviourism I avoid the pitfalls of those that argue indeterminacy comes as a result of Quine's extensionalism *rather* than his behaviourism/naturalism (contradicting Quines own statements); see, for

Frege as we saw in previous chapters, but in Quine it is given very much a naturalistic twist.[342]

This puts a curious spin on the question of how Quine defines truth and factuality. It is immediately obvious that he can't accept the traditional correspondence theory of truth. This is because he takes the surface features of ordinary language for granted and bestows preeminent status on physics. He wants a realist theory of truth, however, but vehemently opposes, even from early on in his career, any reification of meanings.

Objectivity for Quine is explicitly ontological. And how that ontology is achieved is via a system which is in accordance with the scientific spirit. The clear and rigorous language of regimentation is supposed to be the means by which he achieves the specific purpose of philosophy, which is to organise and systematise our knowledge along scientific lines. Regimentation encompasses all the systems of science and thus achieves its goal of being in accordance with science and yet uniquely broader than any specific science.

As stressed earlier, the penultimate goal for Quine in achieving clarity and systematicity is the language of first-order logic. For the knowing agent it is the clarity achieved by theory and not the immediacy of sense data that takes precedence. The freedom afforded to the unencumbered knowing subject – as a substantial entity – allows it to work out a system of knowledge where sense data are theoretically laden. Sense data are never known immediately, but a certain theoretical system must be presupposed in any encounter with them.

---

example, Itay Shani, "The Whole Rabbit: On the Perceptual Roots of Quine's Indeterminacy Puzzle," *Philosophical Psychology* 22, no. 6, (2009): 739-763, https://doi.org/10.1080/09515080903409960

[342] My marrying of Quine's logical relations and theoretical evidential relations with his behaviourism finds further support in statements like this; "…any such interconnections of sentences must finally be due to the conditioning of sentences as responses to sentences as stimuli. If some of the connections count more particularly as logical or as causal, they do so only by reference to so-called logical or causal laws which in turn are sentences within the theory. The theory as a whole – a chapter of chemistry, in this case, plus relevant adjuncts from logic and elsewhere – is a fabric of sentences variously associated to one another and to nonverbal stimuli by the mechanism of conditioned response." Quine, *Word and Object*, 11. And; "…any realistic theory of evidence must be inseparable from the psychology of stimulus and response, applied to sentences." Ibid, 17. In other words, logical implication just is the conditioned responses common between those two sentences.

The trajectory from there should then be for greater and greater levels of clarity and simplicity. This is the goal to which the virtuous theoretician is supposed to orientate their behaviour. These two virtues work hand in hand for Quine such that the regimentation of first-order logic is the paradigm case of how theories should be spelt out. The human agent situated in an ideal state of knowing *acts* in such a way that they will conform to the ideals given in such a state of clarity and according to maximal simplicity.

It is necessary at this stage to pause and consider Quine's own idiosyncratic account of simplicity. Simplicity is a tacit guide for the scientist and its value is ultimately pragmatic.[343] It involves following certain rules for the selection and amalgamation of data so as to minimise the number of entities and their qualities and positional changes. Simplicity works in concert with the formal inference rules of logic so that it is not concerned with the way predicates relate to each other or with the way portions of the data interrelate but rather it is characteristic of the relation between the scientists themselves and the data as a whole. This is a logical simplicity not a simplicity specific to any particular theory.

Quine situates this ideal in a realm beyond what may be cognitively accessible to us due to our limited knowledge and the dichotomy he draws between epistemology and ontology. His working with such a dualistic assumption comes out in statements such as: "It is at this point that we must perhaps acquiesce in the psychophysical dualism of predicates, though clinging to our effortless monism of substance"[344] Quine admits our limited theoretical state, but we are confined to working in it and declaring truth immanent to our limited state of theoretical knowledge. Traditional fields of philosophising like epistemology are now a subset of the scientific enterprise and truth coincides with the natural progression of science. Quine writes:

---

[343] See Quine, *Word and Object*, 19; W. V. O. Quine, "On Simple Theories of a Complex World," in *The Ways of Paradox*, 242-245.
[344] Quine, *From Stimulus to Science*, 87.

"Have we now so far lowered our sights as to settle for a relativistic doctrine of truth – rating the statements of each theory as true for that theory, and brooking no higher criticism? Not so. The saving consideration is that we continue to take seriously our own particular aggregate science, our own particular world-theory or loose total fabric of quasi-theories, whatever it may be. Unlike Descartes, we own and use our beliefs of the moment, even in the midst of philosophizing."[345]

Meaning is therefore very much a matter of *use*. Quine is here echoing the scepticism of Hume who took habits, customs and human nature to be the justification of inference and not in the experiences themselves.[346] He interprets his naturalised epistemology to be a further move in the direction of naturalism than anything envisioned by Hume.[347]

Recall that Russell's Cartesianism existed in the form of acquaintance where the identity and logical conditions of those objects of knowledge were the real underlying essence upon which were cloaked particular sense data such as seeing red, etc. These essences are immediately and internally accessible. Essential to understanding Quine is to recognise that he is forcefully opposing such a picture. Later, when we discuss his "Two Dogmas of Empiricism", we will see that logical and identity conditions are externalised for Quine, and the philosopher is in the – *ideal* – position of conforming behaviourally to such conditions.

Quine rejects propositions and so his particular form of disquotational truth is of the sentential kind. The strings of letters or phonemes, which are inherently meaningless in

---

[345] Quine, *Word and Object*, 24-25.

[346] See his "Response to Hookway," *Inquiry*, 37, (1994): 503. The normativity in our natures independent of facts and experience in Quine's system has parallels with William James' "The Will to Believe," Adelaide: ebooks@adelaide, 2014, accessed 28th July, 2019, https://ebooks.adelaide.edu.au/j/james/william/will/; see also Kant's "Ethics of Belief" and subsequent references in; Robert Hanna, "Kant's Theory of Judgment", *The Stanford Encyclopedia of Philosophy* (Winter 2018 Edition), Edward N. Zalta (ed.), URL = < https://plato.stanford.edu/entries/kant-judgment/supplement2.html>.

[347] He states; "Strawson rallies to the naturalism, as he calls it, of Hume and Wittgenstein. Their position is that belief in external objects is ingrained in human nature and is never really suspended, the skeptics pretensions notwithstanding. It is not open to doubt or, therefore, to substantiation.

If this dismissal of the problem is felt to be lame, I would suggest that the feeling can be relieved by taking a more fully naturalistic stance." W. V. O. Quine, "Four Hot Questions in Philosophy," in *New York Review of Books*, 32, no. 2 (1985). https://www.nybooks.com/articles/1985/02/14/four-hot-questions-in-philosophy/

themselves, derive their meaning elsewhere. (This is the source of the various use–mention confusions). That elsewhere is the physical world and the arrangement of physical states. He writes:

"Both ['Two Dogmas'] and…'The problem of meaning in linguistics', reflected a dim view of the notion of meaning. A discouraging response from somewhat the fringes of philosophy has been that my problem comes of taking words as bare strings of phonemes rather than seeing that they are strings with meaning. Naturally, they say, if I insist on meaningless strings I shall be at a loss for meanings. They fail to see that a bare and identical string of phonemes can have a meaning, or several, in one or several languages, through its use by sundry people or peoples, much as I can have accounts in several banks and relatives in several countries without somehow containing them or being several persons…. I hope this paragraph has been superfluous for most readers."[348]

Thus meaning is derived purely externally and comes about by circling closer and closer to the idealised ontological level – the level of factuality – but never quite getting there. And indeed getting there does not proceed through mental representations. In later sections we will see that this is the lesson taught by his famous doctrines of the indeterminacy of translation, the inscrutability of reference and ontological relativity. What this means, however, is that Quine wants us to maintain a kind of scientific form of virtue epistemology[349] in conforming to a level that physics at least professes to attain. This is what his behaviourism is meant to do and the process by which sentences are infused with meaning (and truth). Our ontology and the level of factuality must discard the particularity inherent in individual facts, but must conform purely by non-cognitive (at least in the mentalistic sense) behavioural disposition to "what minimum catalogue of states would be sufficient to justify us in saying that there is no change without a change in positions or states."[350]

---

[348] W. V. O. Quine, *From a Logical Point of View* 2nd rev. ed. (Cambridge, MA: Harvard University Press, 1980), viii.
[349] A good case is made for Quine's virtue epistemology by Abrol Fairweather, "Duhem-Quine Virtue Epistemology," *Synthese* 187, no. 2, (2012): 673-692. https://doi.org/10.1007/s11229-010-9868-2
[350] W. V. O. Quine, *Essays on the Philosophy of W. V. O. Quine* (Norman: University of Oklahoma Press, 1979) p. 167. Quoted in Gaudet, *Quine on Meaning*, 17.

Along with his rejection of Cartesian dualism, Quine repudiates "mental entities" on scientific grounds. Instead he identifies the mind with the body, but it is an interesting question as to just *how* he does this. He writes:

"Every mental event reflects some bodily one…. [But] it becomes a flagrant breach of…Ockham's maxim of parsimony to admit mind as a second substance at all…. Better to drop the duplication and just recognize mental activity as part of the activity of the body. It is only thus, indeed, that the enigma of mind–body interaction is disposed of."[351]

Despite the ontological identification, however, there is no identification in meaning. Mentalistic predicates and intentions are distinct in meaning from physiological classifications:

"Mental events are physical, but mentalistic language classifies them in ways incommensurable with the classifications expressible in physiological language."[352]

Putting this altogether, what we have with Tarskian sentences and their mentalistic correlates is a picture of *grounding.* Sentences *are* true but only in a derived sense; truth is found ultimately further up-stream in the *process* of learning by social inculcation.[353] An analogy will help. Seated Socrates is an accidental state grounded in the substance that is Socrates. It derives its identity asymmetrically from Socrates. If Socrates was no longer, then so would seated Socrates, but if seated Socrates was no longer, Socrates would still remain. The state of seated Socrates is also contingent vis-à-vis Socrates, who could have existed in any number of other states, such as running Socrates or standing Socrates. The truth and meaning of sentences are the analogue of such accidental states. A sentence may

---

[351] Quine, *Quiddities*, 132.
[352] Ibid, 133.
[353] "We learn to understand and use and create sentences only by learning conditions for the truth of such sentences." Quine, *Roots of Reference*, 78-79. And childhood learning of observation sentences, "is simply a matter of learning the circumstances in which those sentences count as true." Ibid, 79.

be true or false in the way that Socrates may be in a state of being seated or standing. Its truth-value is derived from factuality in the way that seated Socrates would owe its existence to Socrates.

Likewise, definitionally, the meanings of predicates, owing to their very nature *as* predicates, are dependent on their subjects. The predicates owe their existence to their subject, but they have no claim on that subject in any way that could be construed as the subject necessitating the state (as opposed to some other state) represented by the predicate. In the same way, for Quine meanings are not reducible to physical states although they are dependent on them. Mental states are realised in physical states.

For Quine, the identity conditions of each individual sentence is dependent on the ultimate being which is inherent to nature. However, ultimate being is in no sense dependent on or answerable to the individual identity conditions laid out in any particular sentence. It is an asymmetric grounding relation where meaning and truth is conferred on otherwise meaningless sentences through our dispositions and behaviour as truth seekers. In this way we can see *why* Quine states that the sentence points directly to reality. The pointing is the dependency condition.

The foundation of much of Quine's thinking is the external world of physics, where the ultimate underlying conditions are as clear and simple as possible. In other words, it is a pure state of univocality to which our scientific stance is always reaching and upon which the truth of each sentence holistically depends.

This is the true use to which Quine employs quantification. This is how we sort out whether the quantifier should be used in an objectual or substitutional manner. He writes:

"The variable of the 'such that' construction, which is in effect the relative pronoun, is a substitutional variable at its inception. The words 'is a thing x such that' are learned by an equivalence transformation that is explicitly substitutional in character. And this variable, surely, is the variable at its most primitive. It is a regimentation of the relative pronoun. Variables begin as substitutional."[354]

It is only in the initial phases of language learning that the variable and the quantifier are used substitutionally, which means the initial emphasis is on expressions, often names, that can be substituted for the variable. This may seem to work initially, but with regard to statements like "an orange is a fruit" or "a dog is a canine" are we really employing names for each individual dog or orange? Hence it is unworkable to build a quantificational device such that the truth of such statements is dependent on our having names and descriptions for objects when clearly most of the objects we quantify do not.

After this, however, "an irreducible leap in language"[355] occurs. It is in the employment of the "such that" clauses that the variable moves to the objectual state. This is the vital move outwards from the particular to the more general, with the guiding power of *use* extrapolating reference out of univocal being. The in-built generality of the quantifier acts like a promissory note to accompany the variables with progressively more general and simple predicates in language learning and maturing. Quine describes this progress:

"Our theory of nature grades off from the most concrete fact to speculations about the curvature of space-time, or the continuous creation of space-time, or the continuous creation of hydrogen atoms in an expanding universe; and our evidence grades off correspondingly, from specific observation to broadly systematic considerations. Existential quantifications of the philosophical sort belong to the same inclusive theory and are situated way out at the end, farthest from observable fact."[356]

---

[354] Quine, *Roots of Reference*, 99.
[355] Ibid.
[356] W. V. O. Quine, "Existence and Quantification," in *Ontological Relativity*, 98.

It's not clear, however, that the predicates of ordinary empirical usage are dispensable. They serve as a necessary guide, somewhat like signposts on the way to further explication. As Quine states, our limited epistemic state means:

"… our questioning of objects can coherently begin only in relation to a system of theory which is itself predicated on our interim acceptances of objects. We are limited in how we can start even if not in where we may end up."[357]

This is the "meagre input" of our sensory stimulations which mysteriously gets converted into the "torrential output" of theorising via the dispositions of verbal behaviour.[358] This move is analogous to the move from the inexhaustible state of Socrates to the torrent of accidental states of Socrates such as seated Socrates, running Socrates and so on. This is the dependency of our sensory states, and meaning in general, on the being that coordinates the natural world. It is in such an accidental state that explains why meaning goes indeterminate – and attains the status of a "myth" – for Quine. Thus the reconstructive nature of Quinean ontology is reflected in the aforementioned ontological order and consequentially, for Quine:

"To vary Neurath's figure with Wittgenstein's, we may kick away our ladder only after we have climbed it…the proposition that external things are ultimately to be known only through their action on our bodies should be taken as one among various coordinate truths, in physics and elsewhere, about initially unquestioned physical things. It qualifies the empirical meaning of our talk of physical things, while not questioning the reference."[359]

Thus I started this section by pointing out that Quine assumes a Cartesian view of the mind at least for dialectical purposes. What he is stressing in this passage is that we are stuck in such a Cartesian state although we may *act* in accordance with the naturalistic virtues; in such a way as to move according to the epistemological goals of simplicity and clarity in

---

[357] Quine, *Word and Object*, 4.
[358] Quine, "Epistemology Naturalized," in *Ontological Relativity*, 83.
[359] Quine, *Word and Object*, 3-4.

theory and it is in such a state that mental entities attain merely accidental – epiphenomenal status. It is the acting in such a way that conforms to the goals of simplicity and clarity which are ideally embodied in physics and expressed through first-order logic with identity. Mental entities lack referential power owing to their derived ontological status.

Quine puts Parmenidian being in the natural world, and from it we derive our mental states and correspondingly our sentences are mere accidents of such being. *This* is how he qualifies empiricism whilst not questioning the reference, and this is how he is ultimately able to "kick away" any need for a Cartesian mental structure – by reconstructing knowledge naturalistically.

ii) The Analytic-Synthetic Distinction and Indeterminacy

We saw early in this chapter that Leibnizian analyticity is based on the law of identity. The positivists, however, such as A. J. Ayer, accepted the basic notion of analyticity, but not Kant's notion of the synthetic a priori. Ayer insisted that the likes of math and logic had nothing to do with the forms of reality as Kant saw it. Instead, Ayer took these disciplines to be completely devoid of factual content. So something like:

1) $2 + 2 = 4$

would be equivalent to:

2) $a = a$

Such identity statements are devoid of factual information and thus can be known independently of experience. Hence analyticity, for Ayer, is the grounds for a priority. So "a proposition is analytic when its validity depends solely on the *definitions* of the symbols it contains."[360] He concludes that "analytic propositions are necessary and certain...the reason why these cannot be confuted in experience is that they do *not* make any assertions about the external world."[361] A priori knowledge being devoid of factual content remains purely a matter of use and assertion.

Now such a notion of analyticity, and with it the Cartesian basis for knowledge and scepticism about the outside world, comes under heavy fire by Quine in his famous paper "The Two Dogmas of Empiricism". We have already seen that he proposes a naturalist conception of language and hence dismisses the view that meanings are mental entities. Along these lines Quine employs a number of arguments to undercut the identity conditions of such mental entities. But such arguments draws on a number of key assumptions, which were explored in the previous section. These assumptions can be summed up as the following: the relation between language and the world is a product of externalised behavioural conditions that involves engaging in the scientific enterprise in accordance with theoretical virtues that seek out a conception of the world that is maximally general and simple and in accordance with first-order logic with identity.

So how does the naturalist account of language lead to a rejection of the analytic–synthetic distinction? First let us consider an example that relies on the meanings of the words alone:

1) Bachelors are unmarried males

Because this isn't a mere tautology, like "no unmarried man is married", then we have to rely on the notion of synonymy to give us Kant's notion of analyticity. But using synonymy as a criterion for analyticity is of no help to Quine, since it is no clearer than the notion of analyticity itself.

---

[360] Ayer, *Language, Truth, and Logic*, 78.
[361] Ibid, 84.

The problem is that individual meanings have no real identity criteria outside individual overt behavior (and such behaviour is the real source of identity since it puts people into consonance with canonical logic). This is the key assumption Quine makes. One way he brings this out is through the *indeterminacy of translation* which he expresses as:

"Manuals for translating one language into another can be set up in divergent ways, all compatible with the totality of speech dispositions, yet incompatible with one another."[362]

Suppose a field linguist is trying to learn the language of a particular tribe that has never been encountered or communicated with before. Can there be any conidence there is only one way of translating a given expression of that language into English? Quine's answer is no. There may be multiple ways the translation could go that fits with observable behaviour. There is no one correct translation.

For example, the field linguist may observe a situation where "a rabbit scurries by, the native says 'gavagai' and the linguist notes down the sentence 'rabbit' (or 'Lo, a rabbit') as tentative translation, subject to testing in further cases".[363] But when the native points to the rabbit there is no way of knowing by ostension whether the translation should be "rabbit" or, say, "undetached rabbit part".[364] There is no independent tribunal for deciding the correct translation or the correct reference for that matter. There is indeterminacy of translation *and* inscrutability of reference.[365]

This is the logical outcome of his physicalism and the fact that those physical states can assume different translatable states. He asks: "what excuse could there be for supposing that

---

[362] Quine, *Word and Object*, 27. Elsewhere he states the motivation for *indeterminacy*: "What I have challenged is just an ill-conceved notion within traditional semantics, namely, sameness of meaning" W. V. O. Quine, "Indeterminacy of Translation Again" in *Philosophy of Language: The Central Topics*, ed. Susana Nuccetelli and Gary Seay (Lanham: Rowman and Littlefield Publishers, 2008), 10.
[363] Quine, *Word and Object*, 29.
[364] Quine, "Ontological Relativity," in *Ontological Relativity*, 30-31.
[365] On the inscrutability of reference, see ibid, 35 and Quine, *Word and Object*, 51-52 and W. V. O. Quine, "Meaning and Translation," in *On Translation*, ed. R. A. Brower (Cambridge, MA: Harvard University Press, 1959), 153.

the one manual conformed to any distribution of elementary physical states better than the other manual?"[366] So far this may seem rather innocuous from an ontological perspective. But it certainly is not. Quine's conclusion about the nature of language is to say that the indeterminacy prevents any *reifications* of meanings that go above and beyond behavioural dispositions.[367] Even if we settle for one of the many theories that underdetermine the data it does not help. Quine writes:

"However, suppose that we have settled for one of the many over-all theories of nature that fit all possible observation. Translation remains indeterminate, even relative to the chosen theory of nature. Thus the indeterminacy of translation is an indeterminacy additional to the underdetermination of nature."[368]

This means that for any given set of theories, although they may fit all the observations, they are not determined by behaviour and hence they are demoted from the primary realm of being.[369] To revert back to our example, seated Socrates isn't determined by Socrates since it is not part of the essence that makes up Socrates. The former imposes no metaphysical constraints on the latter. Socrates could equally have determined an alternative accidental state like running Socrates. Hence like accidents, surface irritations and mental entities are excluded from the realm of fundamental being.

It is on the basis of meaning indeterminacy that Quine is sceptical of any attempt to clarify the relation of synonymy. Nor will any dictionary be of help in knowing that "bachelor" can be defined as "unmarried man", since that amounts to an appeal to past behaviour:

---

[366] W. V. O. Quine, "Facts of the Matter," in Follesdale, et al, *Confessions*, 284.
[367] Others that interpret Quine's indeterminism as a result of his physicalism/behaviourism are; Michael Friedman, "Physicalism and the Indeterminacy of Translation," *Nous*, 9, no. 4 (1975): 353-374, http://doi.org/10.2307/2214520; John Searle, "Indeterminacy, Empiricism, and the First Person," *The Journal of Philosophy* 84, no. 3 (1987): http://doi.org/10.2307/2026595; Roger Gibson, "Willard Van Orman Quine," in *The Cambridge Companion to Quine*, ed. R. F. Gibson, 1-18. (New York: Cambridge University Press, 2004)
[368] Quine, "Indeterminacy of Translation Again" in Nuccetelli et al, *Philosophy of Language*, 67.
[369] On mental entities he states quite poignantly; "Two men could be just alike in all their dispositions to verbal behaviour under all possible sensory stimulations, and yet the meanings or ideas expressed in their identically triggered and identically sounded utterances could diverge radically, for the two men, in a wide range of cases." Quine, *Word and Object,* 26. Later in that same work he goes so far as denouncing "the baselessness of intentional idioms and the emptiness of a science of intention" (221)

"Clearly this would be to put the cart before the horse. The lexicographer is an empirical scientist, whose business is the recording of antecedent facts; and if he glosses 'bachelor' as 'unmarried man' it is because of his belief that there is a relation of synonymy between those forms, implicit in general or preferred usage prior to his own. The notion of synonymy presupposed here has still to be clarified, presumably in terms relating to linguistic behavior."[370]

So all statements, including analytic ones, are true ultimately by virtue of third-person usage and not first-person meaning.[371] This also means that language is ultimately a "social art" and any notions of meanings as internal representations drop out of the picture. Indeed judgements cannot be made on the basis of semantically isolated units but must proceed holistically:

"My present suggestion is that it is nonsense, and the root of much more nonsense, to speak of a linguistic component and a factual component in the truth of any individual statement. Taken collectively, science has a double dependency upon language and experience; but this duality is not traceable into the statements of science taken one by one."[372]

And so "our statements about the external world face the tribunal of sense experience not individually, but as a *corporate body*."[373] Synthetic statements lie on the periphery of our belief web, while analytic ones lie in the centre. Hence we have a system of interconnected beliefs where:

---

[370] Quine, "Two Dogmas of Empiricism," in *From a Logical Point of View*, 24.
[371] In fact Quine's proposal is so radical that it takes away one's authority over one's own words and meanings as Itay Shani points out; "For, given Quine's picture, agent and interpreter alike have nothing to rely on save for correlations between sensory stimuli and behavioural responses, a fact which makes the agent an 'interpreter' of her own words who, for that matter, is in no better condition than any other interpreter." "The Whole Rabbit: On the Perceptual Roots of Quine's Indeterminacy Puzzle," *Philosophical Psychology*, 22, no. 6, (2009): 744. https://doi.org/10.1080/09515080903409960
[372] Quine, "Two Dogmas of Empiricism," in *From a Logical Point of View*, 42.
[373] Ibid, 41.

"... total science is like a field of force whose boundary conditions are experience. A conflict with experience at the periphery occasions readjustments in the interior of the field. Truth values have to be redistributed over some of our statements. Reevaluation of some statements entails reevaluation of others, because of their logical interconnections..."[374]

This means that the distinction between analytic and synthetic statements is somewhat arbitrary and subject to pragmatic goals:

"Even a statement very close to the periphery can be held true in the face of recalcitrant experience by pleading hallucination or by amending certain statements of the kind called logical laws. Conversely, by the same token, no statement is immune to revision. Revision even of the logical law of the excluded middle [analytic] has been proposed as a means of simplifying quantum mechanics". [375]

Quine's attack on the a priori – a posteriori distinction is part and parcel of his case against first philosophy, and against Cartesian scepticism of the external world. The individual knower is now no longer subject to an internally based system of knowledge founded on the a priori, but becomes merely a bit player – along with their system of knowledge – amongst natural external forces. Thus anything once thought to be a priori – mathematical statements or the laws of logic – are fair game for scepticism. This means no presumption of a priori knowledge can be made, but the presumption is one of knowers already embedded in a naturalistic world explained scientifically.

But there is nothing here to suggest that Quine has surmounted the unbridgeable gulf between the inner Cartesian world of the knowing subject and the outside world of mechanistic forces. Instead of a refutation of scepticism the natural epistemologist assumes its falsity. This is since "the naturalized epistemologist comes out with an account that has a great deal to do with language learning, and with the neurology of perception."[376]

---
[374] Ibid, 42.
[375] Ibid, 43.
[376] Quine, "Five Milestones of Empiricism," in *Theories and Things*, 72.

Elsewhere he appeals to the intelligibility of terms like "reality" and "evidence" as void of meaning without application to the external world.[377]

But this is hardly a surprising result given his metaphysical assumptions, which actually significantly circumscribe the ability of science to investigate the mind-independent world. The Cartesian substantial self and its representations – including terms such as "reality" and "evidence" – bear no essential connection with the outside world. Instead it is the pragmatic necessity of maintaining the simplicity and equilibrium of the theoretical framework of our web of belief – the "maxim of minimum mutilation"[378] – that finds connection with the outside world at the periphery. The substantial thinking self is borne along by those forces totally unrelated to its mental states and not intelligibly connected to its behavioural dispositions.

Quine appears to have no real solution to scepticism.[379] The solution he does propose seems like little more than question begging. Indeed, thought experiments like the indeterminacy of translation seem to guarantee some form of scepticism. Along these lines, Roger Gibson reports on Putnam's position that the "water" in the Ship of Neurath parable resembles something like a Kantian "noumena".[380] In response, Gibson argues that this comparison is false for the simple reason that there is no room for a noumena in Quine's naturalistic world. This misses the essence of the objection, however, which is that the naturalistic world is one that is completely orthogonal to the characteristics of the world delivered to our mental faculties. One could describe Quine's monistic physical world as an analogue to

---

[377] See, for example, quotes like "Having noted that man has no evidence for the existence of bodies beyond the fact that their assumption helps him organize his experience, we should have done well, instead of disclaiming evidence for the existence of bodies, to conclude: such then, at bottom, is what evidence is, both for ordinary bodies and for molecules." W. V. O. Quine, "Posits and Reality," in *The Ways of Paradox*, 233-241.
[378] Quine, *Philosophy of Logic*, 7.
[379] Similar criticisms have been made in the past. For example, Barry Stroud writes:
"What I have meant to deny, with Kant, is that we can regard all our beliefs about the world as 'projections' or as 'theoretical' relative to some 'data' or bits of 'evidence' epistemically prior to them, while at the same time explaining how our knowledge of the world is possible… Quine's project of naturalized epistemology has the interest and the apparent connection with traditional epistemology that it has only because it contains and depends upon such a bi-partite conception of human knowledge of the world. That is what I have argued cannot succeed in explaining how knowledge is possible. But without that conception, 'naturalized epistemology' as Quine describes it would be nothing but the causal explanation of various physiological events." *The Significance of Philosophical Scepticism* (Oxford: Oxford University Press, 1984), 253.
[380] Gibson, "The Key to Interpreting Quine,"

Kant's noumena: "…the proper construal of 'fact of the matter' is neither methodological (i.e. epistemological) nor transcendental; it is naturalistic and physicalistic."

The mental patterns in our minds that seem so integral to our states of knowing – and which inspired Kant's categories – do not relate in any internal sense with the natural world as Quine conceives it and so are rendered epiphenomenal at best or completely eliminable at worst. Indeed the "otherness" of the noumenal world vis-à-vis the phenomenal world – in not having any capacity to make the distinctions delivered by the categories – may be closer to the true spirit of Putnam's objection.

So at the heart of the scepticism towards the analytic–synthetic distinction in the "Two Dogmas" lies Quine's naturalism and ultimately the metaphysical structure where simple, univocal, ultimate being does not uniquely determine any one intensional state. And by its very nature it cannot make such distinctions. Hence the problems that arose for Quine regarding the indeterminacy of translation manuals and scepticism towards intensional states should be no surprise.

The real appeal of Quine's system must ultimately rest on the metaphysical categories he assumes – which he derives ultimately from Parmenides – and the reader has to infer these categories, as Quine does not argue for them. But the heart of Quine's boast was that he did not assume any first philosophy but instead made way for the theoretical advances of science. Thus in assuming metaphysical categories, his system is in danger of contradiction at its core. Additionally, the removal of intensional states and the facts of immediate correspondence must be seen as a negative, since it is a denial of the immediate data of our experience instead of an explanation of it. Russell argued forcefully for the reality of such mental states on the basis of our privileged access to them. So it must count as a virtue for any theory to explain and preserve them rather than follow Quine in eliminating them.

Conclusion

In this chapter, we have situated Carnap firmly within the Frege–Russell tradition by noting his emphasis on employing the Fregean logical apparatus as the structure that grounds the auto-psychological empirical data in the justification of knowledge. In this way, empirical knowledge is not taken at face value but is reconstructed according to the logical machinery of Frege and Russell.

But the question that needs to be asked is whether this whole project can succeed? I have argued that Quine was right that it cannot, but the reason I set out is consistent with the interpretative slant I took to the *LSW*, namely that the Frege–Russell logical machinery lacks the capacity to remove the "is at" connective precisely because it lacks the means to specify the locations of sense data that go together to make up any given object of reference. Such a lack means that the Frege–Russell project cannot make the reconstruction and thus cannot justify any individual instance of empirical knowledge. This also means that Parmenidian being, the Archimedean point upon which knowledge construction was taken to turn for Frege and Russell, fails as an adequate account of the world of sense experience.

The final chapters of this thesis will explicate alternative categories that derive from experience rather than attempting any reconstruction of knowledge. It will not require any radical revision to our ontology by replacing intensional states with its physical substrates. Indeed we saw in the last chapter that Russell argued that our mental states are known in a privileged manner, so surely it is a bonus for an ontology that retains this in agreement with common sense. The last chapters provide an account of knowledge where access to the outside world is not threatened by a radical dualism reminiscent of Kantian scepticism. One in which the categories are not univocal and thus can justify individual knowledge states on the basis of isomorphism through our immediate perceptions.

I have tried to paint a picture of Quine's metaphysics and his naturalistic efforts to reconstruct the relation between our language and the world and have hopefully achieved two key goals. First, I have shown that there are metaphysical assumptions – most notably that of substance and accident – that play key roles in Quine's conceptual scheme. These are ultimately symbolic of the entire structure of his metaphysic, which is that our knowing states are situated in a naturalistic realm of Parmenidian being. Crucially, these assumptions are not drawn from scientific conclusions. They are antecedently assumed and used to circumscribe the application conditions of scientific theories – as well as logic and mathematics – to extend no further than the interlocking web of belief. It thus turns out that Quine has not escaped first philosophy after all and, like Frege and Russell, must be a follower of Parmenidian metaphysics.

My second key goal was to expose the yawning metaphysical gulf between our world of mental representations and that of the univocal state of being as set out in Quine's first-order logic with identity. The normative, goal oriented scientific endeavour embodied in such virtues as simplicity tie his entire ontology to a deflationary definition of existence that is in stark contrast to our world of experience. Thus intensional states are subject to scepticism, but this stands or falls on the basis of assumptions Quine makes. Later, alternative categories will be presented that do not eliminate the entities so basic to our epistemic situation.

Chapter Four - David Lewis and the Ontology of Part–Wholes

Introduction

We saw in the previous chapters that the most basic principles of being for Frege, Russell, Carnap and Quine were thoroughly Parmenidian; that is, being in the most fundamental and primitive sense is essentially unitary and monistic and thus not derived from sense experience. And for Frege and Russell, the very *act* of doing metaphysics is an expression of such being. With Frege it was the act of assertion, whereas with Russell it was in the act of naming the object of acquaintance. Carnap attempted to marry these two systems but failed, and Quine applied being to the naturalistic world and drew attention to some of the consequences of the Frege–Russell system.

The work of the most significant metaphysician of the last 50 years, David Lewis, is a continuation of this tradition. By no means will all of Lewis' vast corpus of work be examined but only his work in mereology. It is here that his Parmenidian assumptions come to the fore. Lewis, like Frege, takes *identity* to be a core principle that is also simple. And as is evident from one of his key principles, Composition As Identity, identity also plays a unifying role and grounds the parthood relationship.

Whilst I intend to present and critique Lewis in this tradition there are elements of his system that I will preserve in my final chapters. Specifically, I intend to preserve the intimacy of the parthood relation. The principles of composition I will present in my final chapters marry part and whole together such that the dependence of each is symmetrical. The main difference I intend to highlight is Lewis' reliance on identity and his holding that the parthood relation is fundamental.

At the heart of Lewis' system is a dualism of form and content that we should be familiar with from the previous chapters. This is a dualism he inherits from Parmenides: a distinction between the fundamental, non-empirically accessed world of being and the world accessed by the senses. The world of senses, for Lewis, is thoroughly Humean which means there are no necessary connections between objects in the world. This is especially apparent in the case of composition since there is nothing in the physical objects themselves that necessitates joining together into more natural wholes to the exclusion of more gerrymandered wholes.

Parts go together to make up a whole in the same way that any object is identical with itself. This is the principle of identity Lewis inherits chiefly from Frege. Identity is simple and unitary and individuates entities and characterises their relation to their parts. The part–whole relations we observe empirically are only accessed by description, and such descriptions are mere epistemic characterisations that do not touch the heart of what it means to be a unitary, self-identical entity.

For Lewis the medium for the expression of being is the *singleton* which, when forming a whole, the class of singletons are nothing over and above each singleton taken as a part. But given the unitary and monolithic nature of all singletons, there is nothing inherent in them that prevents them from applying to any conceivable part–whole relation across the universe. The same monolithic conception of being means that there cannot be any ambiguity or vagueness in composition, a thesis brought out by Lewis in various thought experiments.

But there are several reasons to call into doubt Lewis's ontology and system of composition. First, the notion of Unrestricted Composition, and its application of the parthood relation flies in the face of empirical reality. Rather than being a consistent application of the primitive parthood relation and the truth-functional connectives of first-order logic, we should see it as a *reductio ad absurdum* of the whole Frege–Russell–Quine method of ontology. Second, I argue, in agreement with Wittgenstein, that the identity relation is an empty notion and that the many and varied part–whole relations we observe are just the arrangement of parts observed empirically. Often such relations require being juxtaposed in just the right way and requiring just the right material contents.

Lastly I explore an objection from Peter van Inwagen that we should quantify over wholes as distinct entities to their parts. I take issue throughout this chapter with any conception of a whole that is distinct from its parts. I will, in this chapter, highlight an assumption in Lewis that I will oppose in my own metaphysic: that parts are the values of variables that do not change identity as they enter into a whole for the simple reason that the identity condition is a primitive in Lewis' system of plural logic.

Rounding out the chapter, I give examples of how composition occurs in the real world, involving parts coming together to form macro-emergent entities which have properties that cannot be read off from their material constituents conceived separately. This is not a conception of the whole that is distinct from the parts, however, for a very simple reason that the parts themselves *become* aspects of the whole. This will point the way in later chapters for principles of composition that are more fundamental than the identity relation and the part–whole relation, so that what it means *to be* and *compose* an entity will not just be a simple product of Parmenidian being applied within the system of quantificational logic. On the contrary, the identity of entities will give way to my three proposed categories of being and the part–whole relation will be a product of the application of these principles.

Lewis the Humean

David Lewis was one of the most important metaphysicians of the last 50 years. His fundamental metaphysic was Humean Supervenience (HS), which basically states that all reality is the product of basic spatio-temporal distributions of local natural properties.[381] Here is Lewis' formulation:

"… in a world like ours, the fundamental relations are exactly the spatiotemporal relations: distance relations, both spacelike and timelike, and perhaps also occupancy relations between point-sized things and space-time points. In a world like ours, the fundamental properties are local qualities: perfectly natural intrinsic properties of points, or of point-sized occupants of points…all else supervenes on the spatiotemporal arrangement of local qualities throughout all of history, past and present and future."[382]

---

[381] See his David Lewis, *On the Plurality of Worlds* (Oxford: Blackwell, 1986); David Lewis, "Humean Supervenience Debugged," *Mind,* 103, no. 412, (1994): 474, http://www.jstor.org/stable/2254396.
[382] Ibid.

Lewis isn't prepared to accept that everything just is as it appears to be. Most objects that we come across in the world are fleeting and only superficially real. Everything at the most fundamental level is ultimately made up of smaller, much more durable objects. Lewis positions many of his key theses – on subjects such as causation, chance, counterfactual dependence, etc. – within HS, but it is his mereology and theory of part–whole that is of particular interest in this thesis.

One particularly useful example is the picture that supervenes on its pixels.[383] Take any particular painting, the picture is a product of the arrangement and intrinsic properties of the pixels (most obviously the colours). So for any pictorial depiction of the Mona Lisa, for example, once you have that particular arrangement of pixels, you automatically have the Mona Lisa. So to have the macroproperties of the painting just is to have – is nothing over and above – the base qualities of the bits and pieces of paint and their arrangement.

Now Lewis is vague on what it is that are the points in the mosaic.[384] This may well be to leave the door open to further discoveries from physics that may undermine what we think we know about fundamental physics. But as for the local qualities, Lewis takes a quality to be a perfectly natural property and truths about any particular world to supervene on the natural properties and their relations.[385] One example might be a classical electron which, at least at one time, was thought of as point-sized. It also has natural properties – such as mass, charge and spin – that would qualify it as being part of the fundamental make up of ordinary entities. So a description of the fundamental qualities and the equations of physics gives you a description of everything that is physical. As Daniel Nolan puts it:

---

[383] David Lewis, "Reduction of Mind," in *Papers in Metaphysics and Epistemology*, vol 2, ed. David Lewis, 291-324. (Cambridge, New York: Cambridge University Press, 1999)
[384] David Lewis, "Introduction," *Philosophical Papers* vol. 2 (Oxford: Oxford University Press, 1986), X.
[385] David Lewis, "New Work for a Theory of Universals," *Australasian Journal of Philosophy*, 61, no. 4, (1983): 343-377, https://doi.org/10.1080/00048408312341131; David Lewis, "Putnam's Paradox," in *Papers in Metaphysics and Epistemology*, 56-77.

"Specify the values of the electromagnetic field and the mass function at every point in space and time, in accord with the constraints given by the equations of physics, and you would have specified the entire fundamental physical description."[386]

As the name suggests, HS comes from the Humean notion that there are no necessary connections in the world, that everything is "entirely loose and separate" and that there is no way to "observe any tie between them."[387] But this vast mosaic is overladen with the mereological connections between things that stand in contrast to the contingent point-like spatiotemporal relations between the qualities. Lewis' view of the part–whole is extremely promiscuous: whenever there is more than one thing, there exists a whole out of which those things are parts. But although the arrangement of qualities is contingent, the part–whole relation is necessary, so that however those arrangements turn out, it is necessarily the case that the wholes they make up must also exist.

Parthood and Mereology

A special intimacy between a thing and its parts is assumed throughout Lewis' work. This is intuitively compelling, drawing from Moorean facts about the observational world. My legs, arms, torso and head are intimately connected to me in ways that the hydrogen gas in the Andromeda galaxy is not. Theodore Sider draws on comparisons between relations like these:

- "I own this car
- My hitting the ball caused the window to shatter
- I am taller than my mother
- I am friends with Ned Markosian

---

[386] Daniel Nolan, *David Lewis* (Chesham: Acumen Publishing, 2005), 30.
[387] David Hume, *An Enquiry Concerning Human Understanding* (Oxford: Oxford University Press, 1975), 74.

- My fingertip is three feet from my shoulder"[388]

None of these relations seem particularly special to the subject. Contrast them with these statements:

- My arm is part of me
- I am identical to me

There is something uniquely special about the parthood relation that is not the case with relations that are not intimately connected with the identity of the subject. I could easily have not hit the ball through the window or not been taller than my mother. But it is inconceivable that I could have been non-identical to myself, and it would be a great loss for me to lose my arm or to have been born without it. When war veterans return from service without a limb, we generally think that something of them is missing and say things like "he's a shadow of his former self". Our parts are integral to our identity.

Things existing loosely and separately may appear in tension with the necessity of identity,[389] and it is even harder still to see how such a world sanctions different things standing in an identity relation with a whole. Granted it would be objected by Lewis that the composing entities just are identical with the composed entity. But the identity is only analogous for Lewis, and, as we will see later, the identity relation is a conclusion Lewis draws too quickly.

Lewis lays out a framework with a conception of part–whole that fills in what is missing in his Humean worldview. Three thesis come together for him to derive standard set theory. They are mereology, plural logic and the singleton function.[390] The underlying assumption

---

[388] Theodore Sider, "Parthood," *Philosophical Review* 116, no.1, (2007): 54, http://www.jstor.org/stable/20446938.
[389] Saul Kripke, *Naming and Necessity* (Cambridge: Harvard University Press, 1980)
[390] David Lewis, *Parts of Classes* (Oxford: Blackwell, 1991)

for him is Composition As Identity (CAI), which basically states that a whole is identical with the parts that compose it. For him the parts of a class are not the parts of the ordinary concrete particulars that happen to be members of the class.[391] So my left leg is not a part of my singleton. Instead, the parts of a class are its sub-classes. For example, the singleton {a}, not a, is a part of the class {a, b}.

Composition for Lewis also finds expression in mereology, which he takes "to be perfectly understood, unproblematic, and certain".[392] First it will be useful to give Lewis' definition of "fusion" that defines the primitive parthood relation:

Definition: Something is a *fusion* of some things iff it has all of them as parts and has no part that is disjoint from each of them.[393]

After this, his three axioms of mereology are:

Axiom 1: (Transitivity) If x is part of some part of y, then x is part of y.

Axiom 2: (Unrestricted Composition [UC]) Whenever there are some things, then there exists a fusion of those things.

Axiom 3: (Uniqueness of Composition [UoC]) It never happens that the same things have two different fusions.[394]

These axioms are not all equally popular. Transitivity is a lot less controversial than UC and UoC.

---

[391] Ibid, 81-87.
[392] Ibid, 75.
[393] Ibid, 73.
[394] Ibid, 74.

UC can also be called *e pluribus unum* and gets signified as $\forall xx Ey\ xx=y$. This actually tells us a great deal about the metaphysical assumptions at the heart of mereology. Whenever there are a plurality of objects then each object within that plurality retains the same identity it had when it was singular. In other words, the identity of each particular is absolute. But this is just a case that the identity condition given in a proper name, x, is absolute and fundamental relative to any contingent circumstance it stands in vis-à-vis other objects in the empirical world.

For Russell, the act of proper naming is an expression of being which creates dilemmas when one expresses a proper name of an object that does not exist, such as "Pegasus".[395] But in mereology, the very fact that in *e pluribus unum* the x's remain x's when flanking the identity sign with the whole, y, is an indication that the same Parmenidian assumption is at work. In other words, the a priori conception of being assumed in the naming condition cannot be revoked or usurped by the being that is the whole made up of a collection or set of individuals in the world. To put it succinctly, an instance of being does not change when it becomes part of a whole.

As already alluded by Lewis' axioms of mereology, he regards the parthood relation as a primitive. The classic in this regard is Henry Leonard and Nelson Goodman's paper "The Calculus of Individuals and Its Uses".[396] They developed the definition of part in terms of disjointness, so the latter was taken as primitive. So for x to be disjoint from y just means that they have no part in common. However, the flipside of disjointness is overlap, and this became influential in the definition of parthood.[397] The definition of overlap is:

x overlaps $y =_{df}$ some part of x is part of y

---

[395] Bertrand Russell, "On Denoting," *Mind*, 14, no. 56, (1905): 479-493, http://www.jstor.org/stable/2248381.
[396] Henry Leonard and Nelson Goodman, "The Calculus of Individuals and Its Uses," *Journal of Symbolic Logic*, 5, no. 2, (1940): 45-55, https://doi.org/10.2307/2266169
[397] Peter Simons, on the other hand, takes the proper-part relation as primitive in *Parts: A Study in Ontology* (Oxford: Oxford University Press, 1987), 25-41.

Lewis takes the part–whole relation and identity as the limiting case of overlap. So for two objects that do not overlap, they share no part in common and are entirely distinct, whereas two objects sharing a part are not entirely distinct and partially overlap. If two objects entirely overlap, however, they are identical.[398] He explicitly credits his position on partial identity to David Armstrong and Donald Baxter, and gives the former's example of two terrace houses joined by the same wall as an example of partial overlap.[399]

On the basis of mereology the parthood relation is both reflexive and antisymmetric:

Reflexivity: $\forall x(Pxx)$

Antisymmetry: $\forall x \forall y[(Pxy \ \& \ Pyx) \rightarrow x = y]$

Now as mentioned, the parthood relation has been given as an overlap relation and in fact mereological principles have been analytically tied to location.[400] So a part can be defined as a *subregion* of the whole. This gives extra bite to the challenge to co-locationists who want to argue that two distinct objects, such as a statue and its marble, that do not share parts, can be located at exactly the same region.

There are other powerful arguments from mereology. Consider the Weak Extensionality Principle (WEP): no two objects that have proper parts have the same proper parts at the same time. Now overlap creates a dilemma for co-locationists who think, for example, that a statue and its lump are two coinciding objects. If we take the matter to persist as parts of the lump then there is no part of the statue that does not overlap its matter which would

---

[398] Lewis, *Parts of Classes*, 82-83.
[399] Ibid, 82-85.
[400] See Paul Oppenheim and Hilary Putnam, "Unity of Science as a Working Hypothesis," *Minnesota Studies in the Philosophy of Science* 2, (1958): 3-36, http://hdl.handle.net/11299/184622 and Ned Markhosian, "A Spatial Approach to Mereology," in *Mereology and Location*, ed. Shieva Kleinschmidt, 69-90 (Oxford: Oxford University Press, 2014). See also Lewis' "Inseparability of Location" mentioned in the next section.

seem to imply the statue and lump are identical. Hence two coinciding objects are impossible according to WEP.

Composition as Identity and the Land Sale Argument

UC has attracted controversy precisely because it states that whenever you have some things, any things, you have a sum of those things. So take a bunch of cats:

"Given a prior commitment to cats, say, a commitment to cat-fusions is not a *further* commitment. The fusion is nothing over and above the cats that compose it. It just *is* them. They just *are* it. Take them together or take them separately, the cats are the same portion of Reality either way …If you draw up an inventory of Reality according to your scheme of things, it would be double counting to list the cats and then also list their fusion …The new commitment is redundant, given the old one."[401]

This seems innocuous enough but it has quite bizarre consequences. Lewis' infamous example is the "trout-turkey" which is one thing made up of a trout and a turkey.[402] Lewis argues that it is wrongheaded to see these bizarre monsters lurking about everywhere under his ontology. The *ontological innocence* of composite entities, however, saves UC from such consequences, since it states that we do not really have one disfigured whole distinct from its parts at all. We have not committed ourselves to anything we were not already committed to before. So one of the reasons to accept ontological innocence is that it heads off the threat of UC profligacy.

CAI is supposed to have powerful intuitive appeal. When we stand up and walk around, our parts go with us. I can dispense with articles of clothing and still walk around and it is still

---

[401] Lewis, *Parts of Classes*, 81-82.
[402] Ibid, 7.

me, but it is not so easy for me to dispense with parts of myself. Lewis appeals to our intuitive grasp of such identities by a thought experiment he borrowed from Donald Baxter:

"Suppose a man owned some land which he divides into six parcels. Overcome with enthusiasm for [the denial of CAI] he might perpetrate the following scam. He sells off the six parcels while retaining ownership of the whole. That way he gets some cash while hanging on to his land. Suppose the six buyers of the parcels argue that they jointly own the whole and the original owner now owns nothing. Their argument seems right. But it suggests that the whole was not a seventh thing."[403]

It's hard to deny that the buyers are right. The owner is obviously trying to pull a scam by claiming the whole land is a seventh separate object. So Lewis draws the conclusion that since the six owners are right, *therefore* the owner owns nothing and thus the parts must be identical with the whole. Importantly, Lewis is not arguing for strict identity between parts and whole, the view that was originally advanced by Baxter.[404] But apart from Baxter, the strict view has had very few advocates for the simple reason that it violates Leibniz Law that states that if x and y are identical then every property had by x is had by y. Now by this criterion, a whole cannot be the same as its parts: a whole is one whilst its parts are many as Lewis explicitly acknowledges.[405] Lewis' alternative is an identity that is "strictly analogous".[406] But it is hard to understand exactly what Lewis means by this, which is especially troublesome given that a non-strict identity threatens to imperil UC and UoC: the connection between part and whole isn't strong enough to license innocence or to enforce the exclusive use of parts.

There are two more theses of ontological innocence I wish to mention, theses that, as Karen Bennett points out, can be considered to buttress Lewis' case rather than just being

---

[403] Donald Baxter, "Identity in the Loose and Popular Sense," *Mind* 97 (1988a): 597, quoted in Ibid, 83.
[404] Ibid, and Donald Baxter, "Many-One Identity," *Philosophical Papers* 17, no. 3, (1988b): 193-216, https://doi.org/10.1080/05568648809506300
[405] Lewis, *Parts of Classes*, 87.
[406] Ibid, 84. Peter Van Inwagen also recognizes an analogous form of compositional identity in "Composition as Identity," *Philosophical Perspectives* 8, (1994): 216-219, http://doi.org/10.2307/2214171.

constitutive of the definition of constitution as (analogous) identity.[407] Again, Lewis is priming our already intuitive recognition of part–whole intimacy:

Property Description: A description of the properties and interrelations of the parts is a description of the fusion. Specifying the location of the parts also specifies the location of the fusion. Lewis refers back to the land-sale argument and adds that specifying the ownership of the plots is just to specify the ownership of the original block.[408]

Inseparability of Location: Just as a thing can't be separated from itself so the whole cannot be separated from its parts. If two objects are identical then they occupy the same region of space-time.[409]

I find this account of the intimacy of parthood in Lewis compelling for the most part. I do not think there is anything to a whole that is above and beyond its parts. The issue is whether the constituents of a whole are the same objects in the parthood role as they were before. In other words, is it credible to maintain *e plurubus unum* in this form. Later in this chapter I will provide arguments against the view that the parthood relation is a primitive, pointing the way to more basic composition principles.

Plural Logic and Ontological Innocence

---

[407] Karen Bennett, "'Perfectly Understood, Unproblematic, and Certain': Lewis on Mereology," in *A Companion to David Lewis* ed. Barry Loewer and Jonathan Schaffer, 250-261 (Chichester: Wiley-Blackwell, 2015). But as Bennett and others have pointed out, there is a certain circularity to Lewis' definitions: CAI is taken to buttress ontological innocence but the latter is also taken to buttress the former (and UC); (Ibid, 257).
[408] Lewis, *Parts of Classes*, 85.
[409] Ibid, 85-86.

On the basis of CAI, we have a whole that is "nothing over and above its parts". If we have two plots of land, A and B, then the whole, C, does not make up a third distinct thing. In this case, on the right-hand side we have the four singletons which are the members related non-mereologically – meaning that there is an ontological cost incurred in singleton formation – to their singletons but their joining together, symbolised by +, *is* a mereological whole which is ontologically innocent. Symbolising the identity in such a way gives the nature of CAI.

So a mereological whole can be taken as an identity, such as the class being identical with the members' singletons:

$$\{a, b, c, d, \ldots\} = \{a\} + \{b\} + \{c\} + \{d\} + \ldots$$

There is no way of referring to a many-one identity statement under classical first-order logic. So there is no such identity statement that uses a distinct variable from the parts where the whole is identical to those parts. First-order grammatical rules prohibit one-many identity statements. Only single referring expressions, such as Eric Blair = George Orwell, are acceptable. Under Quine's influence, the quantifier is generally taken as ranging over whatever objects one is committed to, plus their fusion *as a separate* value. So for any two objects you have in the domain, you actually quantify over three objects (n objects, $2^n - 1$). Take something like: There is an a, b and c such that a is a proper part of c and b is a proper part of c then we have three distinct objects under first-order logic and not two. So a and b cannot be identical to c.

By contrast, with plural logic, variables such as xx can be read as composing a single object, such as X, without incurring any extra ontological commitment. Plural logic was developed by George Boolos in response to sentences that could not be expressed in first-order logic (such as the Geach–Kaplan sentence "There are some critics who only admire one another"). Boolos' goal was to quantify over entities in such a sentence without referring to any second-order entities like sets. He states his goal thus:

"The lesson to be drawn from the foregoing reflections on plurals and second-order logic is that neither the use of plurals nor the employment of second-order logic commits us to the existence of extra items beyond those to which we are already committed. We need not construe second-order quantifiers as ranging over anything other than the objects over which our first-order quantifiers range, and, in the absence of other reasons for thinking so, we need not think that there are collections of (say) Cheerios, in addition to the Cheerios. Ontological commitment is earned by our first-order quantifiers; a second-order quantifier needn't be taken to be a kind of first-order quantifier in disguise, having items of a special kind, collections, in its range. It is not as though there were two sorts of things in the world, individuals, and collections of them, which our first- and second-order variables, respectively, range over and which our singular plural forms, respectively, denote, here are, rather, two (at least) different ways of referring to the same things, among which there may well be many, many collections."[410]

Thus Lewis, employing plural logic, can move from the parts of a whole to the whole itself without having to commit to any further entity. Obviously this doesn't completely eliminate abstract objects for him, since he is still stuck with the singleton, which is a basic postulate. But it does mean that he can move from a plurality of singletons to a class of singletons without running up any further ontological cost.

Lewisian Dualism

---

[410] George Boolos, "To Be is to Be a Value of a Variable (or to Be Some Values of Some Variables)," *The Journal of Philosophy* 81, no. 8 (1984): 449, http://dx.doi.org/jphil198481840

The necessary principles which govern the intimate connections between parts and wholes do not, however, sit neatly in a Humean universe. Humean Supervenience denies necessary connections between distinct entities. Everything is built out of local properties that exhibit all their properties at that particular point, so there cannot be any dependence on another space-time point. An example: two trees existing two metres apart. There is nothing in the trees that necessitates their being in that relation. The only fundamental relations that exist are spatio-temporal and these operate on the fundamental properties of the points in space. This is the substance of Lewis' Humeanism, where the world conceived and given to us by empiricism contains just one thing and then another, where no ties can be observed between events and everything is loose and separate.

On such an empirical structure, the concepts of mereology and CAI are theoretical posits brought to bear on the world through the primitive parthood relation and the truth-functional connectives. It may seem obvious that CAI follows from Humean empiricism since the former stipulates that observing the parts implies nothing over and above those parts anyway. There is no requirement for necessary connections between objects that do not form a whole that is distinct from what they are as a collection taken separately, one by one. But as we will see the identity relation for Lewis has significant metaphysical bite and excludes other conceptual approaches to dividing up the world.

One prima facie obvious uneasy fit derives from observed adjacencies of the part–whole relation that display a coherence in contradistinction to their surroundings. When we observe a series of parts of a body – such as the torso, arms, legs, and head – we see a functional unity and coherence that sets it out as distinct from its surroundings. This distinction is not drawn by Lewis' definitions. Consider his infamous example of the trout-turkey:

"I never said, of course, that a trout-turkey is no different from an ordinary, much-heard-of thing. It is inhomogeneous, disconnected, and not in contrast with its surroundings. (Not along some of its borders.) It is not cohesive, not causally integrated, not a causal unit in its impact on the rest of the world. It is not carved at the joints. But none of that has any bearing on whether it exists."[411]

But this is as it should be according to Parmenidian principles of being. Unity is not essentially connected to how things in the empirical world function together. All that passes for existence is atomic unities, and any further thing that might be composed of them is by necessity less fundamental in the order of being. The unity is imposed on the world by a priori principles and not derived empirically.

Being then is an artificial fit owing to the orthogonal nature of the two domains. This is nicely illustrated in the assignment of singletons to any physical object where, say, the same rock can be divided into two different mereological sets covering the same object: one set covers three vertical parts where the other covers three horizontal parts. The content is indifferent to how the part–whole relation is divided up. This is a result of set ontology where distinct sets can cover the same concrete physical aggregate. This was a departure from nominalists such as Goodman who took the content of the set as its individuating conditions. But such a content was not abstract singletons, but the one concrete whole over which it ranged. Thus, unlike Lewis, one could not have two distinct sets occupying the same thing in the world. As Goodman writes:

"If no distinct entities whatever have the same content then a class (e.g. that of the counties of Utah) is different neither from the single individual (the whole State of Utah) nor from any other class (e.g. that of the acres of Utah), whose members exactly exhaust this same whole. The Platonist may distinguish these entities by venturing into a new dimension of Pure Form, but the nominalist recognizes no distinction of entities without a distinction of content"[412]

---

[411] Lewis, *Parts of Classes*, 80.
[412] Nelson Goodman, *The Structure of Appearances* 3rd ed., (Boston: Reidel Publishing, 1977), 36.

Lewis, on the other hand, bites the Platonist bullet and accepts classes of singletons that are distinguished by their content but their content are the singletons. Further, they are indifferent to the joints in nature in that they range over objects in ways that are indifferent to the way the functional parts fit together. Lewis first states:

"The mereological sum of the coffee in my cup, the ink in this sentence, a nearby sparrow, and my left shoe is a miscellaneous mess of an object, yet its boundaries are by no means unrelated to the joints in nature."[413]

But then clarifies that only an "elite minority" of these classes of objects are "carved at the joints".[414] Lewis' atomism obviously plays a strong role here. Mereological sums in themselves do not have a joint cutting function: their intrinsic natures do not select out atomic essences but instead they can encompass any haphazard whole. Properties such as mass, charge, spin, etc., are easily identifiable and delineated from each other. The challenge is in applying mereological wholes to a naturalistic world with its definite and intelligible boundaries that are empirically marked out.

Lewis and Identity

There is a sense of identity which enters into Lewis' first-order quantified statements that has a pedigree stretching back to Frege. However, there is debate and confusion on Lewis' use of identity. The noted work of Byeong-uk Yi[415] and van Inwagen[416] have taken identity in the weakened Lewis version to the point of denying that composition is a form of identity

---

[413] Lewis, "Putnam's Paradox," in *Papers in Metaphysics*, 65.
[414] Ibid.
[415] Byeong-Uk Yi, "Is Mereology Ontologically Innocent?" *Philosophical Studies* 93, no. 2, (1999): 141-160, http://www.jstor.org/stable/4320908.
[416] Van Inwagen, "Composition as Identity,"

at all.[417] Lewis' broadened sense of identity and its ambiguous relation to the principle of the indiscernibility of identicals comes across in this passage:

"…even though the many and the one are the same portion of Reality, and the character of that portion is given once and for all whether we take it as many or take it as one, still we do not really have a generalized principle of the indiscernibility of identicals. It does matter how you slice it – not to the character of what's described, of course, but to the form of the description. What's true of the many is not exactly what's true of the one. After all, they are many whilst it is one."[418]

The crux of the dilemma centres on how it is that something having one property, being one, can be identical with something that has a different property, being many. This objection is usually spelled in the idioms of plural logic, but a more straightforward example will suffice: Take my body. I have arms, legs, a torso and head and these are all identical with my body. But although I can say "my arms are among the parts of my body", there is no way to make sense of a sentence such as "my body is among the parts of my body". Unlike my arms, my body is not among the arms, legs, torso and head.

The second hurdle facing CAI is generalising the indiscernibility of identicals so that it can encompass both sides of the plural identity equation ($xx = y$). But how is it that something which is many can be identical with something that is one? Other commentators have pointed out Leibniz's Law is nonnegotiable for identity claims.[419]

If the commentators on Lewis who take his conception to not really be a case of identity at all are taken seriously then the interesting question to pose is how is it that Lewis is getting the one entity that flanks one side of the identity sign out of the many flanking the other

---

[417] Verity Harte argues that analogous to identity is like being analogous to butter, it really isn't identity at all; *Plato on Parts and Wholes: The Metaphysics of Structure* (Oxford: Oxford University Press, 2002), 23.
[418] Lewis, *Parts of Classes*, 87.
[419] Sider, "Parthood,"

side. The work of Einar Bohn is an illuminating case.[420] He examines certain passages from Lewis, such as this one:

"It does matter how you slice it – not to the character of what's described, of course, *but to the form of the description.*"

What this means, according to Bohn's interpretation of Lewis, is that we have the same "portion of reality" but different forms of description that are both somehow tied by the identity equation.[421] So statements of the generalised principle of the indiscernibility of identicals hold for plural identity but only relative to the descriptions of either the many domain or the one domain. Going back to the example of my body, "my body" and "my arms, legs, torso and head" cannot complete the phase by occupying either side of the "…is one of…" clause on pain of paradox. But if we take such predications as being true only relative to a description, then we can truly say that we have one portion of reality whilst at the same time holding a plural description. So we can describe the one portion of reality as my arms, legs, torso and head, and that predicate will be true relative to the description, D, whereas the description D* takes singular references, such as "my body", and this will also be true relative to description, D*.

Each individual part is a simple and so a manifestation of being, whereas the descriptions just provide the means for us to epistemically pick out the reference. The *grounds* for the unity is given independently of such descriptions. The sum referred to on one side of the identity sign is, by virtue of flanking one side of the identity sign, thereby nothing but a further manifestation of the same principle of being that unifies each part taken individually. The descriptions themselves are really just epistemic access points to the underlying identity predicate that metaphysically grounds the descriptive qualities within the whole identity relation.

---

[420] Einar Bohn, "Commentary on 'Parts of Classes'," *Humana.Mente Journal of Philosophical Studies* 19 (2011): 151-158, https://philarchive.org/archive/BOHCOQ
[421] Frege says something similar; "If, in looking at the same external phenomenon, I can say with equal truth 'This is a copse' and 'There are five trees', or 'Here are four companies' and 'Here are five hundred men', then what changes here is neither the individual nor the whole, the aggregate, but rather my terminology." *Foundations,* § 46.

At this point, it's worth saying something regarding the strict logical demands of Leibnizian identity statements and its variables as the identity condition for the cognitively significant and informative aspects of an object. First take the first-order formulations of Leibnizian identity statements:

(definition) Self-identity   - $\forall x(x = x)$

(definition) Leibniz Law   - $\forall x \forall y[(x=y) \rightarrow (\phi(x) \leftrightarrow \phi(y))]$

Identity is purely a reflexive notion: everything is necessarily identical to itself. Leibniz's Law just states that for two things to be identical, they must share all properties in common. Notice that for Leibniz's Law the conditional moves from the identity condition and universal quantifies on the left to the condition of equality of properties on the right. Leibnizian identity is a logical formulation, which means it is absolute and based on the denoting terms that pick out objects. The properties are part of the identity equation but only because the initial denoting has already done the work independently of them, they are grounded by the object and the logical conditional.[422]

Echoing these definitions, identity statements as they are set out by Frege can take the form of either:

1) $a = b$

---

[422] Armstrong paints a similar picture of identity drawing on a distinction made by Joseph Butler: "strict identity" and identity in the "loose and popular" sense. The latter he illustrates: "Suppose that you are in a zoo and that you see the backside of an elephant in an enclosure. But suppose that you are behind the enclosure and another spectator is at the front and is seeing the front of the elephant. We can properly say that you two are seeing the same elephant. At the same time, though, we could agree that each of you can only see different parts of that one elephant. So in this case talk of seeing the (very) same thing only amounts to talk of seeing different parts of the very same thing. I am inclined to think that when 'the same' or 'the very same' is used in a loose and popular sense, it always involves applying 'the same' to different *parts* of the same thing, where that last phrase 'the same thing' has the sense of *strict* identity. You and the other spectator see different parts of exactly the same, strictly the same, animal." *Universals: An Opinionated Introduction* (Boulder, CO: Westview Press, 1989), 4.

or

2) *a = a*

The "*a*" and "*b*" are either names or descriptions that denote individuals. An example of the first is Frege's famous example of "the evening star = the morning star", and an example of the second is "the evening star = the evening star". Now importantly for Frege, these are both true identity statements but they differ in cognitive significance. We know that "the evening star = the evening star" just by inspecting the terms on either side of the identity sign, whereas "the evening star = the morning star" is an informative statement that requires going out into the world and engaging in an empirical investigation.

What this brings out is that, for Fregean and Leibnizian identity statements, the concepts of "truth" and "identity" do not essentially involve any empirical or phenomenal details of objects, since the true identity of the object is a function of the generic self-identity statements, "*a = a*". What changes, moving from "*a = a*" to "*a = b*", is purely the cognitive significance of the identity, or what is known to the observer, but precisely *what the identity is* of that object – in the strict Leibnizian sense – remains unchanged.

This formal concept of identity – where an abstract, logical and univocal concept of identity does the real heavy lifting in determining *what* that object is – comes across strongly in Lewis' CAI. He takes the identity conditions to be independent, univocal and not dependent on perspective or description. The oneness is an abstract grounding and determining condition, denoted by the identity relation, that cannot be captured in any description that involves the collocation of objects or description of properties.

Lewis also appeals to identity when making the main argument for UC. He writes:

"If Possum exists, then automatically something identical to Possum exists; likewise if Possum and Magpie exist then automatically their fusion exists. Just as Possum needn't satisfy any special conditions in order to have something identical to him, so Possum and Magpie needn't satisfy any special conditions in order to have a fusion."[423]

As this passage indicates, a thing's identity isn't something over and above the object itself, nor is it integral to the object's makeup or essential nature. It is absolutely simple and doesn't involve deep investigations, scientific or otherwise, into a thing's essence. In an earlier publication, Lewis wrote:

"Identity is utterly simple and unproblematic. Everything is identical to itself; nothing is ever identical to anything else except itself. There is never any problem about what makes something identical to itself; nothing can ever fail to be."[424]

Thus identity – and the dictates of mereology that delineate its application to cases of the one and the many – are an expression of ultimate being where descriptions or modes of presentation are really extraneous factors that can only represent our limited epistemic condition. Thus the parthood relation is an expression, via the principle of identity, of the a priori grounding condition given by Frege. And hence a "portion of reality" – which is what that object is independent of descriptive routes to the object – must be an expression of fundamental being – in the Parmenidian sense, that is non-empirical, simple and unitary – as given logically and expressed through the identity sign and the proper names used to refer to the objects themselves.

Lewis on Vagueness

---
[423] Lewis, *Parts of Classes*, 85.
[424] Lewis, *On the Plurality of Worlds*, 192-193.

Another element in Lewis' dualism comes across in one of his main arguments for UC, *vagueness*.[425] Lewis draws a contrast between the identity given by the quantifier and the vagaries and indeterminacies we see in the natural composition of objects. What we have here is essentially an extensionalist theory of semantics, with intensions exorcised as unnecessary abstract, unscientific objects (echoing other philosophers like Quine and Goodman). Quine, as we explored last chapter, took existence "to be the value of a variable" and also the extension of such a variable. Lewis, as discussed, takes identity to be "utterly simple" and inherently tied up with the quantifier, which is absolute, in contrast to the piecemeal and ambiguous data that comes through observations of the world.

The absolute and purely formal truth-functional connectives rules out any kind of vagueness. The apparatus of first-order logic, with identity and the associated truth-functional connectives along with the quantifiers, is not vague, so predicates construed in such a system range over non-vague entities. So the references of both identity and existence, that is "$x=x$" and "$\exists y(x=y)$", are not vague. They are, in fact, examples of absolute identity and existence: there are no shades in between or borderline cases of what definitionally counts as an object.

The vagueness argument takes UC as a way of avoiding arbitrary cut-offs between what may be considered items composing an object and items not composing an object. This is what is known as a sorites series for composition.[426] Take an example of the transition of composition: Suppose we have 20 Lego building blocks randomly scattered on the floor. We take another 20 Lego blocks and put them closer together. Next to those blocks we put another 20 that are even closer. Then we start putting further groups of 20 blocks closer and closer into the dimensions of a table so that the first group we started with looks like a scattered mess compared to the last group perfectly filling out the dimension of a table. At what point along this transition do we say that the blocks compose a table?

---

[425] Ibid, 212-213.
[426] See Theodore Sider, "Four-Dimensionalism." *The Philosophical Review* 106, no. 2, (1997): 212-214, https://www.jstor.org/stable/2998357 and Theodore Sider, *Four-Dimensionalism: An Ontology of Persistence and Time*, (Oxford: Clarendon Press, 2001), 120-132.

If we took one group to be the point where the table is constructed, then what makes that an example of composition where the previous one, which only differed slightly in arrangement, does not? Sider remarks "In no continuous series is there a sharp cut-off in whether composition occurs."[427] Since there is no sharp cut-off, so the argument goes, then everything is an example of composition. So in positing compositions in all cases, we can avoid sharp boundaries, as they prove to be arbitrary. How then do we know when two objects compose a whole?

The vagueness in composition for Lewis is a consequence of the variable nature of the Humean mosaic: things coming together in any way, shape or form cannot constitute a new object that was not there before. This repeats a similar theme I've been highlighting in Lewis' worldview, that of the opposition between the fleeting nature and arrangement of the objects that we observe and the absoluteness of Parmenidian being (which involves uncompromising principles that determine an object's existence conditions). For Lewis, it may be indeterminate whether a particular arrangement of wood makes up a chair, but that there exists something that is indeterminate is not a vague matter. So a statement such as "there exists something that is F" is not vague as to the application of the term "F", the identity conditions of which cannot be vague. But the clause "there exists something" as it applies to any particular case is vague as to the *what* of the object over and above the generic, stipulated identity conditions of a formal existence claim.

But the consequence of this is that the identity of any object is independent of the circumstances under observation. If the object's identity is understood as an immediate and unconditional result of the use of the variable then the observation of concrete parthood as an empirical matter has no input into the identity of the object. As van Inwagen states:

"But suppose someone thinks (as Universalists do) that the arrangement of the blocks is quite irrelevant to the question whether they compose an object: suppose he thinks that the

---

[427] Ibid, 124.

blocks must at any moment at which they all exist compose an object, even if at that moment each of them is thousands of miles from the others, and even if they are moving at high velocities relative to one another, and even if they exert no causal influence to speak of on one another. If the arrangement of the blocks is irrelevant to the question whether they compose anything, why should it be supposed to be relevant to the identity of the thing they compose?"[428]

But this is a consistent Lewisian theme: the identity conditions are supplied by the variable and the logical identity categories are independent of the flux of the Humean mosaic. But is there an alternative? And is the need for sharp and exact boundaries more a consequence of the dualism between the absolute world of Parmenidian being and the unintelligible chaos of the empirical world? Later on in this chapter I put forward principles of composition that involve the whole taking over the identities of the parts. This may not provide a clear cut off for composition, but neither do I feel compelled by the formal (and unnatural) demands of logic and identity.

Critique of Lewis on Identity

Some have taken the extreme generality of identity, in the context of CAI, as a virtue, since being general and non-discriminatory is surely what it means to be fundamental. And this would be an acceptable presupposition to hold if one were taking Fregean logic – with its whole generalisation to instances schema – as basic. The generalised quantifier, and the distinctive inference modes Frege drew on, license precisely such a role for logic and the application of identity categories. But surely one of the most basic elements of identity is precisely that it is *specific*. When we identify something, even in the most obscure sense, we distinguish it from its background – we notice a topology and an internal consistency. Research on pre-linguistic infants confirms this, revealing they "perceive objects as unitary, bounded and persisting bodies".[429]

---

[428] Peter van Inwagen, *Material Beings* (Ithaca: Cornell University Press, 1990), 77.
[429] Elizabeth Spelke, "Principles of Object Perception," *Cognitive Science* 14, (1990): 31, https://doi.org/10.1207/s15516709cog1401_3

Given that one of the most fundamental roles that the concept of identity should play is in distinguishing objects (and their natures) from one another, then how does Lewis' CAI fair? Recall that descriptive elements – and even the numerical properties of "one" and "many" – are not candidates for this role. But when we make use of the *law of identity*, as in "everything is something or other" we expect the "something or other" to be a placeholder for a predicate or a proper name that picks out some sortal or individual that gives content to the identity statement.

Lewis makes considerable heavy use of the logical notion of identity. Identity as a governing term is supposed to pick out objects as distinct from other objects, since to be self-identical is something that, say, Fred has, which is distinct from the relation of self-identity that Bill has. But self-identity as a concept is *univocal* and has no specific content. But then self-identity, $(x)\Box(x=x)$, should be an internal relation if anything.[430] But if it has no content, it is difficult to see how it is internal to anything except in a purely empty logical sense.

To see this consider Frege's use of identity statements: subject–predicate sentences which make use of the "is" as a copula provide a logical role for the monadic predicate, such as "Socrates is wise". But the "is" used in other cases – where there are proper names on either side, such as with "Cicero is Tully" – is not a logical "is", but one of identity.

Now given that a predicate is what remains in a sentence once the proper name is subtracted, then the relation is what remains when "Cicero" and "Tully" are subtracted from "Cicero is Tully". An analogy is a relation such as "John loves Mary". Deleting "John" and "Mary" still leaves the relation "loves" waiting to be completed by two proper names. Any proper name can be substituted for any other proper name and it still constitutes an identity. Quine called such logical constants an "essential occurrence" where, by contrast, the other expressions occur "vacuously", since "its replacement therein by any and every other

---

[430] Kripke, *Naming and Necessity*, 3.

grammatically admissible expression leaves the truth or falsehood of the statement unchanged".[431]

Thus under Frege's system, the logical identity relation is a first-level concept that stands indifferently to its terms in the way that I and my spouse can instantiate the relation of existing ten metres from each other. Obviously any substantial object can occupy such a position without effecting the relation. Likewise, the identity relation in Fregean sentences does not occupy any special connection with the terms that flank it on either side (since it holds itself invariant under permutations). As Colin McGinn describes Frege on identity:

"Identity is such a specific relation, as specific (say) as the successor relation in arithmetic, that it is indeed inconceivable that it might fall into a variety of forms loosely classified together under 'same'. The concept of identity is quite unlike the family resemblance concept expressed by 'game', which is given to us in a highly unspecific form and admits of many subvarieties. Objects that fall under 'game' are not linked by a single common feature, but 'identical' expresses a quite definite concept that remains rigidly the same (!) from case to case."[432]

In contrast to this our ordinary, intuitively given understanding of identity ties completely to the particular. When I observe my spouse, I observe her arms, legs, torso and head and their functioning together as a whole, and that is how, in that instance, I observe the special part–whole relation. All these parts operate together *and they can be empirically observed and explained as a unity.*

The intimacy of parthood is supposed to prime our intuition in precisely such a way that we see this *as* identity and no further considerations, no fundamentally existent add-ons, are needed. There is no transcendental, something-we-know-not-what that operates behind the scenes playing an identity conferring role. Thus if any further considerations are redundant,

---

[431] W. V. O. Quine, "Truth by Convention," in *Ways of Paradox*, 80.
[432] Colin McGinn, *Logical Properties: Identity, Existence, Predication, Necessity, Truth* (Oxford: Clarendon Press, 2000), 6-7.

then the factors which determine *what* an object is are already given and there isn't any real work for something like self-identity to do. The formal identity concept can then be considered to be redundant and nothing over and above the already empirically given conditions.

What about accounting for our common sense knowledge that kinds and objects have individuating conditions that distinguish them from other kinds and objects? This dilemma has both an *epistemological* and an *ontological* dimension.

The epistemological dimension involves how it is that we can *identify* an object in a cognitively meaningful sense as the sort of thing that has such and such characteristics that mark it off from other objects having altogether different characteristics. E. J. Lowe argues:

"For if we do not at least know *what a thing* is, how can we talk or think comprehendingly about it? How, for instance, can I talk or think comprehendingly about Tom, a particular cat, if I simply don't know what cats are and which cat, in particular, Tom is? Of course, I'm not saying that I must know *everything* about cats or about Tom in order to be able to talk or think comprehendingly about that particular animal. But I must surely know enough to distinguish the kind of thing that Tom is from other kinds of thing, and enough to distinguish Tom in particular from other individual things of Tom's kind."[433]

Relatedly, how can we explain our knowledge of numerically different substances? It is far from clear that self-identity can provide such explanations. For one thing, self-identity is supposedly common to all entities. But this creates a dilemma in applying CAI, since one form of self-identity – the whole – cannot usurp the identity of other individual expressions of self-identity – the many. Self-identity as a concept is pure potentiality. In other words, it requires completion by singular terms to mean anything of any substance. This is analogous to the Frege–Russell–Quine view of existence where "*x* exists" expresses a universal

---

[433] E. J. Lowe, "Two Notions of Being: Entity and Essence," in *Being: Developments in Contemporary Metaphysics*, ed. Robin Le Poidevin (Cambridge: Cambridge University Press, 2008), 35-36.

predicate. But to posit such a universal – that is to answer the question "what is there?" with "everything", as Quine did – implies that the meaning is already loaded into the universal. It's the enactment of Parmenidian being in answer to the question. There is no way to individuate out of a univocal archetype. Thus as Mendelsohn points out, there is no room left for informative individual cases:

"The problem with this Redundancy Theory of Existence is that it renders unclear how an existential claim '*F*s exist' can be informative (if true)."[434]

Contrast this with how we normally individuate sets. A set's identity, as dictated by the *axiom of extensionality*, is given by its members. The logical form of the axiom is: $\forall xyz((x < y \leftrightarrow x < z) \rightarrow y = z)$. But this form of the principle just imports the generic identity of the biconditional, which allows any object to be the value of the variables occupying either side of the identity sign. But to know something about the identity of a set, we have to first know some-thing about its members.[435] If we open a carton of eggs we see the set of three eggs, which we infer upon seeing those eggs in that context.[436] We distinguish that set from other sets such as the set of five alley cats which is individuated by those five cats existing in that context.

But if identity is just a logical primitive that plays an identifying role by the existential quantifier, $\exists$, then it is impossible to make such distinctions, and one of the most integral aspects of identity – namely that of individuation – is left unaccounted for. Whilst we could not substitute *one* of the places in the two-place predicate relationship of "*a = a*" with another proper name, such as "*b*", we could replace both places with the same entity and the

---

[434] Mendelsohn, *The Philosophy of Gottlob Frege*, 105.
[435] An example from Lowe; "Consider the following thing, for instance: the set of planets whose orbits lie within that of Jupiter. What kind of thing is that? Well, of course, it is a set, and as such an abstract entity that depends essentially for its existence and identity on the things that are its members – namely, Mercury, Venus, Earth, and Mars. Part of *what it is to be a set* is to be something that depends in these ways upon certain other things – the things that are its members. Someone who did not grasp that fact would not understand *what a set is.*" *Forms of Thought: A Study in Philosophical Logic* (Cambridge: Cambridge University Press, 2013), 146.
[436] The example of the set of eggs comes from Penelope Maddy, *Realism in Mathematics* (Oxford: Clarendon Press, 1990), 58-63.

exact same relation would hold. Self-identity therefore plays no integral role in anything's identity except in the most anaemic, logical sense.

Another epistemological concern is whether we can make *sense* of the concept of identity to begin with. Wittgenstein famously rejects the identity relation in the *Tractatus*. He took it that identity is not a relation[437] and that "…to say of *one* thing that it is identical with itself is to say nothing at all."[438] What Wittgenstein is driving at here is not that self-identity is just a trivial tautology but that any meaning it purports to have is nonsense. Relations *qua* relations must involve individually distinct partners, such as "$a=b$", but this is obviously not the case with self-identity statements such as "$a=a$". The criteria of identity needs to be about any two objects which "$a=a$" is not. But if self-identity really isn't a relation at all then it is not trivially true *but meaningless*. Kit Fine writes:

"It is clear that a criterial principle as some kind of generic import; it is in some sense about *any* two objects of the sort in question. Thus the identity principle for sets tells us what makes *any* two sets the same and the identity principle for persons tells us what makes *any* person at one time the same as a person at another time. The previous gloss on identity claims is general (or universal); it tells us, for any two particular objects of the sort in question, what makes them the same. Thus the generic character of an identity claim is taken to lie in its generality; a generic claim of identity is simply taken to be a general claim of identity."[439]

But if identity presupposes an antecedent grasp of two senses of an individual then it may not be just a "generic claim of identity" we are dealing with here, but that there is no sense we can attach to the identity sign. The logical individuation of objects – which is what we are challenging here – is analogous to the role played by essential natures in the definition

---

[437] Wittgenstein, *Tractatus*, 5.5301
[438] Ibid, 5.5303. Frege states something similar, comparing the contentless ascriptions of "exists" and "self-identical": "[T]he judgments "This table exists" and "This table is identical with itself" are completely self-evident, and that consequently in these judgements no real content is being predicated of this table." In Hermes et al, *Posthumous Writings,* 62-63.
[439] Kit Fine, "Identity Criteria and Ground," *Philosophical Studies* 173, issue 1, (2016): 3-4, https://doi.org/10.1007/s11098-014-0440-7

of kinds. Fine has pointed out that singleton Socrates, {Socrates}, although necessarily connected to Socrates, plays no role in the definition of Socrates.[440] If we listed all the characteristics of Socrates, we would not have to mention his singleton in this regard. Self-identity is a lot like this in that we already know *what* "*a*" is before it enters into the relation with itself and thus it is completely uninformative. Hence the "=", which fixes to a "nothing over and above", signifies nothing and self-identity is epistemically vapid.

Next we come to the ontological challenge. Consider what it is that self-identity is supposed to do. There are no conditions that self-identity imposes on any portion of reality to make it the kind of thing or individual that it is, but its major contribution is that it allows us to conceptualise that portion of reality as *one thing*. But how do we attach any cognitive sense to such a conceptualisation? One way of doing this would be to take Dummett's "amorphous lump"[441] view of reality, which is a world that is completely void of form and thus no items have identity even in the most general sense – as *somethings or other* – sense. David Oderberg argues that what he calls the "law of identity"[442] is falsified by the amorphous lump concept (and vice versa) since according to that law, everything has a nature and can be distinguished in some way but this is a job that the emaciated, uninformative, logical version of identity – necessary self-identity – has absolutely no ability to do.[443]

To paint an even clearer picture, take something like Putnam's "cookie cutter".[444] Imagine there is nothing else in the universe except that homogenous, amorphous dough. Now imagine cutting shapes out of that dough. It may not even be shapes but nonsensical figures. These figures may be completely uninteresting and have no symbolic meaning. But we can differentiate them from one another. Each is an individual in the most generic sense by virtue of the fact that each has clear cut boundaries and borders by which we can

---

[440] Kit Fine, "Essence and Modality," *Philosophical Perspectives* 8. Logic and Language (1994): 1-16, https://doi:10.2307/2214160
[441] Dummett, *Frege: Philosophy of Language*, 577.
[442] I argue in a later chapter that the whole concept of identity is redundant and supervenes on my three most basic categories of being.
[443] David Oderberg, *Real Essentialism* (New York: Routledge, 2007), 86.
[444] Hilary Putnam, *Reason, Truth, and History* (Cambridge: Cambridge University Press, 1981), 52.

distinguish them from each other. Each has a basic unity in the most generic sense of the term.

But the concept of self-identity is nothing like this. A thing's relating itself to itself under an identity does not "carve out" or unify that object and distinguish it from its background. The tautology made famous by Joseph Butler, that "everything is what it is and not another thing", is essential to the definition of identity. Thus the only way I can think of to give an informative account of what it means to *be one* is completely orthogonal to the logical self-identity relation. The unity relation, the sense of being behind the proper name, is reconstructed according to the strictures of Parmenidian being and not one that follows the dictates of the empirical world.

Critique of Composition as Identity

What about CAI as an identity criterion? As was alluded to earlier, the traditional elements of a set retain their distinctive identity conditions so that, for example, a set of six cats can be distinguished from a set of three eggs. But a mereological fusion brings the parts together into a whole in such a way that the parts are incidental to the whole. There are different ways of slicing up the same object. Our rock could be divided vertically into thirds, as in $\{a, b, c\}$, or horizontally into thirds, as in $\{d, e, f\}$, which is a completely different set but the same portion of reality.[445]

There are many different ways the rock can be divided and no set of parts occupies a privileged relationship with the whole – they are all indeterminate. Each way is just a descriptive way of listing the parts fused under mereology. But the fusion into the whole means a submerging of those parts in such a way that they lose their identity relative to the subject. As John Burgess explains:

---

[445] This also follows since the Singleton-to-member relation is not intrinsic; Lewis, *Parts of Classes*, 34.

"Mereological fusion, by contrast, obliterates the separate identities of the fused: A single whole can be taken apart in many ways, and there is no one, canonical way of taking it apart of which it can be said that the genuine parts of which it is composed are just those pieces into which it is disassembled when taken apart in that way and no other."[446]

But Lewis is no emergentist, nor does he embrace any form of hylomorphism (where the parts and whole are a product of their juxtaposition into a suitable arrangement). For example, Aristotle took it that the arrangement of the letters into the word "cat" was an example of a whole being made out of its parts, but the parts had to be arranged in that specific order.[447] Other ways of arrangement, such as "atc" or "cta", do not produce the same whole. For Lewis, these ways of dividing it up are purely descriptive and incidental means to the same whole. The parts become a whole in an entirely different way for Lewis. In fact, the disjoint parts – "c", "a" and "t" – are even arbitrary ways of making the divisions, purely artefacts of our way of describing one portion of reality.

Hence the members within a class are ontologically distinct from the whole in a way that mirrors the way the formal conditions of identity and logic are distinct from any concrete particulars. But this is completely implausible as an explanation for why different compositional relationships hold. The letters "cat" arranged in that order explain the whole in a way that "atc" does not. Lewis' own example of supervenience, where the picture supervenes on the pixels, illustrates the same point. It is only because the pixels are those particular colours arranged in a particular way that explains *why* that particular whole supervenes on those parts. If those pixels had been arranged differently, we would have a different whole. The pixels and arrangement that makes up the Mona Lisa is different to the pixels and arrangement that makes up a portrait of an elephant.

Lynne Rudder Baker points out that mereology is unable to account for our pretheoretic understanding of parts – as conveyed in ordinary language – that makes distinctions between what she calls, following David Sanford, "a part" and "part". Examples of "a part"

---

[446] John Burgess, "Lewis on Mereology and Set Theory," in *A Companion to David Lewis,* 462.
[447] Aristotle, *Metaphysics: Books Z and H*, trans. and commentary by David Bostock, (Oxford: Clarendon Press, 1994), 1041b11.

(and "part"), would be my left kidney and my car's carburettor; an example of a "part" would be the three arbitrary divisions of a rock. She explains:

"But, pretheoretically, x can be part of y without being *a* part of y. For example, a particular molecule may be part of the water in this glass without being *a* part of the water in this glass. Or if part of the silver vase is tarnished, it doesn't follow that *a* part of the silver vase is tarnished. The difference in ordinary language between 'part' and 'a part,' I think, is this: 'x is a part of y' entails that x has some integrity as an object, but 'x is part of y' does not entail that x has any integrity as an object."[448]

But more than just a point about parthood, this is a point about the incommensurable natures of the world and the conception of being – assumed by mereology – that can range over any arbitrary division of any object. Functional unity is not in any way a kind or species of the unity we find in this conception of being, which is Parmenidian in its nature. Univocal notions of parthood cannot differentiate on the basis of the functional integration of parts we normally associate with biological organisms. Hence the locus of unity ranges over objects in the world in a way that is indifferent to the essences of those objects and the properties of its parts.

A further point can be made against making Parmenidian being integral to our concepts of part–whole. The very fact that such a principle cannot explain in any robust sense the different properties and formal principles of wholes – and that a description of those properties and principles *does* tell us all we need to know about the objects in our ontology – means the principle is redundant. If we cannot invoke such a principle in any sort of explanatory role, then it begs the question as to whether it should play any sort of role in our ontology.[449] We could dismiss it not because it abstracts from the quidditative nature of the parts, but because there is no way in which we can conceive of it having any sort of causal impact on the world.[450] If any object can be explained as having the very nature it

---

[448] Lynne Rudder Baker, *Persons and Bodies: A Constitution View* (Cambridge: Cambridge University Press, 2000), 182.
[449] Lowe, E. J. *The Possibility of Metaphysics* (Oxford: Clarendon Press, 2001), 213.
[450] David Armstrong *A World of States of Affairs* (Cambridge: Cambridge University Press, 1997), 41-43.

has without such a principle, then, by Ockham's razor, we should eliminate it from our ontology. The entire edifice of formal conditions passed down from Parmenides fails the test of the basic conditions of empiricism and the scientific approach to the world and should be shaved off our theoretical world view.

Critique of Lewis on Mereological Monism

Lewis' form of mereology is what Sider calls "mereological monism", where we have "a single notion of identity [that] applies to objects of diverse ontological categories."[451] Like self-identity, it is a unitary concept and thus doesn't admit of degrees or, to put it another way, it is not a genus that has certain *differentia*. It is not analogous to such terms as "animal" – where we have different species, such as canine or human – or "blueness", which admits of different shades, etc. The mereology axioms apply up and down the ontological hierarchy and are not necessarily tied to materialism or physicalism. Sider says that this applies even when prefixed to CAI:

"Further, one might construe 'the whole is nothing over and above the parts' as implying that the *features* of the whole are in some sense nothing over and above the features of the parts. This should not be taken to rule out the possibility of irreducibly macroscopic features (for instance quantum states of entangled systems, or, more mundanely, shapes of composite objects, which do not supervene on the properties of the parts). Any irreducibly macroscopic features can be pinned on relations between the parts, and therefore do not essentially involve the whole to the exclusion of the parts."[452]

This is a point about the range of application of the principles, namely that they *only* apply to singletons in classes. That is, the schema only applies to subclasses of classes, which means that their application is carried out regardless of the distinctive nature of the members. Lewis is here following the Frege–Russell–Quine conception of being, where

---

[451] Sider, "Parthood," 72. For Lewis' version of compositional monism see *Parts of Classes,* 75-82.
[452] Ibid, 73

existence is closely allied with the concept of number. For there to be an F is just for the Fs to be 1 or greater.

Singletons pick out a corresponding individual and do it in the most non-discriminatory way, ranging over objects that we ordinarily think of as already pledged to other part–whole relationships, such as my left elbow and the bonnet of my Ford Territory. The axioms of mereology apply indiscriminately to the dappled and pluralistic nature of the concrete world. UC, as an axiom, picks out any object and divides it according to boundaries and lines that are entirely unrestricted and without limit.

If we take UC to mean that any group of objects has a unique fusion that does not exclude those objects from being parts of other wholes, then it can be extended to encompass the whole universe. The part–whole relationship is iterative. Consider my left thumb and left index finger. The minimal whole they occupy is a *fusion* involving just those two parts and no others. But my left thumb and left index finger are also parts of my arm. This, of course, just follows from transitivity and is intuitively right. But it is also the case that my left index finger and left thumb are parts in the whole that involves them and the Andromeda galaxy.

Aside from the sheer absurdity on a spatial scale, and the skipping over of the natural whole – which cries out for explanation as a functionally integrated whole – the part–whole relation is infinitely extendable. For *any* particular object isn't really what we normally consider a particular – with its functional delimitations – but only really a part of some further whole which extends *ad infinitum* until we finally run up against the entire universe. If we take UC as an unconditional postulate:

$$(\exists z)(z = x + y)$$

Then it entails the Universe axiom:

(definition) Universe: $(\exists x)(\Box y)\,(y \leq x)$

The focus on UC in the literature has been almost entirely on the bizarre creatures that come out of unique fusions. Achille Varzi puts it this way:

"For every whole there is a set of (possibly potential) parts; for every specifiable set of parts (i.e., arbitrary objects) there is in principle a complete whole, viz. its mereological sum, or fusion. But there is no way, within the theory, to draw a distinction between 'good' and 'bad' wholes; there is no way to tell an integral whole from a scattered sum of disparate entities by reasoning exclusively in terms of parthood."[453]

But we don't really have "good" or "bad" wholes, since the entire currency of the part–whole exchange is in singletons. So a trout-turkey is no weird creature, since the singletons are no different to the singletons that overlay the parts that make up a tightly integrated whole, such as the heart and kidneys in my body. Our ordinary intuitions of the intimacy of parts means that some things being a part of a certain whole means it shares an identity with that whole. My arm is a part of me in that it is biologically integrated with the rest of my body and is a part of my identity.

This is the logical outcome of the application of a univocal sense of being that is pure Parmenides. Since parthood is an expression of the identity relation and the identity relation just is an application of Parmenidian being, then we would expect its imposition on the world to be completely non-discriminatory. It has no ability to pick out one lot of parthood to the exclusion of any other possible range of the parthood predicate to any other sub-section of the universe.

Now if mereology were applicable absolutely, then the transitivity of parthood would be transparent at every level of the hierarchy. But this is not the case. Consider an example that

---

[453] Achilles Varzi, "Parts, Wholes, and Part–Whole Relations: The Prospects of Mereotopology," *Data and Knowledge Engineering* 20, (1996): 269-270, https://doi.org/10.1016/S0169-023X(96)00017-1

has been given before in the literature against transitivity:[454] A person can be a part of a small military unit and since that small unit would be a part of a large unit then, by transitivity, that person should also be a part of that large unit. But this is not obvious and some have taken this as a reason to deny transitivity.

But as Varzi points out, this does not challenge the general principles of parthood.[455] The reason is that Nicholas Rescher's examples of parts involve an implicit predicate modifier. So a predicate part, "ϕ-part", like a functional subunit of an organ, would fail transitivity even though the unmodified "part" would not, since it applies generally.[456] Parts must be of the same general type as its whole. Concrete parts cannot be part of an abstract whole and vice versa. Likewise, for the natural kind hierarchy: chemical objects cannot be parts of biological kinds.

For a more telling example of Rescher's modified parts, take the set of six cats in my backyard. These six cats can be counted as six objects just by asking how many objects there are in my backyard. But the left paw of my favourite cat Felix is a biologically integrated part of Felix. But if through some unfortunate accident Felix lost her left paw, would we still have six objects in the backyard? In fact, though we may say Felix is a shadow of her former self without the use of her left paw, we would not say that she is any less of a generic object for such a loss. A simpler example: Brad is part of the Sydney Symphony Orchestra, Brad's right kidney is a part of him but not a part of the Sydney Symphony Orchestra.

Thus these lessons should not be taken as a reason to deny transitivity so much as a reason to deny parthood monism. What it means to be a part of a biological whole isn't the same as what it means to be a part of a sequence of numbers under the successor operator. To be a part, in the ordinary sense of the term, does not apply in a unitary manner to all levels of the

---

[454] Nicholas Rescher, "Axioms for the Part Relation," *Philosophical Studies* 6, no. 1, (1955): 8-11, http://www.jstor.org/stable/4318213.
[455] Achilles Varzi, "Mereology," *The Stanford Encyclopaedia of Philosophy* (Winter 2016 Edition), Edward N. Zalta (ed.), URL = <https://plato.stanford.edu/archives/win2016/entries/mereology/>.
[456] Varzi, "Mereology,"

hierarchy of being. It is absurd to say that my hands, legs, torso and head are a set and occupy parts of a set. They are, first and foremost, biological parts and are functionally integrated accordingly.

But the biological fusions we considered earlier are incidental to real mereological fusion which flattens all ontological hierarchies into its logical system. All concatenations of bits and pieces in the universe are transitions on the way to the whole which is designated by the Universe axiom. Literally any division of reality can be made the subject of the axioms and be the values of Lewis' plural quantifiers. This is because of the orthogonal nature of the intensional and extensional domains. More precisely, the structural arrangements of objects that we pay attention to, and are the subjects of our discourse, are completely indeterminate relative to the abstract logical mereology functions.

At the heart of Lewis' troubles then is that mereological monism cannot explain the distinct and varied part–whole relations around us. We learned from Aristotle that certain wholes such as "cat" are in a part–whole relationship precisely because its parts are *specific* and a product of its constituents juxtaposed in just the right manner. We know from the scientific study of natural kinds, such as H_2O, that it's the specific atomic elements arranged in a specific way – in this case the 105° bond – that give it the properties that we observe. Lewis' purely logical strictures – with mysterious singletons and classes as their only focal point – thus have no explanatory power and little relevance for the world around us.

The most notable objection to mereology has been its identifying the parts so closely with the whole. Rudder Baker writes:

"From the point of view of mereology, we would be unable to distinguish between, say, a flag (or any other symbolic or sacred object) and an ordinary piece of cloth: A description of its parts would not distinguish a flag from a scrap of cloth. In any event, a description of the parts of, say, a person is far from a description of the person. So, I see no prima facie motivation to think of persons in terms of mereology."[457]

But I have already argued, contrary to Rudder Baker, that there are good reasons to agree with Lewis on the intimacy of parthood.[458] A description of my head, torso, arms and legs does provide at least some significant clues as to who I am. But a description in terms of the sum of parts that are many-one purely due to plural logic, and the logical axioms of mereology, reduces what is specific to a functional integration of biological parts. But if a constitutive approach to parthood is taken – where what it means to be a part is modified on a kind by kind, or even individual by individual, basis – then there is no problem in moving from a description of my parts to a description of my identity as a whole. What it means to be a part then takes on an organic and functional nature, and instead of dispensing with intimacy, we should instead dispense with monism.

What will emerge in the final chapters of this thesis is an alternative account of the parthood relation and, more importantly, of unity and simplicity: specifically, that objects as constituents of wholes are transformed in their role as parts of the whole. This is an alternative version of *e plurubus unum* where the many, *qua individuals*, are not primitive instantiations of being, but rather become aspects of the whole and thus their identity gets derived from occupying such a place in the whole. The whole, in turn, gets realised as the arrangements of constituents according to an abstract determining pattern. Thus we may observe a whole in distinction from its parts, but only as its parts are considered as separately existing things. For example, we may observe a tree, which is just its molecules arranged appropriately, and not be cognisant of its molecules in the same way that we may not be cognisant of every letter, considered individually, in one of Shakespeare's sonnets or every note in a Beethoven Sympathy. Thus constituents *become* aspects of wholes. This will be discussed in greater detail in the fifth and sixth chapters.

---

[457] Baker, *Persons and Bodies*, 180.
[458] Identity for Baker is partially explained by extrinsic factors; Ibid, ch. 2. So in the case of the flag it would be its national significance derived from the importance conferred on it due to its symbolic significance. But my take would be that a flag is a part of a greater emergent whole, namely the nation state and derives its significance in being a part. My take on wholes and the parthood relation will be discussed in the fifth and sixth chapters.

The van Inwagen Objection

Lewis has been subjected to criticism on the subject of innocence by van Inwagen, who argues that composition as identity doesn't make mereology ontologically innocent.[459] Take, as our domain, the six plots of land as six proper parts and their fusion. Lewis thinks that the fusion, A, is identical to what composes it. Van Inwagen denies this. The truth-value of the existentially quantified statements that range over this domain demand that we conclude that there are seven objects, not six. He says:

"Suppose that there exists nothing but my big parcel of land and such parts as it may have. And suppose it has no proper parts but the six small parcels ... Suppose that we have a bunch of sentences containing quantifiers, and that we want to determine their truth-values: '$ExEyEz(y$ is a part of x & z is a part of x & y is not the same size as $z)$'; that sort of thing. How many items in our domain of quantification? Seven, right? That is, there are seven objects, and not six objects or one object, that are possible values of our variables, and that we must take account of when we are determining the truth-value of our sentences."[460]

As I have already pointed out, the usual way of positing existential quantification means that quantifying over wholes involves adding an extra entity to our inventory of the world that is somehow distinct from its parts. So the truth-values of statements that range over a domain with entities a, b, c means we also need to recognise an extra thing, d, that they compose.

As I see it, there are two lessons to be learnt from van Inwagen's critique. The first is that his interpretation of the domain as being something somehow distinct from its parts is intuitively plausible. Van Inwagen's point regarding the meaning of existentially quantified sentences may have been wholly linguistic. But it does inadvertently highlight that further

---

[459] Van Inwagen, "Composition as Identity,"
[460] Ibid, 213.

considerations based on the collective identity of the whole can be brought to bear on the meaning of those statements, and the *n* entities of the domain over which the quantifiers range are determined accordingly.

But consider what van Inwagen is arguing here. Given the distinction in the size of the land, we have something new in our ontology that can be referred to by a distinct quantifier. He has to appeal to observational facts about a new entity that comes into being by virtue of the contextual organisation of its parts. Even though we normally wouldn't take this as a case of emergence, what we do have is a non-identity claim where the domain of quantification can be interpreted in such a way that the same objects – the plots – can be interpreted under the same domain as a distinct entity – the land – requiring its own distinct variable.

But Lewis doesn't have the conceptual apparatus that allows him to make such a move. Recall that the role of parts for Lewis is played by the singletons which make up a whole (as delineated by plural logical identity statements). The *x*'s, played by the six plots of land, do not collectively make up *y*, a distinct entity. Lewis makes the quite trivial move of reducing plural predicates to statements that can be delineated in a way that makes singular reference to each thing. He writes:

"The plural 'they are books' and 'Isaac has written them' reduce instantly to the singular: 'each one of them is a book', 'Isaac has written each one of them'. The plural 'they are at most 450' reduces less instantaneously: 'for some $x_1,...$, for some x_{450}, each of them either is x_1 or … or is x_{450}'".[461]

There are two key aspects of Lewis' worldview evident here that van Inwagen's argument brings out. The first is Hume's Dictum: that there are no perceived metaphysically necessary connections between distinct, intrinsically distinguished, entities. For the plural logician, the application of plural predicates is arbitrary compared to the application of the singular predicate, since the latter is applied on a one-by-one basis. This is due to the nature

---

[461] Lewis, *Parts of Classes*, 64.

of the elements of sets which, as applied to plural predicates, is reflected in the arbitrary application of the meaning of plural terms. The plural expressions do not find their grounds in the semantics of the terms – which is the sole province of the singular term – but are only constrained by the indeterminacies of contexts that provide purely arbitrary aggregations. For example, a non-singular predicate like "alley cats" may find its reference in a certain back alley in Paris or in a neighbour's yard. Which cats find themselves in such groupings and why is purely an arbitrary matter, and likewise whether we apply plural predicates to such non-ontic entities is purely a matter of choice or convention.

This obviously has implications for *how* objects are introduced as values of plural variables in the first place, since there is no empirically derived unity or oneness to appeal to. Six plots of land, as the values of single variables, cannot come together under any sort of collective functor to form one wholly distinct thing. For Hume, the necessary connections were supplied by the mind; under plural logic the unity of pluralities is a product of our choice, a mere *facon de parler*.

The second key aspect of Lewis' worldview is the atomism that plays a role in the nominalism inherited from Goodman and Quine. Nominalism has its own distinct criteria of identity. Goodman argued that nominalism demands that no two entities can be formed from the exact same elements. Classes are identical when their members are identical. Identity is entirely dependent on "content".[462]

A corollary to this is that the items composing the whole persist in their identity conditions as parts of a whole. Nothing is added to the identity of the constituents as they occupy the parthood roles. All that is required is that the parts exist. Crawford Elder claims that UC is a raw-existence claim and that any substantial relation or structure among the parts is purely incidental:

---

[462] Nelson Goodman, "On Relations that Generate," in *Problems and Projects* (Indianapolis: Bobbs-Merrill, 1977), 171-172.

"For the nature of a mereological object requires no particular relations among that object's parts: the object's existence requires only that each of the individual parts exists… Every conjunct in this specification will say only what some one part of the mereological object intrinsically is like. Mereological objects may *accidentally* bear *richer* structural properties, such that specifying these properties requires indicating, in one or more of the conjuncts, relations among the parts. But the structural property that is essential to any UMC [Unrestricted Mereological Composition] object – the property that characterizes that UMC object's very nature – will be one that incorporates no particular relations among the parts of the object."[463]

This comes out more clearly in the discussions Lewis had with Armstrong on composition. Lewis makes the case against what he calls "magical composition", which is the formation of an atomic whole that has no parts but does have constituents.[464] One example he gives is that of the universal *methane*, which is composed of *carbon* and *hydrogen*. The latter two elements are *distinct* from, and retain their own identities as constituents of, the former. Now if methane does not contain the latter two universals *as parts*, then *how does* it contain them? How under magical composition is it possible to explain the necessary connection between *methane* and *carbon* and *hydrogen*? Under CAI we can easily see how a whole just is its parts, but if the whole is distinct and atomic, then the relationship with the parts is completely mysterious. Lewis draws the conclusion:

"On the magical conception, a structural universal has no proper parts. It is this conception on which 'simple' must be distinguished from 'atomic'. A structural universal is never simple; it involves other, simpler, universals. … But it is mereologically atomic. The other universals it involves are not present in it as parts. Nor are the other universals set-theoretic constituents of it; it is not a set but an individual. There is no way in which it is composed of them."[465]

---

[463] Crawford Elder, *Familiar Objects and their Shadows* (Cambridge: Cambridge University Press, 2011), 154
[464] David Lewis, "Against Structural Universals," *Australasian Journal of Philosophy* 64, no. 1 (1986b): 25-46, https://doi.org/10.1080/00048408612342211
[465] Ibid, 41.

So to sum up Lewis' conundrum: the problem is that we have three entities when really we should only have two, since methane should be nothing but carbon and hydrogen. There are two ways out of this dilemma, which I will label *dissolving* and *emerging*: on the former methane exists in such a "nothing but" relation, on the latter carbon and hydrogen should be blended into methane as one emergent macro-entity. On the latter the newly emerging object retains its integrity as a whole entity where on the former the intimacy between parts and whole is retained, and carbon and hydrogen truly become parts in the mereological sense.

But then what *do* we have with the six plots of land? Simply, they are not merely a plurality but a sum (fusion). The plural reference gets reduced in the way Lewis has already shown us with his example of the 450 books: a sentence such as "they are plots of land" gets reduced to "for some $x_1,...,$ for some x_6 each of them either is x_1 or ... or is x_{450}". If we take Lewis' two cats, Magpie and Possum, conceiving of "Magpie + Possum" as a singular term referring to the fusion is not permitted, since it would mean that Magpie and Possum ≠ Magpie + Possum and that violates ontological innocence.

Under any interpretation of a first-order logic, where identity is taken as a primitive truth-functional connective, one cannot take the individuals – the lowest common denominators – and then refer to those objects as part of a new collective identity. "The soldiers surrounded the palace" takes "the soldiers" in a collective sense that should be translated in plural logic as individual references to each soldier. The reason Lewis cannot take reference to a collective plurality is that it means the objects are identified as part of that collective entity, which is something distinct from the individuals.[466] The grounding of wholeness is the identity relation, "$x=x$", and not some unique circumstantial descriptive event.

A sum is identical to the individuals, not as parts of a collective, but as individuals together in the most innocuous sense, which can take them as individually referred to under a plural logic. For example, the sum $\{a, b\}$ is identical to $\{a\}$ and $\{b\}$ because the former has parts

---

[466] Quine also took semantic reference as indicating his own atomistic metaphysics: "We persist in breaking reality down somehow into a multiplicity of identifiable and discriminable objects, to be referred to by singular and general terms." "Speaking of Objects," in *Ontological Relativity*, 1

in common with the latter. {*a*} and {*b*} sum overlaps {*a*} and {*b*}, but this is just a reformulation of Leibniz identity, where overlap is just identity in the trivial sense that everything overlaps itself. {*a*} and {*b*} do not change in any essential substantive way as parts of the sum.

Returning to van Inwagen's example, the main plot of land that is a result of the collective identity of the six plots cannot be accepted by Lewis since he only wants to quantify over things individually. Hence Lewis takes the *dissolving solution*. The sum isn't something that can add up to something distinct from the parts in the sense that the parts will take on a new identity as a part of a new entity referred to by a singular term, such as "main plot". The parts persist as part of the whole because of the trivial identity.

But then what is to stop Lewis taking "main plot" as a distinct whole in a different context when considering, say, six main plots together and trying to decide whether the six as one – say a "supermain plot" – exists as a distinct entity? The answer is, nothing. This is for the simple reason that it is the a priori applied principle of unity and simplicity that is applied to these cases and not anything abstracted from the world. It also means that the application of such principles is in part a function of our arbitrary interests and focuses within a domain of discourse.

To repeat the lessons of the last section: what we need to recognise here is that there is something of a sleight of hand at play here in that we appeal to wholes that are a consequence of the way the world is arranged, but really what is at work in Lewis' system is the a priori application of being and a Humean atomism that makes any real substantial unitary oneness prohibitive. This is the real lesson of Lewis' argument with van Inwagen. What is more, a consistent approach would be to empirically derive unities *and then* abstract their existence and the principles involved in their being. It also means looking for an alternative account of oneness and the part–whole relation.

Bringing it all together

Lewis avoids positing entities needlessly. He takes an individual and something distinct that is generated, the singleton, and then through plural quantification and CAI he derives everything else. Thus he follows Russell and Quine in seeking the goal of ontological simplicity. But what about the *emerging solution?* In principle, I would argue that this is a much better option and involves the following principles of composition;

New objects are added to our ontological inventory by virtue of some antecedently existing distinct objects. These distinct objects are generated from the old ones by virtue of the way those old ones are arranged. The materials do not persist as those materials once they become parts, but take on structural (contextual) properties and hence new identities. Thus there is no need to deny extensionality, as some would do,[467] when the same objects are used to make different wholes. So "Mary Loves John" is a distinct whole from "John Loves Mary". The parts are different because each object is at least in part defined by its place in the structure.

Returning to a previous example, it now becomes possible to take carbon and hydrogen as parts since they are not distinct from methane due to the fact that they do not retain their identity *as* carbon and hydrogen any longer. Thus we have one entity, methane, with its parts connected into one whole. And that whole has its own unique characteristics due to its contextually organised elements acting together under the unique bonded relation. That bonded relation is of a formal nature and *not* a further element.

Peter Simons makes a similar argument. He asks us to imagine writing down two words, such as "Cardinals" and "Multiply", arranged in a circle. It would be a grammatically viable option for us to read the sentence as either "Cardinals Multiply" or "Multiply Cardinals".[468]

---

[467] E.g. Rescher in "Axioms for the Part Relation," 10.
[468] Simons, *Parts,* 113-114.

We have two different meanings in the distinct ways that the words are juxtaposed. Now Rescher is right that what we have here is something more than the sum of "Cardinals" and "Multiply". But Simons argues that this isn't a violation of extensionality, since a part of a sentence can mean different things. The structure in which the part is embedded could play a role identifying that part. He gives the example of a fragment like "nals Mul" which is a part of "Cardinals Multiply" but not of "Multiply Cardinals".

To take Simons point about parts further, consider the following example. If a house is constructed out of timber, cement and brick, we have something new coming into existence that was not there before. We have the concrete particulars arranged in a way that is complex and not just a mereological sum. We also have the concrete particulars operating under a generative relationship whereby, in occupying the relation, R, they become something distinct.[469] We have one entity, a house, and not a multitude of bits of timber, brick, etc. This reiterates a previous lesson: that identity should not be taken as a logical primitive but instead as a concept that supervenes on – and is "nothing over and above" – the concrete particulars and the way in which they are arranged.

This is not just applicable to artefacts. Suppose there is an alien chemist on another world who is studying the properties of hydrogen and oxygen and yet, being of a strange life form, has had no experience of water. The chemist doesn't know that two hydrogen atoms and one oxygen atom combine to form water. What would the mereological sum of hydrogen, hydrogen and oxygen be? It would be tempting to respond that it would combine to form the substance water. But this would be to tell a story about the formation of water – something substantial and concrete in the universe – that is distinct from its antecedently existing parts, since neither hydrogen nor oxygen have the properties of quenching thirst, being potable or translucent etc. In fact there is little evidence from philosophy of chemistry that such a prediction of macroproperties from microproperties is even possible. Paul Needham writes:

---

[469] Those that have defended an ontology of artifacts see Lynne Rudder Baker "The Ontology of Artifacts," *Philosophical Explorations* 7, no. 2 (2004): 99-112, https://doi.org/10.1080/13869790410001694462 and Crawford Elder *Real Natures and Familiar Objects* (Cambridge, MA: MIT Press, 2004), ch. 7 and Crawford Elder "On the Place of Artifacts in Ontology," in *Creations of the Mind: Theories of Artifacts and Their Representation* ed. Eric Margolis and Stephen Laurence, 33-51 (Oxford: Oxford University Press, 2007)

"Prospects for a purely microscopic description vary, then, from one group of substances to another. The relative ease with which this can be done for the molecular substances of organic chemistry is not a guide to substances in general. This is not to deny, of course, that even in the more recalcitrant cases, there is a microstructure… What doesn't follow from this is that the details of the microstructure of any particular substance are reasonably well known, and certainly not that they are independent of macroscopic constraints or somehow determine the macroscopic features of substances or that substances are in some clear sense 'nothing but' their microconstituents."[470]

Water is not, therefore, a mere additive result of the powers of hydrogen and oxygen. A mereological sum then will not do the work of producing water from its constituents. Sums do not give us the unique arrangement of the H_2O molecule. The only way they can function as a sum is by assuming what needs to be explained.[471]

The crucial distinction to make is between the materials and the parts that they become upon entering the whole. We do not have to be content with either adding the whole to our list of components or not.[472] This is not an example of double counting, since there are no distinct objects except as abstractions from the whole. The "hydrogen", "hydrogen" and "oxygen", have become one object: "H_2O".

A response from Lewis could be that he does not deny any of this and that the sum of, say, the trillion molecules that make up Bill Clinton just are those molecules arranged in that particularly complex way that makes him who he is: his distinct DNA, the signatory brain

---

[470] Paul Needham, "Microessentialism: What is the Argument," *Nous* 45, no.1, (2011): 17, http://doi.org/10.1111/j.1468-0068.2010.00756.x

[471] Barry Smith makes a related charge against what he calls "fantology": "A further problem with set theory is that it deals with combination *per accidens* – drawing no distinction of structure between, say, the set of enzymes, the set of planets in the solar system, and the set of persons whose surnames end in 'E'. It places numbers and popes, molecules and galaxies together in combination and thereby fosters a maximally promiscuous use of the term 'object' that has been detrimental to the advance of ontology in analytic philosophical circles in ways too little appreciated." "Against Fantology," in *Experience and Analysis* ed. Johann C. Marek and Maria E. Reicher, 153-170 (Vienna: öbv&hpt, 2005)

[472] This false choice hasn't only been given by Lewis but also critics of CAI (c.f. Alex Oliver "Are Subclasses Parts of Classes?" *Analysis* 54, issue 4, (1994): 215-223, https://doi.org/10.1093/analys/54.4.215

states that he has, etc. But although Bill Clinton *qua* atomic individual has a singleton, the sum of the trillion molecules that make up Bill Clinton does not. Thus the contextual arrangement – or even enumeration – of such parts is incidental to the whole. Indeed Leonard and Goodman did not see mereology as providing anything other than a thin concept of being, but rather merely a way of *reconceptualising* what already existed:

"…because it provides means for treating many varied entities by means of concepts of a single logical type, the calculus of individuals is a powerful and expedient instrument for constructional work. In addition it performs the important service of divorcing the *logical* concept of an individual from metaphysical and practical prejudices, thus revealing that … wholes is capable of a purely formal definition, and that… all the concepts of logic, are available as neutral tools for the constructional analysis of the world."[473]

In the same way, the Main Plot that van Inwagen argues Lewis cannot quantify over *can* be quantified over under a different interpretation of the quantifier,[474] for example, as the six Main Plots that are all parts of one great Supermain Plot. But the real point of this objection is that these complex arrangements cannot be reduced to sums, and they *do* generate many and varied distinct objects that Lewis can only *assume* exist as values of his variables.[475]

---

[473] Leonard and Goodman, "The Calculus of Individuals," 55.

[474] A discourse dependent or conceptually chosen ontology thus threatens as is evident from Leonard and Goodman: "An individual or whole we understand to be whatever is represented in any given discourse by signs belonging to the lowest logical type of which that discourse makes use. What is conceived as an individual and what as a class is thus relative to the discourse within which the conception occurs." (ibid, 45) And Quine: "Thus I consider, that the essential commitment to entities of any sort comes through the variables of quantification and not through the use of alleged names. The entities to which a discourse commits us are the entities over which the variables of quantification have to range in order that the statements that are affirmed in that discourse be true." ("On Carnap's Views on Ontology," in *Ways of Paradox*, 128). Conceptual relativist conclusions are drawn from the axioms of mereology by Hillary Putnam in *The Many Faces of Realism* (La Salle: Open Court, 1987)

[475] Kathryn Koslicki argues that even the standard fusion of getting one object out of more than one violates ontological innocence: "Those who accept the principle of unrestricted mereological composition, would hold that the world in question also contains a *third* object, c, which is the sum of a and b. All parties agree that the sum, c, is 'in the strict and philosophical sense' numerically distinct from a and b, despite the fact that c is of course not disjoint from a and b. Thus, when "≠" is interpreted in the usual way to denote strict numerical distinctness, then it is true to say that a ≠ c and b ≠ c." in *The Structure of Objects* (Oxford: Oxford University Press, 2008), 42

In addition, the *type of material* used in composition is an essential part of any thing's identity. Carbon has unique properties that suit it for life. Water dissolves sodium precisely because the oxygen and hydrogen atoms have a particular bond strength that produces a polarity at either end which hooks on to the sodium molecule. And some more simpler examples: six plots of asphalt wouldn't give you a Main Plot, you can't build a house from jelly and, as Lynne Rudder Baker points out, a car can't be made from a soap bubble, or a lectern from a block of ice (since it melts too quickly).[476]

But fusions and the axioms of mereology are silent on the intrinsic characters of the parts of a fusion.[477] The material parts are merely placeholders for the real work done by the monistic arrangement of mereological axioms, and the singletons and classes. This is another reason why you can't get properties of wholes from the mereological sum of their parts. But it is also the reason why it is lacking in explanatory relevance.

There are different converging theses in Lewis that bring out one fundamental flaw in his ontology: his logical and axiomatic system does nothing other than overlay the real identity conditions – those empirical conditions I identified earlier in this chapter – of the objects in the world. It therefore assumes what it should explain and force-fits structure rather than deriving it from scientific analysis. Thus it is little more than one complex unproven assumption. An imposing of Parmenidian dualism and its appeal to an other-worldly a priori metaphysic.[478]

---

[476] Baker, *Persons and Bodies*, 32
[477] See Lewis, *Parts of Classes*, 29-35. Some such as Alex Oliver have complained that the mystery of the singleton and its fusion is grounds to question whether Lewis has any understanding at all about the composition of classes from singletons; "Are Subclasses Parts,"
[478] Even some who deny the UoC and provide a definition of "arrangement" where the parts can inhabit different wholes can likewise be committed to definitions within extensional parameters, e.g. "'x is an arrangement of the ys' =def 'x is a composition of the ys, and there is an n-term relation R, such that necessarily, x exists if and only if the ys stand in R to one another,'…"; Douglas Rasmussen, *Defending the Correspondence Theory of Truth* (Cambridge: Cambridge University Press, 2014), 65. In this case the definition of arrangement is subordinated to the biconditional which admits it into the realm of being.

Conclusion

This chapter has explored another significant metaphysician in twentieth century analytic philosophy: David Lewis. His system was an application of the logic of his predecessors – Frege, Russell and Quine – but only in plural form. Nothing in essence changes with Lewis. It is still an application of the law of identity and truth-functional logic, which are expressions of the simplicity and fundamentality of Parmenidian being. In Lewis we see, in several forms, the elevation of this being over that of anything found in the empirical world.

This chapter can therefore be taken as an extension of the criticisms of the Frege–Russell–Quine system. This time it was found to be a failure in the realm of mereology. The identity relation is applied to any system in conjunction with truth-functional logic and singletons applied to anything in the universe despite the inherit intelligibility of the actual physical objects applied together *as wholes*. Such a system may be lauded for its simplicity and broad application, but I have argued that it is simply inadequate as an explanation of what we observe in the world or have discovered through science. On the contrary, it is an artificial imposition on the world that derives no justification from empirical findings.

From here the next step will be to propose alternative principles of composition, principles that do not apply univocally but in concert with empirical findings. A principle of composition where the application of identity underwrites the part–whole relation will be usurped in favour of a system that can explain emergent wholes whilst maintaining the intimacy of parthood.

Chapter Five – Sketch of a Three–Category Ontology

Introduction

As we saw in the last chapter, the rational reconstruction of knowledge that had its origins in Frege's logicist approach had its culmination and ultimate failure in Carnap's *LSW*. The effort to construct an objective and intersubjective account of knowledge based on modern logic failed. Most germane to the following discussion is Quine's objection that an effective reduction cannot be made for mapping the auto-psychological qualities on to physical space-time points. Such a failure to reduce the "is at" of a quality at a space-time point to sense data and logic imperilled Carnap's effort to project knowledge beyond the subjective realm.

This chapter presents an alternative theory, one that provides a grounds for the structure of sense data and an answer to scepticism. This is a theory of being, but it is also a theory of epistemology. Unlike many modern ontologies, it starts where Descartes started – with our status as knowers. So the arrangement of sense data is the gateway to the external world and to an account of ontology. This is based on a further implication of my account: that sense data are intimately connected to the outside world in a way that Descartes believed was impossible.

The categories presented here are fundamental to ontology and can be abstracted from our sensory interactions with objects in the world. Each category has a *being-in-itself* as well as a *being-for-others* aspect to it. The first is the *determiner*, which is a non-spatiotemporal formal condition for any object. It specifies the number, type and arrangement of material constituents. Inherent in its definition is its determining objects within space-time. The second is the *realiser*; which is the material ingredients of an object patterned in some way by the determiner. It is a necessary for the determiner to have any influence in the world. The third is the *communicator*, which is an object presenting itself to other objects in a way that communicates the structural properties of the determiner–realiser (D–R).

I present these categories as an alternative to the Frege–Russell–Quine approach to the reconstruction of knowledge. They are an abstraction from our sensory states of knowledge rather than a replacement of them. The D–R combination provides the basis for the structure of our sense data. In this way we have an explanation of such a structure that is intuitively obvious and superior to the failed attempt that culminated in Carnap's attempt to build sense data from a formal-logical basis.

This approach to ontology focuses on the individual rather than the general and univocal laws of logic central to the Frege–Russell–Quine approach. The vacuous notion of Fregean identity gives way to individual sensory states which are inherently relational – rather than being purely monadic substantial entities – and cause a state of veridical knowledge by communicating the D–R condition of the object known.

I make comparisons with prominent accounts of truth given throughout the last century. First, I consider the redundancy theory proposed by Alfred Tarksi in which individual sentences justify reference through a biconditional. This approach is criticised by Hartry Field for its triviality. Putnam's response is to point to our Kantian – and Quinean – predicament that amounts to just relying on the law of identity to provide linguistic ground for reference. The communicator provides a better alternative since, like Tarski's approach, it focuses on singular instances of justified knowledge and yet explains truth although not in the reductionist manner that Hartry would like. It does not depend on trivial formal conditions for justification, since it relies on our sensory relations to the world.

Second, the account of structure I present cannot vary under permutation since there is no structure that acts as a tribunal for justification that is more fundamental to the individual structures given in veridical experience. This means that the challenge issued by M. H. A. Newman to Bertrand Russell – that his structures are trivially justified merely by meeting the correct cardinality – cannot apply here. In addition, the account of causation given by the communicator means that it is invulnerable to the modern permutation versions given by Putnam.

The specific version of causation given by the communicator provides an answer to scepticism, since it provides a causal account of knowledge in line with the Kripke–Putnam version and thus inherits the realist advantages of that approach. Further, it does not fall prey to the *qua* objection, since the cause of knowledge communicates the structure of the object *as* a kind or species and even those properties arranged according to the specific individual that it is. This also places the justification of knowledge at the level of the individual sensory experience and thus provides a more intuitively acceptable explanation for our veridical states than Lewis' functionalist and holistic approach.

Next, an alternative approach to analysis is given. The abstractive nature of this approach means that analysis proceeds by taking apart our individual sensory states. What gets revealed is a structure analogous to sentence structures. When we analyse we focus on the material conditions given by sense data, which are brought into focus the same way we might focus on a word within a particular sentence. The determiner gives the structure of our sensory states and thus the parts and whole are mutually dependent. This presents a stark contrast to the concept of Parmenidian being given in the reconstruction of knowledge by Frege–Russell–Quine where there is no parthood or analysis within being itself.

I then argue for the D–R combination by comparing it to the supervenience and grounding relations. The realiser is a necessary condition for the determiner, which explains why the properties of the whole supervene on its constituents. However the D–R, unlike supervenience, explains holistic properties, since the determiner arranges the realiser in such a way that a new object emerges among the furniture of the world. But unlike grounding and supervenience, this is not a uselessly general explanatory category, since it structures – and explains – our sensory states and has no truck with Frege–Russell style logical conditionals.

It is important to be clear that the categories are derived on a case-by-case basis. This is an ontology focused on the individual and not the general or universal. Thus I present it as an alternative to any univocal account of being and, instead, point to our ability to see *some* commonality of formal conditions behind objects that can be grouped together under each of the three categories.

Lastly, I present one more argument for the determining conditions specific to this ontology. Quine's indeterminacy of reference blocked the way of justifying the use of any one translation manual above any other. John Searle provided intuitive arguments for the absurdity of such relativism. I argue that the three-category ontology gives the metaphysical ground to marry our metaphysics adequately to what we know intuitively and thus provides a veridical platform for justifying both *the* correct manual of translation and intersubjective knowledge.

Thus the aims of this chapter is expository in laying out the details of each category and their specific functions. The categories also present a superior alternative to that presented in previous chapters. It is also a viable alternative to those answers to scepticism given in recent decades and provides an explanations of the relation between higher level properties and their lower-level constituents.

Determination and Realisation

In this chapter I will sketch a theory of being that is ultimately basic in the sense that (a) it is prerequisite for any entity to be admitted into the realm of existence and (b) characterises any such entity in a way that is exhaustive. Specifically, my aim is to outline a *three-category ontology*, giving details of each and presenting them as at least a viable alternative to the metaphysical pictures presented in the previous chapters. Such categories cover the entire landscape of existence: from the lowliest of entities to the human organism. It is not a theory that tries to compress all other categories and kinds into a single procrustean bed of existence, but is instead abstracted from empirical data.

None of the three categories are more fundamental than the others. Indeed they are all mutually asymmetrically dependent on each other; the unique feature of each acts in a way that is the inverse and yet compliment of the unique feature of the other. These categories are not discoverable a priori but are abstracted from both the ordinary objects of common sense and scientific analysis. Contradicting Quine, we can say that although the terrain between science and philosophy is the same, the division of labour is opposed. We are not devising theories, as Quine supposed, but post-theoretically the philosopher's role is to abstract the various categories and delineate each according to their role in making up the content discovered by science.

The first category to consider is the *determiner* or *unifier*. It's the abstract form of any system that is a collection of objects with certain properties and relations between them.[479] Some examples: a chair, or a human organism, Newtonian Laws and Peano Axioms. It functions somewhat like Aristotle's notion of a formal cause in that it acts on and *informs* matter by transforming each atom into a coherent whole. However, it differs radically from an Aristotelian form in not inhabiting space or time. Nor is it a copy of a concrete individual, as Plato thought. On the contrary, it is a formal condition. The function of the determiner and its formal conditions are identical to those set out in Koslicki's hylomorphic model:[480] (1) the specification of types of entities, somewhat like a list of ingredients, (2) the number of entities and (3) the spatio-temporal arrangement of those entities.

The second category is the *realiser* or *instantiator*. Its function is similar to Aristotle's material cause in that it is the recipient of formal conditions. The realiser is the means by which the determiner has any sort of influence or explanatory power over objects in the space-time world by, inversely, being selected and arranged in a particular way. Also, each realiser has an inherent disposition to realise different states, by virtue of its inherent indeterminacy with regards to alternative forms. For example, ink may instantiate a certain chemical form of its own, but it is also indeterminate relative to various higher-level

---

[479] This is the definition of a system given by Stathos Psillos in "The Structure, the Whole Structure and Nothing but the Structure," *Philosophy of Science* 73, 5 (2004): 560-570, http://doi.org/10.1086/518326 following the work of Michael Dummett in *Frege: Philosophy of Mathematics* (Cambridge, MA: Harvard University Press, 1991) and Stewart Shapiro *Philosophy of Mathematics: Structure and Ontology* (Oxford: Oxford University Press, 1997)

[480] Koslicki, *The Structure of Objects*, 172.

instantiations, (such as a mathematical form, a law of logic, a pictorial representation of a tree and so on).

The constituents of any object are related internally and hence the relata themselves fix the relation. The identity of each entity gets contextualised and hence transformed into its role as a part of the whole. For example, the relata "wife" tells us automatically – without having to spell it out ahead of time – that there is a further relata, "husband", and vice versa. Both, in turn, are aspects of the marital relation *whole* and presumably each lives in the same residence and exhibits certain amounts of affection *towards*[481] each other, etc. In other words, to be aspects of a whole their behaviour is modified accordingly. The existence of each entity fixes the relation, but this does not entail reductionism since it is owing to their place in the context that they have the identity and function that they do.[482] Here is a precisification of relations:

I1: $R(x,y)$ is internal$_1$ iff $R(x,y)$ is essential to x and y.

I2: $R(x,y)$ is internal$_2$ iff "$R(x,y)$" is made true by monadic properties of x and y.[483]

Under the schema I am proposing, the identity transform means I1 is correct but not I2. However, it is not the essential nature of the relata that is explanatorily basic. It is the determining category and the subsequent role the relata occupy in the whole that guarantees the internal relation. The x and y are fixed in their natures by being in such a context set out by the whole. So x and y are essentially related by R, but that state is derived by both x and y being parts of a whole.

---

[481] As will be discussed later the communicator even functions within the whole and in this case the "towards" is the function of the communicator where the determiner functions like an invisible hand to coordinate that influence towards the benefit of the whole. So in this case husband and wife modify their behaviour in marriage but that is not the specific goal of their affections towards each other.

[482] There is actually no conflict here with the physicalist notion that both micro and macro-properties are realised by basic entities Jaegwon Kim, *Mind in a Physical World: An Essay on the Mind-Body Problem and Mental Causation* (Cambridge: MIT Press, 1998), 82. It's just that this picture is incomplete vis-à-vis this proposal since the realisation conditions are specified by a determining form.

[483] David Yates in "Introduction: The Metaphysics of Relations," in *The Metaphysics of Relations*, ed. Anna Marmodoro and David Yates (Oxford: Oxford University Press, 2016), 8.

Some philosophers have taken internal relations to lack any kind of ontological robustness.[484] Thus there is really nothing more to an internal relation than the relata themselves. Now the argument can be spelt out like this:

1) Only objects and their monadic properties exist in the world.

2) Internal relations supervene on their relata and their monadic products.

3) That which supervenes on something else is "no addition of being" in the world.

4) Therefore internal relations are "no addition of being" in the world.

This is entirely consistent with introducing an abstract determiner that fixes the identity of the relata since it is "no addition of being" *in the world*. The above in fact may fail in the same way that supervenience fails – in not being able to explain *why* the relata exist in the state that they are in. Indeed it may well be that the relata so exist in such a state *because* of the relation itself. As Fraser Macbride writes:

"There are true comparative claims of the form *aRb* which are either determined to be true by, or supervene upon, the intrinsic natures of the things they relate, *Fa&Gb*. Philosophers of a reductionist persuasion have argued that this shows there is no need to admit an internal relation (*R*) over and above the intrinsic characteristics or monadic foundations of the things related (*F,G*). But the intrinsic characteristics of the things related only determine the truth of the claim that *aRb*, or the truth of the claim that *aRb* only supervenes upon *Fa&Gb*, because these characteristics stand in an internal relation themselves, *F RG*.

---

[484] For a list of those adhering to a reductionist view of relations see Fraser Macbride's entry "Relations," *The Stanford Encyclopedia of Philosophy* (Winter 2016 Edition), ed. Edward N. Zalta, URL = <https://plato.stanford.edu/archives/win2016/entries/relations/>.

Because the monadic foundations, *Fa* and *Gb*, are only empowered to determine that *aRb* because *F* and *G* lie in this internal relation, *R*, it follows that internal relations still perform an indispensable role in our theorising about the world."[485]

Thus it is the internal relations themselves that stand first in the order of explanation and determine the monadic properties had by its occupants. Which means the monadic properties are at least in part determined by being in the relation. The reductionist case then seems to be little more than question-begging. In response one could point to Armstrong's solution of positing "unsaturated" relations which open up a place within themselves for the bare particular effecting an internally complex state of affairs and can only be analysed out by abstraction from the whole.[486] This avoids any need to posit further entities to tie the relation and particular together. The other advantages is that it allows states of affairs to be ultimate – instead of particulars or universals – and prohibits uninstantiated universals. But what does it mean for a relation or universal to have both an intrinsic nature *and* being inherently dependent on the particular? It seems obscure as to *how* this is actually the case and just labelling it "unsaturated" doesn't help. The obscurity is compounded when it is recalled that, for Frege, unsaturated concepts were not even denizens of the spatiotemporal universe.

But straightforward demonstrations can be made for the D–R categories. Take Koslicki's motorcycle example.[487] We have all the parts shaped out of metal, plastic, leather, etc. We have the seat, the handle bars, the engine, muffler, etc. But the bike does not exist when the parts are scattered randomly across the garage floor. They need to be arranged in the right way. That is, we also need a formal component, the blueprint that the engineer follows in constructing the bike. It is not just another component alongside the muffler and headlights, etc.

But can we deduce that such a formal component is not physical? There are several arguments indicating we can. Firstly, an artefact does not weigh any more than the material

---

[485] Ibid.
[486] Armstrong, *A World of States of Affairs*, 29.
[487] Koslicki, *The Structure of Objects,* 3-4.

stuff that makes it up. If the bike parts weigh 500 kg then the parts arranged into a functioning bike will not weigh an additional 500 kg totalling 1000 kg.[488] Second, there is likewise no principle of additivity when it comes to spatial volume. There is no addition of total spatial volume above and beyond the total comprising the parts of the bike once the bike is fully constructed. Hence the formal component is non-spatial.

But what we *can* say is that this formal component determines the arrangement of the physical parts and is hence dependent on spatiotemporal particulars, and that such a unity makes up an internally related whole. Internal relations do not require further entities to explain the relation holding in the first place. Hence both of Armstrong's worries are relieved – there are no uninstantiated entities and the regress is thwarted – and we have a concept that is experientially demonstrable.

It is also inherent to any analysis of the concept of determination that it be dyadic, since determining involves something doing the determining and something being the recipient of that determination. Thus the existence of such a category, and its inherent relation to the physical universe, is straightforwardly demonstrable.

But then it may be asked where this leaves apparently co-located objects such as a statue and its constituent lump. The solution is very straight forward. There are not two objects here but two principles of composition of the one object: the determining form of the statue and its realising material, clay. The former is non-spatiotemporal and so is not co-located with its matter. The clay does have persistence conditions not attributable to the statue but that is simply because the clay can be smashed and realise an alternate form – that is, go indeterminate relative to the statue form – such as a heap.[489]

---

[488] This argument has been given against the colocation of two objects such as a statue and its lump. E.g. David Lewis writes; "It reeks of double counting to say that here we have a dishpan, and we also have a dishpan-shaped bit of plastic that is just where the dishpan is, weighs just what the dishpan weighs (why don't the two together weigh twice as much?), and so on."; *On the Plurality of Worlds,* 252. See also Dean Zimmerman "Theories of Masses," *Philosophical Review* 104, no. 1, (1995): 87-88, http://doi.org/10.2307/2186012

[489] C.f. Michael Burke's *Dominant Kind View* of material constitution where the copper that enters a constitutive state of a statue goes out of existence leaving not two co-located objects but just one; "Preserving the Principle of One Object to a Place. A Novel Account of the Relations Among Objects, Sorts, Sortals, and Persistence Conditions," *Philosophy and Phenomenological Research* 54, issue 3, (1994): 591-624, https://www-jstor-

Communication

The third category is the *communicator*. It is a basic notion in our conceptual repertoire but it is not primitive in the sense that it cannot be defined. It is only primitive in the way that it can be given an *explication* and shown to be foundational in explaining our experiences. And yet such an explication only allows us to flesh out the concept without the definition itself being sufficient in giving further terms that allow us to dispense with it.

We know that every effect carries some sort of information about its cause and in this respect the communicator functions as a cause and is the means by which the D–R notion conveys its nature to other entities.[490] It is a distinct entity from the object from which it originates and communicates the nature of that entity. A very simple example is the way the nature of a seal implants itself via an outside force (the sealer) into the wax and thus leaves an imprint of itself in the wax.

The role of this category is to communicate the nature of the D–R entity.[491] It does so by entering into the composition of another object. For example, being in a state of knowing that there is a green tree in front of me means I have entered, cognitively, into a unified state of believing – with the proposition "there is a green tree in front of me" – *that* there is in fact a green tree in front of me. The actual communicating entity in this case is the sensory structure had under the state of perception.

---

org.ipacez.nd.edu.au/stable/2108583; "Persons and Bodies: How to Avoid the New Dualism," *American Philosophical Quarterly* 34, issue 4, (1997a): 457-467, https://www-jstor-org.ipacez.nd.edu.au/stable/20009913; "Coinciding Objects: A Reply to Lowe and Denkel," *Analysis* 57, no. 1, (1997b) 11-18, https://www-jstor-org.ipacez.nd.edu.au/stable/3328429. This neutralises the co-locationist's argument from differing persistence conditions for now it is only the dominant kind's – the statue – persistence conditions that remain. But this has the highly odd result that the marble used to sculpt a statue goes out of existence (along with its persistence conditions). It strikes my intuitions as far more plausible to see the marble as merely formed into a statue and taking on the realising condition with the persistence conditions applying to its unformed/unrealised state.

[490] Thus this is a theory of causation that is both forward *and* backward-pointing; that A at t_1 causes B at t_2 and B at t_2 is *about* A at t_1.

[491] C.f. Armstrong's "world of states of affairs," (*A World of States of Affairs,* 1.) where "reality has a propositional structure" (Ibid, 3.)

The arrangement of material entities that make up the tree have no capacity in themselves to communicate their nature, but we can say they are *disposed* to do so owing to their structural nature – and perhaps its molecular reflectance properties – in the same way that a vase is disposed to shatter based on the structure of its molecular make-up, even though it has no power to shatter on its own. Conversely, the communicator is the power that communicates the nature of the D–R categories due to its causal power and the isomorphism[492] it shares with its object of origin.[493] Experience, as structured sense data, makes objects available to us but that structure is explained and justified by the structure of the objects.

Once perception takes place, the knower is in a causally affected state, with the content of the proposition and its intentional properties compelling a state of knowledge. Sense properties bring a commitment to the green tree and forces us into holding that there is a green tree and subsequently admitting it into our ontology. We are placed into the state of knowledge, leaving no room for an inner homunculus or Kantian transcendental ego between our compelled state and the imposing claims of the sensory data. The state of representation supervenes on the existence of the D–R in the mind-external world and our being in an affected state by the representation-inducing sense properties. Consequently, representation is only other-directed. There is in no precondition of a higher-order state of representation, or awareness of awareness, to know that such a correspondence is in place.[494]

---

[492] Another way to put it is to say that the object constitutes the experience in the sense that it "shape[s] the contours of," that experience; M. G. F. Martin "The Limits of Self-Awareness," *Philosophical Studies* 120, no. 1/3, (2004): 64, http://www.jstor.org/stable/4321508.

[493] Evidence that we are intuitively aware that perception is causal in nature is given by William Child: "For example, if one has the concept of vision, one must know that S will stop seeing something if she shuts her eyes, or if we interpose something opaque between her and the object, and if the object is moved away; and to know that is to know that something cannot be seen if it is prevented from, or cannot be, causally affecting S." *Causality, Interpretation, and the Mind* (Oxford: Clarendon Press, 1994), 165.

[494] Keith Allen says colours "impinge" on consciousness to distinguish the causal process involved in perception from the "impact" of causal process that might be involved, for example, in one billiard ball striking another; *A Naïve Realist Theory of Colour* (Oxford: Oxford University Press, 2016), 103. I would, however, see both perception and the collision of billiard balls as examples of communication; Perception compels the state of belief in the perceiver where one billiard ball will compel a state of motion.

i)   **Causation**

It is informative to see how the three-category ontology resolves certain quandaries in various theories of causation. A unitary state was proposed by C. B. Martin to avoid the unwanted conclusion that powers are mere passive states merely awaiting the appropriate stimulus. On his account, the power becomes identified with the mutual manifestation of equal partners in the causal interaction.[495] So there is no longer a stimulus responsible for all the work and a mere passive power, but two equal partners with equal responsibility. For example, the bat hitting the vase is no more responsible for the shattering than the vase itself, for the vase requires the right kind of molecular structure to facilitate the shattering. Another example: the ice in water causes the water to cool, but the water also melts the ice. There seems to be an equal partnering of powers here.

So what we have under Martin's proposal is an identification of the dispositions with the manifestation. In other words, the dispositions do not cause the manifestation: they *are* the manifestation. The example he gives is of two triangle shaped pieces of paper coming together in the right way to form a square. The two triangles arranged appropriately *just are* the square. But as Mumford and Anjum point out, this is essentially an elimination of causation since the coming together – the process we would ordinarily attribute to the cause – now just becomes the manifestation of mutual partnering.[496]

I agree with Martin that such causal encounters *result in* wholes of mutual partners. This is precisely how I explained propositional knowledge: the knower is compelled to a state of justified knowledge by taking on such a state as a property. The proposition and the knower are internally connected. But my account adds a crucial component that Martin reduces to the mutual manifestation. That is the asymmetric causal process whereby sense properties

---

[495] C. B. Martin, *The Mind in Nature* (Oxford: Oxford University Press, 2008), 48-51.
[496] Stephen Mumford and Rani Lill Anjum, "Mutual Manifestation and Martin's Twin Triangles," in *Causal Powers* ed. Jonathan D. Jacobs, 77-89. (Oxford: Oxford University Press, 2017)

act on the knower to induce a state of knowledge. This is the role of the communicator and it is something real and distinct apart from the mutual manifestation of powers.

Martin's manifestation of partners, as mere mereological sums, has also been criticised for lacking the resources to explain novel causal outcomes. As Mumford and Anjum point out:

"To see this, one need only look at what happens when powers of things get combined in the sort of way Martin envisages. If we put together the powers of sodium, for instance, with the powers of chlorine, in the sort of way Martin puts together his two triangular cards, we do not get just their sum. It is hard to argue, then, that the partnered powers are identical with the manifestation. Sodium has a power to ignite spontaneously in water. Chlorine is poisonous. As Rothschild … points out, when we bring together these two substances with their various powers, we do not get something that is both poisonous and explosive. Instead, the two substances transform to become sodium chloride, that is, salt: something that has the powers of being soluble, tasty, and in the right quantities a contributor to human health. This is no simple mereological sum of the powers of the parts. Some powers of the parts are no longer found in the whole and some powers of the whole are not found among the parts."[497]

However, this objection is only a threat to a mereological sum. But the whole *rasion d'etre* of the determining category is to introduce this kind of novelty in unified wholes – a novelty the constituents lacked prior to forming the whole. Returning to Martin's twin-triangles example, the two paper triangles have to be placed in the right juxtaposition to form a square. There needs to be some determination of context to allow the unitary state in the first place.

Mumford and Anjum concur with Martin, and against Hume, that partnered powers act instantaneously. However, this isn't the complete story. The acting of partners may be instantaneous but the full effect may not. The example they give is of sugar dissolving in

---

[497] Ibid, 83.

water: the causal process of the water acting on the sugar may be instantaneous but it may take several minutes for all the sugar to completely dissolve. But then cause does seem to precede effect in some sense, since they concede that the "full effect" is not immediate.[498]

But is this semantic messiness not a result of trying to substitute a metaphysical category like causation for the multifarious and variegated nature of the real physical world? What we have in sugar dissolution is the breaking up of molecules by hot water due to the force asymmetrically applied by the H_2O molecules to the sugar molecules. This process takes time. But it also seems that when a bat is swung at a vase and shatters it, the force built up by the swing preceding contact is crucial to the whole causal process. The temporal element, at least in many instances, seems crucial.

I do not mean here to insist that Hume was right all along and that causes must temporally precede effects. There is a way of looking at sugar dissolution where cause and effect are simultaneous since, on a molecule-by-molecule basis, every molecular act of dissolution simultaneously involves a molecule being broken up. Harre and Madden give the example of a knife going through an orange.[499] The knife's moving through the orange and its separation are simultaneous. What seems undeniably crucial, however, is both the asymmetry or directionality to the process – where temporal precedence is often a factor – and the specific nature of the respective objects. In the case of the orange, the necessary and sufficient conditions seem to be the force applied from the knife to the orange, the arrangement of the steel molecules that ensure a clean incision through the orange, and molecular bonds in the orange that are suitably loose to allow the incision to go through.

The three categories are indispensable for explaining these scenarios. Take the bat shattering the vase. The vase and bat do not seem to be in equal partnership here, contrary to Martin, to the extent that the bat distributes force to the vase asymmetrically and thus cannot remain a partner at all, equal or unequal. It is true that the molecular structure of the

---

[498] Ibid, 82.
[499] Rom Harre and Edward H. Madden, "Natural Powers and Powerful Natures," *Philosophy* 48, no. 185, (1973): 221, http://www.jstor.org/stable/3749407

vase's material base is a crucial component, but this is because of the disposition for indeterminacy in the realising condition to take on different forms.

The formation of sodium chloride from the soft metal sodium hydroxide and the poisonous green gas chloride provides an instance of the formation of a unity from two objects coming together. However, emergentists have used this example since the 19th century as an illustration of the emergence of something distinct from its parts. The properties of the whole cannot be deduced or predicted ahead of time from the properties of the separate elements. C. D. Broad wrote:

"I will merely remark that, so far as we know at present, the characteristic behaviour of Common Salt cannot be deduced from the most complete knowledge of the properties of Sodium in isolation; or of Chlorine in isolation; or of other compounds of Sodium, such as Sodium Sulphate, and of other compounds of Chlorine, such as Silver Chloride."[500]

Thus this is far more than a case of a mereological whole. Interestingly, however, chemists also tell us that both the sodium and chlorine remain and can be extracted. But as parts of a whole their properties do change. Clearly their distinct molecular make up has been contextualised in such a way that the resultant properties of the whole sodium chloride molecule differs from its parts taken separately. But even here the formation of sodium chloride begins with the attraction of an electron from sodium to chlorine, since sodium has only one electron in its outer shell. After donating the electron, positive and negative ions attract each other to form the positive and negative ionic bonds that make up sodium chlorine. Such forces of attraction and repulsion are ubiquitous in chemical interactions and are even said to be basic and unanalysed forces that do not give way to more physical explanations.[501] What appears in this instance is that attraction and repulsion function due to the specific nature of each entity, which results in the formation of a new unity with distinct, emergent properties due to the way the parts are determined. The negative to positive attraction may have been the proximate force initiating the reaction but the

---

[500] C. D. Broad, *The Mind and its Place in Nature* (London & New York: Routledge, 2013), 59.
[501] Janet Stemwedel, "'Causes' in Chemical Explanations," *Chemical Explanation: Characteristics, Development, Autonomy* vol. 988, no. 1, (2003): 217-226, https://doi.org/10.1111/j.1749-6632.2003.tb06101.x

determiner acts, to use a metaphor, like an invisible hand guiding the forces into a coherent, emergent whole.

A distinct role is therefore available for dispositions, based on their structure. But this involves dispensing with the nomenclature of powers and introducing the three-category ontology. Under this schema, specific structures are necessary conditions, since they are disposed towards the cause by virtue of the fact that the cause itself must communicate the relevant aspects of the structure. The clearest example is perception where, for example, a light turned on in a room and the reflection of that light from objects and their specific forms facilitates perception. But even in the case of the bat swung at the vase there must be a certain amount of force applied to effect the shattering *and* the right structural make-up of the bat and vase. In the case of chemical reactions, it is usually the communication of electromagnetic forces involved in attraction and repulsion (with the addition often of a catalyst such as heat). But once the causal process is complete the newly donated electron gets contextualised according to the formal structure set out by the determiner.

Thus we do not *really* have equal partnering as far as causes go. Two factors are indispensable: the structure of the cause and effect, and the communication of some aspect of the cause unilaterally directed towards the effect. And at least in some cases the effect produced leaves both cause and effect as non-mereological parts of a distinct, emergent whole, further susceptible to analysis into determining and realising components of its own. Thus Martin's analysis of mutual manifestation partners more naturally gives way to the three-category ontology which more adequately explains all the factors involved in causation.

ii) **Truth**

As far as the perceptual process is concerned, a redundancy theory of truth is most relevant. Truth, whilst a substantial notion, has no content above and beyond the sense properties themselves. There is no independent criteria for truth. To perceive a cat on the mat is to know that there is a cat on the mat in the mind-independent world and to know such without any antecedent conception of truth or true judgement.[502] Thus it is an embrace of Sellars' myth of "the given"[503] and an attempt at bridging the gulf, traditionally seen since the time of Galileo and Descartes, between mind and world.

But that isn't to give way to deflationism either. Truth is a condition of existent entities. It is *of* these entities, but it is not *among* the existent entities. It is not just "one more thing" among the range of existents within the domain. To know what truth is, is to look at specific examples of true propositions.

The relation between knower and proposition is internal. The knower must be in a compelled state of knowledge of that proposition whilst that proposition has been incorporated into the knowledge base of the knower. This sets up an interesting contrast with the correspondence theories rejected by Frege and Russell. For Frege, as we saw, it is not possible to be in a correspondence state of knowledge of an object without setting off a regress, since to be in such a state requires *knowing* that one is in such a state and that in turn requires us being in a correspondence state with *that* relation of correspondence.[504]

But under *communication*, the connection is internal: the state of knowing is internal to the knower and the proposition known. Hence this view is vastly different to the Cartesian view of the mind, where the knower occupies something akin to a homunculus reflecting on its internal mental states. Such a relation is external and allows what Edmund Husserl calls an

---

[502] Echoing Dummett we can say that truth and sense are intertwined in the same way as playing a game and winning that game are; "Truth," *The Aristotelian Society* virtual Issue no.1 (2013): 7, https://www.aristoteliansociety.org.uk/pdf/dummett.pdf

[503] Wilfrid Sellars, "Empiricism and the Philosophy of Mind," in, *Minnesota Studies in the Philosophy of Science, Volume I: The Foundations of Science and the Concepts of Psychology and Psychoanalysis*, ed. Herbert Feigl and Michael Scriven (Minneapolis, Minn: University of Minnesota Press, 1956), 253-329. But this system does not fall into Sellar's trap since, as the bulk of this thesis has been at pains to show, the space of reasons and sense data are interlocked – that is, phenomenal properties are *determined* - so that concepts are identified with suitably structured sense data. They are intelligible causal impacts on the perceiver and not "mere brute impact[s] from the exterior" as John McDowell has put it; *Mind and World*, 8

[504] This is an old problem as Hillary Putnam sees the same dilemma for William of Ockham who's mental particulars are "signs" for the outside world where any concept of such a relation requires a further sign and so on; "Realism and Reason," *Proceedings and Addresses of the American Philosophical Association* 50, no. 6, (1977): 483-498, http://doi.org/10.2307/3129784.

epoche: the freedom of the internal self to commit or not commit to states of knowing the world outside itself. It is precisely such an external relation that sets off a regress of demands for correspondence conditions.

Traditionally, states of propositional attitude and their "aboutness" were specified independently of phenomenal content. By contrast, on my proposal a proposition is a formal unity of sense properties – perception being the paradigmatic example – that have as the object of their communication the mind-independent externally specified object (made up of the D–R categories). Sense qualities have an intentional content and there is a match between the object's structure and the structure of the representative sense properties. The arrangement of such sense properties reflects the structural arrangement of realising states according to the abstract form of the determiner.[505] Implicit in our cognition of sense properties is the recognition first, that those sense properties originate from the object they are about, and second, that those properties are arranged in such a way that reflects the structural arrangement of the object that is the subject of its aboutness.[506]

States of experiential consciousness are not reduced states, but are one-level phenomena and any attempt at defining them must mention their being in a state of consciousness of objects. Echoing Fred Dretske, we can say that conscious mental states are states we are conscious *with* not conscious *of*.[507] That is, they are not dependent on any second-order

---

[505] This is broadly similar to what George Pitcher called "correspondence-as-congruence" (as opposed to mere "correspondence-as-correlation"); "Introduction," in *Truth* ed. George Pitcher (Englewood Cliff: Prentice-Hall, 1964), 10.

[506] I say "implicit" because it takes a more cognitively sophisticated ability to grasp these two properties of sense perception. What is *most* basic to sense perception is the intentionality of the communicator, the referring to the object in the world. This is something young children and animals would have no problem grasping. This gives my own account of perception advantage over Searle's internalist "causal self-referentialist" account of the intentionality of visual experience where it is part of the conditions of satisfaction of the visual experience that it must be *caused* by the state of affairs that is a constituent of that condition of satisfaction; John Searle *Intentionality: An Essay in the Philosophy of Mind* (Cambridge: Cambridge University Press, 1983), 48-49. Specifically, Searle's theory is far too cognitively sophisticated and would exclude animals and children from having the sort of perception he describes; David Armstrong, "Intentionality, Perception, and Causality," in *John Searle and His Critics,* ed. Ernest Lepore and Robert Van Gulick, 149-158 Oxford, Basil Blackwell, 1991 and Tyler Burge, "Vision and Intentional Content," in ibid, 195-213.

[507] Fred Dretske, *Naturalizing the Mind* (Cambridge, MA: MIT Press, 1995), 100-101.

mental state being directed at it. Our consciousness is not a substance as Descartes thought.[508] It is a "being in-itself" but equally it is a "being for-others".[509]

The unified state of knower and proposition known gives us the intrinsic state of believing there is an object given in immediate perception.[510] The explanation of *how* such a knowledge state comes about is based on the asymmetric cause of the communicative category that is originally responsible for such a belief state. Analogously, we could give a description of the length of a shadow cast by a flag pole based on the height of the flag pole and the position of the sun. The explanation would involve some optics and basic trigonometry and thus be a mixture of formal and material factors. But this does not grant us the explanatory factors in this process since it would be equally possible to deduce the length of the flag pole from the length of the shadow. Thus the directionality of the sun's rays bearing down on the flag pole is a crucial factor accounting for the asymmetric causal explanation of the shadow.

The object out in the world, therefore is not a truth-maker, since the *communicator* presents the truth as basic and ultimate and hence it is not derived from anything else. It is its structural form that is derived from the structural form of the D–R entity, although the latter is disposed to be communicated to other entities.[511]

---

[508] It will be recalled from the previous chapters that the notion of substance that Descartes inherits from Aristotle is an example of Parmenidian Being: a simple, independent and fundamental package of Being.

[509] There is consonance here with Amie Thomasson's *adverbial* theory of conscious awareness; "If I am conscious that there is an orange tree before me, it is because it *seems to me* that there is an orange tree there. But although the focus of my attention is the orange tree…nonetheless, the experience is itself conscious, not in the sense that I am aware *of it*…; but in the sense that it has the phenomenal qualities that make me aware of the tree: it is what makes me see *consciously*." (emphasis original) "After Brentano: A One-Level Theory of Consciousness," *European Journal of Philosophy* 8, issue 2, (2000): 203-204, http://doi.org/10.1111/1468-0378.00108

[510] The intrinsic connection between knower and mental content also grounds the infallibility of knowledge of our own mental states.

[511] Scientifically this could be specified in terms of the reflectance properties of the molecules in the objects in the world and how they interact with photons/light waves, etc.

iii) Sense Data Structure

The third chapter detailed the culmination of the Frege–Russell logical project as reaching its zenith in the work of Carnap's *LSW*. I agreed with Quine that Carnap failed in his attempt to eliminate any reference to the predicate that locates each sense datum and therefore failed to adequately reconstruct empirical knowledge. However, contrary to Quine, I consider the source of that failure to be Carnap's acceptance of Frege and Russell's approach.

The communicator is a property of our structured sensory states. It is a means for the justification of knowledge that is not based on a structure that is independent and superimposed on the world of senses. To have knowledge of a particular in front of oneself is not to be in a state that is ultimately grounded in the logical superstructure, but it is the sensory structure that one is caused to be having that puts one in a state of knowing with certainty.

Since there is no Archimedean point on which to base our knowledge states, there is no need for the reconstruction to take place in order to meet such a standard in the first place. Instead, the structure of appearances derives from the structure of things in the world. A necessary condition of communication requires our sensory states to be structured in a way that is isomorphic with the entities communicated. The nature of communication is derived from the nature of the object communicated. For example, the structure of my sensory state of seeing a tree derives from the arrangement of the molecules that constitutes the tree. Thus we have a ready explanation for the arrangement of sense data by taking it as given and not demanding a reconstruction and in turn deriving our metaphysical categories in such a way that explains such sense data structures rather than explaining them away.

Realism and Subsequent Debates

i)   Tarski, Putnam and Field on Truth

Ever since the time of Aristotle one very prominent way of expressing what it means for a statement to be true is just to say that there is a relation of correspondence between what is said and the facts out there in the world. But the definition of correspondence carries the connotation is of a two-place relation between propositions and facts. But how do we characterise such a relation? How do we define what it means to be a fact?

John Locke, drawing on a tradition begun with Galileo and Descartes that saw our sense data as being purely mind-dependent, and as having no intrinsic connection with the outside world, could not ground general and universal notions in sense data and thus relied on linguistic notions expressed in public communications.[512] As we saw in the third chapter, Cartesianism was very much an assumption of Quine's even though he tried hard to remove its ontological implications from his system. A heavy emphasis has been laid on linguistics since Frege and we saw in the first chapter that he too inherited a form of Cartesianism and denied, through strong use of the context principle, any correspondence theory of truth. These sorts of developments have seen a need for a linguistic expression of correspondence. Ralph Walker writes:

"Colloquially, 'corresponds with the facts' can function as a long-winded way of saying 'is true'..."[513]

---

[512] He states; "General and Universal, belong not to the real existence of Things; but are the Inventions and Creatures of the Understanding, made by it for its own use, and concern only signs, whether Words or Ideas." John Locke, *An Essay Concerning Human Understanding*, (Pennsylvania: Pennsylvania State University, 1999), 399.

[513] Ralph Walker, "Theories of Truth," in *A Companion to the Philosophy of Language* ed. Bob Hale and Crispin Wright (Oxford: Blackwell, 1997), 309.

And he goes on to state that such a definition "becomes an empty tautology".[514] As a result of the linguistic approach leading to vacuity, many have tried to free the correspondence theory of what they see as its excess metaphysical baggage. One prominent way of doing this was with the "semantic conception" of truth advocated by Tarski.[515] Tarski was working during the time when logical positivism was preeminent, with its thrust to banish all metaphysical notions that could not be empirically derived. Tarski aimed to satisfy the Aristotelian idea of correspondence with reality and he did so with his famous *adequacy condition*. This condition relieved the anxieties that the correspondence theory provoked. As Karl Popper writes:

"It was not so much the antinomy of the liar which frightened me, but the difficulty of explaining the correspondence theory: what could it be that constituted the correspondence of a statement to a fact?"[516]

The formula that has to be satisfied for a sentence to be true must conform to the following schema:

1) x is true if and only if p

The right-hand side of the biconditional gives the non-semantic term that is supposed to satisfy the schema. If we take a statement like "the moon is blue", we cannot generalise this without the truth predicate, which gives us:

2) If "the moon is blue" is true, then the moon is blue

We can then generalise this formula as:

3) X is true if, and only if, p

---

[514] Ibid.
[515] Alfred Tarski "The Semantic Conception of Truth and the Foundations of Semantics," *Philosophy and Phenomenological Research* 4, no. 3, (1944): 341-376, http://doi.org/10.2307/2102968 and Alfred Tarski "The Conception of Truth in Formalised Languages," in *Logic, Semantics, Metamathematics; Papers from 1922 to 1938*, trans. Joseph Woodger, ed. John Corcoran (Oxford: Clarendon Press, 1956), 152-278.
[516] Karl Popper, *Objective Knowledge: An Evolutionary Approach*, reprint with corrections and new appendix 2 (Oxford: Clarendon Press, 1979), 320.

So '*p*' is a sentence token and 'X' is the name of the sentence token '*p*'. This provides an advantage over just saying:

4) "The moon is blue" refers to the moon is blue

The reason the satisfaction relation is advantageous is that it applies to *n*-place formulas and so a number of instances can be substituted for the variables to give us objects that satisfy the truth predicate. So "'the moon is blue' is true iff the moon is blue" and "'the sun is bright' is true iff the sun is bright" and so on. Such satisfaction conditions are given extensionally as the appropriate objects are assigned to variables and truth is given by the sentential function. Each instance is only a partial truth, since a full definition can only be given if the full sequence from the object language is also given.[517]

It is important to note that Tarski took his adequacy condition to be metaphysically neutral:

"We may accept the semantic conception of truth without giving up any epistemological attitude we may have had; we may remain naïve realists, critical realists or idealists, empiricists or metaphysicians – whatever we were before. The semantic conception is completely neutral toward all these issues."[518]

Now what was touted as an advantage of Tarski's scheme – its ambiguity among a number of different formulations of realism and anti-realism – and may have endeared it to the logical positivism around at the time, I see as a disadvantage. The adequacy condition gives us a semantic formula that allows us to state conditions at the purely linguistic level only. There is no explanation as to *how* the satisfaction relation obtains. If the logical connectives are taken classically to do the work demanded by Aristotle, then the right-hand side of the biconditional just gives us variables and we are left asking whether the names

---

[517] Leon Horsten argues that Tarski has actually given up on giving us a definition of truth and instead interested in questions like "how is truth used?", "how does truth function?" and "how can its functioning be described?" *The Tarskian Turn; Deflationism and Axiomatic Truth* (Cambridge, MA: MIT Press, 2011), 15-16.
[518] Tarski, "The Semantic Conception of Truth," 362.

occupying those variables can function themselves, in a context independent way, to refer to the world or if it is purely the axiomatic structure itself at work.

An objection levelled at Tarskian truth is that in giving us a list of truths that are relative to a given language, there is no way to apply a truth criterion to new cases.[519] We need to have some sort of antecedent grasp of truth in order to subsume new cases where the truth predicate applies. But that is a demand for a universal notion of truth that subordinates the particular which, from the three-category ontology perspective, has things backwards. But that is not my main focus here.

In a similar vein, Hartry Field takes issue with the Tarskian method for providing no commonality between the sentences but only an enumeration of sentences that fulfil the relation of satisfaction.[520] The reduction effected by Tarski, argues Field, does so in a way that sheds no light on the nature of truth. Field provides the example of a comparable reduction in chemistry: for the "valence of a chemical element" we could give the following list:

"$\forall E \forall n(E$ has valence $n \leftrightarrow E$ is potassium and n is +1, or..., or E is sulphur and n is -2)"[521]

All that is being given here is a list of every element, and its associated valence and the rules whereby the valence of compound elements derive their valence from their constituent atoms. Field believes that we need more than this. We need an account of the physical properties and an explanation of the nature of the bonding process itself. All we get in the quantified statement is a list of conjuncts and, since Wittgenstein, we have been alerted to the fact that logical connectives such as conjunctions add nothing above and beyond the mere list.

---

[519] Donald Davidson, "The Folly of Trying to Define Truth," in *Truth*, ed. Simon Blackburn and Keith Simmons, 308-322. (Oxford: Oxford University Press, 1999)
[520] Hartry Field, "Tarski's Theory of Truth," *Journal of Philosophy* 69, no. 13, (1972): 347-375, http://doi.org/10.2307/2024879.
[521] Ibid, 363.

In responding to Field, Putnam first draws a comparison between statements of reference, such as "'Electron' refers to electron" and Tarskian satisfaction statements like "'snow is white' is true if and only if snow is white".[522] He then goes on to specify the "Criterion of Adequacy" (referred to as criterion T below) for the latter case as:

"(Call the result 'Criterion S'– 's' for Satisfaction) An adequate definition of satisfies-in-L must yield as theorems all instances of the following schema: ⌜ $P(x_1,...,x_n)$ ⌝ is satisfied by the sequence $y_1,...,y_n$ if and only if $P(y_1,...,y_n)$.

Rewriting (1) ['Electron' refers to electron] above as

(1`) 'Electron (x)' is satisfied by y_1 if and only if y_1 is an electron – which is how it would be written in the first place in Tarski-ese – we see that the structure of the list Field objects to is determined by Criterion *S*. But these criteria – T, or its natural generalization to formulas containing free variables, S – are determined by the formal properties we want the notions of truth and reference to have, by the fact that we *need* for a variety of purposes to have a predicate in our meta-language that satisfies precisely the Criterion S."[523]

There does not seem to be much to this response, however, other than a long question-begging reiteration of the logical nature of Tarski's theory, since the class of statements fulfilling the satisfaction condition are just derived analytically – by the law of identity – given by the biconditional acting on the domain; "⌜ $P(x_1,...,x_n)$ ⌝ is satisfied by the sequence $y_1,...,y_n$ if and only if $P(y_1,...,y_n)$."[524] He stresses our "*need*" to satisfy the criterion of adequacy and such a fulfilment gives the references in the resultant trivial matter. But we are still left with a mystery as to exactly *what* the satisfaction condition *is*, the lack of an answer for which we might say offends *our need* for scientific detail and the concordance

---

[522] Hillary Putnam, *Meaning and the Moral Sciences* (London: Routledge and Kegan Hall, 1978), 31.
[523] Ibid.
[524] Ibid.

with experience. At least Field attempts an answer that doesn't appeal to underlying logical form. However, Putnam then gives away the heart of the matter, which is the Kantian predicament:

"'Electron' refers to electrons – how else should we say what 'electron' refers to from within a conceptual scheme in which 'electron' is a primitive term? Given the Quinean (Kantian predicament?) that there is a real world but we can only describe it in terms of our conceptual system (Well? We should use someone else's conceptual system?) is it surprising that primitive reference has this character of apparent triviality?"[525]

The point he is making is that the only real work that the Tarskian sentences are able to do is to link terms up with objects *within our conceptual scheme.* And under such a conceptual scheme there is no way to reach the outside world except through terms embedded in the deductive logical machinery of first-order logic. Such a process abstracts completely from the content of the terms. This means the true sentences give us a mere list and do not tell us *why* just that list is true and not some other list. As A. C. Grayling describes the problem:

"[Tarski's truth] definition seems to contain material for supporting a correspondence construal...it proceeds in terms of a definition of satisfaction, and satisfaction is a relation between sentences and sequences of objects. But the difficulty is that Tarski's definition states that true and false sentences are respectively satisfied by all sequences and none, with no appeal being made to specific sequences."[526]

In other words, Tarski does not tell us *why* those particular sentences are true and that is because his system lacks the explanatory means to do so.[527] It is the biconditional and the conferring of mere extensional equivalence justifying the satisfaction relation for the list of

---

[525] Ibid, 32.
[526] A. C. Grayling, *An Introduction to Philosophical Logic* (Oxford: Blackwell, 1997), 156.
[527] Quine exploited the difference between sentences about sentences and sentences about the world to lay the ground of truth in the naturalistic/behaviouristic world so no intelligible explication of truth could be given by any individual sentence (see ch. 3 of this thesis). So Quine converts intentionality into a naturalistically conceived logical grounding relationship. Similarly for Frege, the first redundancy theorist, truth ultimately resided not with any particular sentence but at the level of assertive judgement (see ch. 1 & 2 of this thesis).

Tarski sentences and there is nothing inherent to such formal conditions that will select any particular list of sentences over any other.[528]

But this is a poor answer to Field's challenge. The heart of the problem remains that concepts cannot refer beyond themselves, as Putnam points out, because of the metaphysical and epistemic predicament we have been placed in by the works of Kant and Quine. What we need is a propositional system that is not tainted by the Cartesian predicament, one where the propositions in which our concepts are embedded *can refer* beyond themselves to the outside world. That condition is given by the *communicator* and thus gives us an advantage over the positions of Putnam and Quine. With such a category we get an explanation of truth (though not a reduction) as Field wants and avoid the unwanted consequences of allowing the underlying logic to play the truth-functional role.

ii) **Structuralism**

I would be remiss at this point not to engage with the version of realism known as *structuralism*. Reference is usually made to Russell's *The Analysis of Matter* as the original formulation of a structural theory of scientific realism.[529] There is much in his causal theory of perception – which states that our experiences are causally related to the objects of perception – that I find congenial, especially what Stathis Psillos calls the "Helmholtz–Weyl Principle".[530] This holds that differences in stimuli are responsible for differences in percepts and together with spatio-temporal continuity gives us knowledge of the structure of stimuli.

---

[528] This is far from a new observation. Dummett, in his seminal paper, "Truth," pointed out the deficiency in the Tarskian equivalence in providing any sort of explanation for the truth conditions of a sentence in the object language since one must already have a grasp of the sense of the sentence to know whether it is true which is precisely what was needed to be explained; "Truth," 6-7. See also (Wilfrid Sellars, *Science and Metaphysics* [Routledge & Kegan Paul, 1968], ch. 3) where he reanalyses notions like satisfaction in a way that doesn't involve a word-to-world relation. See also ("Correspondence between Wilfrid Sellars and Gilbert Harman on Truth," Sellars Archives, accessed 25th of May, 2019, http://www.ditext.com/sellars/sh-corr.html) for further defense/reiteration of his criticism that Tarskian semantics does not explain the referential relation.
[529] Bertrand Russell, *The Analysis of Matter* (London: Kegan Paul, 1927)
[530] Stathis Psillos, "Is Structural Realism Possible?" *Philosophy of Science* 68, no. S3 (2001): S14, https://doi.org/10.1086/392894

Interestingly, however, although the isomorphism between our percepts and stimuli allow knowledge of the structure of the latter, it does not allow for knowledge of the intrinsic natures of the stimuli themselves. All we can know about the world is its structure and not the things-in-themselves.

So far, however, there is nothing to adequately constrain the proliferation of structure beyond what is given, since the only requirement is that as stimuli differ then so must our percepts. There is no reason, as Psillos notes, not to expect some structure at the unobservable level, the level not manifested in phenomena. Hence he suggests this is more of an embedding than a strict isomorphism.[531] However, this scenario is ruled out by the functional integration of the three categories. The different categories work in tandem so that there is no possibility of any one functioning independently. Because the three categories form a unity that makes up a single act of perception such that the connection is necessary and isomorphic then there is no possibility of having undetected entities or perceptions without correlates in the world.

There was a fatal dilemma for Russell's structuralism, however, and it was pointed out by M. H. A. Newman.[532] Newman's objection is that actually knowing the structure of the world only gives us very trivial knowledge. If we take *TC* to be a combination of the *theoretical postulates* – containing theoretical but not observational terms – and *correspondence rules* – containing both theoretical and observational terms – then we have the open sentence:

$TC(t_1,\ldots,t_n,o_1,\ldots,o_m)$

---

[531] Ibid.
[532] M. H. A. Newman, "Mr Russell's 'Causal Theory of Perception'," *Mind* 37, no. 146, (1928): 137-148, https://doi.org/10.1093/mind/XXXVII.146.137

By substituting the theoretical terms for variables, we get a Ramsey Sentence (RS) with a truth-value:

$$\exists x_1\ldots\exists x_n TC(x_1,\ldots,x_n,o_1,\ldots,o_m)$$

This states that there exists $x_1,\ldots,x_n$ such that they have the features attributed to (the domain) $t_1,\ldots,t_n$ by the theory. Having the variable there means that there is some unspecified relation such that the theory holds of both the observable and unobservable relations. But the predicate *TC* is just a logical predicate and hence a function of the *m* integers + *n* integers. The RS can be formulated in short as $\exists x\, TC(x,o)$.

But the purely logico-mathematical nature of the predicate *TC* confers triviality, since we cannot know the nature of the structure between the observable and unobservable domains but only a set of ordered tuples of each domain. Merely saying that there is some relation such that the unspecified structure of the unobservable realm is *W* tells us little other than it is constrained by having the same cardinality. But any relation-in-extension can be arranged such that it fulfils the right amount of *n* tuples and therefore fulfils the *W* criteria. Newman concludes "[a]ny collection of things can be organised so as to have structure W, provided there are the right number of them".[533] This can be spelt out in symbolic form:

$$X \subseteq Y \leftrightarrow \forall z \in X.\, z \in Y$$

This is basic second-order logic and states that X is a subset of Y if and only if every element of X is an element of Y. In this case it is the natural number structure exhibited by the variables and observation terms. Any organisation of any relation-in-extension into the right *n*-tuples will automatically give the correct structure. This is just a more complicated version of the identity relation given in set form. Hence since all relations are encompassed – given that they can all exhibit the right numerical value – it is a trivial matter to identify any particular relation.

---

[533] Ibid, 144.

There have been different responses to the Newman critique. Some critics retain RS but deny one of the premises in Newman's argument, others consider the RS to be a deficient expression of a theory's content.[534] My interest here is how the truth-value of the RS is derived. We have established that we can derive little more about the unobservable realm than its cardinality. The theoretical terms and predicates play no role in the making of judgements. The entities in a RS as bound variables are pure existents and nothing needs to be known about them to derive the truth-value. As Psillos explains:

"However, the Ramsey-sentence $\exists u\, TC(u,o)$ of the theory implies more than the empirical content of the original theory: it implies that not all statements of the form 'u stands in relation TC to o' are false, and hence it implies that TC is realised. In other words, it implies that there are classes (and classes of classes) which realise the Ramsey-sentence. But the Ramsey-sentence does not commit one to the existence of some particular set of such entities. On Ramsey's view, the cognitive (i.e. truthvaluable) content of the theory is captured by its empirical content together with the abstract claim of realisation."[535]

Ramsey is employing Russell's account of quantification which centres on the propositional function, so a function like *everything is self-identical* will map all existing objects to a true proposition.[536] The crucial point is that existence is not predicated of the object said to exist but is grounded outside the object. This is the identity condition which we have identified with Parmenidian being throughout this thesis and which grounds the existence of specific objects. The Ramsey sentence functions in much the same way where theoretical entities are not given by proper names but by the variables within the sentence (which will map at least one existing relation to a true proposition). Moreover, the variables which are the existing objects are the ground for the *o*-terms through the numerical equivalence relation. Thus the *TC* predicate gets instantiated in such a grounding relation that functions, and may be true, irrespective of what gets substituted for the variables.

---

[534] These approaches are spelt out in Peter Ainsworth's "Structural Realism: A Critical Appraisal," PhD Thesis (London: University of London, 2009)
[535] Stathis Psillos, *Scientific Realism: How Science Tracks Truth* (London: Routledge, 1999), 49-50.
[536] Russell, "On Denoting,"

The very fact that two participants in a debate over exactly what plays the role of the variable can disagree and yet the consequences of the RS follow means that the specific character of the filler in the theoretical role is irrelevant to the logical deduction. Explicit definitions giving intensions are unnecessary. As Frank Ramsey writes:

"Clearly in such a theory judgment is involved, and the judgments in question could be given by the laws and consequences, the theory being simply a language in which they are clothed, and which we can use without working out the laws and consequences. The best way to write our theory seems to be this $\exists \alpha, \beta, \gamma$: dictionary · axioms. Here it is evident that α, β, γ are to be taken purely extensionally. Their extensions may be filled with intensions or not, but this is irrelevant to what can be deduced in the primary system"[537]

The passage of judgement therefore passes irrespective of the intensions or non-extensional meanings within the theory. But this is consistent with Russell's analysis of propositions into quantification, identity and truth functions. The integration of variables means the truth-valuableness of a sentence occurs in such a manner that the empirical qualities themselves are variable and hence dispensable.

To avoid these unwanted consequences the truth of theories needs to be tied to the intensional nature of the observations revealed in scientific experimentation. It is in making sense experience both a necessary and sufficient condition for presenting the object – and not the formal structure of first-order logic – in the world in a way that is unique and *sui generis* that blocks substitution and the trivialisation of theoretical structure. Theory needs to be inferred directory from experience where common sense observation consists in nothing more than noticing that it is our causal interactions with, say, a dog that causes us to exclaim "dog!" Being in a particular perceptual state is *ipso facto* to be in a veridical state of knowing.

Hence being in a state of knowing is not a trivial matter: a bland form of set-theoretic structural isomorphism is not enough. On this account the compositional arrangement of parts that makes up an intensional state must be sufficiently determined by mirroring the

---

[537] Frank Ramsey, "Last Papers: Theories," in *The Foundations of Mathematics and Other Essays* ed. Richard Bevan Braithwaite (London: Routledge and Kegan Paul, 1931), 231.

structure of the entity that is its object of knowledge. If one is in a state of believing that there is a horse in the far distance despite there being inadequate lighting, then if the cause of the belief is in fact a cow, one is not in a state of knowing "there is a horse". The reason is simply that our perceptual state is indeterminate. Our sense properties, as they find themselves in the cognitive state of the knower, are not sufficiently determined by the particular structure of the horse. So in a perceptual causal encounter with a horse, under the proviso that observation conditions are sufficiently clear, then we will exclaim "horse!" where in the same circumstances we could not exclaim "cow!" In this way, the distinct nature of a cause is necessary, there can be no substitution of alternate structures if that condition of knowing is to remain veridical.[538]

Hence the theory of truth I am offering does not depend on an underlying supersystem of Frege-style logical axioms in which a consistent set of permutations can be offered for terms in the original language. Truth is inherently tied to the particular and is given at that level primarily. Knowledge of any particular entity does not emerge out of a structure foreign to that entity but is given purely in the act of perception embedded in a structure unique to that individual.

iii) **Putnam's Case Against Realism**

At one stage in his career, Putnam offered a modern version of Newman's permutation argument, concluding that any sense of correspondence with reality is indeterminate.[539] The details of this argument are not important, for the simple reason that it offers nothing new beyond the Newman permutation challenge. The response is essentially the same: the internal connections between sense and reference, and the supervenience of truth on each specific instance of knowledge, do not permit permutations.

---

[538] Elizabeth Anscombe has noted another problem with isomorphic accounts of knowledge in her criticism of Wittgenstein's picture theory of the proposition in the Tractatus. Namely, that isomorphisms are symmetrical relations so there is no determining which is pictured and which is picturing; "Cambridge Philosophers II: Ludwig Wittgenstein," *Philosophy* 70, no. 273 [1995]: 398, http://www.jstor.org/stable/3751665. For a similar criticism of Sellars' version of set-theoretic isomorphism and his "picturing" model of knowledge, see John O'Callaghan, "The Identity of Knower and Known: Sellars's and McDowell's Thomisms," *Proceedings of the American Catholic Philosophical Association* 87, (2013): 8, 10.5840/acpaproc201481318. My account doesn't suffer such a problem due to the asymmetric function of the communicative category.
[539] See Putnam, *Reason, Truth, and History*, 33-35 and 217-218

A response to Putnam's sceptical arguments may utilise what Timothy Button calls the "causal constraint"[540] where a causal relation to a cat may be the basis for that cat being the object of reference. This was actually the solution that Field offered to the failure of the Tarski reduction.[541] Specifically, the causal-historical theory of reference[542] hooks the objects in the world to the terms that refer to them. This method proceeds independently of any conceptual intermediaries and so is a rejection of the concept-to-world interface embraced by Putnam.

The causal theory of reference was developed in response to the descriptivist theories developed most notably by Frege and Russell. Briefly, the causal theory targets two key assumptions of this theory: 1) that the knowledge of the meaning of a term is a matter of being in a certain psychological state and 2) that the meaning or intension (that is, sense) of a term determines its extension. The sense can play a singular referring role as in "the brightest star in the morning sky". It can also play a general referring role as when a term for a natural kind such as "water" is given descriptively, as in "the transparent liquid that fills lakes and streams, that is required for sustaining life, quenches thirst, boils at 100°C and freezes at 0°C".

The first assumption of the causal theory is targeted famously by Putnam with his "Twin Earth" thought experiment.[543] Here we are asked to imagine an alternative world called "Twin Earth" that is qualitatively indistinguishable from Earth, the only difference being that the substance that satisfies the description of water given in the last paragraph has the chemical composition XYZ and not H_2O as it is on Earth. Now despite "water" on Earth and "water" on Twin Earth referring to a substance that is qualitatively identical, "water" on the former refers to H_2O whereas "water" on the latter refers to XYZ. Thus the meanings

---

[540] Timothy Button, *The Limits of Realism* (Oxford: Oxford University Press, 2013), 3.1.
[541] Field, "Tarski's Theory of Truth,"
[542] See Kripke, *Naming and Necessity*
[543] Hilary Putnam, "The Meaning of 'Meaning'," *Philosophical Papers, Vol II: Mind, Language, and Reality* (Cambridge: Cambridge University Press, 1975)

of terms are not tied to the psychological states of their referrers. Meanings, according to Putnam, "just ain't in the head" and thus assmption 1) is false.

As for assumption 2), it is useful to recap some of the discussion from chapter one. In the following identity statements involving proper names:

1) "Hesperus is Hesperus"

2) "Hesperus is Phosphorus"

The cognitive significance given by 1) differs from that given by 2) because the sense of "Hesperus" is not the same as the sense of "Phosphorus". For Frege, it is possible for one extension to have two different senses, but it is not possible for the same sense to have two different extensions. But to repeat a point made in chapter two: It is Frege's context principle in conjunction with the law of identity that grounds such a result. So if we have an identity statement such as "$a = b$", it is due to each variable occupying such a context that confers identity on them. The identity is fixed metaphysically by being in that sentence. And in such a context, each sense is attached to the same extension whilst it is not possible for one sense to attach to two different extensions. This is, in essence, what Frege meant for sense to determine reference. If sense does not vary, then by necessity reference does not vary. But it is only in such a semantic context – the grounding relation – that this holds in the first place.

Russell takes less of a semantic path than Frege, although the laws of logic are still integral to his system. The reference that pertains to names for Russell must be one of immediate acquaintance, and the epistemological state of knowledge must be incorrigible. Hence our psychological state of knowing and being in immediate sensory contact is an indispensable element. But this constrains epistemological possibilities by not allowing names that refer to anything not known incorrigibly.

Now the innovations from Kripke and Putnam's causal theory of reference attack Fregean senses and Russell's knowledge by acquaintance. The target in Russell's epistemology was the Cartesian standard of incorrigibility where the reference of names is given by acquaintance. Instead, Kripke proposes that a reference is fixed by a metaphysical necessity called a "rigid designator" that is initially picked out by a "baptism".[544] In the process, an object is given a name by someone in immediate contact with that object and subsequent reference(s) is maintained with that event by causal links.

Now for Frege, sense is not "in the head", so to speak, so it may be confusing as to what Putnam is targeting in Frege's epistemology. But as Putnam later clarified, being "in the head" meant "transparent to reason"[545] and, as we have seen, Fregean senses are fixed by occupying either side of the identity sign and are known through reason.

So the Kripke–Putnam theory involves the fixation of a term through the initial baptism and a natural kind, then derives its meaning from being in the sameness relation to that object given in ostension. Hence for a natural kind like water, we may begin by pointing at the paradigmatic example of the stuff and then, after a significant amount of scientific investigation has revealed the micro-physical essence to be H_2O, we can conclude that the initial baptism of the stuff called "water" actually took H_2O to be its reference whether or not we were aware of it at the time. This is a far cry from Frege, in the sense that the constitution of the world and its causal behaviour is integral to meaning, whereas Frege at best saw the physical world and our empirical interactions as promptings for our rational faculties to derive essences that are only transparent to reason.

What is interesting about Kripke–Putnam semantics is that meaning is fixed in the mind-independent world and not through acquaintance or by being transparent to reason. It takes natural kinds to be real entities in the world that may or may not be essentially characterised

---

[544] Kripke, *Naming and Necessity*, 91.
[545] Hillary Putnam personal correspondence quoted in Sanjit Chakraborty, *Meaning and World: A Relook on Semantic Externalism* (London, UK: Cambridge Scholars Publishing, 2016), 16.

in the way they are presented to us. So on Twin Earth, "water" refers to the microphysical essence of XYZ or, under a different scenario here on Earth, Aristotle may not have been the tutor of Alexander the Great and yet we would still say that "Aristotle" picks out the same individual. Obviously it is not essential to Aristotle to be the tutor of Alexander the Great.

This theory of reference and its version of causation is deficient, however, since it seems as though some sort of descriptive element is necessary to pick out the right *kind of thing* within our reference frame. We saw with Quine in the last chapter that there is an indeterminacy when referring to "rabbit" between a rabbit part or a temporal stage of a rabbit. The reference could equally pick out a lower genera, such as its being an animal or a living organism of some undefined type. As Preston Stanford and Philip Kitcher state the problem, "it is utterly mysterious how, without something more than our causal relation to the sample, we can pick out one, rather than another, of the many kinds the sample instantiates."[546]

So we need to supplement ostension with a descriptive element to specify the right nature that exists under the sameness relation. Michael Devitt and Kim Sterelny point out that the cause of the experience must fit the general categorical term used to characterise *the whole object* or we may be stuck with our encounter of a momentary time slice or spatial part of the object.[547] Alternatively, the supplementation could come from the conceptual side as Amie Thomasson points out:

"Some associated conceptual content is also needed to supply frame level coapplication conditions for our nominative terms – that is, rules that (supposing the term to have been successfully applied) specify under what conditions the term would be applied again to one and the same entity. (For singular terms – unlike sortals – these are of course just the same as conditions under which it could be successfully applied again at all.) For it is only this

---

[546] Preston Stanford and Philip Kitcher, "Refining the Causal Theory of Reference for Natural Kind Terms," *Philosophical Studies* 97, no. 1, (2000): 101, https://doi.org/10.1023/A:1018329620591
[547] Michael Devitt and Kim Sterelny, *Language and Reality: An Introduction to the Philosophy of Language* (Oxford: Blackwell, 1999), 80.

that disambiguates, for example, the attempt to refer to an animal from the attempt to refer to a mass of cells, or a time-slice of an animal, and so on. These coapplication conditions (like the application conditions) may incorporate a great deal of deference to the world (i.e. it is the same animal only if death is not undergone, but what empirical conditions establish death may be left for discovery), but nonetheless, at the basic, frame level, this conceptual content establishes what basic conditions are and are not relevant to when the term may be reapplied to one and the same entity."[548]

But this is moving things in a decidedly antirealist direction, one that runs contrary to the strongly realist implications of the D–R–C framework. Another approach would be to supplement the causal side by making causation a reflection of the successive hierarchy of entities in the external world *that is specific to each individual*. This would be a pluralist theory of causation that is geared to communicating the various entities in nature in cooperation with the descriptive properties given in sensation. The reason that "rabbit" references the specific species level individual *rabbit* and not *animal* is because the D–R entity communicated by our sensory data applies at the individual level, and the lower categories play the role of realisers for the determined higher categories. Thus the application conditions of the D–R applies at the most specific and information-rich level.[549] Lower categories can only be abstracted from the more specific individual level.

The D–R–C framework, therefore, whilst being a version of the causal theory of reference, supplies what is lacking in the Kripke–Putnam model. It is the fact that the communicator, in its structure, interacts with foreign objects by communicating the nature of the D–R that we have an explanation for how our acts of perception hook on to the right kind of object in the world.[550]

---

[548] Amie Thomasson, *Ordinary Objects* (Oxford: Oxford University Press, 2007), 40.

[549] There is some support for this from the invariants within the science of perception; specifically that of Gestalts which are relational wholes made out of their constituent elements. Itay Shai writes; "Breidbach and Jost are at pains to emphasize that, so defined, a Gestalt is neither a concrete pattern, nor a function of the sum of whatever patters belong to it. Rather, it designates 'a structural property of the patterns in that class . . . expressed in the relationships between elements of the patterns'. While individual patterns may *exemplify* a Gestalt, the Gestalt itself is an underlying covert reality inherent in the relational structure left unaffected by a group of transformations."; "The whole rabbit," 756. A crucial feature of Gestalts is the "spatial integrity" of the object perceived which in the case of a rabbit would be specific to its particular phenotype; Ibid, 757.

[550] Putnam (*Reason, Truth, and History*, 37 – 38) gives the example of an exploding pressure cooker to show that causes are actually interest relative and find no home in the world. Here we tend to single out the stuck

iv) Lewis' Response

Lewis' response to Putnam's model-theoretic argument is to propose the world itself as a constraint on our choice of theories.[551] He finds a voluntarism at the heart of Putnam's referential scheme that involves the speaker's intentions determining reference rather than objects in the mind-external world.[552] This commits Putnam to the homunculus fallacy, where our knowledge of the outside world does not constrain our theoretical interpretations but a separate self, independent of our representations. Lewis has two reactions to this:

First, although there are endless ways of carving up the world into arbitrary, gerry-mandered things and classes – such as Lewis' Trout-Turkey – the lesson is not that any grouping of objects under any predicate is as good as any other. Rather, Lewis proposes a standard of objective sameness and difference in nature where only elite natural properties that are sparse are allowed to form objectively existing classes in the world and these constrain our theories.[553]

Second, his account of mental representation is holistic in denying that representations come in individual atoms and that we can only be agnostic regarding the relations between

---

valve as causing the explosion but ignore other causes that are equally salient, such as the lack of holes to release pressure, relegating them to mere background conditions. But is it the case that because we take one aspect of an event as causally relevant for psychological reasons that it is therefore obviated as playing a causal role altogether? If we break down the pressure cooker example into the three-category ontology then we are not so much contrasting the blocked valve with the lack of holes, but rather contrasting the pressure cooker as a unit with the event of the explosion. The explosion itself is a result of the nature of the cooker being such that it traps excess heat, on the one hand, and the adding of pressure through the input of power, on the other. The explosion is a communication of the state the pressure cooker was in since the release of energy will be proportional to the amount of energy built up in the cooker. We may focus our interest on the blocked valve but regardless of this we can credibly analyse the event into the three categories.

[551] Lewis, "New Work for a Theory of Universals," and Lewis, "Putnam's Paradox," in *Papers in Metaphysics*, 56-77.

[552] Ibid, 228. Putnam's voluntarism can be seen in "Models and Reality," *Journal of Symbolic Logic* 45, no. 3. (1980): 482, http://doi.org/10.2307/2273415 where he states "we interpret our language or nothing does".

[553] Lewis, "New Work for a Theory of Universals,"; Lewis, "Putnam's Paradox," 56-77; Lewis, *On The Plurality of Worlds,* 59-63

parts of a representation and their wholes.[554] Lewis professes agnosticism on the medium of representation for individual beliefs, but proposes that intentional states should be seen as explanations of our rational actions and behaviours. So the picture of representation as being something like the arrangement of sense properties picking out an individual in the world is rejected by Lewis. Rather, "You have beliefs the way you have the blues, or the mumps, or the shivers".[555]

This second response was a way in which the interactions that an individual has with their environment fixes the narrow content – that which is accessible internally to the mind – of our meanings, such that narrowness now becomes a specific attitude with a content of its own. So we are not accessing the world through individual mental states but as rational agents in the world, and his *functionalist* view of the mental life is very much involved:

"Narrow content is independent of what you are acquainted with, but that does not mean that it is altogether intrinsic to you. For it still depends on the causal roles of your brain states; … it is the typical causal role of your brain states that matters. But you may be an atypical member of your kind; hence what is typical of your kind is not intrinsic to you. So I can only say this: if X and Y are intrinsic duplicates, and if they live under the same laws of nature, and if they are of the same kind, then they must be exactly alike in narrow content."[556]

This is, in a nutshell, how Lewis takes the mind-external world of broad content – that which may be H_2O on earth or XYZ on Twin Earth – to fix the mind-accessible world of narrow content: the phenomenally accessible qualities of water such as its being transparent, odourless, inhabiting lakes and rivers and so on. This metaphysical picture carries over from the early modern philosopher's distinction between primary and secondary qualities, where there is an intelligibility gap between the latter (being simple ideas of our mental life that are only derived relationally from the objects of experience) and the former (which describe the mechanistic world of corpuscles that are intrinsic to

---

[554] Lewis, "Reduction of Mind," in *Papers in Metaphysics*, 291-324.
[555] Ibid, 311.
[556] Ibid, 315.

objects in the mind external world). The idea of God as a *deus ex machina* was invoked by many of the early moderns to bridge this gap via a pre-established harmony.

The response from Putnam to any constraints such as naturalness or causation is to label them as "just more theory",[557] which will itself require interpretation and hence be an addendum to our total theory. But then the model-theoretic argument will just be applied to the new addition to our theory. The homunculus is trapped behind the veil of senses and has no way out except by interpreting whatever senses become available.[558] This is why the sceptical Putnam of the late 1970s and 1980s derided the scientific essentialist arguments he himself put forwarded in the early 1970s as a "magical theory of reference."[559]

It is important to note that Lewis, like Quine, embraces the Cartesian dilemma. However, unlike Quine, he does not reject intensions but instead assigns narrow content a role in his materialist functionalist view of the mind in its interactions with the world. His scepticism, in fact, extended to the scientific enterprise itself in an essay he wrote called "Ramseyan Humility".[560] There he argues that although we can know the relational "role" of properties, we cannot know their intrinsic "realizers". Science puts us in touch with such relational properties, such as the effects of negative charge, without getting us to the thing in itself – just what it is that realises the negative charge role. Thus Lewis draws the Kantian conclusion that we cannot know things in themselves.

Returning to the model-theoretic response, I would say that Lewis, by integrating referencing into the functional behaviour of holistic brain states and away from the homunculus model, has successfully avoided falling into the model-theoretic trap. But at what cost? His alternative is quite costly for, as it turns out, propositional attitudes such as

---

[557] See, for example, his "Realism and Reason," 486-487.
[558] Carsten Hansen indeed makes the point that Putnam's "just more theory" move depends on a Lockean veil of senses where the realist has "only access to representations" in "Putnam's Indeterminacy Argument: The Skolemization of Absolutely Everything," *Philosophical Studies* 51, no. 1 (1987): 90 – 95, http://www.jstor.org/stable/4319877.
[559] Putnam, *Reason, Truth and History,* 47.
[560] David Lewis, "Ramseyan Humility," in *Conceptual Analysis and Philosophical Naturalism* ed. David Braddon-Mitchell and Robert Nola, 203-222. (Cambridge, MA: MIT Press, 2009)

belief states are always towards *specific content* and Lewis is forced to deny this. But this is a false account of mental representation. As Robert Stalnaker notes:

"But this is not right, since whatever the nature of the vehicle or vehicles of mental representation, the plural noun 'beliefs' does not refer to that vehicle, or to those vehicles. What it refers to is the contents of a representation – to the propositions that are believed."[561]

Thus for Lewis, information is represented in such a way that it blends into the functioning nature of the organism. But it is different from the nature of knowing given in this chapter, since that state of knowing – and the knower-propositional unity – preserves the epistemic integrity of particular sensory states and puts us into an internal relation – no Lockean intelligible gap – with the *specific* object of knowledge.

There is also the added virtue of quelling the need for Ramseyian humility, for there is an internal connection between relational role and realiser since the *communicator* is an asymmetric act of causation that communicates the nature of the object itself. Thus there is no need to venture into Kantian scepticism. There is also no gap between narrow and wide content. Contrary to Putnam and Lewis we *can* proceed from the narrow content to the wide content, since the very nature of our sensory properties are intrinsically tied to the mind-external world of physical particulars. This makes science fiction scenarios like Twin Earth impossible and ties the essential natures of natural kinds to this worldly individuals.

Analytic – Synthetic and A Priori – A Posteriori

We saw in the previous chapter that analytic statements, such as "bachelors are bachelors", are manifestations of the law of identity and justified a priori. But the pertinent question is whether such an underlying logical scheme is relevant as a system of epistemic justification in light of the new categorical system proposed. In this section a new method of analysis will be clarified and, following Quine, I will dispense with the analytic–synthetic

---

[561] Robert Stalnaker, "Lewis on Intentionality," *Australasian Journal of Philosophy* 82, no. 1, (2004): 208, https://doi.org/10.1080/713659796

distinction but for different reasons. Specifically, replacing of the univocal concept of identity with the three-category ontology demands a method of analysis that is in concert with these categories. Basically, analysis is an operation performed on empirical data in a way that leaves whole entities intact, that is, it doesn't bottom out at a simple, opaque ground level of being the way atomistic ontologies do.

The three categories are ultimate in the metaphysical *and* epistemic sense. This means that any justification of knowledge is constituted by the *communicative* category, which is structured in a way that is isomorphic with the D–R categories. This relation is necessarily both dyadic and irreflexive, whereas analytic statements are, in the parlance of truthmaker theory, truthmakers of themselves.

Wittgenstein criticised the law of identity for being senseless, but this is really just a function of its univocal status and the fact that literally anything in both the real and imagined world that occupies its variables returns a value of true. In contrast, the communicator cannot be senseless or in any way content-free, since it is an abstraction from the sense data of any particular sense experience (whether from ordinary experiences or scientific investigation).

This is not to say that any of the categories are deduced from, or are in any way justified by, sense experience. The relationship is far more intimate than that. To be in a state of justified knowledge of an object *just is* to have a particular sense experience. In other words, the metaphysics proposed here does not involve any kind of superstructure above and beyond what is given in sense experience. This process constitutes the justification of knowledge.

What is the best way to proceed with analysis then? The answer is by abstraction operating on empirically derived items of knowledge through common-sense and scientific methods.[562] The reason that a posteriori necessary identities required such a method of

---

[562] Experience, as opposed to mere thoughts or memories of the experience, gives the possibility of a "continuing informational link" between the knower and the object known, Evans, *The Varieties of Reference*, 146

knowing in the first place rested on the difference between what is given to us in sensation and the world of atoms and molecules revealed by science. But it is because whole states of atoms are arranged in certain ways according to their determination conditions that the gap becomes explainable. For example, water is wet not because it is a feature of hydrogen or oxygen as separate entities, but because these elements form a whole with new emergent properties.

The ancients had no idea about molecular composition because they lacked the scientific and theoretical tools of analysis to understand the underlying molecular composition. The communicative state of a sensory whole breaks up under scientific analysis to reveal the details of the underlying micro-compositional features that are determined in such a way that as realising states they are a *necessary* condition of the whole. Water cannot be XYZ because we know nothing of the nature of XYZ and science fiction scenarios cannot help us. But we know that water's macro-features require just those atoms of hydrogen and oxygen organised in a specific way. For example, solubility depends on the polarity in the structure of the molecule that creates a slight negative and positive charge on either side of the molecule.

Analysis, then, is somewhat akin to *focusing*[563] in the way that we might focus on the characters of a sentence. This can give the mistaken impression that all there is to a sentence is a concatenation of its parts. But a sentence is a whole and each word is placed in a specific sequence that results in a whole that has an ontological status of its own. So an analysis of water reveals the individual hydrogen and oxygen atoms in their appropriate contextual arrangement. This does not reveal anything new, just a greater level of detail.

---

[563] There is some similarity here with (John Campbell's *Reference and Consciousness* [Oxford: Clarendon Press, 2002]) theory of conscious *attention* as key to a grasp of reference. Without selective attention, argues Campbell, we are not able to pick out a particular reference, or details of an object, in a sea of images in our visual field and unite such an image to the propositional content. Selective attention does a lot of work for Campbell; specifically, it enables a "selection of information for further processing". So one might pick one's daughter's face out of a school photo by selective attention to the details of her face. The difference is Campbell wants the neural activity of our conscious attention to *explain* the organization of phenomenal properties at the focused point in one's visual field. This further step, however, is a kind of neural Kantianism that does not resemble what I am arguing for here. On my take conscious attention would be a correlate of an already present underlying phenomenal content that is necessary for cognitive processing but does not causally explain such a structure or its referential features in the first place.

To continue the example: the definition of each word is derived from being in that whole, but not just any word will do. For example, in "rattle snake" each word is modified by being juxtaposed with the other: both "rattle" and "snake" can have somewhat different definitions in different contexts. So being in that whole modifies the definition of each term but still it is those terms that are necessary (but not sufficient) for the meaning of the whole. To repeat: determining (the structure of the whole) *and* realising (each word) conditions are necessary. This seems like a repeat of Frege's context principle, but the main difference is the categories are abstractions from our sensory – not linguistic – states of knowledge.

Substances and Properties

In his *Metaphysics*, Aristotle was not so concerned with existence as with which things are *substances* – the most basic of entities – and which things are dependent on substances.[564] Substances are independent and durable and may be subject to change in losing or acquiring new properties. But they do not change from being *essentially independent* to being *essentially dependent* parts of a whole. This follows from their fundamentality, since if they could be altered by being in some state of relation, then that state or relation would be fundamental.

Cracks have appeared in modern formulations of substance. Michael Gorman proposes the following definition of a substance:

"x is a substance=df x is a particular, x is unified in the right way, and there is no particular y such that y is not identical with x, y is not one of x's parts, and the identity of x depends on the identity of y."[565]

---

[564] Aristotle, *Metaphysics: Books Z and H*
[565] Michael Gorman, "Substance and Identity-Dependence," *Philosophical Papers* 35, no. 1, (2006): 116, https://doi.org/10.1080/05568640609485174

Thus *x* has to have a certain unity. Koslicki goes even further and argues that a theory of substance shouldn't rule out its being a non-particular, a proper part or a hylomorphic compound.[566]

Under the system I am proposing, however, the three categories are not substantial entities. They are what W. Norris Clarke calls "Substance-In-Relation": "To be a substance and to be related are distinct but complementary and inseparable aspects of every real being. The structure of every being is indissolubly dyadic: it exists both as in-itself and as toward others."[567] Thus they do have "in-itself" being and "towards-others" being, but whereas Clarke takes this to be features of creatures in the world, I am taking them to be characteristics of the formal parts of each thing. Thus what it is to *determine* is to determine something distinct from itself. Likewise, what it is to *realise* is to realise something distinct from itself. And what it is to *communicate* is to communicate something distinct from itself.

The determiner, then, cannot be classified neatly as either an *ante rem* or *in re* structure, as Stewart Shapiro labels them.[568] There is overlap in both categories. Like the former, the determiner is a non-spatiotemporal category and it is a free standing entity, but only in the sense that it has an in-itself reality. It also has *in re* characteristics since it is dependent on the material content of the structure in order to be realised and needs to be abstracted out of that structure.

So the three categories on this scheme, acting in unison compose each independent entity and are a substitute for the long held tradition of substance. The three categories exhaustively compose an entity: once their functions are accounted for, the singular entity is fully accounted for. Each category is *internally related* to the other: built into each category is the implication that the other exists. Thus since the determiner organises its matter in such a way that that matter becomes a space-time realiser of that formal determining

---

[566] Kathrin Koslicki, "In Defence of Substance," *Grazer Philosophische Studien* 91, issue 1, (2015): 59-80, https://doi.org/10.1163/9789004302273_004
[567] W. Norris Clarke, "To Be Is to Be Substance-in-Relation," in *Explorations in Metaphysics: Being-God-Person* (Notre Dame, Indiana: University of Notre Dame Press, 1992), 102-122.
[568] Shapiro, *Philosophy of Mathematics*, 84-85

condition, and since both acting in unity are communicated by being structurally mirrored by the communicator, then the whole of all three acting in unison singularly and exclusively compose – and epistemologically ground – the whole. Thus analysing the whole in terms of these formal parts is a case of what Armstrong has called "no addition of being".[569] To be aware of each category independently necessitates abstracting it out from the whole, but it is a whole that is nothing over and above its formal parts.[570]

Thus entities that enter into wholes become realisers of the formal specifications of the abstract determiner. In this way substance, and even identity, gives way to more fundamental categories. An entity that enters into a whole becomes a part of that whole. But, as Verity Harte argues, in becoming a part it takes on a "role" formally specified for the entity that occupies that particular "slot". As she puts it: "Parts get their identity only in the context of the structure of which they are part."[571] Harte is identifying the whole with the structure.

On this model we can propose a part–whole relation where the whole is not merely a function of its parts but is a case of symmetrical supervenience: the whole supervenes on the parts and the parts supervene on the whole.[572] Ted Sider complains that with such an account of reciprocal supervenience it would make the single whole identical to the many parts.[573] Harte's position, however, is immune from such an objection, since the parts just become slots specified by the one structure.

But in identifying the whole with the structure, the material content that occupies these roles drops out of the picture entirely. Koslicki complains that for Harte, structure already gives all the identity conditions to the "slots" in the whole and so has no room for the

---

[569] Armstrong, *A World of States of Affairs,* 12. In contrast to this, Armstrong's States of Affairs (SoA) are non-mereological wholes composed of a particular and a property, or a relation between two or more particulars (Ibid, 122). So a SoA *is* an ontological addition over and above its parts.

[570] Although each formal part necessitates the other two that doesn't mean each individual entity exists necessarily (c.f. David Armstrong, *Truth and Truthmakers* [Cambridge: Cambridge University Press, 2004], 49.)

[571] Harte, *Plato on Parts and Wholes,* 174.

[572] C.f. Armstrong, *A World of States of Affairs,* 12.

[573] Theodore Sider, "Another Look at Armstrong's Combinatorialism," *Nous* 39, no. 4 (2005): 691, http://www.jstor.org/stable/3506116.

"structure/content *dichotomy*".[574] This is in fact apparent from Harte's example of the dinner party seating arrangement where the whole is identified with the structure as the specification of the seating plan.[575] In a nutshell, Koslicki's complaint is that the whole gets identified with the structure – the seating plan – and the guests, which we would ordinarily think of as being indispensable to a party, drop out as irrelevant.

Harte's position is akin to my own, but without the realising category. The determining category does specify a single structure that manifests in the way the parts are arranged and so, as a result, renders those parts *context sensitive*. This means that we have an identity transform in the occupation of such positions and hence, since they no longer retain their previous identities but instead have become parts, then those parts together can only really be counted as *one thing*. Analysing them as parts, thus, depends on abstracting them from the whole. Hence, contrary to Sider, we do not have many parts that are many things, but many parts that are aspects of the singular whole. And in retaining the realiser as a vital formal part of this whole, we are not left in the equally absurd position where guests are irrelevant to the identity of dinner parties.

Thus there is a reciprocal relation of dependence between both categories. There is at least superficial affinity with Frege's context principle here. Recall that for Frege a word may occupy different sentences and its semantic value is in part determined by being in such a sentence. But the resemblance is only superficial, since the parts, for Frege, ultimately derive their identity from being placed in the context of a whole sentence. This is especially evident given that the reference of a thought is the Platonic primitive: the True. As argued in the second chapter, particular sentences emerge and are ontologically derivative from their truth condition. The simple and abstract status of the truth-value affords no possibility for analysis into parts due to the opacity of that conception of being.

The model offered in this chapter presents an alternative for analyzing wholes into parts not possible for Aristotelian substances. Objects are essentially dependent on their parts whilst

---

[574] Koslicki, *The Structure of Objects,* 115 (emphasis original)
[575] Stewart Shapiro's "places-are-objects" position is similar since for *ante rem* structures the objects that fill the roles set out by the abstract structure can be characterised purely by the places they occupy; *Philosophy of Mathematics*, 10.

the parts are dependent on the whole in the sense that they derive their identity by being in the whole. As we have seen from the dinner guest example, it is not plausible to dispense with the content in favour of the structure. Both are indispensable and both are accounted for by the D–R model.

Supervenience and Grounding

For many modern philosophers of the physicalist variety, psychological properties and events are problematic since they present, prima facie at least, as conceptually and nomologically distinct from the physical realm. *Supervenience* has been proposed as one way of accounting for the dependence of the mental on the physical without needing a reduction, and sets up an interesting contrast with the three-category ontology. Supervenience states that if A properties supervene on B properties then it is redundant to specify the A properties if the B properties have already been specified. Davidson's particular formulation is interesting for our purposes:

"[P]sychological characteristics cannot be reduced to the others, nevertheless they may be (and I think are) strongly dependent on them. Indeed, there is a sense in which the physical characteristics of an event (or object or state) *determine* the psychological characteristics…"[576]

Davidson wants to say that although the psychological doesn't reduce to the physical, the relation is still one of dependence and determination. Being "dependent" seems pretty straightforward: it appears to mean that mental properties require physical properties to be instantiated in the world. To "determine", however, seems a little more complex. Quine taught us in the last chapter that mental states are indeterminate relative to physical states. Kim points out that this is a sufficiency condition:

"If the modal qualifier 'necessarily' is understood as metaphysical necessity, the base property is metaphysically sufficient for – it 'necessitates' or 'entails' – the supervenient

---

[576] Donald Davidson, "The Material Mind," in *Essays on Action and Events: Philosophical Essays,* 2nd ed. (Oxford: Oxford University Press, 2001), 253.

mental property; if it is understood to mean nomological necessity, the base property will be sufficient, as a matter of empirical law, for the mental property."[577]

The trouble with terms like "necessitates" and "entails" is that they apply logically across the board and are void of any information content that might allow us to explain the uniqueness of the mental. Consider the necessity condition as it applies to the Uniqueness of Composition: "wherever there are some things there exists a fusion of those things".[578] This is as bland and all-encompassing as could be.

As for the state of "nomological necessity" it relies on the logical conditional. We learnt from Frege and Quine that the logical constants supplemented by the law of identity are univocal notions that are likewise devoid of information. So take an example like "$M \rightarrow T$" which is a regularity or law expressing that when a particular neural state holds there will be a mental state such as a ticklish sensation. The problem, as Kim points out, is that the conditional only goes through if sensations like "ticklish" are already contained in the vocabulary of the basic physical sciences.[579] In other words, we need a solution that is similar to a straight analytic statement, like "a bachelor is an unmarried male", which is an expression of the law of identity.

Supervenience has been broadly recognised to be nothing more than mere modal correlation that lacks any explanatory value. As Kim states:

"Supervenience itself is not an explanatory relation. It is not a 'deep' metaphysical relation; rather, it is a 'surface' relation that reports a pattern of property covariation, suggesting the presence of an interesting dependency relation that might explain it."[580]

But if the supervenience relation demonstrates the need for explanation rather than providing it then what is missing? Lewis, one of the few who thinks supervenience is reductive, gives us a clue with the following example:

---

[577] Jaegwon Kim, *The Philosophy of Mind* (Colorado: Westview Press, 1996), 224.
[578] Lewis, *Parts of Classes*, 74.
[579] Ibid, 174.
[580] Jaegwon Kim, "Postscripts on Supervenience," in *Supervenience and Mind: Selected Philosophical Essays*, ed. Ernest Sosa. (Cambridge: Cambridge University Press, 1993), 167.

"Imagine a grid of a million tiny spots – pixels – each of which can be made light or dark. When some are light and some are dark, they form a picture, replete with interesting gestalt properties. The case evokes reductionist comments. Yes, the picture really does exist. Yes, it really does have those gestalt properties. However, the picture and the properties reduce to the arrangement of light and dark pixels. They are nothing over and above the pixels. They make nothing true that is not made true already by the pixels. They could go unmentioned in an inventory of what there is without thereby rendering that inventory incomplete. And so on."[581]

So far so good. But he goes on to say:

"The picture reduces to the pixels. And that is because the picture supervenes on the pixels: there could be no difference in the picture and its properties without some difference in the arrangement of light and dark pixels. Further, the supervenience is asymmetric: not just any difference in the pixels would matter to the gestalt properties of the picture. And it is supervenience of the large upon the small and many. In such a case, say I, supervenience is reduction. And the materialist supervenience of mind and all else upon the arrangement of atoms in the void – or whatever replaces atoms in the void in true physics – is another such case."[582]

So to get the correct gestalt properties, we need the pixels plus their arrangement in the right way. The gestalt properties are asymmetrically dependent on such an arrangement. I take this as an obvious Moorean truth and yet it has far reaching consequences for ontology and the debate over emergence and reductionism. Pixels being inert and indeterminate in themselves[583] require being arranged in the right way and as a result – and only as a result – of such an intervening of determinacy can the painting be said to exist. This is a crucial lesson from Lewis' own example that he doesn't mention.

I am taking what is lacking in supervenience as an indication that what is needed is an abstract principle of determination that provides the specificity that matter does not provide itself. But what other metaphysical responses have there been? Some have looked to what is

---

[581] Lewis, "Reduction of Mind," in Lewis, *Papers in Metaphysics*, 294.
[582] Ibid.
[583] This is especially so in the Humean universe assumed by Lewis.

known as a *grounding* principle for saying how it is that those entities that are not the most fundamental are grounded in the entities that are. As Schaffer describes it:

"Grounding is an unanalyzable but needed notion – it is the primitive structuring conception of metaphysics. It is the notion the physicalist needs to explicate such plausible claims as 'the fundamental properties and facts are physical and everything else obtains in virtue of them'. It is the notion the truthmaker theorist needs to explicate such plausible claims as: 'Must there not be something about the world that makes it to be the case, that serves as an ontological ground, for this truth?'"[584]

Other stock examples have been given using similar terminology, such as "depends" or "in virtue of",[585] as in a set being dependent on its members[586] and a smile being dependent on its particular face. But of what explanatory value can a notion that is primitive and encompasses such a broad array of metaphysical positions have? For example, one who concurs in Aristotelian terms that an accident is grounded in its substance may not concur that mental states reduce to brain states.

Thomas Hofweber has objected to grounding as an example of "esoteric metaphysics".[587] He claims that metaphysicians who appeal to grounding are guilty of a "bait and switch" involving the illicit move from a claim of ordinary grounding to one of distinctly metaphysical grounding. He gives an example from Kit Fine who appeals to a true disjunction as grounded by its true disjunct.[588] Hofweber's complaint is that this amounts to nothing more than logical priority and that other examples fail for the same reason.

---

[584] Jonathan Schaffer, "On What Grounds What," in *Metametaphysics; New Essays on the Foundations of Ontology* ed. David Chalmers, David Manley, and Ryan Wasserman (Oxford: Clarendon Press, 2009), 364-365.
[585] Aristotle writes; "By the emotions, I mean desire, anger, fear, confidence, envy, joy, friendship, hatred, longing, jealousy, pity; and generally those states of consciousness which are accompanied by pleasure or pain. The capacities are the faculties in virtue of which we can be said to be liable to the emotions, for example, capable of feeling anger or pain or pity. The dispositions are the formed states of character in virtue of which we are well or ill disposed in respect of the emotions; for instance, we have a bad disposition in regard to anger if we are disposed to get angry too violently or not violently enough, a good disposition if we habitually feel a moderate amount of anger; and similarly in respect of the other emotions." "Nichomachean Ethics" Book 2, chapter V, in *Greek Philosophy Thales to Aristotle* 3rd ed. Trans. Harris Rackham, ed. Reginald Allen (New York: The Free Press, 1991), 401.
[586] This is often assumed to be the case without argument; for example, see Kit Fine "Ontological Dependence," in *Proceedings of the Aristotelian Society* 95, issue 1, (1995): 269-290, http://www.jstor.org/stable/4545221 and Tuomas Tahko and Jonathan Lowe "Ontological Dependence," *Stanford Encyclopaedia of Philosophy*. (Winter 2016) https://plato.stanford.edu/entries/dependence-ontological/
[587] Thomas Hofweber, "Ambitious, Yet Modest, Metaphysics," in Chalmers et al, *Metametaphysics,* 260-289
[588] Example from Fine is "The Question of Realism," *Philosopher's Imprint* 1, no. 2, (2001): 1-30, http://hdl.handle.net/2027/spo.3521354.0001.002

Hofweber seems right here, but my complaint is that grounding is insufficient for the same reason as supervenience: what we have are ultimately logical or mathematical relationships of dependence that do nothing to explain the distinctive nature of things. So the true disjunct *p* implies the true disjunction *p* v *q*. But this relation is asymmetric since the true disjunction *p* v *q* does not imply *p*. But my complaint goes deeper than Hofweber's since such a logical relation fails to single out any particular intension and is therefore vapid. It also bears remembering that much of Frege's logical system amounted to particular instances of sentences depending on logical axioms in the same way that accidents are grounded in substances.[589] Grounding on this account then is vacuous.

Jessica Wilson complains that grounding isn't fine-grained enough to do the discriminatory work needed to distinguish between different notions of metaphysical dependence. As a result, she argues, it cannot "do the work of appropriately characterizing metaphysical dependence on its own, failing to distinguish importantly different (eliminativist, reductionist, non-reductionist, emergentist) accounts of such dependence, not to mention small-g variations on these themes."[590]

So some grounded facts like a conjunction may be accepted as really existing whereas applied to other objects, such as a lectern – under the assumption of naturalism – obliges us to say the lectern is not "ultimately real".[591] On the issue of how it is that fundamental facts acceptable to naturalism relate to derivative facts, Rosen gives us a picture of how that might work:

"A path in such a tree is naturalistic when there is a point beyond which every fact in the path is non-normative and non-intentional. A tree is naturalistic when every path in it is

---

[589] Jerrold Katz, drawing on Wittgenstein, attacked Frege's conception of analyticity precisely because it is just such logical connections such as *p* → *p* v *q* that imply the equivalent of *s* v *s*` where *s*` stands for any possible sentence; *Sense, Reference, and Philosophy* (New York: Oxford University Press, 2004), 30-31.
[590] Jessica Wilson, "No Work for a Theory of Grounding," *Inquiry* 57, no. 5-6 (2014): 540, https://doi.org/10.1080/0020174X.2014.907542
[591] Gideon Rosen, "Metaphysical Dependence: Grounding and Reduction," in *Modality: Metaphysics, Logic, and Epistemology* ed. Bob Hale and Aviv Hoffman (Oxford: Oxford University Press, 2010), 112.

naturalistic. Metaphysical naturalism is then the thesis that every fact tops a naturalistic tree."[592]

Consider this definition of grounding from Fine:

"A number of philosophers have recently become receptive to the idea that, in addition to scientific or causal explanation, there may be a distinctive kind of metaphysical explanation, in which explanans and explanandum are connected, not through some sort of causal mechanism, but through some form of constitutive determination."[593]

This is not just a derivation of principles immediately given in experience and Rosen's metaphor certainly is not. It is an application of a priori metaphysical principles to the structure of reality. The Aristotelian notion of substance was attacked earlier for resembling a metaphysical atom rather than anything analysable in the scientific world. Grounding likewise seems an imposition, especially as an auxiliary to other metaphysical doctrines such as naturalism.

Grounding is given as a primitive notion and so admits of no definition in more basic terms. This in itself does not strike me as troubling, since my own categories are basic.[594] The problem seems to be that it functions more like a metaphysical interpretative superstructure that is void of any substantial content. This is why it does not give details on the *how* of why some facts depend on others. As Wilson explains:

"Grounding alone leaves open questions that are crucially relevant to characterizing metaphysical dependence and the structure of reality... But the deeper concern...is not just that Grounding (failure of Grounding) claims leave some interesting questions open; rather, it is that such claims leave open questions that must be answered to gain even basic

---

[592] Ibid, 111-112.
[593] Kit Fine, "Guide to Ground," in *Metaphysical Grounding: Understanding the Structure of Reality* ed. Fabrice Correia and Benjamin Schneider (Cambridge: Cambridge University Press, 2012), 37.
[594] Although they can be *elucidated* with examples from our ordinary and scientific knowledge base.

illumination about or allow even basic assessment of claims of metaphysical dependence, or associated theses such as naturalism."[595]

It is for these reasons that I concur with Quine's aversion to first philosophy, since it imports assumptions not warranted from the data and attempts to force-fit that data into categories that are content-free and provide no explanations. Notions of grounding and substance are open to such criticisms. The starting point should be the empirical data, where the non-epistemic structures are given and are the basis for the fact that A causes B.

As should be evident from this section, both the grounding and supervenience relations are formulated in ways that draw on the Frege–Russell logical superstructure and thus inherit the lack of explanatory specificity that taints that conception of logic. In fact, supervenience is an *ex post facto* statement of dependence of higher level properties on their subvenient base, in which case it explains nothing. On the other hand, the D–R categories explain the dependency of emergent wholes on their physical base, since the determiner, in order to be realised, must function as a principle organising its physical constituents in such a manner that a distinct whole emerges. In this way, the realising base is a necessary but not a sufficient condition for the properties of the whole.

Hierarchy of Non-Univocal Being

The first thing to note is the abstraction of the three categories starts and finishes in the terrain of empirical data. The three categories compose, and are specific to, each individual: from the most general kinds of things to the most specific at the species level. But at the level of species we see a differentiation from the genera level and hence an increase in information content which would make species extrinsic to the categories. Such differentiation rules out univocal being. This makes sense from ordinary observation where we see a clear structure in ordinary objects like tables and chairs right through to the complex arrangement of particles that make up the human nervous system. They all exhibit the D–R–C categories in greater and greater degrees of specificity.

---

[595] Wilson, "No Work," 544-545.

However, the application of terms like "organisation" and "form" across different objects of varying specificity, signals that there is *some commonality* between heterogeneous objects. We know that the form of a table and the form of a motorcycle both organise matter according to different specifications but the difference isn't like the difference between equivocal terms such as a river "bank", or a financial "bank".

We are drawn to the conclusion, then, that there are varying manifestations of the categories and in fact there is something of a hierarchy of greater and greater levels of *determination* in the natural world. The first level we may call the *unit* which is purely an object of counting; it is the most basic way that we differentiate objects from each other. Moving up the hierarchy we have greater and greater levels of specificity. The subjects of physics and chemistry being relatively low in the hierarchy relative to the biological forms and finally the level of human consciousness.[596] The latter examples being far more complex examples of structures.

For Frege the material world as expressed in our psychological states were functionally inadequate to carry knowledge of logical laws. Such was dismissed as psychologism. Concomitant with such a dismissal was a rejection of all particularity expressed in empiricism and thus anything above the level of the purely logical did not enter into the domain of ultimate existence. For Quine being took on a similarly strict formal structure but it was naturalised such that any knowledge of the empirical – that is, empirical as derived from sense data – was eliminated in favour of exchanges at the purely behavioural level.

Thus for the present work empirical conscious perceptual data is the starting point and our ontology takes the objects of our experience as given, not to be reduced to any normative preconceived superstructure. This is a form of "easy ontology"[597] embraced by Carnapians

---

[596] It is important to appreciate that the Determiner is both non-spatial and non-temporal which means the formal component can function across time by regulating the number and types of entities that come in and out of the organism.

[597] A modern day Carnapian doing "easy ontology" would be; Amie Thomasson, *Ontology Made Easy* (Oxford: Oxford University Press, 2014)

but without the Cartesian trappings and haunting of verificationism that came along with that viewpoint. The *communicator* category provides the internal connection that immediately places the knower into a state of knowledge without needing any principle akin to verificationism vulnerable to accusations of a priority.

For Aristotle being could not be said to exist in any equivocal sense in the way that "bank" can be defined either as a money repository or a riverside. Even what we would normally, in common parlance, consider a kind of artefact, *chair* for instance, can only each have individual senses equivocal relative to one another; since chairs come in many shapes and sizes and serve slightly different functions.

Aristotle saw no significance in terms of ultimate being in the similarities across members of such a kind. Instead he systematically unified equivocal statements around each of their "pros hen" manifestations.[598] For example, to use the expression "is healthy" can be said in many ways all of which are systematically connected according to their singular *focal meaning*. We can say that broccoli is healthy, and jogging is healthy, and Socrates was healthy. But broccoli and jogging are only healthy relative to the state of health they induce in the individual. Socrates, on the other hand, is healthy in a way that is not derivative and constitutes the *central sense* of healthy.

Aristotle's hierarchy of senses of being, however, reflect the metaphysical order of being. So Socrates being in a state of ingesting broccoli, running a marathon, or having healthy complexion are all accidental state of Socrates.[599] But Socrates himself, however, is a substance and so for that reason his health is non-derivative. The three-category ontology also reflects its ontology in each semantic instance. So in perceiving a dinner chair the specific dimensions and properties are determined by the three categories. But the dimensions of a bar stool are slightly different. It is the *individual manifestations* that are

---

[598] Aristotle, *Metaphysics: Γ, Δ, and E*, 2nd ed. Trans. Christopher Kirwin, (Oxford: Clarendon Press, 1993), 1003a34-b4.
[599] He states; "For some are called things that are because they are substances; some because they are affections of a substance; some because they are a route to a substance, or destructions, or lacks, or qualities, or productive, or generative of a substance..." Ibid, 1003b6.

fundamental since even though we can categorise each instance under the genus of chair such an abstraction of a universal category of chairness has only derivative ontological status relative to each individual case. To state it bluntly; there is no universal determiner, realiser, or communicator category that applies across individual instances. Abstractions can be made but they are only abstractions there is no subsisting singular category that has instances.

So in each individual the D–R–C categories are only explicated in specific, case-by-case contexts, according to each individual and its qualities and dimensions.[600] Despite the specific differences at each level of the scientific hierarchy, and even more pronounced, the variances amongst human individuals,[601] there is a structural arrangement unique to each existent. The categories are not univocal but strictly speaking equivocal relative to each other and located within an ontology applicable most fundamentally at the individual level.[602]

---

[600] C.f. Gilbert Ryle's pluralism and contextualising of the definition of existence; "It is perfectly proper to say, in one logical tone of voice, that there exist minds, and to say, in another logical tone of voice, that there exist bodies. But these expressions do not indicate two different species of existence, for 'existence' is not a generic word like 'coloured' or 'sexed.' They indicate two different senses of 'exist,' somewhat as 'rising' has different senses in 'the tide is rising,' 'hopes are rising' and 'the average age of death is rising.' A man would be thought to be making a poor joke who said that three things are now rising, namely the tide, hopes and the Hand Wednesdays and public opinions and navies; or that there exist both minds and bodies."; *The Concept of Mind* (London: Hutchinson, 1949), 23.

[601] C.f. David Armstrong's argument against universals at this level; "Biologically considered, human beings are extremely complex structures. And it is sufficiently obvious that, despite resemblances, these structures will not be *identical* (strictly identical) in all, or indeed in any two, human beings. Using once again the powerful truism that a universal must be strictly identical in each instance, it seems that there is no biological structure that will serve as the universal required." (*A World of States of Affairs*, 66) I agree that therefore the universal *humanness* is undermined but I don't agree with Armstrong that we should ontologically prioritise objects at the level of fundamental physics. I would issue the same qualified endorsement of Brian Ellis' brand of *natural kind* "scientific essentialism"; "As human beings, we are members of a natural kind cluster. But most of us are *sui generis* within that cluster. That is, we belong to a microspecies of the cluster defined by our own unique genetic constitutions, and have only ourselves as members. The genidentical species to which we belong are certainly variable natural kinds, since our causal powers and capacities are not fixed by our genetic constitutions…As we move to yet more complex systems, from biological organisms up to ecological or social systems, natural kinds analyses become much less interesting. There are no natural kinds that satisfy the strict criteria applicable to chemical kinds that can readily be distinguished, and there are no sets of intrinsic characteristics of ecological, economic, social or other high-level systems that could plausibly be used to define appropriate microspecies." *The Philosophy of Nature: A Guide to the New Essentialism* (Chesham: Acumen, 2002), 31-32.

[602] I do not discuss universals in this thesis because I take them to have secondary ontological importance. Hence this position may be comparable to those that stress the importance of the individual over that of the universal; see, for example, Nancy Cartwright's endorsement of the medieval philosopher Duns Scotus; "This book takes its title from a poem by Gerard Manley Hopkins. Hopkins was a follower of Duns Scotus; so too am I. I stress the particular over the universal…" *The Dappled World: A Study of the Boundaries of Science*, (Cambridge: Cambridge University Press, 1999), 104.

Determinacy of Reference

The lesson that Quine wanted us to take away from his thesis of the indeterminacy of reference was that our sentences and their relations to our sensory stimulations do not nail down any one particular reference. Ascribing different references are a trivial matter for him precisely because of the logical machinery he employs: He uses the mathematical function operator, *f*, where a sentence that is about x can instead be about *f*(x) where *f* maps any referent of x on to its "cosmic complement", which is just the entirety of space-time excluding that object.[603] This fits in to Quine's use of the quantifier and its indiscriminate use in applying to any conceivable way of carving up the universe.

So Quine exhorts us to eliminate intensions and the first-person authority which they carry in our mental lives. But this is a conclusion from the joint assumptions of the univocality of being and the physicalist assumptions at play in translating observation sentences and truth functions in response to stimulus meanings. The threat of scepticism emerges from this as Quine concedes:

"It is meaningless to ask whether, in general, our terms 'rabbit', 'rabbit part', 'number', etc., really refer respectively to rabbits, rabbit parts, numbers, etc., rather than to some ingeniously permuted denotations. It is meaningless to ask this absolutely; we can meaningfully ask it only relative to some background language."[604]

But of course Quine doesn't embrace scepticism but instead takes meaning and reference to be a function of behaviourism accessed only from the third-person perspective. But Putnam pushes Quine's views to what one may consider to be their logical conclusion – conceptual

---

[603] Quine, *From Stimulus to Science*, 71-73.
[604] Quine, "Ontological Relativity," in *Ontological Relativity*, 48.

relativism. The Frege–Russell–Quine thesis ties existence up with number and yet, as Putnam points out, there is no way to even answer questions such as "how many objects are there?" This is because for him there are no objective ways of defining, independent of one's own conceptual scheme, concepts like "exists" or "object". He states

". . . it is no accident that metaphysical realism cannot really recognize the phenomenon of conceptual relativity – for that phenomenon turns on the fact that the logical primitives themselves, and in particular the notions of object and existence, have a multitude of different uses rather than one absolute 'meaning'."[605]

It may be quite tempting to look with suspicion on the whole Frege–Russell–Quine venture as being hopelessly in contradiction with our intuitions that seem to tell us quite unequivocally that there is a rabbit in front of us and not just its part or temporal slice. The solution then would be to reject the former and not intensions. Searle's response to the indeterminacy argument is to deny that meanings are indeterminate and conclude that there are facts other than stimuli behind our meanings.[606] His main objection is with the arbitrariness of which translation manual to select under Quine's scenario.

To support his case Searle offers up a thought experiment. He imagines two French friends, Henri and Pierre who are unfamiliar with the English word "rabbit". They offer two French translations both of which are bad, in response he objects that it is "just a plain fact about me that when I said 'rabbit,' I did not mean *stade de lapin* or *parti non-détachée d'un lapin*".[607] He then goes on to elaborate that a bad translation does not mean that there is not a residual core of common understanding:

"That is, if, for example, Henri means by stade de lapin what I mean by lapin, then he understands me perfectly; he simply has an eccentric way of expressing this understanding. The important thing to notice is that, in either case, whether they are right about my original

---

[605] Putnam, *The Many Faces of Realism*, 19.
[606] Searle, "Indeterminacy, Empiricism, and the First Person,"
[607] Ibid, 133.

meaning or I am right in thinking that they are wrong, there is a plain fact of the matter to be right or wrong about."[608]

Searle also attacks Quine's reliance on the relativity of reference frames for his semantic case for the relativity of meaning on the basis of different linguistic frameworks. He asks us to imagine Henri and Pierre estimating the speed of the car they are travelling in. Suppose they come to wildly different estimates based on whether one is gauging speed relative to the road, where the other is gauging relative to a truck they are passing. To gauge they are both right requires taking into account reference frames but it is absurd, Searle thinks, to carry this analogy over to semantics: "...are they analogously both right about the translation of 'rabbit' once the coordinate systems have been identified? Is it a case of moving at different semantic speeds relative to different linguistic coordinate systems? It seems to me that these absurdities are just as absurd when relativized".[609]

But Searle's case seems to be little more than intuition pumping and appealing to our common sense that we in fact *do* have independent knowledge of semantic meanings and hence *the* correct translation relative to the others. He says "the problem we are trying to deal with is that we know independently that both of their translation manuals are just plain wrong".[610] He then goes on to explain the problem with the physics analogy:

"In physics the position and motion of a body consist entirely in its relations to some coordinate system; but there is more to meaning than just the relations that a word has to the language of which it is a part; otherwise the question of translation could never arise in the first place. We can't detach the specific motion or position of an object from a reference to a specific coordinate system and translate it into another system in the way we can detach a specific meaning from a specific linguistic system and find an expression that has that very meaning in another linguistic system."[611]

---

[608] Ibid, 134.
[609] Ibid.
[610] Ibid, 135.
[611] Ibid.

But again there seems to be little to Searle's case other than appeals to common sense and intuition. He merely states the plane fact of objective semantic meaning and expects the reader to acquiesce. The more robust solution, I suggest, is to meet Quine's objection that there is a dearth of reasons for accepting intensions. More precisely by providing a metaphysic that justifies intensional mental states.

The category system I am proposing does just this since communication is a property of our sensory states that hooks our epistemic states up with objects in the mind-independent world. On this account meanings are not a function of their place in the structure of our web of belief systems. Each meaning is a product of the richness of its structure, conferring a veridical and determinately justified epistemic state that cannot be permuted into any cosmic complement or any complement at all. Quine's use of the mathematical function operator relies on the singular univocal notion of being that allows such permutations since its functions operate independently of the sensory world.

So the categories provide instances of knowledge that are each unique and grounded in the D–R conditions of each *individual knowledge instance*. Hence real world entities that correlate with our sensory states – intensions – form the basis for which we can have confidence that our intentional states are about the real world and that there are good grounds for a normative and intersubjectively reliable standard of translation.[612]

The communicative feature of each particular sensory state confers on it an inherently relational disposition that makes not only knowledge of external objects possible but also knowledge that others in foreign linguistic settings are likely in the same state of knowledge owing to their own intrinsically relational mental states. Thus a proper metaphysic owing to categories abstracted from our sensory states aligns theory and intuition and provides a compliment to just the intuition pumping arguments provided by Searle.

---

[612] Again I would recommend the interested reader consult the science of Gestalts in perception. See Itay Shai for a defence of intensional modes of knowledge against Quine's extensional approach drawing on Gestalt invariances; "The whole rabbit," (see also ft note. 545.)

Conclusion

This chapter has offered up a detailed metaphysic in the form of three categories that together are meant to exhaustively explain what we observe in common sense and scientific practice. Those categories are the *determiner*, *realiser*, and *communicator*. These are non-univocal concepts since the nature of each structure applies (somewhat) differently throughout the hierarchies in nature and from individual to individual. We do notice, however, some commonality but the emphasis is on their application on a case-by-case basis.

The first two categories explain how it is that entities we witness in the world are organised in such a way that physical constituents are all we witness and yet new objects appear among the furniture of the world from the way those physical entities are organised. Entities determined are inherently related to each other but it is the determiner that is explanatorily basic and not the relation.

The communicator functions like a cause communicating the nature of the D–R to entities other than itself whilst the latter has the structure that explains the structure of the former. Thus the communicator is inherently intentional in nature but does so by either forming new unities with another object – by being determined in that whole – or by destroying unities and thus actualising the disposition of the constituents to manifest alternate forms. All three categories have both "in-itself" and "for-others" aspects to them which means that they are internally related to each other. Thus any relational regress is halted since an extra entity relating the relations is not required.

The categories provided a solution to the "is at" flaw in Carnap's system that was a culmination and downfall of the Frege–Russell system of logic. Sense properties are a reflection and communication of the structure of the D–R which provide the organisational form for the arrangement of sense data. This alone should recommend this method – over Frege–Russell style reconstruction – along with its approach to abstraction of form rather than an imposition of a univocal form on to sense experience.

Now such a metaphysic grants us a concept of sense data that allows our perceptual states to do what modern philosophy has forbidden – to refer beyond itself to entities in the mind-independent world. This communicative aspect is not an independent Platonic entity from which individual perceptual states derive their intentional properties but is intrinsic to each perception itself. Such a focus on the individual perceptual state avoids the pitfalls that came with the Tarski method and its defence by Putnam which amounted to a triviality that failed to determine which sentences are true. The asymmetric nature of the communicative explanation of truth also filled in the lack of explanation provided by extensional equivalence highlighted by Field.

Next was a comparison with the structuralism proposed by Russell. The structures put up by the three-category ontology are, again, focused primarily on each individual perceptual state where knowledge supervenes on the structure of each instance of sense structure and does not derive from a supremely general logical structure. Newman's triviality objection does not succeed here since there is simply no way for permutation to occur between one perceptual state and another since each structure differs and communicates different natures in the world.

As was already stated the three categories provides the knower with an intrinsic connection to the mind-independent world. Thus it inherits the virtues of anti-Cartesian approaches such as the Kripke-Putnam causal theory of reference and yet it had the added virtue of avoiding the *qua* problem since communication is a reflection of each individuative structure of entities known. The knowing agent is also intrinsically connected to its perceptual states which compels a state of knowledge and thus avoids any inner-homunculus as with Putnam's account, but also avoids the pitfalls of Lewis' holistic approach.

Analysis, following this approach, is thoroughly empirical and is a matter of focusing on the parts of structures within our perceptual field. In this way it is likened to the way that we might focus on individual words within a sentence which one may not be immediately conscious of on first reflection. Extending the analogy to macro-properties of a natural kind like water, analysis can proceed by revealing its molecules but it is not possible for it to reveal other micro-constituents – in other possible worlds – precisely because the macro-properties are a result of the constituents contextualised in the right way. Thus we have a unique and scientifically respectable method of analysis where parts and whole mutually supervene. This is in stark contrast to the Parmenidian analysis of Frege, Russell, Carnap and Quine where being was inherently simple and primitive.

Moving on I compare the three categories to the supervenience and grounding relation. The determiner-realiser unit simultaneously explains why new emergent properties come into being on the basis of physical entities arranged in the right way whilst also explaining why there is a dependence on the basal properties; determiners structure entities but require physical entities in order to be realised. But the non-univocality of the categories means it is empirically adequate and unlike both supervenience and grounding does not cover Frege–Russell style logical derivation which renders the latter two approaches vapid.

Lastly I compare this system to the indeterminacy inherent to reference under Quine's account. Quine works out a holistic system of meaning where it is possible for a mathematical function to map all reference to its cosmic complement. Thus reference is more a function of mathematical consistency within each linguistic system given by translation manuals where internal meanings, which will give behaviourally and verifiably consistent results, will vary. Searle responds to Quine's argument by appeals to intuition in grounding objectively right answers between linguistic systems. I find that only through the three-category ontology, however, do we have a metaphysical account that answers Quine's quandary whilst maintaining consistency with intuition.

Summing up we have found that the three-category ontology explains an enormous amount of data that does not require reconstructing our knowledge base. It overcomes many and varied challenges to realism and is vastly more useful and consistent with the structured entities we observe in nature through our structured perceptions. What remains now is to apply the categories to a specific scientific example and see how it compares with other metaphysical accounts.

Chapter Six – Three-Category Ontology Applied to the Natural Sciences

Introduction

Care has been taken throughout this thesis to distinguish the methodology offered in the last chapter from that offered by Frege and Russell. Specifically, the three categories are abstracted from science and common sense rather than being an a priori imposition on the empirical data and hence demanding a reconstruction of knowledge. It is vital to the success of this project to test how well the categories apply to a specific scientific discipline.

I first set the scene by discussing the debate between reductive and non-reductive physicalism. To the uninitiated it might seem that Fodor's non-reductive account would be in line with my own, but it is not, since it characterises kinds across disjuncts of physical realisers. The Frege–Russell style logical apparatus is a poor substitute for real kinds of things due to its generality – to the point of being completely vapid. Donald Davidson's anomalous monism likewise suffers by not explaining how the interactions between levels of sciences proceeds. Kim makes the pertinent point that the causal powers of macro-entities under non-reductive physicalism get usurped by the causal powers of their physical realisers. Kim's vulnerability, however, is in claiming physical atoms retain their identity within the system they realise.

Quantum mechanics has long been plagued by mysteries and philosophers have sought to devise conceptual characterisations of quantum phenomena. I argue here that the first two categories nicely explain key quantum properties: firstly, determined physical states are inherently relational in being organised along certain channels that characterise the whole entity. But the physical entities are necessary conditions due to their role in realising the determining form. This nicely explains the *relational holism* detailed by Paul Teller and the *fusionism* advanced by Paul Humphreys. But retaining physical realisers within the larger context does not, unlike fusionism, blot out the lower-level entities.

The determining category is then brought in as the abstract explanatory feature of whole systems. The determining category explains the transformation of identities of constituents but retains an intelligible connection with the physical realisers highlighted by Kim's definition of emergence. But there are two key differences with Kim's account: the categories are an abstraction from the whole and explain the complexity that uniquely characterises each individual entity. Kim, on the other hand, *identifies* the macro-properties with the functionally given physical realisers. Kim's account woefully underdetermines the complexity of entities, since the physical realisers are retained only as a class of entities.

This brings us to the second key difference with Kim. His physical realisers are retained in their essential identity. This is a key feature of physicalist ontology: the basic entities are fundamental and immutable in identity. Quantum Mechanics (QM), however, shows this to be empirically inadequate, and the identity transform given by the three categories has the added advantage of avoiding the causal exclusion argument that results only if the physical realisers are retained as separately identifiable entities.

Reduction and Non-Reductionism

The three categories apply across the entire spectrum of sciences and common sense objects, and the vast majority of objects show some difference in the dimensions of each structure and the level of complexity. Object structures come in all sorts of shapes and sizes: individual dogs are many and varied in their exact natures and biological structures, which differ even further from human organisms, and human brain structures differ from individual to individual. The non-univocality and straightforward abstraction of the categories from the sciences and ordinary objects of perception implies a non-reductionist standard for ontology.

In concert with the many and varied kinds of objects in the world are distinct kinds of events and processes that are communications of the nature of the different kinds of objects in the world. This is the basis for the interactions between all objects. It is also the basis for scientific realism, since the way objects interact with scientific instruments and the way photons and microparticles interacts with our senses through the communicative process transmits natures from distinct objects. This gives way to a kind of causal pluralism, further evidenced by the different verbs used to describe them. As Nancy Cartwright writes: "The pistons compress the air in the carburettor chamber, the sun attracts the planets, the loss of skill among longterm unemployed workers discourages firms from opening new jobs".[613] And yet we still see these things as "causes" in some way or another. Each is just contextualised according to the make-up and distinct properties of each individual thing.

This is, therefore, an ontological picture that is robust both in the sense of embracing real causal relations in the world but also a variety of different types of things each with distinct causal powers; from artefacts like tables and statues to individual human organisms. But this differs radically from the reductionist picture of the sciences embraced since at least the time of the logical positivists with their talk of the "unity of the sciences". David Papineau points out that during the 1950s and 60s, the majority of philosophers had reached the conclusion that "physicalism" was the correct scientific picture of the world.[614] They had noted the widespread tendency to invoke the four fundamental forces – the weak and strong nuclear forces, the electromagnetic force and the gravitational force – to explain physical

---

[613] Nancy Cartwright, "Causation: One Word, Many Things," *Philosophy of Science* 71, no. 5. (2004): 814, https://doi.org/10.1086/426771
[614] David Papineau, "The Rise of Physicalism," in *Physicalism and its Discontents* ed. Carl Gillett Barry Loewer, 3-36. (Cambridge: Cambridge University Press, 2001)

phenomena. They also noted that explanation in the biological sciences was increasingly becoming mechanised, dispensing with "vital" or "mental" forces.

One of the most influential accounts of the period was Paul Oppenheim and Putnam's paper "Unity of Science as a Working Hypothesis,".[615] Oppenheim and Putnam developed a system of reductionism with three essential goals: the explanations achieved by the reduced theory had to be accounted for by the reducing theory, the reducing theory had to have more "systematic power" than the reduced theory, and all the entities referred to by the reduced theory had to be decomposed into entities referred to by the universal discourse of the reducing theory. But it is the formal method of decomposition that they say is "of great importance for the program of Unity of Science".[616] Here is the formal account:

"The relations 'micro-reduces' and 'potential micro-reducer' have very simple properties: (1) they are transitive (this follows from the transitivity of the relations 'reduces' and 'Pt'); (2) they are irreflexive (no branch can micro-reduce itself); (3) they are asymmetric (if B_1 micro-reduces B_2, B_2 never micro-reduces B_1)."[617]

It is important to appreciate that the latter two conditions are the reverse of the formal conditions of identity. Identity ordinarily employs transitivity – if A is identical to B and B is identical to C then A is identical to C – reflexivity – everything is identical with itself – and symmetry – if A is identical to B then B is identical to A. So although this account makes use of empirical theoretical accounts, the reduction and decomposition itself comes about by a purely formal application of the concept "micro-reduces".

The basic entities in the physicalist reduction are atomic and substance-like, forming a floor below which the part–whole division cannot continue any further. Their identity conditions, as values of variables – such as (x) – are also primitive and immutable, and represented with accompanying predicates as $(\exists x)(Px)$. One of the leading modern physicalists,

---

[615] Oppenheim and Putnam, "Unity of Science as a Working Hypothesis,"
[616] Ibid, 7
[617] Ibid.

Jaegwon Kim, describes an atomist-style ontology thus: "The core of contemporary physicalism is the idea that all things that exist … are bits of matter and structures aggregated out of bits of matter".[618] On this basis the real causal work of any macro-object gets usurped by the basic entities of physics and their primitive identity conditions.

One of the major challenges to this picture of the world came from Jerry Fodor in his 1974 paper "Special Sciences".[619] Fodor argued that the special sciences, with special emphasis on psychology, cannot be reduced to physics. He takes aim at the notion that physics is the basic science and that any theories in the special sciences must be reduced to those in physics. Now the theoretical terms in the reduced and reducing theories in order to be interesting must be disjoint. So take a law like this:

1) $S_1 x \rightarrow S_2 y$

S_1 being a predicate in the special sciences entails a further predicate in the special sciences, S_2. But according to reductionism, special science predicates are just special instances of a law in physics. Thus the S predicates reduce to the P predicates such as:

2) $P_1 x \rightarrow P_2 x$

Fodor, drawing on Ernst Nagel's 1951 work "The Structure of Science", defines reduction in terms of equivalences between the laws of the reduced and reducing sciences where the antecedents and consequences of each are equivalent. Thus we have a case of identity, and statements describing these equivalences are called "bridge laws" where the predicates can be exchanged and a biconditional holds, as in:

---

[618] Jaegwon Kim, *Physicalism or Something Near Enough* (Princeton: Princeton University Press, 2005), 149-150.
[619] Jerry Fodor, "Special Sciences (Or: The Disunity of Science as a Working Hypothesis)," *Synthese* 28, no. 2 (1974): 97-115, http://doi.org/10.1007/BF00485230

3) $S_1x \leftrightarrow P_1x$

4) $S_2y \leftrightarrow P_2y$

Hence Fodor spells out his account in terms of natural kinds where every natural kind is linked to a co-extensive physical kind by a bridge law. He concludes that "the natural kind predicates of a science are the ones whose terms are the bound variables in its proper laws."[620] So we are talking about a much stronger connection than just saying that every token individual thing is a physical thing where the universal type of that thing is not physical. Rather, the reductionism he wants to attack is the much stronger thesis that says the very being of an individual thing and its laws ultimately *just are* physical properties and laws.

But he argues that such a correspondence between natural kinds and physical kinds cannot possibly be true for the following reasons:

"(A) interesting generalizations (e.g., counter-factual generalizations) can often be made about events whose physical descriptions have nothing in common, (b) it is often the case that whether the physical descriptions of the events subsumed by these generalizations have anything in common in an obvious sense, is entirely irrelevant to the truth of the generalizations, or to their interestingness, or to their degree of confirmation, or indeed, to any of their epistemologically important properties, and (c) the special sciences are very much in the business of making generalizations of this kind."[621]

Fodor draws on an example from economics known as Gresham's Law which says, in simple terms, that bad money drives out good money. A reductionist would have to say "that any event which consists of a monetary exchange (hence any event, which falls under Gresham's law) has a true description in the vocabulary of physics and in virtue of which it

---
[620] Ibid, 102.
[621] Ibid, 103.

falls under the laws of physics."[622] But, as Fodor notes, there is nothing in Gresham's law that can relate terms such as "is a monetary exchange" with a predicate derived from physics.

Now "money" may refer to a kind of thing in economics which may be instantiated in a particular physical kind. But there are multiple physical kinds that can take on the monetary role, such as paper, silver and gold. So we can express a bridge law for Gresham's law thus:

$$M \leftrightarrow P_1 \vee P_2 \vee P_3 \vee P_4 \ldots \vee P_n$$

But such a disjunction of physical kinds is not an expression of any physical law. The set of physical entities picked out share nothing in common. The functional aspects of economic conditions and what holds as a result of them cannot be captured in any interesting way by their physical instantiations. So Fodor concludes that even if there is a co-extension between psychological and neurological natural kinds, it cannot be lawlike contrary to what we saw with 3) and 4) above.

The problem here is that 3) and 4) are ambiguous as far as reduction goes. It could be that the biconditional means that the special science predicate and the physical predicate are extensionally equivalent (that is, the very same thing has both the S predicate and the P predicate). But as Fodor points out, this does not go far enough for reduction purposes, since it is not saying the properties and laws themselves are identical, but only that they are properties of the same thing. Basically, P_1 could be a physical property (or event) whilst S_1 could still be a non-physical property (or event). Fodor concludes that all we will have is a nomologically necessary correlation between P and S. He writes:

"On this interpretation, the truth of reductionism does not guarantee the generality of physics vis-à-vis the special sciences, since there are some events (satisfaction of S

---

[622] Ibid.

predicates) which fall in the domain of a special science (S), but not in the domain of physics.... The upshot would be a kind of psychophysical dualism of a non-Cartesian variety, a dualism of events and/or properties rather than substances."[623]

In other words, the bridge laws need to give us identities of properties and not just extensional equivalence. So from here we can formulate a "token physicalist" style reduction where each individual event mentioned in the special sciences is an event mentioned in the physical sciences. But Fodor claims that reductionism needs more. It also needs to say that it is not just the tokens that are physical, but that all types (or properties) are physical types (or properties). Consider:

T   T

What we have here are two different tokens of the same type of thing. Now there is obviously an identity at the individual level between the letter and its physical characteristics. But the fact that it can be instantiated in *other* physical instances means that we have a universal aspect to it that gets instanced at more than one location and/or time. Hence there is more to T than just that which is physically instantiated. The argument from Fodor is that a physical token reductionism is insufficient since it does not capture these laws and properties of the special sciences applicable at the type-instanced level. The most we can get from the outcomes of scientific practice is token style reductionism where non-physical substances are ruled out and therefore reductionism as a full generality thesis fails:

"...the classical construal of the unity of science has badly misconstrued the goal of scientific reduction. The point of reduction is not primarily to find some natural kind predicate of physics coextensive with each kind predicate of a special science. It is, rather, to explicate the physical mechanisms whereby events conform to the laws of the special sciences."[624]

---

[623] Ibid, 99.
[624] Ibid, 107.

What we quite clearly have here under Fodor's explication are special science laws and properties that are somehow instantiated in each physical particular but at the same time are ontologically distinct from each physical particular owing to the fact that the one law or property finds itself instantiated in many heterogenous physical particulars. But then how are we supposed to identify the law or property in each particular case? We know that the claims of current physics do not subsume the "laws" of the special sciences, but what positive knowledge can we have about the special science "natural kinds" themselves? What epistemic conditions can we identify that will characterise the law or property that justifies us in having such a knowledge? How are we supposed to abstract out the law from the physical accidents? Or is it the case that we cannot have any knowledge of the special science and its ontological condition unless we have observed multiple instances?

The epistemic and ontological conditions of the special sciences under this conception seem murky at best. This may at least in part be owing to the fact that the biconditional and truth functional apparatus Fodor makes use of operates at a level of generality that abstracts from any scientific or empirical content. The problems here have been rehearsed throughout this thesis, but the upshot is that such a thin conception of ontology that appeals to the formal biconditional as a model for co-instantiation lacks the ontological resources to provide any interesting characterisation or identification of laws or properties coinciding in any one particular. Kim puts the objection in more concrete terms and extends it to causal powers:

"We should remember that UP [P_1 v P_2 ...] is, or can be, an extremely heterogeneous and unmanageably huge disjunction; this makes it unclear what causal-nomological import UP can have. Consider two properties, each with a specific set of causal powers, say having a temperature of 100° C. and having a mass of one kilogram. What causal powers are to be associated with the disjunctive property of having a temperature of 100° C. or having a mass of one kilogram? What causal powers does an object have in virtue of having this disjunctive property? It isn't clear what we should say. All we can say appears to be that if an object has this disjunctive property – that is, if it either has a temperature of 100° C. or has a mass of one kilogram – then it either has the causal powers associated with the temperature or those associated with the mass. The last 'or' in the preceding sentence is sentence disjunction, not a special operator designating some kind of 'disjunction' operation on properties.

That is, to say that something has causal powers C_1 or causal powers C_2 is to say only that either it has C_1 or it has C_2; there is no need to posit a disjunction of C_1 and C_2, which one might denote as $[C_1 \vee C_2]$, and say that the thing has this disjunctive causal power $[C_1 \vee C_2]$. If such disjunctions are to be posited, we will need an explanation of what the disjunctions stand for in terms of what each of their disjuncts stands for. But such an explanation is exactly something we don't have. In consequence, we are without an understanding of what causal powers are to be associated with disjunctive properties, or with their instances."[625]

Thus we do not have any substantial unity across the individual disjuncts but just a set of physical individuals with wildly differing causal properties. There is no basis here for any kind of nomological or causal unity. Disjunction as one of the apparatus of truth-functional logic implies that any heterogeneous group of objects may take up the place of the variables.

Another prominent form of non-reductive physicalism is Davidson's *anomalous monism* where mental events can cause physical events but only on the basis of physical laws *not* mental laws. The mental can only be characterised descriptively, hence it is a way to avoid the ontological dilemma of reductionism that seeks to make all things purely a result of physical laws. Davidson states: "The principle of the anomalism of the mental concerns events described as mental, for events are mental only as described".[626] So the mental descriptions of such an event conveniently avoid any kind of competition with its role within the physical laws.

But this account, like Fodor's, lacks clarity regarding how it is that the distinct realms of physical laws and mental descriptions are supposed to relate to each other. The point seems to be that mental descriptions *qua* descriptions are excluded from the physical realm and thus cannot compete ontologically. But this is unsatisfactory from the point of view of

---

[625] Jaegwon Kim, "Reduction and Reductive Explanation: Is One Possible Without the Other?" in *Being Reduced: New Essays on Reduction, Explanation, and Causation* ed. Jacob Hohwy and Jesper Kallestrup (Oxford: Oxford University Press, 2009), 108-109.
[626] Donald Davidson, "Mental Events" in *Essays,* 215.

doing real ontology and holding to a realist view of the special science laws. As Kim explains:

"Davidson's anomalous monism says no more about the relationship between the mental and the physical than the claim that all objects with a color have a shape says about the relationship between colors and shapes."[627]

What we need instead is a positive account of how the different levels, such as the mental and the physical, relate to each other. Kim again:

"I believe we want our mind-body theories to tell us more, a positive story about how mental properties and physical properties are related, and hopefully also explain why they are so related. We don't get such a story from anomalous monism."[628]

Another well-known argument against non-reductive physicalism is the *causal exclusion argument*. This states that there cannot be more than a single sufficient cause for any given event.[629] If a causal role is filled by both mental and physical properties, then an overdetermination threatens. Positing more than one necessary and sufficient cause of an event is not possible, as dictated by the Causal Inheritance Principle:

"If M is instantiated on a given occasion by being realized by P, then the causal powers of this instance of M are identical with (perhaps a subset of) the causal power of P."[630]

How can mental properties play a causally robust role in bringing about real differences to temporally distinct mental properties and their physical realisers when we also want to say that it is really just the physical realisers themselves that are playing the causal role as base properties? In such a case, the physical properties usurp the causal powers of the mental, thus rendering the latter superfluous. Hence the causal powers of higher-level properties must be given up at risk of violating causal overdetermination.

---

[627] Kim, *Mind in a Physical World*, 5.
[628] Ibid.
[629] Kim, *Physicalism*, 42.
[630] Jaegwon Kim, "The Non-Reductivist's Troubles with Mental Causation," in *Supervenience and Mind*, 355.

The Quantum Mechanical Challenge

As we have seen, reductionists like Oppenheim, Putnam and Kim believed that reality ultimately reduces to aggregates of, as Kim puts it, "bits of matter".[631] Along with this is the presupposition that the causal power of aggregates ultimately derives from the causal powers of their more basic physical constituents. In the fourth chapter we saw that, according to mereologists like David Lewis, individuals are combined into fusions which have no real ontological being over and above the mere sum of their parts. Whereas my own definition of parthood embraced a symmetry of dependence between part and whole, the dependence relation for Lewis and other materialists is entirely asymmetrical: the whole is dependent on its parts and not the other way around. Such a metaphysical picture gives us a conception of the whole that is nothing but its immutable atomic parts. Any entity does not experience any change in identity when combined into a whole.

But is such a picture of metaphysical atomism – based on fundamental physical entities and their causes – consistent with scientific revelation at the micro-level, that is, at the level of quantum mechanics? The challenge is that our ordinary conception of a "thing" or a "part" conflicts empirically with what is known as *quantum entanglement*. Consider a property of elementary particles like *angular momentum* (spin). Any given particle can be in a state that is either "up" or "down".

Now under an atomistic metaphysic, we would generally think that basic atomic building blocks would have a certain degree of independence and determinacy in their basic properties. But under entanglement this does not seem to be the case. Experiments have shown that two particles radiated from the same source in different directions will have either an "up" or a "down" state, but the surprising thing is that each state is coordinated with each other such that if one is measured in one of the two possible states, then the other will be measured in the opposite state. But what is coordinating the particles such that if

---

[631] Kim, *Physicalism,* 150.

one is in an "up" state then the other must be in a "down" state? There is no physical mechanism that can be pointed to as the means by which such a coordination could occur.

Thus these entangled states appear to show that the particles and the properties that inhere in them are non-separable, that is, they are not determined in any independent way separable from the whole. The intrinsic states of each particle as conceived prior to the whole do not fix the states that each particle finds themselves in as parts of the whole. As Paul Humphreys writes:

"It frequently has been noted that one of the distinctive features of quantum states is the inclusion of non-separable states for compound systems, the feature that Schrodinger called 'quantum entanglements'. That is, the composite system can be in a pure state when the component systems are not, and the state of one component cannot be completely specified without reference to the state of the other component."[632]

What is even more interesting, however, is that such a holistic function, where the fixing of the one spin state automatically corresponds to the fixing of the opposite spin state, constitutes *immediate* action at a distance. Physics tells us that the speed of light is a limiting velocity for any event in space-time, so the immediacy of the apparent communication of quantum entanglements would seem in violation of such which led Einstein to famously describe such a process as "spooky action at a distance".[633] As Schaffer states: "Entangled particles seem as if telepathic. They act as a unit."[634]

Now this would seem to run contrary to the basic thesis of physicalism, where it is presumed that the basic physical building blocks are the fundamental units of reality. If those units do not seem to preserve their identity and are in some way determined by the whole of which they are a part, then this would suggest the whole ought to instead be

---

[632] Paul Humphreys, "How Properties Emerge," in *Emergence: Contemporary Readings in Philosophy and Science* ed. Mark A. Bedau and Paul Humphreys (Cambridge, MA: MIT Press, 2008)
[633] Quoted in Jonathan Schaffer, "Monism: The Priority of the Whole," *The Philosophical Review* 119, no. 1 (2010): 52, https://doi.org/10.1215/00318108-2009-025
[634] Ibid, 52.

regarded as fundamental. The atomic units, as it turns out, are not units at all since they derive their being from the whole. In fact since the properties are not fixed by the intrinsic properties of the parts, this can be classed as a case of emergence. As Schaffer argues:

"[Q]uantum entanglement is a case of emergence, in the specific sense of a property of an object that has proper parts, which property is not fixed by the intrinsic properties of its proper parts and the fundamental relations between its proper parts."[635]

Paul Teller, in his seminal piece "Relational Holism and Quantum Mechanics", speaks of quantum states as derived from fundamentally relational entities, and even if we regard them as distinct entities, they are nonetheless *inherently related to each other*: "by relational holism I will mean the claim that objects which in at least some circumstances we can identify as separate individuals have inherent relations, that is, relations which do not supervene on the non-relational properties of the distinct individuals."[636] Hence the intrinsic quantum properties are only so characterised due to the relational whole of which they are an aspect, which runs contrary to the atomistic thesis that individuals give rise to uninteresting aggregates or sums.

Ontology, as Teller sees it, makes quantum entangled relational states basic and the individual and its properties derivative from that state. As he says:

"The step we may need to take to advance our physical theory and our conceptual scheme for the physical world may be to come to terms with inherent relations and to understand how they give rise to (or come to be seen as) the non-relational properties which have so far formed the basis of our physical world view."[637]

---

[635] Ibid, 56.
[636] Paul Teller, "Relational Holism and Quantum Mechanics," *The British Journal for the Philosophy of Science* 37, no. 1 (1986): 73, http://www.jstor.org/stable/686998.
[637] Ibid, 81.

But Teller's account seems to leave something out and this goes back to the issue of relations and what it is that is explanatorily basic. Along these lines we can ask *why* it is that entities that seem to have individuative characteristics before entering a holistic state somehow lose them once they become parts of the whole. Indeed it seems to be the case that the identity of an object suffers indeterminacy once it meshes with a whole. As Jonathan Lowe points out, quantum theory tells us that there is no way to determine or keep track of particular entities that are parts of atomic conditions.[638] So no sense can be made of statements such as "x is the same electron as y" and this is not just a result of an epistemological limitation, but it is a basic ontological condition that there is no determinacy to these individual entities. So an electron captured by a helium ion (where another electron is already present) and the subsequent release of an electron provides no means for us to know if the released electron is the same as the one that just entered the atom or the one that was there originally. There is no way of knowing because there is *no ontological fact of the matter*.

But as Lowe also points out, it is not as though we cannot make a countable distinction between the two electrons in the helium atom.[639] We know there are precisely two electrons in a helium atom: it is just that there is no fact of the matter as to which one is which. The electrons do not appear to be just lower-level correlates in the system but are aspects of the system such that they have not retained their original identity conditions. But they are still present in some form or another since helium atoms form chemical bonds on the basis of the negative charge of their electrons. Likewise water molecules dissolve sodium chloride due to a slight net negative electrical charge at the end of its dipole structure.

It is also the case that these entities have distinct properties as classes of entities. The individuating conditions of quantum entities are not altogether threatened. For example, electrons are fermions and hence obey the Pauli Exclusion Principle – the state we have discussed whereby no two fermions can be in the same quantum state – and thus have properties that are distinct from other classes, such as bosons. Lowe writes:

---

[638] Lowe, *The Possibility of Metaphysics*, 62.
[639] Ibid.

"…it would be wrong to assume that quantum theory poses problems for the synchronic individuation and diachronic identity of electrons *quite generally*, and hence casts doubt upon the legitimacy of our description of the preceding example in terms of an identifiable electron *a* existing prior to the interaction and an identifiable electron *b* existing subsequent to it."[640]

So we can draw two preliminary conclusions here. The first is that we have identifiable entities existing prior to entangled quantum states and the second is that we appear to need a means of explaining *why* it is that that entity ceases to exist as a separate independently identifiable entity after entering entanglement. In other words, the entity seems to disappear and reappear as a part or aspect of the whole.[641]

Humphreys usefully introduces a term, *fusion*, to describe the process by which the atomic states become the entangled states.[642] Fusion operates at the level of the whole by conferring properties on that whole, M, from the properties of the lower-level instances, P and P`. There is a sense in which each separate property instance loses its identity when it jointly composes the whole. It loses some of its causal powers whereupon, as Humphreys states, some of these powers "… have been 'used up' in forming the fused property instance. Hence, these i-level property instances no longer have an independent existence within the fusion."[643] And "[t]he lower-level property instances go out of existence in producing the higher-level emergent instances."[644]

Thus we can characterise such a state of the whole as supervening on the intrinsic properties of the relata where such intrinsic properties are inherently relational. But the catch is that such intrinsic states are not the same intrinsic states as the separate property instances. This is the conclusion we reached in the fifth chapter: just positing relata is

---

[640] Ibid, 61.
[641] Non-emergentists have complained that emergentists have been unable to bear the explanatory burden of how it is that emergent properties come into being; John Heil writes "Any conception of emergence is incomplete without an account of the *bearers* of emergent properties" in *The Universe as We Find It* (Oxford: Clarendon Press, 2012) 28 (original emphasis)
[642] Humphreys, "How Properties," in Bedau et al, *Emergence*, 111-126.
[643] Ibid, 117.
[644] Ibid.

insufficient as it is the identity transform itself that needs explaining, and doing so requires reference to the entity as a whole which is the locus of the higher-level properties. Humphreys, by introducing fusion, at least goes some way to explaining such a transform.

Humphreys also emphasises the fact that the fused state of the whole acts causally *qua* whole entity – introducing novel causal powers in place of the ceased separate causal powers – and not as the mere sum of the physical property instances. So the higher level properties are causally powerful higher level properties and hence we have one inseparable causally powerful state that communicates such a state to other entities.

There are two further advantages to fusion emergentism. First, it does not fall prey to logicism or the mathematicisation of the physical world. Fusion is a "real physical operation, not a mathematical or logical operation on predicative representations of properties."[645] Humphrey's model respects the fact that there are not just logico-mathematical structures in the world, but real properties of individual things and real distinctions between the levels of the sciences outside our methods of representation. This is, in fact, a necessity owing to the *ontic* indeterminacy we see in quantum entanglements.

Second, a highly attractive feature of Humphrey's brand of fusion emergentism is that it provides an answer to Kim's causal exclusion argument. The removal of the base causal powers of the separate entities means the removal of any threat of causal competition for the higher-level causal powers. Thus the causal powers of the base properties are simply eliminated and hence not there to compete with the emergent powers in the first place.

We may, at this preliminary stage, state some features of QM well explained by the three-category ontology. First, physical structures are realising conditions of the abstract determining principle. This means that a physical constituent is, in part, defined by its context within the whole. Hence there is an identity transform of any entity within its structure. But it is contextualised by the abstract determiner and hence retains its physical

---

[645] Ibid.

properties – but only to the extent that they are channelled and organised according to the characteristics of the whole. Here we are given the *why* behind inherently related entities.

Second it is an interesting feature of the determiner that it is non-spatio-temporal and thus formally determines the physical parts instantaneously. There is no "action at a distance" because the formal component is not acting through space and does not therefore violate any physical laws. Hence an "up" state can be determined for one entity simultaneously with the "down" state of the other entity within the entangled system.

Critique of Fusion Emergentism and the Three-Category Solution

It is one thing for a model of emergentism to base itself on quantum phenomena, it is entirely another question whether the model will adequately explain larger-scale objects. One significant challenge is raised by Hong Yu Wong concerning the loss of basil causal powers by the emergent state.[646] His main objection is this: the lower-level properties in a system often form the structural properties of the system that contributes vitally to the emergent properties. Eliminating these lower-level properties means eliminating the structural properties and hence a vital component in the system that ensures the existence and functioning of the emergent powers themselves.

This is, for the most part, a fairly simple and non-controversial point. I raised earlier the fact that the causal powers of electrons are integral to the functioning of the wholes of atoms like helium or molecules like H_2O. Wong gives a more sophisticated example from neuroscience:

"An example is feedback control, which is ubiquitous in the nervous system, both in motor areas and sensory systems. In sensory systems, it is clear that information fed back for control purposes is not solely for controlling these sensory systems but also contributes to

---

[646] Hong Yu Wong "Emergents from Fusion," *Philosophy of Science* 73, no. 3 (2006): 345-367, http://doi.org/10.1086/515413.

behavioral decisions, emotional states, and motor control. Hence feedback control is a phenomenon that should be maintained independently of the emergence of mental or other complex states. Consider, for example, how duration and trajectories of saccadic eye movements can be explained by optimization processes where the nervous system tries to extract maximal information from the sensory input. However, since N_1 and N_2 expire in fusing into $[N_1*N_2]$, all other structural states they underwrite will also expire."[647]

Humphrey's choice of the term "fusion" means he is not unaware of such problems, since clearly the connotation of such a term implies that the separate powers are still retained in some way in the newly emergent state. The problem is how they can still be retained whilst also being extinguished as separate causal powers. Idioms such as "used up" are of little clarifying value. The gist of the problem is that there is nothing in Humphrey's account that singles out the basil properties in their structural roles.

But there is a way of reframing the solution in terms of the basil properties occupying a contextual role such that they are now not identical with the separate basil properties but are aspects of the newly integrated whole. But in doing so the role of the basil powers as newly contextualised organisational powers needs to survive in some manner. The D–R categories conceptually specify a way of doing just this. The base powers obtain new identities and new causal powers by being in a context – forming an inseparable web of component parts – and by realising the structure as specified by the determining category.

An analogy will help. The basil powers do not entirely disappear in the same way that words can be given a slightly new meaning in new sentence contexts. Recall our example of the sentence "rattle snake" where each term is defined slightly differently within the context of the sentence. The words are organised in a specific way – and thus newly determined in such a role – that integrates them into the whole sentence. In a similar way, the atoms of hydrogen and oxygen – which taken separately are gas – are organised in such a way in a H_2O molecule that their powers are different – although necessary – and different because they are realising an abstract determining form placing them in a specific structural context.

---

[647] Ibid, 355.

Kim gives a useful summary of some of the necessary features of emergentism.[648] He notes that the old Nagelian method of deduction utilised bridge laws as auxiliary premises to derive the reduced entity from the reducing base. But this, Kim claims, leaves unanswered the basic question that older emergentists like Broad proposed, which was *why* a particular higher-level property will arise from a particular lower-level property. For example, why does pain in particular – as opposed to tickles or itches – correlate with C-fibre excitation? The Nagelian derivation does not explain this. Furthermore, given that the Nagelian methods utilise the truth functional conditional, this should not be a surprise, since such a formal method – given its univocal nature and the permutation potential in its relata – lacks the explanatory resources to characterise the intimacy we would expect from such identities between higher-level properties and their realisers.

Kim proposes another form of reduction, called *functional reduction*, that does not suffer from the explanatory deficiencies that plagues the Nagelian brand.[649] It first involves identifying the neural state, N_1, as the property of a system caused by damaged tissue that in turn causes aversive behaviour. Pain is then *defined* as that physical state, P_1, which is caused by tissue damage and which in turn causes aversive behaviour. Here we have a conceptual definition of pain where the physical property is placed conceptually in the pain role and therefore no further questions are needed as to *why* pain is P_1 since conceptually it is defined as such.

Kim then proposes the following two principles as functional reductionist principles that the emergentist should embrace:

`(1) Instantiations of M can be predicted on the basis of information concerning neural and behavioral processes alone (including laws concerning these processes).

---

[648] See Jaegwon Kim, "Being Realistic About Emergence," in *The Re-Emergence of Emergence: The Emergentist Hypothesis from Science to Religion* ed. Philip Clayton and Paul Davies (Oxford: Oxford University Press, 2006), 189-202 and Jaegwon Kim, "Emergence: Core Ideas and Issues," in *Essays in the Metaphysics of Mind* (Oxford: Oxford University Press, 2010), 66-84
[649] Ibid.

`(2) Similarly, why an organism instantiates M at a time can be explained on the basis of information concerning facts at the lower level, namely neural and behavioural facts."[650]

Thus Kim thinks superveniece is a necessary condition of emergence. In the last chapter it was argued that the three-category ontology explains supervenience: given that higher-order properties such as being in pain are structural states, we would expect that an adequate description of the physical and chemical properties of the central nervous system and its structural arrangement will automatically give us the higher-level properties. To be in an emergent state just is to be in a state that is physically structured in the appropriate way. But now consider the last two principles Kim thinks define emergentism:

"(3) Each occurrence of pain has the causal powers of its neural realizer; thus if pain occurs by being realized by N_1, this occurrence of pain has the causal powers of N_1. In general, if M occurs by being realized by N_1 on a given occasion, the *M*-instance has the causal powers of the *N*-instance....
(4) If M is instantiated in virtue of the instantiation of its realizer N_1 on a given occasion, the M-instance is identical with the N_1-instance.
We have, therefore, identified a second condition of emergence:

Irreducibility of emergents: Property M is emergent from a set of properties, $N_1,..., N_n$, only if M is not functionally reducible with realizers at the level of the *N*s."[651]

So the argument proceeds by making N_1 the realiser for the mental state pain, M, where M thus has the causal power derived from N_1 which then gives the identity of M with its realiser N_1. Emergentism, according to Kim, is the denial of such a functional reduction. But notice Kim wants to retain N_1 as the physical substrate of the higher-order emergent mental states as an entity in its own right with its own identity conditions and causal powers. This is something Humphreys and myself would deny. N_1 should be identified with

---

[650] Ibid, 76.
[651] Ibid, 77.

an aspect of M, since it is now playing such a role and its identity is so laden within such a higher-order context.

Thus the key difference with Kim's criteria can be given. That emergence as given by the three categories does indeed entail a non-reductionist account of the causal properties of the whole but much more than that it is the identities themselves that are altered by becoming parts of the whole. Also, the elimination of the basal properties – or its conversion into realising conditions – allows for the emergent account to avoid Kim's causal exclusion dilemma.

Thus the three-category ontology agrees with Kim's account of emergence in the characterisation of the entity given by the structured and functionally irreducible supervenience state of the physical realisers. But the realising condition utilises the entities and their properties in so far as they are in their set role, unlike Humphrey's fusionism. But the crucial difference is that in the giving of causal powers at the neuronal level, we have a case of the physical realisers operating in the context of the whole such that the identity of the entity is defined by such a role. There is not even the question of there being any class of physical entities retained to reduce the macro-properties.

Emergentism and the Three-Category Ontology

We will now consider further the definitions of emergentism that Kim gives, Kim draws from the work of Robert van Gulick.[652] The first, called "specific value emergence", is the uninteresting version where, for example, an object of mass 1 kg is emergent on its parts since none of the parts weigh 1 kg. The second is called "modest kind emergence" on which Kim quotes van Gulick thus: "The whole has features that are different in kind from those of its parts ... For example, a piece of cloth might be purple in hue even though none

---

[652] See both ibid., and Kim, "Being Realistic," in Clayton et al, *The Re-Emergence of Emergence*, 189-202.

of the molecules that make up its surface could be said to be purple. Or a mouse might be alive even if none of its parts (or at least none of its subcellular parts) were alive".[653]

The third form of emergentism is "radical kind emergentism" in which, like the previous form, the emergent whole is a distinct kind from its parts. But what is new is the denial of supervenience; that is, the parts and their law-like connections are not necessary conditions for at least some features of the emergent states. So two systems that have identical microstructure may have different emergent properties.

As Kim points out, it was the second kind of emergentism that the traditional British emergentists such as Broad embraced. The ontology argued for in this thesis most closely resembles this form. But the major difference is that for modest kind emergence there is a wide gap between the emergent whole and its parts. Of course we would not want to say that a mouse's cells are "alive", but it is the case that they are *aspects* of the whole. In the same way, the compound noun "rattle snake" is not contained in either the word "rattle" or word "snake" taken separately. But each word *in the specific context of referring to a venomous reptile* is modified to the extent that we can say that its identity is fused with its role.

Given the inseparable connection between determining and realising conditions, the third form of emergentism would be ruled out *tout court*. There are no emergent properties that would not find some realising condition in its base constituency. And given that the nature of a particular entity supervenes on its structure – given form by the determining condition – it would not be possible for two entities having the same structure to manifest different properties. The implausibility of this is pointed out by Kim with an example: "If the connection between pain and its neural substrate were irregular, haphazard, or coincidental, what reason could there be for saying that pain 'emerges from' that neural condition rather than another?"[654] In other words, the categories give us the necessary intelligible connection between the macro-state and its physical realisers.

---

[653] Kim, "Emergence," in *Essays*, 68.
[654] Kim, "Being Realistic," in the Clayton et al, *Re-Emergence of Emergence*, 193.

But then to what epistemological considerations can we appeal to identify a genuine case of emergence? Consider first the premises Kim sets out to derive functional reductionism:

"System s is in neural state N_1 at t.

N_1 is such that tissue damage causes s and systems like s to go into N_1, and N_1 causes these systems to emit aversive behavior.

By definition, a system is in pain iff it is in some state P such that P is caused by tissue damage and P in turn causes aversive behavior.

Therefore, s is in pain at t."[655]

Now the first thing to be aware of with this argument is that the premises are organised along a priori and a posteriori lines. The third premise is purely conceptual and a priori where the concept *pain* is analysed as an identity with a physical property in a causal relation to tissue damage and is in a causing relation with aversive behaviour. It can be expressed thus:

1) Pain = (pRt & pRa)

This is just an identity statement. The second premise is an appeal to facts: the neurological conditions are given empirically. This is a restatement of the distinction between "relations of ideas" and "matters of fact" which was embraced by Frege and Russell under the title of Hume's principle. Now recall that the use of the biconditional in Nagelian bridge laws was insufficient to connect the emergent and base properties because they invited further questions as to why they held. Fodor also invoked the biconditional in expressing the multiple realisation argument. But Kim's conceptual definition likewise relies on the biconditional, which is really underwritten by the identity relation. What gives such a logical relation any further powers to marry the concept of pain with the basal physical conditions just because Kim has placed such a connection at the a priori level?

---

[655] Kim, "Emergence," in *Essays*, 76.

An alternative approach to such an ontological and epistemological method is to call into question the entire conceptual edifice in the first place. That between the truth-functional structure and the representations of particulars filling the roles in the class. Notice that in Kim's definition of neural particulars they are set out as a class: $N_1...N_n$. But the organisational structure of the brain is far more interesting than that! Ned Block proposes a useful principle against the heterogeneity of higher-level properties:

"In Walt Disney movies, teacups think and talk, but in the real world, anything that can do those things needs more structure than a teacup. We might call this the Disney Principle: that laws of nature impose constraints on ways of making something that satisfies a certain description."[656]

Now Kim argues forcefully for the necessity of tying emergent states to their physical realisers. But why not extend such a requirement to the nature of the structure itself? The structure of brains and central nervous systems are far too complex to be captured by mere classes, which are just the extensions of place-holders at the truth-functional level.

How might the three-category ontology handle such conditions? We have already covered the structural conditions, which are just the interplay of determining and realising conditions that jointly produces an emergent state with the basal physical conditions playing role-fillers within the structural web. But on this account, expressions of pain – such as wincing and crying out – and even scientific tests such as MRI scans are the communicating conditions of the structural pain state. In particular, MRI scans reveal the structure of the brain, with certain areas experiencing greater structural intensity than others. The image communicates a structure, but it is a structure that is far more complex and informationally rich than any purely extensional class of particulars.

---

[656] Ned Block, "Anti-Reductionism Slaps Back," *Nous* 31, no. 1, (1997): 120, http://doi.org/10.1111/0029-4624.31.s11.5

It may be objected that this leaves out the first-person conditions of mental states, which cannot be identified with behaviour or any necessarily third-person scientific methodology. This has generally been thought of as the *problem of other minds* and comes down to us from Descartes. It is a dilemma that finds resolution in the connection between communicating categories and the D–R entities which are disposed to be revealed. Every case of communication is necessarily mediated by the communicating category. Under conditions of perception, the object is perceived through light waves. Electrons and other submicroscopic phenomena are detected through scientific instruments.

Under normal conditions of communication, people communicate their own thoughts, emotions, or desires, etc. In the classroom, a good teacher will have the disposition to communicate certain aspects of their own mental life that are considered relevant to the students' learning. Two people in love will communicate their feelings to one another by acting on each other in certain ways. There is a communicated aspect, the thing-for-others, but there is also the thing-in-itself. Thus, the advantage of the three-category ontology is that it resolves a problem thought unique to our mental life.

Thus the three-category ontology offers an alternative way of conceptualising structure, one that does not reduce to truth-functional logic in the style of Frege and Russell. This rich non-univocal way of abstracting the relevant categories accounts for the complexities in structured entities. It also offers a plausible account of "modest kind emergence" that takes into account the functional intimacy between macro-properties like pain and its physical realisers.

Conclusion

I have attempted to provided an example in this chapter of how one can practise metaphysics in a way that is answerable to science instead of trying to reconstruct science along metaphysical lines. The focal point was the first two categories: the determiner and realiser. The specific issues considered were a) whether those categories could shine light on the debate between reductive and non-reductive physicalists and emergentism and b) how they fared explaining quantum mechanical phenomena.

Physicalists like Kim and Fodor were found to be doing their analytic work in the grip of Fregean and Russellian logical methods and, for Kim in particular, it was atomistic assumptions that further hampered his metaphysics. Such logical methods of drawing inferences are too simple and univocal to provide adequate explication of each individual object and its structure. With Kim it was the fact that his atomic basal entities were immutable in identity – where the neural substrate retained the same identity within the causal system as a whole – that created the conundrum with causal exclusion that prevented the success of any non-reductive or emergent competing account.

On the other hand, the categories were found to offer plausible explanations of quantum phenomena for several reasons. First, they are not univocal characters so they cohere well with the non-logical, non-mathematical concept of fusion. Second, they explain the inherently relational nature of each quantum entity that Teller's account merely assumed to be the case. Third, given that determined entities as realisers within wholes change identity when entering the whole, the categories explain why individuating quantum entities after entering a whole is an impossibility even whilst counting them as parts of that whole is possible. Fourth, determined entities obtain new emergent properties and yet are emergent by being contextualised and so are still retained (much in the same way that words are retained if slightly redefined when becoming parts of sentences). This explains the behaviour of entities within macro-states, such as chemicals in brains or atoms in molecules, in a way that fusionism could not. Lastly the categories provided a richness to structures not evident in Kim's class based alternative.

Conclusion

What I have presented in this work is a new theory of being *qua* being called *the three-category ontology*. It is in rather stark contrast to theories of being that have come before it. I concentrated on contrasting it with the specific method of philosophical analysis that was predominant throughout the twentieth century. Philosophers who adopted that method mostly focused on epistemology but, as I showed, their work was dripping with metaphysical assumptions that had their roots in the Pre-Socratic era. Most notable was the assumption that being is simple, univocal and primitive – and hence opaque to analysis.

My work also started with epistemology, but a robust metaphysic was developed by considering our ordinary perceptual states and scientific practice. That metaphysic was abstracted from experience rather than by imposing a univocal theory of being on experience and then attempting a reconstruction of knowledge on the basis of that theory. Chapter one focused on Frege's theory of logical analysis and explication, which is thoroughly rationalist in nature and involves grounding in such a way that cannot, in any essential way, involve sense experience. Instead, knowledge is constructed and particulars differentiated by occupying either side of the identity sign and being in the context of a sentence that takes the True for a reference. Thus empirical data are not taken at face value, but are conceptually interpreted as constructed from the one true theory of being that is known through reason. Also of note is the metaphysical motif of accident and substance that informs his theory of grounding.

Chapter two brought the theory of Parmenidian being into sharper focus in the work of Frege and Russell. Frege's theory of the True and Russell's proper names and theory of acquaintance are examples of Parmenides' influence on their work. Frege's primitive Platonic conception of the True implied that no individual instance of propositional knowledge could be known to be true in any underived sense. Wittgenstein identified problems with any theory that does not tie truth to individual propositions in a way that is intrinsic to the proposition itself. Russell's thesis was also plagued by dilemmas, such as there being nothing in his metaphysical armoury to act as a unifying agent of propositions, and his method of logical construction only produced logical fictions that were no substitute for the real complexities found in experience. Russell's image theory of the proposition was a step in the right direction but ultimately fails as an explanation of the unity of experience.

Chapter three sought an interpretation of Carnap's *LSW* as a reconstruction of knowledge that is based on Frege–Russell logic but attempts to connect such reconstruction with our empirical knowledge. The *LSW* is an elaborate system marrying Frege and Russell together in the reconstruction of knowledge but, contrary to Russell, maintaining a more pure auto-psychological basis. But such a project was found to be a failure by Quine, since the analytic basis of Carnap's system cannot determine sense data in such a way that allows for the elimination of the "is at" predicate. Carnap's system then is a failure of determinacy and represents a failure of the whole Frege–Russell project.

I then analyse Quine's system of being, which is a naturalistic application of Parmenidian being. Quine situates the knowing agent in behavioural correspondence to being that acts in a manner that dispenses with the internal a priori – a posteriori distinction. The process of regimentation involves adhering to such scientific virtues as simplicity and clarity, through spelling out via the quantifier the univocal theory of identity. Quine adopts – and naturalises – Fregean identity and integrates it into his quantification of first-order logic. Central to Quine's naturalism is the eschewing of first philosophy, but here I show that his theory of truth draws on metaphysical assumptions that are such that they cannot differentiate between manuals of translation. The Tarskian sentences function akin to accidents relative to the real substantial being in nature derived behaviouristically. My second critique is that it fails to make the relevant distinctions in our perceptual experience failing to enable us to identify ordinary objects in our acts of judgement and making sense data dispensable in the naturalistic reconstruction of knowledge.

Chapter four extends the Frege–Russell project into the latter part of the twentieth century and into the area of mereology and composition. I focus on the work of Lewis and show that his assumption of the intimacy of parthood is correct and intuitively obvious. I assume it in my own theory of being. But the application of the truth-functional apparatus, the identity relation, and Lewis' singletons makes the parthood relation non-discriminatory in a way that is intuitively jarring. It represents an imposition on reality rather than a derivation from what is actually experienced.

The fifth chapter explains the three-category ontology. The first two categories are the determiner and the realiser. The determiner is a non-spatiotemporal entity involved in specifying the structure of the entity and applying determinacy to the otherwise indeterminate second category, the realiser. The latter category exists in space-time with its primary function being the realisation of the determiner.

The third category is communication and its primary function is to communicate, through causation, the determining–realising entity to other entities it comes into contact with. Thus the entity doing the causing has a specific nature that is isomorphic with the entity from which it originates (or at least with one of its properties), and it is that nature or property that it communicates. Such instances of causation may form new unities or liberate the dispositions in matter to further states of indeterminacy or new determination conditions.

These categories present an alternative to the old approach to analysis. In contrast to Parmenidian being, the sense of being expounded here can be broken up into parts. Analysis involves focusing in on the arrangement of matter that is given form by being in a certain role within the web of the structure as a whole. The analogy was given with words that, when placed in a sentence, acquire a new meaning by being within the context of that particular sentence. But the sentence structure as a whole requires the words in order to be realised in the world. Analysis by focus then means that such beings can be broken up into parts, but the parts are also supervenient on the whole.

Each category also differs significantly from Parmenidian being by being essentially relational. Each category has a "for-itself" and "for-others" aspect to it: the determiner is something in-itself yet an aspect of its essential nature involves determining its realising matter; the realiser is a something in-itself yet an aspect of its essential nature involves realising the determiner, the communicator is a something in-itself yet an aspect of its essential nature is communicating the determiner–realiser structure. Analysis involves abstraction, and analysis of each category and any whole supervenes on the three categories without remainder (or need for any further entities to glue each category together).

Thus every object in the world, in order to classify as an object, must be a function of determiner and realiser and all are involved in some manner in communicating that structure via causal interactions. I went on to apply the categories to various problems in twentieth century philosophy. Primary emphasis was placed on the individual, and thus every instance of knowledge and truth was not of a univocal nature, with perception granting knowledge due to its inherently relational nature. This meant knowledge was not of a trivial nature and permutations with other truth instances within the system not possible. Thus the categories do not succumb to the threat of sceptical arguments, since the metaphysical system does not make them viable in the first place.

The causal nature underlying perception and its structure were of such a nature that they reflected the object the perception was directed at. Thus it acquired the advantages of the causal theory of perception – robust realism – without falling prey to the *qua* problem. The inherently relational nature of perception also means that it was not plagued by the homunculus dilemma that plagued Descartes' and Putnam's models and yet also avoided the pitfalls in Lewis' holistic model.

I went on in the fifth chapter to compare the categories on composition. Supervenience is not an explanation of why new properties come into existence in a way that is dependent on the basal-level entities. Both dependence and supervenience are given explanation by the determiner and realiser acting in unison, where properties of the whole supervene on the realising matter arranged in the right way. Grounding was a far too general and esoteric concept, where determiner and realiser *are* related asymmetrically and are explanatorily robust principles and derive empirically from particular experience.

The sixth chapter tested the first two categories against debates between reductive, non-reductive and emergent accounts. The first obvious advantage was in avoiding the Frege–Russell logical categories employed by reductionists like Kim and non-reductionists like Fodor. The latter was not able to explain individual objects and structures and the former employed an atomistic physics and a primitive concept of identity. By making identity for matter less fundamental than the determining and realising conditions, the categories were able to explain whole entities without falling prey to the causal exclusion problem.

The categories also excelled in explaining the quantum phenomena of entanglement. Through the added formal conditions the change in identity – yet remaining countable – of entities entering quantum relational states are explained. They also explain how such quantum objects can share information at a distance in a way that non-quantum objects cannot. Additionally the entities were only transformed in identity after entering the context of a whole and thus are retained and causally active by being organised in ways specific to the functional make-up of whole states. This avoided the pitfall that other explanatory concepts (like fusion) fell into by blotting out the lower-level entities altogether.

Thus the three-category ontology avoids the explanatory dead-ends in which alternative conceptions of being found themselves. But it is more than that. It's a metaphysic focused primarily on the individual encountered in perception. It justifies knowledge by explaining the structural make-up specific to that particular individual. It also explains the varied objects encountered in our experience instead of explaining them away, and thus accords with a robust non-reductive realism that is scientifically integrated instead of imposing logical categories on the items of our experience.

The introduction of a new metaphysic opens up the possibility that it may have application to other metaphysical puzzles. The Christian doctrine of the Trinity – that espouses the one God divided into the three persons of Father, Son and Holy Spirit – has traditionally drawn on Greek philosophical categories to give it adequate expression and consistency. The following is a brief exposition of that doctrine in light of the three-category ontology leaving open the possibility for further research on how these various themes intersect.

I suggest that the three categories and their functional natures described in this thesis correlate remarkably well with the three functional natures of the three persons within the Trinity. This gives a metaphysical exposition of the Trinity that is coherent and biblically faithful. But this requires revising the key metaphysical devices traditionally used in its exposition. Consider these commonly given trinitarian claims:

1) The Father is God
2) The Son is God
3) The Holy Spirit is God
4) The Father is not the Son
5) The Father is not the Holy Spirit
6) The Holy Spirit is not the Son
7) There is only One God

The references given on either side of the "is" in 1) – 3) are proper names and so these are identity statements. The transitivity of identity makes 1) – 3) inconsistent with the other four claims. For example, if the Father is God and the Son is God then, by transitivity, the Father is the Son, which contradicts 4). Traditionally this is how the key dilemma for the Trinity is spelt out, but it requires taking identity as an absolute and exclusive concept.

Another key metaphysical category historically applied to the divine essence is the notion of "*ousia*", which Aristotle defined with his phrase "*protai ousiai*" meaning "primary substance". Such a term has presented a difficulty, however, since it is a reference to *primary* being, which means it cannot be divided up or analysed into parts. Given that there has been no avenue for differentiation within *ousia*, one common approach has been to separate the divine persons from the divine nature so as to retain the three distinct persons from the divine being which is one and undivided.

For example, William Lane Craig and J. P. Moreland locate the oneness of God in the "immaterial substance or soul" such that divinity somehow permeates the whole triune nature. They provide a helpful analogy: take the three-headed mythical dog, Cerberus. What we have is one dog, since it has one body, but three distinct centres of consciousness, each with its own unique self-consciousness, intentionality and will. Thus the three persons are retained within the one essential nature.[657]

Whatever criticisms can be levelled at this approach, there is a conspicuous ontological distinction drawn between the divine nature taken as a whole and each of the divine selves. Criticisms have been made to the effect that they have left the divine nature without any form of personhood at all.[658] The response by Craig has been to say that God *does* possess personhood, since he is a soul which *possesses* the rational faculties sufficient for such.[659] In other words, God – the divine nature – inherits personhood from his parts – the three persons. But what sort of part–whole model is this? Clearly the whole remains something over and above its parts and that whole is the soul of God. The divine nature is therefore something ontologically distinct from its parts and hence in its essential nature is not personal.

Another model is Social Trinitarianism whose most prominent exponent in recent years is Richard Swinburne.[660] On this approach, each person of the trinity is a separate loci of consciousness, with the divine substance divided up into three parts of one collective. He attempts to mend the division through an elaborate account of causal interdependence and strict unity in actions amongst the members. This has unsurprisingly faced criticisms of tritheism[661] but he has attempted to neutralise such attacks by appealing to references such

---

[657] James Portland Moreland and William Lane Craig, *Philosophical Foundations for a Christian Worldview* (Illinois: InterVarsity Press, 2003), 393.
[658] See Daniel Howard-Snyder, "Trinity Monotheism," *Philosophia Christi* 5, no. 2 (2003): 375-403, http://doi.org/10.5840/pc20035245 where numerous other objections are offered to Moreland and Craig's model.
[659] William Lane Craig, "Trinity Monotheism Once More: A Response to Daniel Howard-Snyder," *Philosophia Christi* 8, no. 1, (2006): 105, http://doi.org/10.5840/pc2006817
[660] Richard Swinburne, *The Christian God* (Oxford: Clarendon Press, 1994), 170-191.
[661] For example, William Alston, "Swinburne and Christian Theology," *International Journal for Philosophy of Religion* 41, no. 1 (1997): 35-57, http://www.jstor.org/stable/40019081 and Ed Feser "Swinburne's Tritheism," *International Journal for Philosophy of Religion* 42, no. 3 (1997): 175-184, https://doi.org/10.1023/A:1003015616503

as 7) in the Athanasian Creed as a denial of three *independent* beings rather than an affirmation of strictly one God. He provides argumentative support for such a claim by placing the Father in the supreme legislative position laying down divine rules for the three persons to avoid any clash of wills.

But Swinburne's model suffers in the same way as Craig and Moreland's but for different reasons. The trinity as a unit is not a personal being since it is a mere collective or sum of three persons. Brian Leftow writes: "One who worships addresses someone. So worship makes sense only if directed to someone who can be aware of being addressed."[662] The metaphysical issue is the way the three persons are united, and in Swinburne's case that unity is not one that involves the essential natures of each person such that each nature is essentially related to each of the others. Literally anything can enter into a collective, which is why Leftow goes on to draw a comparison with the Greek gods who could have formed a similar monotheism by being more alike or better integrated: morally and causally. As Leftow alludes, we need a conception that preserves the three selves united in love, but where the mutual cooperation and procession is at a deep metaphysical level.[663]

But what may be frustrating attempts to explain such a unity are the metaphysical categories employed to individuate the members of the trinity and how they relate to one another. With Swinburne's account in particular, the Son is dependent on the Father in being preserved in existence which in itself creates the threat of Arianism. But despite such causal dependence, the Son, for Swinburne, is a discrete substance it its own right. There is nothing in the Son's metaphysical nature that unites it to the other two members.

Can an essential definition of each member of the Trinity provide a grounding for unity? It can if we reify each member's distinct functional attribute as the nature of that member and identify such a nature as the locus of self-consciousness. First, we identify the Son as "begotten" of the Father (John 1:18) which means the latter somehow causes the former. The Father is also cast in the executive role throughout Jesus' earthly ministry (for

---

[662] Brian Leftow, "Anti Social Trinitarianism," in *The Trinity* (Oxford: Oxford University Press, 1999), 228.
[663] Ibid, 232.

example, John 5:19, 6:37–38, 8: 28–29), whilst the Son is the exclusive revelation of God and his will (Matt. 11:27, John 14:6). The Holy Spirit originates, on the other hand, from the Father (John 14:26) and the Son (John 16:7) and has the unique function of communicating the will of both to any being exterior to God.

So the Father, although not creating the son *ex nihilo*, somehow determines the Son. But the question is, how? The extra detail is given in Colossians 1: 15 which says the Son is "the image of the invisible God, the firstborn of every creature." In being the image of the invisible Father, we can say that in realising the nature of the Father, the Son is formed in such a way by the Father that he embodies that nature. Similarly we can say that the Holy Spirit communicates the nature of the joint entity of Father and Son to all other beings by sharing the form of the Son.

Note that the unity is an essential by-product of each nature in two notable ways. First, as has been explained, determining is an inherently dyadic action. To determine there must be a determiner and object determined. The same goes for the other two categories. Second, the relatedness is inherent to the distinct nature of each category.

For example, the determiner of a chair informs the wood in accord with its nature such that no other form could enter into such a unity and, in the same sense, the wood realises the determiner in the world in accordance with its own nature. Perception of the chair involves sense data arranged in such a way that it is formally identical to the determining and realising conditions of the chair, but the sense properties refer beyond themselves to the chair such that in the act of perception we are grasping *one thing*. The whole act of perception, therefore, supervenes on the formal parts of determiner, realiser and communicator. The whole is an ontological free lunch.

This avoids many of the pitfalls of the other models. First, on this account the Son is not created for the same reason that the realiser is not created but merely formed by the determiner. In fact, although the Father is cast in the executive role, he is also dependent on the Son in order to be realised in the world. The Father and Son are also dependent on the Holy Spirit for communication and the latter is dependent on the former for its structure. Hence we have an explanation for all three being equally interdependent. Second, three distinct selves are maintained on this account, since all three categories are distinct. Third, we can also say there is only one personal God, since all three are fully integrated according to their distinct will, intellect and personality, for the Holy Spirit and Son are formally identical to the Father. This makes the references to one personal God in the Old Testament perfectly accurate. Thus God is both personal in its threeness and in its oneness. Such an integral unity avoids Swinburne's mere collective unity and, since the whole supervenes on the essential natures of each then the whole is an integrated whole that is personal in nature (there is no divine nature separate from its personal parts). Fourth, given the supervenience between persons and whole, there is no fourth entity, a problem that plagues some models. Fifth, the model of perichoresis – the mutual indwelling or interpenetration – is not mysterious, as direct analogies can be drawn with the beings of ordinary objects in the world.

Such an account requires further explication and comparisons with other models, but there is not enough space here to do so. It may also be possible that this model could inform a cosmological argument for God's existence. But this will have to await further developments. The goal here is merely to give a foretaste of possible further research and in applying the three-category model to various areas of metaphysics and thus make clear the fruitfulness and fecundity of this ontology.

Bibliography

Ainsworth, Peter. "Structural Realism: A Critical Appraisal." PhD Thesis. University of London, 2009

Allen, Keith. *A Naïve Realist Theory of Colour*. Oxford: Oxford University Press, 2016

Alston, William. "Swinburne and Christian Theology." *International Journal for Philosophy of Religion* 41, no. 1 (1997): 35-57. http://www.jstor.org/stable/40019081.

Anscombe, Elizabeth. *An Introduction to Wittgenstein's Tractatus*. London: Hutchinson University Library, 1959

Anscombe, Elizabeth. "Cambridge Philosophers II: Ludwig Wittgenstein," *Philosophy*, 70, no. 273 (1995): 395-407. http://www.jstor.org/stable/3751665

Aristotle. "Nichomachean Ethics." In *Greek Philosophy Thales to Aristotle* 3rd ed. Translated by Harris Rackham. Edited by Reginald Allen, book 2, chapter V. New York: The Free Press, 1991

Aristotle. *Metaphysics: Γ, Δ, and E*, 2nd ed. Translated by Christopher Kirwin. Oxford: Clarendon Press, 1993

Aristotle. *Metaphysics: Books Z and H*. Translated and commentary by David Bostock. Oxford: Clarendon Press, 1994

Armstrong, David. *Universals: An Opinionated Introduction*, Boulder, CO: Westview Press, 1989

Armstrong, David. "Intentionality, Perception, and Causality." In *John Searle and His Critics,* edited by Ernest Lepore and Robert Van Gulick, 149-158. Oxford: Basil Blackwell, 1991

Armstrong, David. *A World of States of Affairs.* Cambridge: Cambridge University Press, 1997

Armstrong, David. *Truth and Truth-Makers*. Cambridge: Cambridge University Press, 2004

Ayer, A. J. *Language, Truth, and Logic*, 2nd ed. New York: Dover Publications, 1946

Bacon, Francis. *The New Organon*, edited by Lisa Jardine and Michael Silverthorne. Cambridge: Cambridge University Press, 2000

Baker, Lynne Rudder. "The Ontology of Artifacts." *Philosophical Explorations* 7, no. 2 (2004): 99-111. https://doi.org/10.1080/13869790410001694462

Baker, Lynne Rudder. "On the Place of Artifacts in Ontology." In *Creations of the Mind: Theories of Artifacts and Their Representation*, edited by Eric Margolis and Stephen Laurence, 33-51. Oxford: Oxford University Press, 2007

Baxter, Donald. "Many-One Identity." *Philosophical Papers* 17, no. 3, (1988): 193-216. https://doi.org/10.1080/05568648809506300

Bennett, Karen. "'Perfectly Understood, Unproblematic, and Certain': Lewis on Mereology." In *A Companion to David Lewis*, edited by Barry Loewer and Jonathan Schaffer, 250-261. Chichester: Wiley-Blackwell, 2015

Block, Ned. "Anti-Reductionism Slaps Back." *Nous* 31, no. 1 (1997): 107-132. http://doi.org/10.1111/0029-4624.31.s11.5

Bohn, Einar. "Commentary on 'Parts of Classes'." *Humana.Mente Journal of Philosophical Studies* 19 (2011): 151-158. https://philarchive.org/archive/BOHCOQ

Boolos, George. "To Be is to Be a Value of a Variable (or to Be Some Values of Some Variables)." *The Journal of Philosophy* 81, no. 8, (1984): 430-449. http://dx.doi.org/jphil198481840

Bradley, F. A. *Appearance and Reality*. Oxford: Clarendon Press, 1893

Bradley, F. H. "Coherence and Contradiction." In *Essays on Truth and Reality*. Oxford: Clarendon Press, 1914: 219-244

Bradley, F. H. "Relations." in *Collected Essays* vol. 2. Oxford: Clarendon Press, 1935: 628-676

Broad, C. D. *The Mind and its Place in Nature*. London & New York: Routledge, 2013

Burge, Tyler. "Frege on Knowing the Third Realm." In *Early Analytic Philosophy: Frege, Russell, Wittgenstein: Essays in Honor of Leonard Linsky*. La Salle: Open Court, 1997: 1-18

Burge, Tyler. "Frege on Sense and Linguistic Meaning." In *The Analytic Tradition: Meaning, Thought and Knowledge,* edited by David Bell and Neil Cooper, 30-60. Oxford: Blackwell, 1990

Burge, Tyler. "Intentionality, Perception, and Causality." In *John Searle and His Critics,* edited by Ernest Lepore and Robert Van Gulick, 195-213. Oxford: Basil Blackwell, 1991

Burgess, John. "Lewis on Mereology and Set Theory." In *A Companion to David Lewis*, edited by Barry Loewer and Jonathan Schaffer, 459-469. Chichester: Wiley-Blackwell, 2015

Burke, Michael. "Preserving the Principle of One Object to a Place: A Novel Account of the Relations Among Objects, Sorts, Sortals, and Persistence Conditions," *Philosophy and Phenomenological Research* 54, issue 3, (1994): 591-624. https://www-jstor-org.ipacez.nd.edu.au/stable/2108583

Burke, Michael. "Persons and Bodies: How to Avoid the New Dualism," *American Philosophical Quarterly* 34, issue 4, (1997a): 457-467. https://www-jstor-org.ipacez.nd.edu.au/stable/20009913

Burke, Michael. "Coinciding Objects: A Reply to Lowe and Denkel," *Analysis* 57, no. 1, (1997b) 11-18, https://www-jstor-org.ipacez.nd.edu.au/stable/3328429.

Button, Timothy. *The Limits of Realism*. Oxford: Oxford University Press, 2013

Campbell, John. *Reference and Consciousness*. Oxford: Clarendon Press, 2002

Candlish, Stewart. *The Russell/Bradley Dispute and its Significance for Twentieth-Century Philosophy*. New York: Palgrave Macmillan, 2007

Carnap, Rudolph. *The Logical Structure of the World and Pseudoproblems in Philosophy*. Translated by Rolf A. George. Chicago and La Salle, Illinois: Open Court, 1967

Cartwright, Nancy. *The Dappled World: A Study of the Boundaries of Science.* Cambridge: Cambridge University Press, 1999

Cartwright, Nancy. "Causation: One Word, Many Things." *Philosophy of Science* 71, no. 5. (2004): 805-820. https://doi.org/10.1086/426771

Chakraborty, Sanjit. *Meaning and World: A Relook on Semantic Externalism*. London, UK: Cambridge Scholars Publishing, 2016

Clarke, W. Norris. "To Be Is to Be Substance-in-Relation." In *Explorations in Metaphysics: Being-God-Person*, Notre Dame, Indiana: University of Notre Dame Press, 1992: 102-122.

Cook, John. *The Metaphysics of Wittgenstein*. Cambridge: Cambridge University Press, 1994

Coxon, A. H. *The Fragments of Parmenides: A Critical Text with Introduction and Translation, the Ancient* Testimonia *and a Commentary*, revised and expanded edition with new translations by Richard McKirahan. Las Vegas, Zurich, and Athens: Parmenides Publishing, 2009

Craig, William Lane. "Trinity Monotheism Once More: A Response to Daniel Howard-Snyder." *Philosophia Christi* 8, no. 1, (2006): 101-113. http://doi.org/10.5840/pc2006817

Davidson, Donald. "Truth and Meaning." *Synthese* 17, no. 1, (1967): 304-323. http://www.jstor.org/stable/20114563.

Davidson, Donald. "The Folly of Trying to Define Truth." In *Truth*, edited by Simon Blackburn and Keith Simmons, 308-322. Oxford: Oxford University Press, 1999

Davidson, Donald. "Mental Events." In *Essays on Action and Events: Philosophical Essays,* 2nd ed. Oxford: Oxford University Press, 2001: 207-224.

Davidson, Donald. "The Material Mind." In *Essays on Action and Events*, 245-260

Davidson, Donald. *Truth and Predication*. Cambridge, MA: Belknap Press, 2005.

Dejnozka, Jan. *The Ontology of the Analytic Tradition and its Origins: Realism and Identity in Frege, Russell, Wittgenstein and Quine*. New York: Rowman and Littlefield, 1996

Dennett, Daniel. "Artificial Intelligence as Philosophy and as Psychology," in *Brainstorms: Philosophical Essays on Mind and Psychology*. Cambridge, MA: MIT Press, 1978, 109-126

Dennett, Daniel. *Consciousness Explained*. New York: Black Bay Books, 1991

Descartes, Rene. "The Philosophical Writings of Descartes." vol. II, translated by John Cottingham, Robert Stoothoff, Dugald Murdoch. Cambridge: Cambridge University Press, 1984

Descartes, Rene. *Meditations on First Philosophy*. Translated by Michael Moriaty. Oxford: Oxford World's Classics, 2008

Devitt, Michael and Sterelny, Kim. *Language and Reality: An Introduction to the Philosophy of Language*. Oxford: Blackwell, 1999

Dretske, Fred. *Naturalizing the Mind*. Cambridge MA: MIT Press, 1995

Dummett, Michael. "An Unsuccessful Dig." *The Philosophical Quarterly* 34 no. 136 (1984): 377-401. http://doi.org/10.2307/2218768.

Dummett, Michael. "Truth," *The Aristotelian Society* Virtual Issue no. 1, (2013): 1-17. https://www.aristoteliansociety.org.uk/pdf/dummett.pdf

Dummett, Michael. *Frege: Philosopher of Language*. London: Duckworth, 1981

Dummett, Michael. *Frege: Philosophy of Mathematics*. Cambridge, MA: Harvard University Press, 1991

Dummett, Michael. *The Interpretation of Frege's Philosophy*. London: Duckworth, 1981

Elder, Crawford. *Familiar Objects and their Shadows*. Cambridge: Cambridge University Press, 2011

Elder, Crawford. *Real Natures and Familiar Objects*. Cambridge: MIT Press, 2004

Ellis, Brian. *The Philosophy of Nature: A Guide to the New Essentialism*. Chesham: Acumen, 2002

Evans, Gareth. *The Varieties of Reference*. Oxford: Oxford University Press, 1982

Fairweather, Abrol. "Duhem-Quine Virtue Epistemology," *Synthese* 187, no. 2, (2012): 673-692. https://doi.org/10.1007/s11229-010-9868-2

Feser, Ed. "Swinburne's Tritheism." *International Journal for Philosophy of Religion* 42, no. 3 (1997): 175-184. https://doi.org/10.1023/A:1003015616503

Field, Hartry. "Tarski's Theory of Truth." *Journal of Philosophy* 69, no. 13, (1972): 347-375. http://doi.org/10.2307/2024879.

Fine, Kit. "Essence and Modality." *Philosophical Perspectives* 8, (1994): 1-16. https://doi:10.2307/2214160.

Fine, Kit. "Ontological Dependence." *Proceedings of the Aristotelian Society* 95, issue 1, (1995): 269-290. http://www.jstor.org/stable/4545221.

Fine, Kit. "The Question of Realism." *Philosopher's Imprint* 1, no. 2, (2001): 1-30. http://hdl.handle.net/2027/spo.3521354.0001.002

Fine, Kit. "Guide to Ground." In *Metaphysical Grounding: Understanding the Structure of Reality*, edited by Fabrice Correia and Benjamin Schneider, 37-80. Cambridge: Cambridge University Press, 2012

Fine, Kit. "Identity Criteria and Ground." *Philosophical Studies* 173, issue 1, (2016): 1-19. https://doi.org/10.1007/s11098-014-0440-7

Fodor, Jerry. "Special Sciences (Or: The Disunity of Science as a Working Hypothesis)." *Synthese* 28, no. 2 (1974): 97-115. http://doi.org/10.1007/BF00485230

Frege, Gottlob. *Foundations of Arithmetic* 2nd rev. ed. translated by John Langshaw Austin, New York: Harper & Brothers, 1953

Frege, Gottlob. "The Thought: A Logical Inquiry." *Mind* 65, no. 259 (1956): 289-311, http://www.jstor.org/stable/2251513

Frege, Gottlob. "On Concept and Object." In *Translations from the Philosophical Writings of Gottlob Frege*, edited and translated by Peter Geach and Max Black, 42-55. Oxford: Basil Blackwell, 1960

Frege, Gottlob. "On Sense and Reference." In Geach et al, *Translations from the Philosophical Works of Gottlob Frege*, 56-78.

Frege, Gottlob. "Frege Against the Formalists." In Geach et al, *Translations from the Philosophical Writings of Gottlob Frege*, 182-233.

Frege, Gottlob. *The Basic Laws of Arithmetic*. Translated and edited by Montgomery Furth. Berkeley: University of California Press, 1964

Frege, Gottlob. "Begriffsschrift, a formula language, modeled on that of arithmetic, for pure thought." In *From Frege to Godel: A Source Book in Mathematical Logic, 1879-1931*. Translated by Stefan Bauer-Mengelberg, edited by Jean van Heijenoort, 1-82. Cambridge: Harvard University Press, 1967.

Frege, Gottlob. "Conceptual Notation." in *Conceptual Notation and Related Articles*. Translated and edited by Terrell Ward Bynum, 101-203. Oxford: Clarendon Press, 1972

Frege, Gottlob. "Logic" in *Posthumous Writings*, edited by Hans Hermes, Friedrich Kambartel, Friedrich Kaulbach, 1-8. Translated by Peter Long and Roger White. Oxford: Basil Blackwell, 1979

Frege, Gottlob. "Boole's Logical Calculus and the Concept-Script." In Hermes et al, *Posthumous Writings*, 9-46

Frege, Gottlob. "Dialogue with Punjar on Existence." In Hermes et al, *Posthumous Writings*, 53-67.

Frege, Gottlob. "Logic." In Hermes et al, *Posthumous Writings*, 126-151.

Frege, Gottlob. "A Brief Survey of my Logical Doctrines." In Hermes et al, *Posthumous Writings,* 197-202.

Frege, Gottlob. "Logic in Mathematics." In Hermes et al, *Posthumous Writings*, 203-250

Frege, Gottlob. "[Notes for Ludwig Darmstaedter]." In Hermes et al, *Posthumous Writings*, 253-257

"Frege to Husserl 30.10-1.11.1906." In *The Philosophical and Mathematical Correspondence*, edited by Gottfried Gabriel, Hans Hermes, Friedrich Kambartel, Christian Thiel, Albert Veraart, 66-69. Translated by Hans Kaal. Oxford: Basil Blackwell, 1980

Frege, Gottlob. "Frege to Husserl 9.12.1906." In Gabriel et al, *The Philosophical and Mathematical Correspondence*, 70-71.

Frege, Gottlob. "Frege to Jourdain undated." In Gabriel et al, *The Philosophical and Mathematical Correspondence,* 78-80.

Frege, Gottlob. "Frege to Jourdain 28.1.1914." In Gabriel et al, *The Philosophical and Mathematical Correspondence,* 81-84

Frege, Gottlob. "Frege to Marty 29.8.1882." In Gabriel et al, *The Philosophical and Mathematical Correspondence*, 99-102.

Frege, Gottlob. "Frege to Russell 28.7.1902." In Gabriel et al, *The Philosophical and Mathematical Correspondence*, 139-141

Frege, Gottlob. "Frege to Russell 13.11.1904." In Gabriel et al, *The Philosophical and Mathematical Correspondence*, 160-166

Frege, Gottlob. "Function and Concept." In *Collected Papers on Mathematics, Logic, and Philosophy*, edited by Brian McGuinness, 137-156. Translated by Max Black, V. H. Dudman, Peter Geach, Hans Kaal, E. –H. W. Kluge, Brian McGuinness, R. H. Stoothoff. Oxford: Basil Blackwell, 1984

Frege, Gottlob. "On the Foundations of Geometry: Second Series." In McGuiness et al, *Collected Papers*, 293-340

Frege, Gottlob. "Thoughts." In McGuiness et al, *Collected Papers on Mathematics, Logic, and Philosophy*, 351-372

Frege, Gottlob. *On the Foundations of Geometry and Formal Theories of Arithmetic*. Translated by Eike-Henner Kluge. New Haven: Yale University Press, 1971

Friedman, Michael. "Physicalism and the indeterminacy of translation." *Nous* 9, no. 4 (1975): 353-374. http://doi.org/10.2307/2214520

Friedman, Michael. "Carnap's *Aufbau* Reconsidered." In *Reconsidering Logical Positivism*. Cambridge: Cambridge University Press, 1999: 89-93.

Gaudet, Eve. *Quine on Meaning: The Indeterminacy of Translation*. London: Continuum International Publishing Group, 2006

Geach, Peter. "Frege." In (with Elizabeth Anscombe) *Three Philosophers*, 127-162. Oxford: Blackwell, 1961

Gibson, Roger. "The Key to Interpreting Quine." *The Southern Journal of Philosophy* 30, issue 4, (1992): 17-30. https://doi.org/10.1111/j.2041-6962.1992.tb00644.x

Gibson, Roger. "Willard Van Orman Quine." In *The Cambridge Companion to Quine*, edited by R. F. Gibson, 1-18. New York: Cambridge University Press, 2004

Godel, Kurt. "Russell's Mathematical Logic." In *Philosophy of Mathematics, Selected Readings* 2nd ed, edited by Hillary Putnam and Paul Benacerraf. Cambridge: Cambridge University Press, 1983

Goodman, Nelson. "On Relations that Generate." In *Problems and Projects*. Indianapolis: Bobbs-Merrill, 1977a

Goodman, Nelson. *The Structure of Appearances*, 3rd ed. Boston: Reidel Publishing, 1977b

Gorman, Michael. "Substance and Identity-Dependence." *Philosophical Papers* 35, no. 1, (2006): 103-118. https://doi.org/10.1080/05568640609485174

Grayling, A. C. *An Introduction to Philosophical Logic*. Oxford: Blackwell, 1997

Haack, Susan. *Deviant Logic, Fuzzy Logic: Beyond the Formalism*. Chicago: University of Chicago Press, 1996

Hanna, Robert. "Kant's Theory of Judgment", *The Stanford Encyclopedia of Philosophy* (Winter 2018 Edition), Edward N. Zalta (ed.), URL = < https://plato.stanford.edu/entries/kant-judgment/supplement2.html>.

Hansen, Carsten. "Putnam's Indeterminacy Argument: The Skolemization of Absolutely Everything." *Philosophical Studies* 51, no. 1 (1987): 77-99. http://www.jstor.org/stable/4319877.

Harre, Rom and Edward H. Madden. "Natural Powers and Powerful Natures." *Philosophy* 48, no. 185, (1973): 209-230. http://www.jstor.org/stable/3749407.

Harte, Verite. *Plato on Parts and Wholes: The Metaphysics of Structure*. Oxford: Oxford University Press, 2002

Heck, Richard and Robert May. "The Composition of Thoughts." *Nous* 45, no. 1 (2011): 126-166. https://doi.org/10.1111/j.1468-0068.2010.00769.x

Heil, John. *The Universe as We Find It*. Oxford: Clarendon Press, 2012

Hofweber, Thomas. "Ambitious, Yet Modest, Metaphysics." In *Metametaphysics; New Essays on the Foundations of Ontology*, edited by David Chalmers, David Manley and Ryan Wasserman, 260-289. Oxford: Clarendon Press, 2009

Horsten, Leon. *The Tarskian Turn; Deflationism and Axiomatic Truth*. Cambridge, MA: MIT Press, 2011

Howard-Snyder, Daniel. "Trinity Monotheism." *Philosophia Christi* 5, no. 2 (2003): 375-403. http://doi.org/10.5840/pc20035245

Hume, David. *Enquiries Concerning Human Understanding and Concerning the Principles of Morals*, 3rd ed. Oxford: Oxford University Press, 1975

Humphreys, Paul. "How Properties Emerge." In *Emergence: Contemporary Readings in Philosophy and Science*, edited by Mark A. Bedau and Paul Humphreys, 111-126. Cambridge, MA: MIT Press, 2008

Hylton, Russell. *Russell, Idealism, and the Emergence of Analytic Philosophy*. Oxford: Clarendon Press, 1990

James, William. "The Will to Believe," Adelaide: ebooks@adelaide, 2014; accessed 28th July, 2019. https://ebooks.adelaide.edu.au/j/james/william/will/

Johnston, Mark. "Better Than Mere Knowledge?: The Function of Sensory Awareness." In *Perceptual Experience*, edited by Tamar Szabo Gendler and John Hawthorne, 260-290. Oxford: Oxford University Press, 2006

Kant, Immanuel. "To Marcus Herz, February 21, 1772," in *Philosophical Correspondence, 1759-1799*, ed. and trans. Arnulf Zweig, 70-75. Chicago: The University of Chicago Press, 1970

Kant, Immanuel. *Kant: Groundwork of the Metaphysics of Morals*. Translated and edited by Mary Gregor. Cambridge: Cambridge University Press, 1997

Kant, Immanuel. *The Critique of Pure Reason*. Translated by Paul Guyer and Allen W. Wood. Cambridge: Cambridge University Press, 1998

Kanterian, Edward. *Frege: A Guide for the Perplexed*. London and New York: Continuum, 2012

Katz, Jerrold. *Sense, Reference, and Philosophy*. Oxford: Oxford University Press, 2004

Kenny, Anthony. "The Homunculus Fallacy." In *The Legacy of Wittgenstein*. Oxford: Basil Blackwell, 1984, 125-136

Kenny, Anthony. *Frege: An Introduction to the Founder of Analytic Philosophy*. London: Penguin 1995

Kim, Jaegwon. "Postscripts on Supervenience." In *Supervenience and Mind: Selected Philosophical Essays*, edited by Ernest Sosa, 161-172. Cambridge: Cambridge University Press, 1993

Kim, Jaegwon. "The Non-Reductivist's Troubles with Mental Causation." In Sosa, *Supervenience and Mind*, 336-357

Kim, Jaegwon. *The Philosophy of Mind*. Colorado: Westview Press, 1996

Kim, Jaegwon. *Mind in a Physical World: An Essay on the Mind-Body Problem and Mental Causation*. Cambridge: MIT Press, 1998

Kim, Jaegwon. *Physicalism or Something Near Enough.* Princeton: Princeton University Press, 2005

Kim, Jaegwon. "Being Realistic About Emergence." In *The Re-Emergence of Emergence: The Emergentist Hypothesis from Science to Religion*, edited by Philip Clayton and Paul Davies, 189-202. Oxford: Oxford University Press, 2006

Kim, Jaegwon. "Reduction and Reductive Explanation: Is One Possible Without the Other?" In *Being Reduced: New Essays on Reduction, Explanation, and Causation*, edited by Jacob Hohwy and Jesper Kallestrup, 93-114. Oxford: Oxford University Press, 2009

Kim, Jaegwon. "Emergence: Core Ideas and Issues." In *Essays in the Metaphysics of Mind*. Oxford: Oxford University Press, 2010: 66-84

Koslicki, Kathryn. *The Structure of Objects*. Oxford: Oxford University Press, 2008

Koslicki, Kathrin. "In Defence of Substance." *Grazer Philosophische Studien* 91, issue 1, (2015): 59-80 https://doi.org/10.1163/9789004302273_004

Kripke, Saul. *Naming and Necessity*. Cambridge, MA: Harvard University Press, 1980

Leftow, Brian. "Anti Social Trinitarianism." In *The Trinity*. Oxford: Oxford University Press, 1999: 203-249.

Leibniz, Gotfried Wilhelm, *The Monadology*, translated by Robert Latta. Adelaide: ebooks@adelaide, 2014; accessed 1st June, 2019.
https://ebooks.adelaide.edu.au/l/leibniz/gottfried/l525m/

Leonard, Henry and Nelson Goodman. "The Calculus of Individuals and Its Users." *Journal of Symbolic Logic* 5, no. 2, (1940): 45-55. https://doi.org/10.2307/2266169

Levine, Joseph. "Analysis and Decomposition in Frege and Russell." *The Philosophical Quarterly* 52, no. 207 (2002): 195 – 216. http://www.jstor.org/stable/3542843.

Lewis, David. "New Work for a Theory of Universals." *Australasian Journal of Philosophy* 61, no. 4, (1983): 343-377. https://doi.org/10.1080/00048408312341131

Lewis, David. *On the Plurality of Worlds*. Oxford: Blackwell, 1986a

Lewis, David. "Against Structural Universals." *Australasian Journal of Philosophy* 64, no. 1 (1986b): 25-46. https://doi.org/10.1080/00048408612342211

Lewis, David. *Philosophical Papers* vol. 2. Oxford: Oxford University Press, 1986c

Lewis, David. *Parts of Classes*. Oxford: Blackwell, 1991

Lewis, David. "Humean Supervenience Debugged." *Mind* 103, no. 412, (1994): 473-490. http://www.jstor.org/stable/2254396.

Lewis, David. "Putnam's Paradox." In *Papers in Metaphysics and Epistemology*, vol 2, edited by David Lewis, 56-77. Cambridge: Cambridge University Press, 1999

Lewis, David. "Reduction of Mind." In Lewis, *Papers in Metaphysics and Epistemology*, 291-324

Lewis, David. "Ramseyan Humility." In *Conceptual Analysis and Philosophical Naturalism*, edited by David Braddon-Mitchell and Robert Nola, 203-222. Cambridge, MA: MIT Press, 2009.

Linsky, Bernard. "The Unity of the Proposition." *Journal of the History of Philosophy* 30, no. 2 (1992): 243-273. https://muse.jhu.edu/article/226223

Locke, John. *An Essay Concerning Human Understanding*. Pennsylvania: Pennsylvania State University, 1999

Lowe, E. J. *The Possibility of Metaphysics*. Oxford: Clarendon Press, 2001

Lowe, E. J. "Two Notions of Being: Entity and Essence." In *Being: Developments in Contemporary Metaphysics*, edited by Robin Le Poidevin, 23-48. Cambridge: Cambridge University Press, 2008

Lowe, E. J. *Forms of Thought: A Study in Philosophical Logic*. Cambridge: Cambridge University Press, 2013

Lynsky, Leonard. *Referring*. New York: Humanities Press, 1967

Macbride, Fraser. "Relations." *The Stanford Encyclopedia of Philosophy* (Winter 2016 Edition), ed. Edward N. Zalta, URL = <https://plato.stanford.edu/archives/win2016/entries/relations/>.

Macfarlane, John. "Frege, Kant, and the Logic in Logicism." *The Philosophical Review* 111, no. 1 (2002): 25-65. http://doi.org/10.1215/00318108-111-1-25

Maddy, Penelope. *Realism in Mathematics*. Oxford: Clarendon Press, 1990

Makin, Gideon. *The Metaphysics of Meaning: Russell and Frege on Sense and Denotation*. London and New York: Routledge, 2000

Markhosian, Ned. "A Spatial Approach to Mereology." In *Mereology and Location*, ed. Shieva Kleinschmidt, 69-90. Oxford: Oxford University Press, 2014

Martin, D. M. *The Mind in Nature*. Oxford: Oxford University Press, 2008

Martin, M. G. F. "The Limits of Self-Awareness." *Philosophical Studies* 120, no. 1/3, (2004): 37-89. http://www.jstor.org/stable/4321508.

McDowell, John. *Mind and World*. Cambridge, MA: Harvard University Press, 1994

McGinn, Colin. *Logical Properties: Identity, Existence, Predication, Necessity, Truth*. Oxford: Clarendon Press, 2000

Mendelsohn, Richard. "Frege's *Begriffsschrift* Theory of Identity." *Journal of the History of Philosophy* 20, no. 3 (1982): 279-299. http://doi.org/10.1353/hph.1982.0029

Mendelsohn, Richard. *The Philosophy of Gottlob Frege*. Cambridge: Cambridge University Press, 2005

Miah, Sajahan. *Russell's Theory of Perception (1905-1919)*. London and New York: Continuum, 2006

Moore, G. E. "The Nature of Judgment." *Mind* 8, no. 30 (1899): 176-193. http://www.jstor.org/stable/2247657.

Moore, G. E. *Principia Ethica*. Cambridge: Cambridge University Press, 1903

Moreland, James and William Lane Craig. *Philosophical Foundations for a Christian Worldview*. Illinois: InterVarsity Press, 2003

Mumford, Stephen and Rani Lill Anjum. "Mutual Manifestation and Martin's Twin Triangles." In *Causal Powers*, edited by Jonathan D. Jacobs, 77-89. Oxford: Oxford University Press, 2017

Neale, William and Martha. *The Development of Logic*. Oxford: Clarendon Press, 1962

Needham, Paul. "Microessentialism: What is the Argument." *Nous* 45, no.1, (2011): 1-21. http://doi.org/10.1111/j.1468-0068.2010.00756.x

Newman, M. H. A. "Mr Russell's 'Causal Theory of Perception'." *Mind* 37, no. 146, (1928): 137-148. https://doi.org/10.1093/mind/XXXVII.146.137

Nolan, Daniel. *David Lewis*. Chesham: Acumen Publishing, 2005

O'Callaghan, John. "The Identity of Knower and Known: Sellars's and McDowell's Thomisms." *Proceedings of the American Catholic Philosophical Association* 87, (2013): 1-30. 10.5840/acpaproc201481318

Oderberg, David. *Real Essentialism*. New York: Routledge, 2007

Oliver, Alex. "Are Subclasses Parts of Classes?" *Analysis* 54, issue 4, (1994): 215-223. https://doi.org/10.1093/analys/54.4.215

Oppenheim, Paul and Hilary Putnam. "Unity of Science as a Working Hypothesis." *Minnesota Studies in the Philosophy of Science* 2, (1958): 3-36. http://hdl.handle.net/11299/184622.

Papineau, David. "The Rise of Physicalism." In *Physicalism and its Discontents* edited by Carl Gillett and Barry Loewer, 3-36. Cambridge: Cambridge University Press, 2001

Pincock, Christopher. "Russell's Influence on Carnap's *Aufbau*." *Synthese* 131, no. 1, (2002): 1 – 37. https://doi.org/10.1023/A:1015066427566

Pitcher, George. "Introduction." In *Truth*, edited by George Pitcher, 1-15. Englewood Cliffs: Prentice-Hall, 1964

Popper, Karl. *Objective Knowledge: An Evolutionary Approach*, reprint with corrections and new appendix 2. Oxford: Clarendon Press, 1979

Potter, Michael. *Wittgenstein's Notes on Logic*. Oxford: Oxford University Press, 2009

Proops, Ian. *Logic and Language in Wittgenstein's Tractatus*. New York: Garland Publishing, 2000

Proops, Ian. "Russellian Acquaintance Revisited," *Journal of the History of Philosophy* 52, no. 4 (2014): 779-811. https://doi.org/10.1353/hph.2014.0098

Psillos, Stathis. *Scientific Realism: How Science Tracks Truth*. London: Routledge, 1999

Psillos, Stathis. "Is Structural Realism Possible?" *Philosophy of Science* 68, no. S3 (2001): S13-S24. https://doi.org/10.1086/392894

Psillos, Stathos. "The Structure, the Whole Structure and Nothing but the Structure." *Philosophy of Science* 73, no. 5 (2004): 560-570. http://doi.org/10.1086/518326.

Putnam, Hillary. "The Meaning of 'Meaning'." In *Philosophical Papers, Vol II: Mind, Language, and Reality*. Cambridge: Cambridge University Press, 1975: 215-271

Putnam, Hillary. "Realism and Reason." *Proceedings and Addresses of the American Philosophical Association* 50, no. 6, (1977): 483-498. http://doi.org/10.2307/3129784.

Putnam, Hillary. *Meaning and the Moral Sciences*. London: Routledge and Kegan Hall, 1978

Putnam, Hillary. "Models and Reality." *Journal of Symbolic Logic* 45, no. 3. (1980): 464-482. http://doi.org/10.2307/2273415.

Putnam, Hillary. *Reason, Truth, and History*. Cambridge: Cambridge University Press, 1981

Putnam, Hillary. *The Many Faces of Realism.* La Salle, Illinois: Open Court, 1987

Quine, W. V. O. "Empirical Content." In *Theories and Things*, 24-30. Cambridge, MA: Harvard University Press, 1981

Quine, W. V. O. "Meaning and Translation." In *On Translation*, edited by R. A. Brower, 148-172. Cambridge, MA: Harvard University Press, 1959

Quine, W. V. O. *Word and Object*. Cambridge, MA: MIT Press, 1960

Quine, W. V. O. "On What there is." In *From a Logical Point of View: Logico-Philosophical Essays*. New York: Harper and Row, 1963: 1-19

Quine, W. V. O. "Two Dogmas of Empiricism" in *From a Logical Point of View*, 20-46

Quine, W. V. O. "The Ways of Paradox." In *The Ways of Paradox and Other Essays*. Cambridge: Harvard University Press, 1966: 3-20

Quine, W. V. O. "Truth by Convention." In *The Ways of Paradox*, 70-99

Quine, W. V. O. "On Carnap's Views on Ontology." In *The Ways of Paradox*, 126-134

Quine, W. V. O. "Posits and Reality." In *The Ways of Paradox*, 233-241

Quine, W. V. O. "On Simple Theories of a Complex World." In *The Ways of Paradox*, 242-245.

Quine, W. V. O. "Speaking of Objects." In *Ontological Relativity and Other Essays*. New York: Colombia University Press, 1969: 1-25

Quine, W. V. O. "Ontological Relativity." In *Ontological Relativity*, 26-68

Quine, W. V. O. "Epistemology Naturalized." In *Ontological Relativity*, 69-90

Quine, W. V. O. "Existence and Quantification." In *Ontological Relativity*, 91-113

Quine, W. V. O. *Philosophy of Logic*, 2nd ed. Cambridge, MA: Harvard University Press, 1970

Quine, W. V. O. *Roots of Reference*. LaSalle, Il: Open Court, 1974

Quine, W. V. O. *From a Logical Point of View* 2nd rev. ed. Cambridge, Massachusetts: Harvard University Press, 1980a

Quine, W. V. O. "The Variable and its Place in Reference." In *Philosophical Subjects: Essays Presented to P. F. Strawson*, edited by Zak van Straaten. 164-173. Oxford: Clarendon Press, 1980b

Quine, W. V. O. "Five Milestones of Empiricism." In *Theories and Things*, 67-72. Cambridge, MA: Harvard University Press, 1981

Quine, W. V. O. "Four Hot Questions in Philosophy," in *New York Review of Books*, 32, no. 2 (1985). https://www.nybooks.com/articles/1985/02/14/four-hot-questions-in-philosophy/

Quine, W. V. O. *Quiddities: An Intermittently Philosophical Dictionary*. Cambridge, MA: Harvard University Press, 1987

Quine, W. V. O. *Pursuit of Truth*. Cambridge, MA: Harvard University Press, 1992

Quine, W. V. O. "Response to Hookway," *Inquiry* 37, (1994): 495-506

Quine, W. V. O. "Things and Their Place in Theories." In *Contemporary Materialism: A Reader*, edited by Paul Moser and J. D. Trout, 199-215. New York and London: Routledge, 1995

Quine, W. V. O. *From Stimulus to Science*. Cambridge: Harvard University Press, 1998a

Quine, W. V. O. "Reply to Harold N. Lee." In *The Philosophy of W. V. O. Quine* expanded edition, edited by Lewis Edwin Hahn and Paul Arthur Schilpp. 315-318, La Salle, Il: Open Court, 1998b

Quine, W. V. O. "Reply to Hillary Putnam." In Hahn et al, *The Philosophy of W. V. O. Quine*, 427-432

Quine, W. V. O. "Facts of the Matter." In *Confessions of a Confirmed Extensionalist and Other Essays*, edited by Dagfinn Follesdal and Douglas B. Quine, 271-286. Cambridge, MA: Harvard University Press, 2008a

Quine, W. V. O. "Indeterminacy of Translation Again." In *Philosophy of Language: The Central Topics*, edited by Susana Nuccetelli and Gary Seay, 64-68. Lanham: Rowman and Littlefield Publishers, 2008b

Ramsey, Frank. "Last Papers: Theories." In *The Foundations of Mathematics and Other Essays*, edited by Richard Bevan Braithwaite, 212-236. London: Routledge and Kegan Paul, 1931

Rasmussen, Joshua. *Defending the Correspondence Theory of Truth*. Cambridge: Cambridge University Press, 2014

Rescher, Nicholas. "Axioms for the Part Relation." *Philosophical Studies* 6, no. 1, (1955): 8-11. http://www.jstor.org/stable/4318213.

Richardson, Alan. *Carnap's Construction of the World: The Aufbau and the Emergence of Logical Empiricism*. Cambridge: Cambridge University Press, 1998

Ricketts, Thomas. "Objectivity and Objecthood: Frege's Metaphysics of Judgment." In *Frege Synthesized: Essays on the Philosophical and Foundational Work of Gottlob Frege*, edited by Leila Haaparanta and Jaakko Hintikka, 65-95. Dordrecht: D. Reidal Publishing Company, 1986

Ricketts, Thomas and James Levine. "Logic and Truth in Frege." *Aristotelian Society Supplementary Volume* 70, Issue 1, (1996): 121-175. https://doi.org/10.1093/aristoteliansupp/70.1.121

Ricketts, Thomas. "Concepts, Objects, and the Context Principle." In *The Cambridge Companion to Frege*, edited by Thomas Ricketts and Michael Potter, 149-219. Cambridge: Cambridge University Press, 2010

Rosen, Gideon. "Metaphysical Dependence: Grounding and Reduction." In *Modality: Metaphysics, Logic, and Epistemology*, edited by Bob Hale and Aviv Hoffmann, 109-136. Oxford: Oxford University Press, 2010

Rudder-Baker, Lynne. *Persons and Bodies: A Constitution* View. Cambridge: Cambridge University Press, 2000

Russell, Bertrand. "On Denoting." *Mind* 14, no. 56, (1905): 479-493. http://www.jstor.org/stable/2248381.

Russell, Bertrand and Alfred North Whitehead. *The Principia* 2nd ed. 3 vols. Cambridge: Cambridge University Press, 1910-1913

Russell, Bertrand. *The Problems of Philosophy*. Indianapolis, Cambridge: Hackett Publishing Company, 1912

Russell, Bertrand. "The Nature of Sense-data: A Reply to Dawes Hicks." *Mind* 22, no. 85 (1913): 76-81

Russell, Bertrand. "The Relation of Sense-data to Physics." in *Mysticism and Logic and Other Essays*. London: Allen and Unwin, 1917: 145-179

Russell, Bertrand. *Introduction to Mathematical Philosophy*. New York: Dover Publications, 1919

Russell, Bertrand. *The Analysis of Matter*. London: Kegan Paul, 1927

Russell, Bertrand. "The Philosophy of Logical Atomism." In *Logic and Knowledge*, edited by Robert Charles Marsh, 175-282. London: Unwin Hyman, 1956

Russell, Bertrand. "On Propositions: What They Are and How They Mean." In *Logic and Knowledge*, 283-320.

Russell, Bertrand. *Our Knowledge of the External World*. New York: The New American Library, 1960

Russell, Bertrand "Meinong's Theory of Complexes and Assumptions." in *Essays in Analysis*, edited by Douglas Lackey, 21-76. London: Allen & Unwin, 1973

Russell, Bertrand. *The Collected Papers of Bertrand Russell,* Vol. 6: *Logical and Philosophical Papers 1909-1913*. London, Routledge, 1992a

Russell, Bertrand. *An Inquiry into Meaning and Truth*. London and New York: Routledge, 1992b

Russell, Bertrand. *The Analysis of Mind*. PA: Pennsylvania State University, 2001

Russell, Bertrand. *A History of Western Philosophy*. London and New York: Routledge, 2004

Russell, Bertrand. *A Critical Exposition of the Philosophy of Leibniz*. Nottingham: Spokesman, 2008

Russell, Bertrand. *Principles of Mathematics*. London and New York: Routledge, 2010

Ryle, Gilbert. *The Concept of Mind.* London: Hutchinson, 1949

Schaffer, Jonathan. "On What Grounds What." In *Metametaphysics; New Essays on the Foundations of Ontology*, edited by David Chalmers, David Manley and Ryan Wasserman, 347-383. Oxford: Clarendon Press, 2009

Schaffer, Jonathan. "Monism: The Priority of the Whole." *The Philosophical Review* 119, no. 1 (2010): 31-76. https://doi.org/10.1215/00318108-2009-025

Searle, John. *Intentionality: An Essay in the Philosophy of Mind,* Cambridge: Cambridge University Press, 1983

Searle, John. "Indeterminacy, Empiricism, and the First Person." *The Journal of Philosophy* 84, no. 3 (1987): 123-146. http://doi.org/10.2307/2026595.

Sellars, Wilfrid. "Empiricism and the Philosophy of Mind." In *Minnesota Studies in the Philosophy of Science, Volume I: The Foundations of Science and the Concepts of Psychology and Psychoanalysis*, edited by Herbert Feigl and Michael Scriven, 253-329. Minneapolis, Minnesota: University of Minnesota Press, 1956

Sellars, Wilfrid. "Correspondence between Wilfrid Sellars and Gilbert Harman on Truth, 1970" Sellars Archives, accessed 25th of May, 2019, http://www.ditext.com/sellars/sh-corr.html

Shani, Itay. "The Whole Rabbit: On the Perceptual Roots of Quine's Indeterminacy Puzzle," *Philosophical Psychology* 22, no. 6, (2009); 739-763. https://doi.org/10.1080/09515080903409960

Sider, Theodore. "Four-Dimensionalism." *The Philosophical Review* 106, no. 2, (1997): 197-231. https://www.jstor.org/stable/2998357

Sider, Theodore. *Four-Dimensionalism: An Ontology of Persistence and Time*. Oxford: Clarendon Press, 2001

Sider, Theodore. "Another Look at Armstrong's Combinatorialism." *Nous* 39, no. 4 (2005): 679-695. http://www.jstor.org/stable/3506116.

Sider, Theodore. "Parthood." *Philosophical Review* 116, no.1, (2007): 51-91. http://www.jstor.org/stable/20446938.

Simons, Peter. *Parts: A Study in Ontology*. Oxford: Oxford University Press, 1987

Simons, Peter. "Frege and Wittgenstein, Truth and Negation." in *Wittgenstein: Eine Neubewertung/Wittgenstein – Towards a Re-Evaluation*, edited by Rudolf Haller and Johannes Brandl, 119-129. Munich: J.F. Bergmann-Verlag, 1990

Sluga, Hans "Frege and the Rise of Analytic Philosophy." In *Inquiry* 18, no. 4 (1975): 471-487. https://doi.org/10.1080/00201747508601779

Sluga, Hans. "Frege as a Rationalist." In *Studies on Frege,* vol 1., edited by Matthias Schirn, 27-47. Stuttgart and Bad Cannstatt: Frommann-Holzboog, 1976

Sluga, Hans. *Gottlob Frege: The Arguments of the Philosophers*. London: Routledge, 1980

Smith, Barry. "Against Fantology." In *Experience and Analysis*, edited by Johann C. Marek and Maria E. Reicher. Vienna: öbv & hpt, 2005

Smith, Nicholas J. J. "Frege's Judgement Stroke and the Conception of Logic as the Study of Inference not Consequence." *Philosophy Compass* 4, issue 4, (2009): 639-665. https://doi.org/10.1111/j.1747-9991.2009.00219.x

Spelke, Elizabeth. "Principles of Object Perception" *Cognitive Science* 14, issue 1, (1990): 29-56. https://doi.org/10.1207/s15516709cog1401_3

Stalnaker, Robert. "Lewis on Intentionality." *Australasian Journal of Philosophy* 82, no. 1, (2004): 199-212. https://doi.org/10.1080/713659796

Stanford, Preston and Philip Kitcher. "Refining the Causal Theory of Reference for Natural Kind Terms." *Philosophical Studies* 97, no. 1, (2000): 97-127. https://doi.org/10.1023/A:1018329620591

Stemwedel, Janet. "'Causes' in Chemical Explanations." *Chemical Explanation: Characteristics, Development, Autonomy* vol. 988, no. 1, (2003): 217-226. https://doi.org/10.1111/j.1749-6632.2003.tb06101.x

Stern, David. *Wittgenstein on Mind and Language*. Oxford and New York: Oxford University Press, 1995

Stevens, Graham. "Russell and the Unity of the Proposition." *Philosophy Compass* 3, issue 3. (2008): 491-506. https://doi.org/10.1111/j.1747-9991.2008.00142.x

Shapiro, Stewart. *Philosophy of Mathematics: Structure and Ontology.* Oxford: Oxford University Press, 1997

Stroud, Barry. *The Significance of Philosophical Scepticism.* Oxford: Oxford University Press, 1984

Sullivan, Peter. "The Sense of a Name of a 'Truth Value'." *The Philosophical Quarterly* 44, no. 177 (1994): 476-481. http://doi.org/10.2307/2220246.

Swinburne, Richard. *The Christian God.* Oxford: Clarendon Press, 1994

Tahko, Tuomas and Jonathan E. Lowe. "Ontological Dependence." *Stanford Encyclopaedia of Philosophy.* (Winter 2016). Edited by Edward N. Zalta. https://plato.stanford.edu/entries/dependence-ontological/

Tarski, Alfred. "The Semantic Conception of Truth and the Foundations of Semantics." *Philosophy and Phenomenological Research* 4, no. 3, (1944): 341-376. http://doi.org/10.2307/2102968.

Tarski, Alfred. "The Conception of Truth in Formalised Languages." In *Logic, Semantics, Metamathematics; Papers from 1922 to 1938*, translated by Joseph Woodger, edited by John Corcoran, 152-278. Oxford: Clarendon Press, 1956

Teller, Paul. "Relational Holism and Quantum Mechanics." *The British Journal for the Philosophy of Science* vol. 37, no. 1 (1986): 71-81. http://www.jstor.org/stable/686998.

Textor, Mark. *Frege on Sense and Reference*. London and New York: Routledge, 2011

Thomasson, Amie. "After Brentano: A One-Level Theory of Consciousness." *European Journal of Philosophy* 8, issue 2, (2000): 190-210. http://doi.org/10.1111/1468-0378.00108

Thomasson, Amie. *Ordinary Objects*. Oxford: Oxford University Press, 2007

Thomasson, Amie. *Ontology Made Easy*. Oxford: Oxford University Press, 2014

Uebel, Thomas. "Neurath's Influence on Carnap's *Aufbau*." In *Influences on the Aufbau*, edited by Christian Dambock, 51-76. Dordrecht: Springer, 2016

Van Inwagen, Peter. "Composition as Identity." *Philosophical Perspectives* 8 (1994): 207-220. http://doi.org/10.2307/2214171.

Van Inwagen, Peter. *Material Beings*. Ithaca: Cornell University Press, 1990

Varzi, Achille. "Parts, Wholes, and Part–Whole Relations: The Prospects of Mereotopology." *Data and Knowledge Engineering* 20, issue 3, (1996): 259-286. https://doi.org/10.1016/S0169-023X(96)00017-1

Varzi, Achilles. "Mereology." *The Stanford Encyclopaedia of Philosophy* (Winter 2016 Edition), Edward N. Zalta (ed.), URL = <https://plato.stanford.edu/archives/win2016/entries/mereology/>.

Walker, Ralph. "Theories of Truth." In *A Companion to the Philosophy of Language*, edited by Bob Hale and Crispin Wright, 309-330. Oxford: Blackwell, 1997

Wilson, Fred. "On the Hauseman's 'A New Approach'." in *Berkeley's Metaphysics: Structural, Acquaintance, Ontology, and Knowledge: Collected Essays in Ontology,* edited by Robert Muehlmann, 67-88. University Park, PA: Pennsylvania State University Press, 1995

Wilson, Jessica. "No Work for a Theory of Grounding." *Inquiry* 57, no. 5-6 (2014): 535-579. https://doi.org/10.1080/0020174X.2014.907542

Wittgenstein, Ludwig. *Philosophical Grammar*, edited by Rush Rhees and translated by Anthony Kenny. Berkeley, CA: University of California Press, 1974

Wittgenstein, Ludwig. *Notebooks, 1914-1916*, edited by George Henrik von Wright and edited and translated by Elizabeth Anscombe. Oxford: Blackwell, 1979

Wittgenstein, Ludwig. *Tractatus Logico-Philosophicus*. Translated by David F. Pears and Brian F. Mcguinness. London and New York: Routledge, 2002

Wong, Hong Yu. "Emergents from Fusion." *Philosophy of Science* 73, no. 3 (2006): 345-367. http://doi.org/10.1086/515413.

Yates, David. "Introduction: The Metaphysics of Relations." In *The Metaphysics of Relations*, edited by Anna Marmodoro and David Yates, 1-18. Oxford: Oxford University Press, 2016

Yi, Byeong-Uk "Is Mereology Ontologically Innocent?" *Philosophical Studies* 93, no. 2, (1999): 141-160. http://www.jstor.org/stable/4320908.

Zimmerman, Dean. "Theories of Masses." *Philosophical Review* 104, no. 1, (1995): 53-110. http://doi.org/10.2307/2186012.

Printed in the USA
CPSIA information can be obtained
at www.ICGtesting.com
LVHW080422261023
762083LV00010B/40